Constitutional Democracy *in* Indonesia

Constitutional Democracy *in* Indonesia

Edited by
MELISSA CROUCH
University of New South Wales

Great Clarendon Street, Oxford, OX2 6DP,
United Kingdom

Oxford University Press is a department of the University of Oxford.
It furthers the University's objective of excellence in research, scholarship,
and education by publishing worldwide. Oxford is a registered trade mark of
Oxford University Press in the UK and in certain other countries

Published in the United States of America by Oxford University Press
198 Madison Avenue, New York, NY 10016, United States of America

British Library Cataloguing in Publication Data

Data available

Library of Congress Control Number: 2022941393

ISBN 978–0–19–287068–1

DOI: 10.1093/oso/9780192870681.001.0001

Printed and bound in the UK by
TJ Books Limited

Preface

In November 2019, I organized a series of panels on constitutional democracy in Indonesia at the biennial Indonesia Council Conference, hosted by the Australian National University. The Indonesia Council is the leading subregional council for Indonesian Studies in Australia and is affiliated with the Asian Studies Association of Australia. Little did we know of the enormous global challenges to come, nor of the way in which the pandemic would exacerbate the decline of constitutional democracy and academic freedom in Indonesia.

I acknowledge the great challenges and hardships that Indonesian authors and our research collaborators—academics, civil society, students—have faced since 2020 as a result of the Covid-19 pandemic. I acknowledge those who lost their lives, and those who cared for sick ones amid the horrific shortages of oxygen, lack of access to hospitals and healthcare, as well as related medical supplies. I acknowledge those who juggled their academic duties with caring for sick relatives and for children while Indonesia's schools remained closed for most of 2020–2021. This project was delayed to account for these challenges. Unfortunately, some authors who had originally joined the project were no longer able to contribute.

The Covid-19 pandemic raises many critical issues for constitutional democracy around the world, including for Indonesia. During the pandemic, debate continued over whether to amend the Constitution or even return to aspects of the initial 1945 Constitution. At the time of writing, we do not yet know whether these debates will lead to a formal move for constitutional amendment. The debate does indicate that there remains serious contention over ideas and institutions central to constitutional democracy in Indonesia. Regardless, there have been some incredible achievements towards constitutional democracy in Indonesia over the past few decades. This book affirms these achievements and those who have struggled to consolidate and maintain this commitment to constitutional democracy, even in the midst of real setbacks and the decline of constitutional democracy.

This book builds on and extends several earlier collaborations on Indonesian law through the Southeast Asia Law and Policy Forum. The volume on *The Politics of Court Reform: Judicial Change and Legal Culture in Indonesia* (2019, Cambridge University Press) reflected on court reform initiatives and specialized courts over twenty years. Since then, I have collaborated with a range of Indonesian universities and spoken at seminars, including the University of Brawijaya, University of Diponogoro, University of Indonesia, Sultan Agung State Islamic University, and Gajah Madah University. This volume follows on from these various initiatives and offers a reflection on the state of constitutional democracy since 2002 and the amendments to the 1945 Constitution, over twenty years ago.

A brief note on constitutional terminology. In this volume, authors distinguish between the original or initial 1945 Constitution that was in place from 1945 to 1949 and from 1959 to 1998, and the amended 1945 Constitution (also referred to as the current or incumbent constitution) that has been in place since 2002 as a result of constitutional amendments during 1999 to 2002. I acknowledge that there is debate over how to refer to the first 1945 Constitution, because those who seek to return to this first constitution and the authoritarianism it facilitated tend to use the word 'original constitution' to imply that it is superior. For this reason, the late lawyer Adnan Buyung Nasution suggested the term 'initial 1945 Constitution', to avoid the idea that the constitution is so sacred it cannot be amended (see Crouch, this volume). Nevertheless, in this volume whether authors use the term original or initial 1945 Constitution is not necessarily used to indicate their agreement or disagreement with that first constitution. Chapters may simply refer to 'the Constitution' where the context is already clear. All Indonesian legal references cited in this volume are in Bahasa Indonesia, from court decisions to laws and regulations.

Finally, I would like to extend my sincere thanks to Oxford University Press for their support of this volume. There were two goals for this edited volume. The first goal was to profile the case of constitutional democracy in Indonesia to a broader audience of comparative constitutional law and politics scholars. The second goal was to provide a space to highlight the research of many emerging Indonesian scholars of comparative constitutional studies, political science, and law and society. The future of constitutional democracy in Indonesia lies with these scholars and the policy and advocacy networks and debates to which many of them contribute.

Melissa Crouch
Sydney, August 2022

Contents

PART 2. THE CONSTITUTIONAL COURT AND RIGHTS

List of Indonesian Abbreviations

ABRI   *Angkatan Bersenjata Republik Indonesia* [Armed Forces of the Republic of Indonesia]
AILA   *Aliansi Cinta Keluarga* [Love Family Alliance]
AMAN   *Aliansi Masyarakat Adat Nusantara* [The Alliance of Indigenous Peoples of the Indonesian Archipelago]
AMDAL   *Analisis Manajemen Dampak Lingkungan* [Social and Environmental Impact Assessment]
APHI   *Assosiasi Penasehat Hukum dan Hak Asasi Manusia Indonesia* [Indonesian Human Rights Lawyers Association]
Bawaslu   *Badan Pengawas Pemilihan Umum* [General Election Supervisory Board]
BAZ   *Badan Amil Zakat* [government supported *zakat* agency]
BAZNAS   *Badan Amil Zakat Nasional* [National Board of Zakat]
BFO   *Bijeenkomst voor Federaal Overleg* [Federal Consultative Assembly]
BHP   *Badan Hukum Pendidikan* [education legal entity]
BOS   *Bantuan Operasional Sekolah* [School Operational Assistance]
BPK   *Badan Pemeriksa Keuangan* [National Audit Office]
BPSK   *Badan Penyelesaian Sengketa Konsumen* [Consumer Dispute Settlement Board]
BPUPKI   *Badan Penyelidik Usaha Persiapan Kemerdekaan Indonesia* [Investigating Committee for Preparatory Work for Indonesian Independence]
BSM   *Bantuan Siswa Miskin* [Assistance for Poor Students]
CPI   Competent Person Indonesia
DIM   *Daftar Inventarisasi Masalah* [list of issues]
DKH   *Dewan Kehormatan Hakim* [Judges Honorary Board]
DKPP   *Dewan Kehormatan Penyelenggara Pelimu* [Honorary Council of Election Organizers]
DKR   *Dewan Kesehatan Rakyat* [Peoples Health Council]
DPD   *Dewan Perwakilan Daerah* [Regional Representative Council]
DPR   *Dewan Perwakilan Rakyat* [People's Representative Council]
DPRD   *Dewan Perwakilan Rakyat Daerah* [Regional People's Representative Council]
ELSAM   *Lembaga Studi & Advokasi Masyarakat* [Institute for Policy Research and Advocacy]
FPBB   *Fraksi Partai Bulan Bintang* [Crescent Star Political Party]
FPPP   *Fraksi Partai Persatuan Pembangunan* [United Development Political Party]
GBHN   *Garis-Garis Besar Haluan Negara* [Broad Guidelines of State Policy]
HIR   *Herziene Indonesisch Reglement* [Revised Indonesian Regulation]
HMI   *Himpunan Mahasiswa Islam* [Islamic Student Association]
HPH   *hak pengusahaan hutan*
IAGI   *Ikatan Ahli Geologi Indonesia* [Association of Geologists Indonesia]
ICJR   Institute for Criminal Justice Reform

ICMI	*Ikatan Cendekiawan Muslim Indonesia* [Indonesian Muslim Intellectual's Association]
ICW	Indonesian Corruption Watch
IDI	Indonesian Doctors Association
IKAHI	Indonesian Judges Association
ILR	Indonesia Legal Roundtable
IPKI	*Ikatan Pendukung Kemerdekaan Indonesia* [League of Supporters of Indonesian Independence]
KAJS	*Komite Aksi Jaringan Sosial* [Action Committee for Social Security]
KIP	*Komisi Informasi Pusat* [Central Information Commission]
KMB	*Konferensi Meja Bundar*
KNIL	*Koninklijk Nederlands Indisch Leger* [Royal Netherlands East Indies Army]
Konstitusi RIS	*Konstitusi Sementara Republik Indonesia Serikat 1949*
KOPKAMTIB	*Komando Operasi Pemulihan Keamanan dan Ketertiban* [Operational Command for the Restoration of Security and Discipline]
KPA	*Konsorsium Pembaruan Agraria* [Consortium for Agrarian Reform]
KPK	*Komisi Pemberantasan Korupsi* [Corruption Eradication Commission]
KPU	*Komisi Pemilihan Umum* [General Election Commission]
KUHAP	*Kitab Undang-Undang Hukum Acara Pidana* [Code of Criminal Procedure]
KUHP	*Aliansi Nasional Reformasi* [National Alliance for Reform of the Criminal Code]
LAZ	*Lembaga Amil Zakat* [private zakat agency]
LBH	*Lembaga Studi & Advokasi Masyarakat* [Jakarta Legal Aid]
LGBTI	lesbian, gay, bisexual, transgender, and intersex
LPSK	*Lembaga Perlindungan Saksi dan Korban* [Witness and Victims Protection Agency]
LPU	*Lembaga Pemilihan Umum* [General Election Institute]
MKRI	*Mahkamah Konstitusi Republik Indonesia* [Constitutional Court of the Republic of Indonesia]
MORA	Ministry of Religious Affairs
MPPH	*Majelis Penelitian dan Pertimbangan Hakim* [Council of Judge's Research and Consideration]
MPR	*Majelis Permusvawarahan Rakyat* [People's Consultative Assembly]
MUI	*Majelis Ulama Indonesia* [Indonesian Council of Ulama]
NGO	non-governmental organization
NU	*Nahdlatul Ulama*
NVMS	National Violence Monitoring System
PAN	*Partai Amanat Nasional* [National Mandate Party]
Panwaslu	*Pengawas Pemilu* [Election Supervisory Committee]
PBB	*Partai Bulan Bintang* [Crescent Moon and Star Party]
PDI-P	*Partai Demokrasi Indonesia Perjuangan* [Indonesian Democratic Party of Struggle]
PDKB	*Partai Demokrasi Kasih Bangsa* [Love the Nation Democratic Party]
PDU	*Perserikatan Daulat Umat* [Union of Muslim Sovereignty]

PERHAPI	*Perhimpunan Ahli Pertambangan Indonesia* [Indonesian Association of Mining Experts Indonesia]
PERLUDEM	*Perhimpunan Pemilu dan Demokrasi* [Association for Elections and Democracy]
PETA	*Pembela Tanah Air* [Japanese Defenders of the Fatherland]
PGRI	*Persatuan Guru Republik Indonesia* [Indonesian Teachers Union]
PK	*Partai Keadilan* [Justice Party]
PKB	*Partai Kebangkitan Bangsa* [National Awakening Party]
PKH	*Program Keluarga Harapan* [Family Hope Programme]
PKI	*Partai Komunis Indonesia* [Indonesian Communist Party]
PNI	*Partia Nasional Indonesia* [Indonesian Nationalist Party]
POLRI	*Kepolisian Republik Indonesia* [National Police Force]
PPKI	*Panitia Persiapan Kemerdekaan Indonesia* [Preparatory Board for Indonesian Independence]
PPP	*Partai Persatuan Pembangunan* [United Development Party]
RIS	*Rupublik Indonesia Serikat* [Federated Republic of Indonesia]
SRMI	*Serikatan Raykat Miskin Indonesia* [Indonesian Poor People's Union]
SV	*Wetboek van Strafvordering* [Code of Criminal Procedure]
TNI	*Tentara Nasional Indonesia* [Indonesian National Military]
TURC	Trade Union Rights Centre
UPZ	*Unit Pengumpul Zakat* [Zakat Collecting Unit]
UUDS	*Undang-Undang Dasar Sementara Republik Indonesia 1950* [Provisional Constitution of the Republic of Indonesia 1950]
WALHI	*Wahana Lingkungan Hidup Indonesia* [Indonesian Environmental Forum]
YLBHI	*Yayasan Lembaga Bantuan Hukum Indonesia* [Indonesia Legal Aid Foundation]
YLKI	*Yayasan Lembaga Konsumen Indonesia* [Indonesian Consumers Foundation]

List of Contributors

Fachrizal Afandi is a lecturer at the Law Faculty of University of Brawijaya (UB), Malang, Indonesia, where he teaches courses on Indonesian criminal procedure, criminology, and anthropology of law. He is a PhD researcher at the Leiden Law School in the Netherlands, and has been involved in various academic activities in the Indonesian criminal justice system and social-legal issues. Fachrizal is currently an executive director at the UB Centre for Criminal Justice Research (PERSADA UB). He completed his bachelor's and master's degrees in law at UB and received his BA from the Faculty of Psychology, Islamic State University of Malang, Indonesia.

Adhy Aman is a senior programme manager at the International Institute for Democracy and Electoral Assistance (IDEA). He was exposed to electoral processes in Indonesia upon being appointed First Secretary of the Central 1999 General Elections Supervisory Committee (Panwaslu 1999 Pusat) by the Supreme Court. Adhy has since been involved in electoral reform research and advocacy in Indonesia and beyond. At International IDEA, he has been involved in the development of publications and databases, such as on Direct Democracy and Electoral Justice. His current research interests are how to leverage the use of technology for elections and other democratic processes.

Yance Arizona is a lecturer at the Department of Constitutional Law, Universitas Gadjah Mada, Indonesia. He accomplished his PhD studies at the Van Vollenhoven Institute for Law, Governance and Society, Leiden University, the Netherlands. Prior to his PhD, Yance obtained a master's in constitutional law from the University of Indonesia and Master of Arts from Onati International Institute for the Sociology of Law, Spain. He has published many articles regarding the constitution, agrarian and natural resources, and indigenous communities' rights in Indonesia. In 2019, he visited the University of New South Wales Law School as part of the Sylff Young Leaders Fellowship Fund Program.

Adriaan Bedner is a professor at the University of Leiden. His research has a particular focus on access to justice, dispute resolution, and the judiciary. He is the author of *Administrative Courts in Indonesia* (Kluwer Law 2001) and *Court Reform* (Leiden University Press 2008). He has published numerous book chapters and journal articles, including for the *Asian Journal of Law & Society*, the *Journal of Legal Pluralism*, the *Hague Journal on the Rule of Law*, and the *Utrecht Law Review*. Adriaan has been project leader and/or steering board member of several research projects in Indonesia sponsored by the Royal Dutch Academy of Sciences, the Dutch Research Council, and the Dutch Department of Foreign Affairs. He has been involved in extra-curricular teaching within the framework of the Indonesian-Netherlands' legal cooperation programmes.

Mark Cammack is a professor at Southwestern Law School. He studied both law and Southeast Asian history in the Department of South Asian Studies at the University of Wisconsin. Mark received a Fulbright grant to conduct field research on Indonesia's Islamic court system. He is the author of numerous journal articles and book chapters, particularly on the Indonesian religious courts. His publications include *Islamic Law in Modern Courts* (with Haider ala Hamoudi) (Wolters Kluwer 2018), 'Islamic Professionals in Southeast Asia' (with R Michael Feener and Clark Lombardi) (2012) 21 *Pacific Rim Law Journal* 1, and *Islamic Law in Contemporary Indonesia: Ideas and Institutions* (co-editor with R Michael Feener) (Harvard University Press 2007).

Melissa Crouch is a professor and associate dean research at the Law School, University of South Wales (UNSW). She leads the Southeast Asia Law and Policy Forum at UNSW Law. Melissa is the author of *Law and Religion in Indonesia: Conflict and the Courts in West Java* (Routledge 2014) and *The Constitution of Myanmar* (Hart 2019). She has published in a range of peer-reviewed journals including the *Law & Society Review*, the *International Journal of Constitutional Law*, the *Oxford Journal of Legal Studies*, the *Sydney Law Review*, and the *Asian Studies Review*. She is the editor of several volumes including *Women and the Judiciary in the Asia Pacific* (Cambridge University Press 2021) and *The Politics of Courts: Judicial Reform and Legal Culture in Indonesia* (Cambridge University Press 2019).

Rachael Diprose is the Director-International and a senior lecturer at the School of Social and Political Sciences at the University of Melbourne. Also formerly of the University of Oxford, Department of International Development, Rachael's mixed-methods research traverses two inter-related streams. First, her research is concerned with the dynamics of rapidly changing political and social contexts and the implications of such change for populations, the environment, governance, policy, and political order. Second, her research focuses on international development, especially understanding poverty and inequalities, with a particular focus on inclusion, gender, and empowerment. She has published in a range of peer-reviewed journals including *Governance*; *Review of International Political Economy*; *Third World Quarterly*; *The Extractive Industries and Society*; the *Journal of Contemporary Asia*; *Conflict, Security and Development*; *Oxford Development Studies*; and *Ethnopolitics*. Rachael continues to collaborate in research, teaching, publications, public engagement, and other initiatives with colleagues from universities, civil society, and government in Asia, Europe, the US, and West Africa, having led large mixed-methods research programmes and held roles as an international advisor in a number of countries, especially in Indonesia.

Stefanus Hendrianto studies the Indonesian constitutional system from legal, comparative, philosophical, historical and theoretical perspective. Currently, he is a lecturer at Pontifical Gregorian University in Rome, Italy. In recent years, he served as a visiting professor at Santa Clara University School of Law and a guest scholar at the Kellogg Institute for International Studies at the University of Notre Dame. He holds a Ph.D. degree from University of Washington School of Law in Seattle, an LLM from Utrecht University in the Netherlands, and an LLB degree from Gadjah Mada University, Indonesia. In addition, he also holds an MDiv and ThM degrees from Boston College. Hendrianto is the author of *Law and Politics of Constitutional Court: Indonesia and the Search for Judicial*

Heroes (Routledge, 2018). His work has been published in the Notre Dame Journal of Law, Ethics and Public Policy, Washington International Law Journal, the Australian Journal of Asian Law, Journal Law and Method, and several edited book volumes.

Nadirsyah Hosen is a senior lecturer at the Faculty of Law, Monash University. He holds two PhDs. Nadir is an expert on Shari'a and Indonesian law. His articles have been published in internationally recognized and refereed journals, such as the *Nordic Journal of International Law*, the *Australian Journal of Asian Law*, the *European Journal of Law Reform*, the *Journal of Islamic Studies*, and the *Journal of Southeast Asian Studies*. He is the author of *Human Rights, Politics and Corruption in Indonesia: A Critical Reflection on the Post Soeharto Era* (Republic of Letters 2010), and *Shari'a and Constitutional Reform in Indonesia* (ISEAS 2007); a co-editor (with Joseph Liow) of *Islam in Southeast Asia*, 4 volumes (Routledge 2010) and a co-editor (with Richard Mohr) of *Law and Religion in Public Life: The Contemporary Debate* (Routledge 2011). His recent book (co-written with Ann Black and Hossein Esmaeili) is *Modern Perspectives on Islamic Law* (Edward Elgar 2013).

Marcus Mietzner is an associate professor at the Department of Political and Social Change, Coral Bell School of Asia Pacific affairs, Australian National University. Having lived and researched in Indonesia for over a decade during the democratic transition of the 2000s, he has published widely on the country's military politics. Marcus is the author of *Military Politics, Islam, and the State in Indonesia: From Turbulent Transition to Democratic Consolidation* (KITLV Press 2009) and the editor of *The Political Resurgence of the Military in Southeast Asia: Conflict and Leadership* (Routledge 2011). His latest publication on the Indonesian military is 'The Indonesian Armed Forces, Coalitional Presidentialism, and Democratization' in Robert W Hefner (ed), *Routledge Handbook of Contemporary Indonesia* (Routledge 2018).

Ahmad Rofii is a senior lecturer at the State Institute of Islamic Studies (IAIN) Cirebon, West Java. He teaches Islamic law and human rights, Islamic legal theory, and comparative family law. He holds a PhD in law from Monash University. Ahmad's thesis was on the place of Islamic law in the Indonesian Constitution. He holds two masters degrees, one in Islamic law from UIN Syarif Hidayatullah Jakarta, and the other in law from the University of Melbourne, Australia. His main fields of research and publication are Islamic law and Islamic legal theory, law and religion, Indonesian law, and comparative legal studies.

Dian Rositawati is a researcher at the Indonesian Institute for Independent Judiciary (LeIP). She was involved in the drafting of the Supreme Court Blueprints in 2003 and 2010 and has played an important role in their implementation efforts ever since. Dian provides assistance to the Supreme Court in various reform programmes in the area of judicial training, case management, and supervision. She completed her PhD at the Tilburg University in the Netherlands. In addition to teaching courses at the Indonesia Jentera School of Law, she is also a programme director for Indonesia at the Center for Human Rights and International Justice at Stanford University.

Andrew Rosser is professor of Southeast Asian Studies and deputy director at the Asia Institute, University of Melbourne. His research concerns the political economy of development focusing in particular on Indonesia and Timor Leste. His work has been published in leading book outlets and journals such as *World Development, Third World Quarterly,* the *Journal of Development Studies, Pacific Review,* and the *Journal of Contemporary Asia*. Andrew has won grants from the Australian Research Council, Australia's Department of Foreign Affairs and Trade, the Developmental Leadership Program, and the Australia-Indonesia Governance Research Partnership. Between 2012 and 2015, he was an Australian Research Council Future Fellow. In addition to the University of Melbourne, Andrew has worked at the University of Adelaide, the Institute of Development Studies (Sussex), the University of Sydney, and Murdoch University. He has also acted as a consultant for various development agencies.

Abdurrachman Satrio is a researcher at the Institute for Migrant Rights, Cianjur, Indonesia. He graduated from the Faculty of Law Universitas Padjadjaran, Indonesia, with an LLB in 2018. Shortly after that, he worked at the Center for State Policy Studies (*Pusat Studi Kebijakan Negara*) in the same faculty. In 2021, Satrio was awarded his LLM with distinction from the Central European University, Vienna. His thesis focused on the influences of the family state concept on the Indonesian and Singapore constitutions. Satrio's research interest is in comparative constitutional law, with a special focus on the constitutional practices of Southeast Asian states. His works have been published in journals such as the *Vienna Journal on International Constitutional Law* and the *Australian Journal of Asian Law*. He often writes reports on the development of Indonesian constitutional law in constitutional law blogs.

Stephen Sherlock is a visiting fellow at the Department of Political and Social Change at the Australian National University (ANU) and former director of the Centre for Democratic Institutions (CDI) at ANU. His research interests are in Indonesia and Southeast Asia, focusing on the political economy of elections, political parties, parliaments, and women's political empowerment. Currently an international political governance consultant, he has wide experience working on training, policy development, evaluation reports, research publications, and capacity-building in the Indonesian parliament, government ministries, civil society organizations, and political parties. He has worked extensively within Indonesian state institutions and has published widely on Indonesian governance and democratic development.

Fritz Siregar is an alumnus of UNSW Law and a former visiting fellow at UNSW Law (2017). In 2017, he was appointed by the President of Indonesia to an important post on the Indonesian Elections Supervisory Board (*Bawaslu*, 2017–2022). Fritz completed his LLB at the Faculty of Law, University of Indonesia. He holds a Master of Laws degree from Erasmus University of Rotterdam and the University of New South Wales. In 2016, he completed his SJD at UNSW on judicial behaviour and the judicialization of the Indonesia Constitutional Court. Prior to this, from 2004 to 2009, he was part of the founding generation of staff on the Indonesia Constitutional Court as a justice assistant to Justice Maruarar Siahaan. In 2006, Fritz was selected as the first foreigner to work as an intern as Judicial Associate at the High Court of Australia. He also previously worked at the International Monetary Fund's project on legal reform in Indonesia. Fritz is the author of several articles, the most recent published in the *Australian Journal of Asian Law*.

Dirk Tomsa is an associate professor in the Department of Politics, Media and Philosophy at La Trobe University, Melbourne. His main research interests include electoral and party politics in Indonesia as well as comparative Southeast Asian politics. Dirk is the co-author (with Ken Setiawan) of *Politics in Contemporary Indonesia: Institutional Change, Policy Challenges and Democratic Decline* (Routledge 2022) and has published extensively in peer-reviewed journals such as the *Political Research Quarterly*, the *International Political Science Review*, and the *Journal of East Asian Studies and South East Asia Research*. He is also the co-editor of two volumes on Indonesian and Southeast Asian politics.

1

The Limits of Transformational Authoritarian Constitutions

The Indonesian Experience

Melissa Crouch

Introduction

The Indonesian Constitution is an important text that governs the world's third largest democracy. In 1998, after decades of authoritarian rule, the initial 1945 Constitution underwent a series of major constitutional amendments. During the constitution-making process from 1999 to 2002, constitution-makers introduced profound changes to the legal and political system, including a bill of rights and a Constitutional Court. A culture of constitutional democracy has developed, driven by a robust civil society, media, and lawyers who mobilize advocacy campaigns for the rule of law and social justice.

In this volume we explore an ongoing set of debates over the meaning and practice of the Indonesian Constitution. This includes debates about the role of the security forces, the powers and term of the president, the powers of the legislature, the role of decentralization in promoting democracy, the scope of rights and the ability of the state to limit rights, the importance and challenges of elections, the role of accountability agencies, the impact of corruption on legal and political governance, and the role of the Constitutional Court as guardian of the Constitution. We address these issues against a social, political, and economic environment that has seen a decline in tolerance, freedom, and respect for minorities, and shrinking space for the exercise of rights including the rights to freedom of speech, freedom of association, and freedom of the press. Indonesia's decline in democracy reflects trends facing politics around the globe, from Hungary to India.

The contributors in this volume consider how the legal reforms post-1998 have fostered constitutional democracy in Indonesia, and at the same time how constitutional democracy is under threat. Indonesia has shifted from a period of democratic transition to consolidation or stagnation, and then to decline. In particular, some members of the legislature have called for amendments to the Constitution and to revert, in part or in whole, to the initial 1945 Constitution. The threat of formal reversal of Indonesia's democratic gains through constitutional amendment remains real, while the actual decline in constitutional democracy is tangible. The chapters in this book are written in light of these threats to constitutional democracy, that is, democratic governance through a constitutional text that ensures competitive elections and limits on

Melissa Crouch, *The Limits of Transformational Authoritarian Constitutions* In: *Constitutional Democracy in Indonesia*. Edited by: Melissa Crouch, Oxford University Press. © Melissa Crouch, 2023. DOI: 10.1093/oso/9780192870681.003.0001

power. The normative and practical content of constitutional democracy is contested in Indonesia, and while some Indonesians may associate constitutional democracy with liberalism and the protection of individual rights, others do not. Despite competing claims to constitutional democracy, what is clear is that the calls to return to the initial 1945 Constitution are distinctly anti-democratic, illiberal, and authoritarian.

In this chapter I seek to address two main lines of inquiry around the idea of transformational authoritarian constitutions. How is the amended 1945 Constitution a transformational authoritarian constitution? How does the case of Indonesia demonstrate both the possibilities and limits of transformational authoritarian constitutions? To explore the case of Indonesia, I offer a genealogy of its constitutional past, identifying five authoritarian elements of the initial 1945 Constitution and, correspondingly, five transformational elements of the amended 1945 Constitution. The contemporary debate over whether to return to the initial 1945 Constitution exposes the limits of transformational authoritarian constitutions, which may be limited in time and provoke a backlash that risks inspiring a return to the authoritarian constitution.

The Idea of Transformational Authoritarian Constitutions

Can a constitution drafted by an authoritarian regime, or used to support authoritarian rule, instead later facilitate a transition to democracy? Is it necessary for a country to completely replace an authoritarian constitution as part of its democratic transition? Many countries have made the transition to democracy without necessarily replacing their constitution wholesale. This suggests that it is possible to retain an authoritarian constitution during a transition to democracy. The use of an authoritarian constitution to facilitate a political and legal transition holds both possibilities and risks.

One way to understand such a constitution is the idea of transformational authoritarian constitutions. If something is transformational, it causes or generates significant change. A transformational authoritarian constitution is a constitution that has in the past been drafted by authoritarian rulers and/or been used to sustain and justify authoritarian rule, but has since been amended to facilitate a transition to constitutional democracy (Ginsburg 2020). The amendments to the constitution may occur at the start of the transition or gradually and incrementally over time. A transformational authoritarian constitution is set in contrast to an authoritarian constitution, that is, a constitution that has been drafted by authoritarian rulers to further an authoritarian regime and/or a constitution that is used to advance and legitimate authoritarian rule.

Ginsburg suggests that there are three aspects to a transformational authoritarian constitution (2020: 244). First, the constitution is based on the idea of popular sovereignty and facilitates the resumption of competitive democratic elections. Second, the constitution articulates mechanisms that set limits on the democratic state, that is, the constitution puts in place key democratic policy goals that bind the government. Third, there must be a process to enforce the provisions of the constitution as stipulated by the constitution, such as judicial review through a constitutional court. These can be understood as generic and relatively high-level criteria common to all transformational authoritarian constitutions. The precise ways in which an authoritarian constitution facilitates transformation and is itself transformed will depend on the features of that authoritarian constitution. Ginsburg identifies other examples of transformational authoritarian constitutions from Latin America, Africa, Europe, Asia, and the Pacific, including Panama's 1972 Constitution, Mexico's 1917 Constitution, and Turkey's 1982 Constitution (Ginsburg 2020: 243). Ginsburg explores this idea of a transformational authoritarian constitution in the context of Chile's 1980 Constitution, which was used to facilitate the transition from Pinochet's authoritarian regime to democracy in 1990 (Ginsburg 2020).

The idea of transformational authoritarian constitutions is distinct from the idea of transitional constitutionalism or transformative constitutionalism. One of the differences between transformational authoritarian constitutions and the notion of transformative constitutionalism (Klare 1998) is that in the former the authoritarian constitution persists in order to facilitate the transition to constitutional democracy. This is exemplified in cases like Chile and Indonesia that retained their pre-existing constitution but made amendments to it. In contrast, Karl Klare's idea of transformative constitutionalism is developed in the context of South Africa, where a new constitution was created as part of the end of apartheid. In addition, Ginsburg suggests that transformational authoritarian constitutions are distinct from Ruti Teitel's (2000) idea of transitional constitutionalism because the latter seeks to do justice for the past, while the former may in fact protect the previous regime or the constitution-makers through immunity clauses or prevent other efforts at transitional justice and criminal prosecutions (Ginsburg 2020: 246). A transformational authoritarian constitution is not necessarily explicit in granting immunity or preventing action to address past human rights abuses; the constitution may also simply be silent about any prospects for transitional justice. By deferring the issue of transitional justice, past abuses may in fact never be accounted for. Examples of this include the poor record of Indonesia's ad hoc human rights courts (Setiawan 2019), and the Constitutional Court's decision to annul the Truth and Reconciliation Commission Law.

There are potential advantages to maintaining an authoritarian constitution while transforming it over time during a period of political transition away from authoritarian rule. This approach does not require constitution-makers to start the constitutional design process from the beginning. It potentially helps make amendment more agreeable where actors from the former regime would otherwise oppose wholesale constitutional reform. For example, well-known lawyer Adnan Buyung Nasution (1934-2015) suggested that the amendment of the 1945 Constitution, rather than drafting a new constitution, was the middle-way approach acceptable to most stakeholders (Nasution 2011). The authoritarian constitution may have broad legitimacy, for example, because it was the first post-independence constitution or because it is associated with an important historical moment in the history of the country. Maintaining the authoritarian constitution may also help to avoid an open-ended discussion about constitutional possibilities, closing off certain models or options and helping to focus the debate.

Ginsburg's account of transformational authoritarian constitutions charts some of the possibilities to facilitate constitutional democracy. I expand this concept by exploring some of the limitations of transformational authoritarian constitutions. The contemporary case of Chile's new constitution-making process suggests one limitation—that transformational authoritarian constitutions may be temporary and only last for a period of time and then be replaced by a new constitution. This is not necessarily negative, but rather an example of how a transformational authoritarian constitution may function to defer and delay major constitutional reform to a later point in time. As I will show, the case of Indonesia also indicates the temporal nature of transformational authoritarian constitutions.

The case of Indonesia also sheds light on another limitation—that the transformational authoritarian constitution stands as a reminder of the constitutional past and its original form may be a rallying point for constitutional reform. That is, there may be groups within society that prefer to revert to the authoritarian constitution for the greater political control and reduced limits on power it would offer. Such an argument may be steeped in populism, originalism, or the idea that the initial constitution was a sacred document and should not have been amended. In short, authoritarian elites or key political groups, such as the military or political parties, use or misuse the idea of the authoritarian constitution as a binding social contract that should be returned to and cannot be amended. This may be related to formerly high hopes for the promise of constitutional democracy that have not been realized, or disillusionment when constitutional democracy sidelines some elites, or anticipated social and economic progress are not realized. Calls to return to the initial authoritarian constitution may be a persistent source of opposition and alternative vision for the future. These calls are likely to gain greater momentum during times of emergency or crisis, or when such changes might strengthen the power of the sitting government and that government has sufficient support in the legislature to pass a constitutional amendment. In short, transformational authoritarian constitutions contain within themselves the seeds of its own discontent and are at risk of provoking democratic decline as the past model remains visible and, for some, viable.

In this chapter I show that in Indonesia the authoritarian constitution was used as the basis for amendment and to transform the state's commitments to constitutional democracy. While the military did not draft Indonesia's initial 1945 Constitution, the military is now supportive of this Constitution. I add to our understanding of transformational authoritarian constitutions by exploring the case of Indonesia in detail and by showing that the transformation can be undone or is at risk by the potential for the initial constitution to remain a viable constitutional alternative. In contemporary Indonesia, the initial 1945 Constitution is a constitutional touchstone for those in support of authoritarian rule who seek to revert back to some or all aspects of the initial 1945 Constitution. A constitutional touchstone is a document that articulates alternative constitutional proposals and is a symbolic resource in discussions of constitutional reform (Crouch 2020). These proposals to return to the initial 1945 Constitution, enhance the power of the People's Consultative Assembly, remove the term limit of the president and reduce direct democracy, which I discuss later in detail, pose a significant threat to constitutional democracy in Indonesia.

The case of Indonesia shows both the possibilities and limits of transformational authoritarian constitutions to facilitate the transition to constitutional democracy. I first reflect on how Indonesia arrived at this period of constitutional democracy by characterizing constitutional developments in five main stages from 1945 to the present.

A Genealogy of Indonesia's Constitutions

Constitutions face different challenges over time. One particular challenge facing all new constitutions is the first period challenge, that is, the challenges in the immediate years following the introduction of a new constitution that involves implementing and socializing a new constitution, building its legitimacy and credibility. There is no one definition of a first period, and there are different events that may mark the end of the first period, such as two cycles of free elections or from the time when constitution-makers are no longer in politics (eg Ginsburg & Huq 2020). What counts as a first period may also differ within the same country over time. The first period of a new constitution is a crucial time, especially when it coincides with a transition from authoritarian rule. In addition, most countries including Indonesia have had multiple constitutions, and so the first period of a constitution is inevitably influenced and shaped by the constitutional past.

I characterize the genealogy of constitutional developments in Indonesia into five main stages: the first and second period of the revolution constitution (1945–1949; 1959–1999); the interim period of constitutional democracy under two interim constitutions (1949–1959); the first period of constitutional democracy under the amended 1945 Constitution (1999–2019); and the second period of the amended 1945 Constitution marked by a decline in constitutional democracy (2019–present). I place particular emphasis on the first and second period of the amended 1945 Constitution as a transformational authoritarian constitution. This genealogy sets the present constitution in contrast to the authoritarian constitution of the past, acknowledges the past existence of other liberal constitutional models, and demonstrates that the illiberal constitutional model of the initial 1945 Constitution lingers as a potential disruptor for the future of constitutional democracy.

A Temporary Constitution for the Revolution: The First Period of the 1945 Constitution (1945–1949)

The first stage of constitutional developments from 1945 to 1949 involved the inauguration of the initial 1945 Constitution, a period of revolution as Indonesia fought against the Dutch for its independence. The drafting of the 1945 Constitution stretched across two political eras. From 29 May to 17 July 1945, the Investigating Body for Preparatory Work for Indonesian Independence initiated the first period of constitution-making. This occurred towards the end of World War II during Japanese occupation. On 18 August 1945, after independence from the Dutch was declared, the Preparatory Committee for Indonesian Independence (*Panitia Persiapan Kemerdekaan Indonesia*, PPKI) met to finalize the process of constitution-making in one day.[1] There was an inevitable sense of uncertainty and urgency to this constitutional endeavour that partly

---

[1] For speeches and documents of the 1945 constitution-making process, see Kusuma 2004.

explains the lack of representative processes or consultation, and was the reason that constitution-makers intended the Constitution to be a temporary constitution.

The initial 1945 Constitution was the constitution of Indonesia from 1945 to 1949 and again from 1959 to 1999. The Constitution is historically significant because it was introduced by Indonesian nationalists upon the declaration of independence, despite the refusal by the Dutch to recognize independence. It is therefore a revolutionary Constitution and one that formed part of the struggle against the Dutch for the right to be an independent state.

The Constitution was intended to be temporary and for the period of the revolution, until such time as independence was consolidated and a new constitution could be drafted for the postcolonial nation. For these reasons, it was a bare bones constitution, its brevity apparent at just thirty-seven articles. Yet the Constitution played little role during this first period. This is because in October 1945 a vice-presidential decree was issued to establish the presidential advisory body, the Central Indonesian National Committee. The Committee held legislative power until the legislative bodies under the Constitution were established (Nasution 1992: 15–17).[2] After a struggle between the president and this Committee, the president dissolved the cabinet and appointed a new cabinet to regain control. As a result, the Constitution was effectively sidelined.

Further, political elites in the first period focused on the revolutionary struggle against the Dutch, as well as parallel political negotiations with the Dutch on a future constitution for an independent Indonesia. I suggest that the more important period of the initial 1945 Constitution is the second period, the period from 1959 to 1998, which includes president Soekarno's Guided Democracy from 1959 to 1966, and president Suharto's New Order from 1966 to 1998. But first, I consider the brief interim period from 1949 to 1959 under two other provisional constitutions that cast a very different vision from the initial 1945 Constitution. These two temporary constitutions illustrate the history of ideas of liberal constitutionalism in Indonesia, in contrast to the vision and political practices of the 1945 Constitution.

The Interim Constitutional Period 1949–1959

The second stage in Indonesia's constitutional development from 1949 to 1959 was one of liberal constitutional democracy. As a condition of gaining independence, the Dutch effectively required Indonesia to adopt the federal Constitution of the Republic of the United States of Indonesia 1949 (*Konstitusi Sementara Republik Indonesia Serikat 1949, Konstitusi RIS*). Indonesian elites swiftly replaced this Constitution with the similar but unitary Provisional Constitution of the Republic of Indonesia 1950 (*Undang-Undang Dasar Sementara Republik Indonesia 1950*, UUDS 1950). Both documents were intended to be temporary and anticipated that a Constituent Assembly would be set up as soon as possible to draft a permanent constitution. Yet what was common across both these constitutions was a commitment to liberal constitutionalism and human rights. This demonstrates that such ideas are not alien to

---

[2] Vice-Presidential Decree X, 16 October 1945.

independent Indonesia but have always been part of debates about the constitutional future.

In 1949, after Indonesians won the support of the international community for its struggle for independence, a Roundtable Conference (*Konferensi Meja Bundar*, KMB) was held to draft a provisional constitution. The roundtable was held in the Netherlands, rather than in Indonesia, which is one indication of Dutch control over the process. The Dutch had significant influence over the constitution-making process, insisting on a federal constitutional model.

The 1949 Constitution differed in fundamental ways from the 1945 Constitution. The 1949 Constitution endorsed a liberal, federal democratic state with a comprehensive list of civil and political rights with a number of socio-economic rights (Droogelever 1997). The Constitution established a representative civilian parliament, and the courts were guaranteed judicial independence. The fact that the Constitution endorsed democracy and liberalism meant that it stood in contrast to the 1945 Constitution, which I come to shortly. The 1949 Constitution, at least in its original form, lasted less than six months.

Indonesian elites replaced the 1949 Constitution with the 1950 Constitution. One of the main differences was that the 1950 Constitution removed the federal articles of the 1949 Constitution and replaced them with a unitary system. The anticipated Constituent Assembly was also released from any constitutional obligations to adhere to the provisional 1949 Constitution. From 1956 to 1959, the elected Constituent Assembly met to draft a new constitution (see Nasution 1992). This was a time of social and political instability, and by 1957 the president had declared martial law across the entire country. Further, by 1958, the army sought to undermine the Constituent Assembly by calling instead for a return to the 1945 Constitution (see Lev 2009: 253–297). At this time, local rebellions had arisen across several islands. By 1959, President Soekarno had come on board with the military's agenda and alleged that the Constituent Assembly had failed to come to an agreement on a constitution, although this is disputed. On 5 July 1959, the president issued a decree that revived the 1945 Constitution, effectively disbanding the Constituent Assembly and ignoring the Assembly's work towards a democratic constitution. The president took this action with the support of the military. This is the most controversial use of presidential decree power in Indonesia's history and marks the infamous return to the 1945 Constitution.

Back to the Future: The Second Period of the 1945 Constitution (1959–1999)

The third stage of constitutional development from 1959 to 1999 was the second period of the initial 1945 Constitution. The initial 1945 Constitution was an authoritarian constitution because it was used to justify and legitimate the authoritarian regime of Soekarno's Guided Democracy (1957–1966) and Soeharto's New Order (1966–1998).

The period from 1959 to 1966, Soekarno's Guided Democracy, was the first direct period of authoritarian rule. Soekarno's decree unilaterally reinstated the 1945 Constitution.[3] Soekarno manipulated the Constitution to his advantage, dissolving

---

[3] There is some debate over precisely when this period began. See, eg, discussion of this debate in Indrayana 2008: 106–108; Nasution 2011: 6.

the legislature and appointing replacements, overriding the need for elections. The composition of the People's Representative Assembly (*Dewan Perwakilan Rakyat*, DPR) shifted from a civilian body to one mixed with military officers, although it was later under Soeharto that the representation of the military in politics expanded further. Soekarno used the 1945 Constitution to further his regime, but also failed to adhere to the Constitution (Indrayana 2008: 110–111).

In 1966, Soeharto took over as president from Soekarno, setting his 'New Order' in contrast with Soekarno's 'Old Order'. Again, the Constitution was a key aspect of Soeharto's authoritarian regime. There were five key features of the Constitution that in theory or practice facilitated authoritarianism. These features of the 1945 authoritarian Constitution include a powerful and unlimited executive; an undemocratic legislature; subordinate courts; the absence of protection for rights; a highly centralized governance system; and the ideology of integralism. These features contrast with the transformational authoritarian constitution that later followed.

The first feature of the Constitution that enabled authoritarianism was the almost unlimited powers of the executive. The Constitution created a strong president with wide powers intended for maximum flexibility during the revolution, although these powers were open to abuse. The president had powers to make laws; issue regulations to implement laws; exclusive powers to appoint ambassadors, grant amnesty, and pardon; and authority over ministers and the formation of cabinet, as well as broad emergency powers. The president was not accountable to the DPR, the elected legislature. In theory the president was accountable to the People's Consultative Assembly (*Majelis Permusyawaratan Rakyat*, MPR), but as it was only required to meet once every five years, this was a weak form of accountability. There were no limits on the number of terms a president could serve, which enabled Soeharto to rule for several decades.

The role of the president was also supported by an expansive role for the military. During Soeharto's New Order, the military operated along the lines of its *dwifungsi* ideology. The dual function of the military involved its external role in defence and its socio-political function, or its internal role (Lubis 1994: 194–205). The lines between the role of the military and the police were blurred.

The second feature of the Constitution was a weak and compromised legislature in contrast to the power of the president and executive. There were two aspects to this: the composition and role of the MPR as the highest lawmaking body, and the composition and role of the DPR, a weak legislative body. The DPR in theory consisted of elected members, but political parties were limited and elections manipulated. Both Soekarno and Soeharto acted as if members of the DPR did not all need to be elected and instead appointed some representatives.[4] While Soekarno was the first to appoint miliary representatives to the DPR, over time, Soeharto increased the number of military representatives (see Mietzner, this volume). The DPR was, in practice, a weak institution, especially due to the manipulation of elections through the reduction of political parties, suppression of political opposition, and restrictions on freedom of speech and association, among other tactics. There were no free elections

---

[4] The initial 1945 Constitution did not specifically mention that the members of the DPR were to be elected.

under Soekarno's Guided Democracy or Soeharto's New Order. The 1955 general elections is regarded as the last free and fair election up until 1999.

Related to the DPR, the text of the initial 1945 Constitution established the MPR as the supreme and sovereign lawmaking body, acting on the sovereign power of the people. The MPR consisted of members of the DPR but also various groups, including the military. The MPR had in theory two crucial powers: to appoint the president and to set the terms of the Broad Guidelines of State Policy (*Garis Besar Haluan Negara*, GBHN). The Broad Guidelines of State Policy were set every five years and contained centralized policy plans that government agencies and lower levels of government were expected to follow. On one view, the president reported to the MPR and followed the Broad Guidelines of State Policy. However, in practice, neither presidents Soekarno nor Soeharto after him operated this way. Both acted as if the president was the highest institution and the MPR had little or no power over them. The president's ability to legislate was one example of the weakness of the DPR, the absence of a clear separation of powers, and a lack of strong checks and balances on executive power. Further, in practice, president Soeharto set the Broad Outlines of State Policy and the MPR approved it. Under Soeharto's New Order, the MPR was effectively powerless. However, the MPR had the power to remove the president, and in 1967 the MPR did in fact exercise this power to remove Soekarno.[5]

The third feature of the initial Constitution is that there was no constitutional separation of powers, the courts were subordinate to the executive and there was no explicit reference in the Constitution to judicial independence.[6] The courts were under the administrative and financial control of the Ministry of Justice. This was known as the two roofs system (*dua atap*). The military courts were not responsible to the Supreme Court, and there was no right to appeal from the military courts. There was no judicial review, so courts could not review law for constitutionality. There was no bill of rights in the Constitution, although there was provision for the right to work, equality before the law, and a right to education. Freedom of association, assembly, and expression were to be provided for in law, but could also be limited by law. There was no means to enforce the rights that were set out in the Constitution.

There was a constitutional right to freedom of religion, in part to reassure minorities who were nervous about their future in a country with a majority Muslim population. This right was not without contention. The drafters debated the idea of the Jakarta Charter, that is, whether seven words would be inserted into the preamble of the Constitution to oblige all Muslims to uphold Islamic law. However due to the concerns of minorities, the drafters removed these words and instead included the Pancasila with its acknowledgement of Belief in One God (see Drooglever 1997; Elson 2013). Proposed by Soekarno, the Pancasila is the state ideology with five pillars: belief in (one) Almighty God; a just and civilized humanity; national unity; representative politics based on deliberation; and social justice (Morfit 1981). These five principles are mentioned in the preface to the Constitution. Soeharto promoted the five principles as a national ideology. In fact, while Soekarno's authoritarian regime was built under

---

[5] MPR Decree No XXXIII 1967 on the Revocation of Presidential Powers of President Soekarno.
[6] The Elucidation referred to independent courts, but the status and legitimacy of the Elucidation is debated.

the guise of Guided Democracy, Soeharto claimed his regime was one of 'Pancasila Democracy'. Soeharto referred to the idea of the family principle and used Pancasila to qualify democracy and ultimately destroy it (Lubis 1994: 174–193).

The fourth feature of the Constitution that facilitated authoritarianism is the high degree of centralization of power at the national level, particularly in the office of the president. The initial 1945 Constitution was set in contrast to the 1949 federal Constitution, and emphasis was placed on the idea of a unitary state and the mantra of national unity, as reflected in the Pancasila.

Finally, those who sought to use the Constitution to justify authoritarian rule increasingly referred to the ideology of integralism, as articulated by its main proponent, Soepoemo.[7] Integralism was not specifically mentioned in the constitutional text, but Soepomo advocated for the idea during the constitutional debates of the 1940s. Those in favour of the rule of law argued that integralism did not gain support in the drafting of the 1945 Constitution, and that Soepomo was also one of the drafters of the more liberal 1950 Constitution. Yet supporters of Soepomo's integralism point to the persistence of this idea underlying the 1945 Constitution (Lubis 1994: 91–93).

Integralism was later taken up under Soekarno's Guided Democracy and Soeharto's New Order (Lubis 1994: 94–96). According to Soepomo, an integralist state was based on the idea that the state was all citizens, and so the interests of the state and citizens were the same. Soepomo also openly referred to the integralistic state (*negara integralistik*) as a totalitarian state (*negara totaliter*) (Kusuma 2004: 127–128). He claimed that the integralistic state knows what is best for the people and would promote harmony between the state and citizens. Soepomo illustrated the idea of integralism with reference to Imperial Japan and the role of the Emperor, as well as Hitler's totalitarian Germany (Kusuma 2004: 126).

Soepomo also sought to localize integralism by claiming that it was derived from Javanese philosophy and village customary law (Bourchier 2015). Integralism has been used to support the assertion that Indonesian culture, or Javanese culture in particular, is authoritarian in nature. However Indonesian scholars and lawyers such as the late Adnan Buyung Nasution have rejected this culturally determinist approach (Nasution 1992), instead insisting that democracy is necessary and fits the Indonesian context. The thinking of key Indonesian nationalists reflected a mix of local traditions and European philosophy and can be traced to prominent colonial intellectual Cornelis van Vollenhoven. As a leading example of the Leiden school of thought, van Vollenhoven emphasized the importance of a state that reflected local culture and a communal approach that valued harmony (Bourchier 2015). The Leiden school of thought can be traced back to early nineteenth-century German romanticism and the organic state, with society perceived as a coherent whole held together by custom (Burns 2004: 242–249). On an organicist view of the state, the state represents society as a collective and law emerged from within the unique conditions of that society. Integralism glorified a centralized and absolutist state. Integralism did not limit the power of the state, and it rejected the need to offer constitutional protection for rights, because it assumed that the state would act in the best interests of the people.

---

[7] See Soepomo's speech to the Investigating Body for Preparatory Work for Indonesian Independence of 31 May 1945 in Kusuma 2004: 123–133.

The idea that the 1945 Constitution facilitated authoritarian rule was legitimated through integralism. This view of the Constitution was contested and further debate arose over the relevance and meaning of the Elucidation. Written by Soepomo, the Elucidation was a document that accompanied the Constitution yet it appeared well after the Constitution was endorsed. The Elucidation, for example, mentioned that the state was based on 'hukum (rechtsstaat)', referring to both the Indonesian word and the continental European idea for 'rule of law', and contrasted this with a state based on 'kekuasaan belaka (Machtsstaat)', or power.[8] Many lawyers committed to democracy and the rule of law insisted that mention of rechtsstaat in the Elucidation was reference to a substantive idea of the rule of law. Supporters of the New Order, however, preferred the thinner interpretation of rechtsstaat or hukum as law, without the need for substantive commitments to human rights or even representative democracy (Nasution 1992; Butt and Lindsey 2012).

Under both Soekarno and Soeharto, the 1945 Constitution was used to further authoritarian rule.[9] Yet in 1998, after significant pressure from pro-democratic protestors and students, Soeharto stepped down from office. This created space for a political and legal sea change, a shift to constitutional democracy and, more than that, to the possibility of a liberal constitutional state.

A Transformational Authoritarian Constitution: The First Period of the Amended 1945 Constitution (1999–2019)

The fourth stage in constitutional developments was from 1999 to 2019. This era was the first period of the amended 1945 Constitution. Indonesia was a late entrant to the third wave of democracy. The fall of Soeharto's authoritarian regime in 1998 created space for new thinking on the Constitution. After the 1999 elections, the MPR led a constitutional amendment process that was widely heralded as introducing a democratic constitutional framework.[10] Only twenty-nine provisions of the 1945 Constitution stayed the same; the constitutional text was greatly expanded to 166 new provisions. For the most part, it was a new constitution. The amended Constitution was intended to be a dramatic break from the past and a document that would guide the transformation of the state to a constitutional democracy. Constitution-makers transformed aspects of the 1945 Constitution in order to promote constitutional democracy. The constitution-makers began with the 1945 Constitution, rather than draft a new one, in order to preserve the symbolism and legitimacy of the revolution Constitution, avoid the potential challenges of drafting an entirely new constitution, and as a compromise to those who wanted to maintain the 1945 Constitution in its initial form (Indrayana 2008; Nasution 2011). There are five broad ways in which the amended 1945 Constitution was a transformational authoritarian constitution.

---

[8] Elucidation to the 1945 Constitution, System of Government, Art 1 (*Penjelasan tentang Undang-undang Dasar Negara Indonesia, Sistem Pemerintahan Negara*).

[9] Bedner (2017: 170) argues that integralism was more prominent under Soeharto than Soekarno.

[10] For an early assessment, see Lindsey (2006).

First, there was a transformation from a powerful and unlimited president to a reduced role for, and limitations on, the role of the president and executive. Under the amended 1945 Constitution, the president could not pass laws, unlike in the past. The president was limited to two terms in office. Since 2004, the president is directly elected, involving the people in the choice of the head of state. The president may be removed through clear impeachment procedures. These reforms maintained the presidential office but attempted to curb the dominance and supremacy of the president. This was a direct response to the authoritarian regimes of both Soekarno, who in 1960 declared himself president for life, and Soeharto who ruled from 1965 to 1998, thirty-three years. The presidential term limit was particularly important and was designed to prevent another long-term dictator. Susilo Bambang Yudhoyono was the first president to serve two terms and then step down after the end of his second term (2004–2014).

Executive power was also rendered subordinate to civilian control. The military was brought under the control of civilian authorities and removed from its legislative positions, although not without resistance. The constitutional reforms effectively sought to end the army's *dwi-fungsi* ideology and civilianize the state. Constitutional and legal reforms distinguished between the military's role as an external force, and the role of the police in internal security. The military became subject to criminal law and military court trials could go on appeal to the Supreme Court.

Second, there was a transformation from a weak and co-opted legislature to a strong, representative legislature. The DPR's role as primary lawmaker was clarified and affirmed. The DPR, rather than the president, now had the final say in lawmaking. If the president did not sign the DPR's bill within thirty days, it automatically became law. The role and powers of the MPR were revised and it no longer selected the president nor had legislative powers, ensuring instead that these powers were exercised by the people and democratically through elected representatives. The MPR plays a symbolic role of inaugurating the president, although it also has the power to review the Constitution. Two new legislative bodies were established—the Regional Representative Council (*Dewan Pimpinan Daerah*, DPD) at the national level and the subnational Regional Representative Councils (*Dewan Perwakilan Rakyat Daerah*, DPRD) as unitary provincial legislatures. The national government retained power to legislate on select key areas, but otherwise legislative power was decentralized with provinces and regencies/cities making laws. A new electoral system was introduced as a pillar of the democratic system.

Third, there was a transformation from a compromised and subordinated court system to judicial independence, understood as the separation of the courts from the executive; in addition, a landscape absent of rights was transformed with a bill of rights and judicial enforcement of these rights. The general courts were removed from the administration of the Ministry and full control was given to the Supreme Court. The Supreme Court was given a role in the granting of pardons, rather than it being the sole power of the president. A new Judicial Commission was created to enhance judicial accountability, with the power to propose judicial candidates and to supervise judges to ensure adherence to ethical standards (see Rositawati, this volume). Over the past two decades, the balance between judicial independence and judicial accountability has been the subject of significant debate and contestation.

A new Constitutional Court was established with powers of judicial review and individuals could bring cases, realizing long-held demands for the protection of rights through judicial review. A bill of rights was introduced in the Constitution to ensure protection for human rights. The amended Constitution protects a range of rights including civil and political rights; equal treatment before the law; economic, social, and cultural rights; the right to a healthy environment; and the right to receive health care and social security. The state has various constitutional obligations, such as the obligation to commit a minimum of 20 per cent of the state budget to education.

Many of the chapters in this volume show that the meaning of these rights comes down to how the Constitutional Court has interpreted the right and the scope of any permissible limitations on rights, as well as how the administration may practically circumvent these rights. For example, the chapter by Bedner and Afandi shows that the police and prosecutors circumvent the constitutional protections for the accused by claiming that the arrest of an accused does not in fact amount to an 'arrest' according to the amended Constitution. Other chapters reflect on gains and limits to social and economic rights, the rights of indigenous peoples, and religious freedom (see Rosser; Arizona; Hosen and Rofii, this volume). The Constitutional Court has also had its challenges and critics, from Nasution's claims that the Court is too conservative (Nasution 2011) to judges found guilty of corruption, and a lack of equal female judicial representation on the bench (Crouch 2021), among other criticisms.

Fourth, there was a transformation from a highly centralized administration to decentralization and special rights for some areas. By geographic area including land and sea, Indonesia is the largest archipelago in the world, with 6,000 of its 17,000 islands inhabited. This means that governance is a challenge both in terms of the fragmented land mass, as well as the vast resources on land and at sea. The most populous island is Java, and other major islands include West Papua, Kalimantan, Sumatra, and Sulawesi. Decentralization responds to the long-held debate in Indonesia about how to hold the country together, cutting through the dichotomy between the idea of a unitary state in the 1945 Constitution and federalism in the 1949 Constitution. The constitutional amendment process introduced decentralization to distribute greater power to the regions.

Since 2002, the creation of new provinces has been a common occurrence. In 2021, there were thirty-four provinces. A key change is that governors, regents, and mayors are all democratically elected positions. In 2014, a law was passed that would have abolished direct elections for regional heads, although the president then used his power to overturn the law. Both the provinces of Aceh and West Papua were granted special autonomy status and wider powers than other regions, although there remain serious ongoing human rights issues in West Papua. One aspect of decentralization is the local competition over natural resources, an issue that Diprose considers in her chapter in this volume.

The fifth aspect of the transformation was from an ideology of integralism as a justification for authoritarianism, to the aspiration for and realization of constitutional democracy through the constitution. This commitment to constitutional democracy is the collective achievement of the above major changes. The key characteristic of the transformational authoritarian constitution was the limits it set on government, realized through new accountability and integrity institutions, including the General

Election Commission, as well as the previously mentioned Judicial Commission and Constitutional Court.[11] Through legislation, other accountability institutions including the National Human Rights Commission, the Anti-Corruption Commission, and the National Ombudsman were formed.

From the mid-2010s there has been persistent warnings of deconsolidation or the decline of democracy and the rise of authoritarianism (see, eg, Bourchier 2019; Diprose, McRae, and Hadiz 2019; Mietzner 2015; Mietzner 2018; Power 2018). Part of the debate about the decline of democracy in Indonesia concerns the issue of the legacy of Soeharto's New Order in the *reformasi* era (Fealy and Aspinall 2010). A fuller explanation of the challenges and threats to constitutional democracy is found in the chapters that follow in this volume. I highlight three of the challenges for constitutional democracy.

The first challenge is the persistence and increasing influence of illiberalism and its negative effect on the protection of rights. Intolerance and resistance to political liberalism has a long history and can be traced to the emergence and use of Soepomo's idea of integralism. Since 1998, there have been intermittent threats and physical attacks on various minority groups, including religious, ethnic, and sexual minorities. At the local level, religious regulations emerged based on Islam that often discriminated against minorities, while criminal charges of blasphemy were often used to target critics of Islam (Crouch 2013). In 2005, this campaign against liberalism was made concrete in a fatwa issued by the Indonesian Ulama Council against religious liberalism, secularism, and pluralism. In 2008, a violent demonstration at the National Monument in Jakarta against a minority Islamic sect, Ahmadiyah, led ministers to issue a regulation that in effect limited their freedoms. By 2017, no less than the former governor of Jakarta, a Chinese Christian and former running mate of Jokowi, was found guilty for the crime of blaspheming Islam after large street demonstrations by Islamists and a concerted political campaign to ensure he could not run in the 2017 elections for governor of Jakarta (Mietzner 2018). These and many other challenges, from attacks on and discrimination against the lesbian, gay, bisexual, transgender, and intersex (LGBTI) community to violence in West Papua, marked the second half of the 2010s.

The second challenge is the persistence of corruption and the disempowerment or cooptation of independent accountability institutions, as well as the politicization of leadership positions within law enforcement agencies and the use of law to target political opposition. Corruption in elections has only become more pervasive over time (Aspinall and Berenschot 2019). There have been concerted efforts to subdue and co-opt the Anti-Corruption Commission, the main independent organization in the way of a corrupt political elite that has often targeted members of the legislature, the police, and public prosecutors. The Anti-Corruption Commission has faced numerous challenges to its role and its Commissioners have faced fabricated criminal charges and even physical attacks. In 2019, the Anti-Corruption Commission's powers and structure were amended in a way that is widely understood to have curtailed its strength and role in addressing gross corruption in high office. Further, in 2011, the

---

[11]   Constitution, Arts 22E(5); 23E, F, G 24B; 24C.

Constitutional Court faced legislative changes to its mandate and again in 2020, with the latter changes granting sitting judges a longer tenure, raising concerns that this would potentially make judges more favourable to the agenda of the government. The posts of law enforcement agencies such as the police and the Attorney General's office have also been politicized and these offices have increasingly used their powers to target political opponents (Mietzner 2018; Power 2018).

The third challenge is the support for a return to authoritarianism, embodied by the calls to revert to some aspects of the initial 1945 Constitution, which I discuss next.

The Limits of a Transformational Authoritarian Constitution: The Second Period of the Amended 1945 Constitution (2019–present)

The fifth stage of constitutional developments in Indonesia is from 2019. The period since 2019 is characterized by tangible legal and political threats to constitutional democracy. The year 2019 marks the beginning of the second term of president Joko Widodo (Jokowi) after a period of significant democratic decline. Jokowi was endorsed in office despite a first term marked by the intensification of threats and criminal allegations against political opponents and restrictions on freedom of speech, association, and the press, including online speech.

I suggest that this era is the second period of the amended 1945 Constitution, because one of the most prominent threats to constitutional democracy is the calls to amend the Constitution and revert to aspects of the initial 1945 Constitution. The idea propagated by illiberal nationalists and populists, as well as the military, is that the initial 1945 Constitution is somehow sacred and that the 1999–2002 amendments violated that sacred constitutional bargain. These groups often deliberately refer to the initial 1945 Constitution as the *original* 1945 Constitution, implying it has greater legitimacy and salience compared to the amended version. By co-opting the idea of the 'original 1945 Constitution', proponents suggest that the Constitution is sacred and should not have been amended. Legal advocates such as the late Adnan Buyung Nasution have argued that the use of the word 'original' is problematic, and instead the first Constitution should be referred to as the 'initial 1945 Constitution' (Nasution 2011), in order to avoid any suggestion that constitutional amendment is illegitimate.[12] Nasution associated Soepomo's idea of integralism with the myth of the sacred 1945 Constitution.

Since at least 2002, there have been intermittent calls to amend the Constitution and return to the initial 1945 Constitution. Around 2002, these calls began with the military's response to constitutional amendments , and several years later, in 2008, a new political party, the Greater Indonesia Movement (*Gerakan Indonesia Raya*, Gerinda), picked up the mandate. Since then, these calls have come from all sides of politics, including minority political parties, members of the government, and the military. The reasons for these calls are complex and motivated by different goals, although the ends they wish to achieve—including strengthening the power of the

---

[12] For this reason I have used the term 'initial 1945 Constitution' in this chapter.

executive, reducing limits on the power and term of the president, and reinstating the position of the MPR—are similar.

First, discussions on amending the Constitution are framed around the idea of reinstating the five-year economic development plan known as the Broad Guidelines of State Policy (*Garis-Garis Besar Haluan Negara*), commonly referred to in Indonesia by the acronym 'GBHN'. This proposal would in theory return greater power to the MPR, which once had the power to set state guidelines under the initial 1945 Constitution. Members of the two largest political parties in Indonesia, Golkar and PDI-P, have been proponents of this proposal. For example, in 2014, former president and member of Golkar BJ Habibie (1998–1999, d 2019), ironically known for the speed and scale of his liberalizing reforms, endorsed the idea of returning to the GBHN (Tempo 2014). He repeated this message at several events and argued that such an approach would enhance long-term national development (Antara News 2017). In 2016, the chairperson of the political party Indonesian Democratic Party of Struggle (*Partai Demokrasi Indonesia Perjuangan*, PDI-P), Megawati Sukarnoputri, proposed the idea of returning to the 1945 Constitution in a speech to the PDI-P Congress (Razak 2016; Ihsanuddin 2016), which is the second largest political party in Indonesia. A few months later, a majority of political parties in the People's Representative Assembly (MPR) and the Regional Representatives Council (DPR) drafted a proposal with two options for constitutional amendment. One option was to grant the MPR the authority to issue guidelines in the form of a decree, while the second option was to insert an explicit power to formulate GBHN as an article in the Constitution.

These proposals to reinstate the power and status of the MPR display a paradox. On one hand, during the regimes of Soekarno and Soeharto as mentioned earlier, political elites never followed the wording of the initial 1945 Constitution in practice. That is, while the text of the 1945 Constitution did position the MPR as the highest institution, in practice the president was the most powerful office. The idea that the president was accountable to the MPR, or that the MPR set state policy, was never realized. The impotence of the MPR was a key element of authoritarian constitutional politics of the past. On the other hand, this constitutional amendment proposal appears to be motivated by the desire to centralize political power, affirm the role of the president, and ensure political parties and not the people select the president. Some contemporary actors want to reinstate not the actual text of the constitution, but the type of politics it permitted and facilitated, that is, centralized authoritarian rule similar to the regimes of Soekarno and Soeharto.

Second, there are related constitutional amendment proposals to enhance the power and term of the president, and changes to the appointment process. There are proposals to remove direct presidential elections and instead return to a selection process whereby the MPR has the power to appoint the president. There have been ongoing debates over the presidential election process and dissatisfaction with the process which generally only sees two candidates run for office. There are also calls to remove the presidential term limit. This would allow president Joko Widodo, known as Jokowi, to run for a third term in office, as he is currently serving his second and final term. Jokowi has declined to endorse such a proposal to date.

Minority political party Gerinda openly advocates for amendment to the Constitution. The objective of restoring the initial 1945 Constitution is a goal in the preamble of Gerinda's founding document. In 2008, Gerinda was established as a political party led by former disgraced military general, Prabowo Subianto. Prabowo is a key advocate for returning to the initial 1945 Constitution and he has specifically called for a return to the Broad Outlines of State Policy (Aspinall 2015). Aside from former military officers in politics such as Prabowo, the military is also a key actor in the calls to return to the 1945 Constitution (Mietzner, this volume).

Due to Indonesia's history of authoritarianism, civil society harbours wide suspicions about the calls to amend the Constitution. For example, there are concerns that starting such a process even with a narrow purpose may lead to much larger charges to the Constitution that would threaten the future of constitutional democracy. On the other hand, the military perceives the return to the initial 1945 Constitution as an opportunity for the restoration and expansion of its role in national politics.

The process for amendment requires a proposal to be made in writing that specifies both the articles to be amended and the justification and basis for the amendment. The proposal must be put to a session of the MPR and submitted with the support of at least one-third of MPR representatives. At the session, at least two-thirds of the representatives must be present. The proposal must be approved by a simple majority (50 per cent plus one). Since 2019, Jokowi's government could garner the support needed for such an amendment.

Calls to amend the Constitution and return to the 1945 Constitution have not been the only proposals for reform. In contrast, the late human rights lawyer Adnan Buyung Nasution argued that the amended 1945 Constitution was in need of further amendment in order to advance democratic reforms (Nasution 2011). Many others, including authors in this volume, have suggested democratic reforms to the text or practise of the Constitution. Nevertheless, it is the debate about returning to the 1945 Constitution that remains prominent.

In the lead up to the 2024 elections, many questions remain. Will the Constitution be amended before the elections and, if so, how? Will Jokowi step down after the end of his second term as president? Will the next president be directly elected? How will other issues—such as social and economic recovery from Covid-19 and moving the capital city—affect the future of constitutional democracy? Given that the issue of returning to the 1945 Constitution has been raised since 2002, this proposal is unlikely to go away. The real question is whether the government will choose to act on these calls or not.

Challenges and Prospects for Constitutional Democracy: Themes in this Volume

In this volume, many of the chapters review and assess the state of the field and developments in constitutional democracy over the past twenty years. The volume is divided into two parts, 'Legal and Political Foundations and Institutions', and 'The Constitutional Court and the Protection of Rights'. The chapters in Part 1 primarily focus on key constitutional institutions including the legislature, the executive, the military, the Judicial Commission, the Supreme Court, the General Election Commission, and the General Election Supervisory Agency (*Bawaslu*).

In Chapter 2, Stephen Sherlock focuses on Indonesia's legislature, the centrepiece of the law reform process. He questions the impact that constitutional reforms had on the role of the legislature and assesses its performance over more than twenty years. He suggests that the perception that the reform process gave significant powers to the legislature is in fact incorrect. He argues that the constitutional reform process only partially transferred legislative power to the legislature. Legislature power is in fact still shared between the president and legislature, it is not the sole remit of the legislature. Further, the lawmaking process by the legislature is overseen by a representative from the president, ensuring close involvement of the president's office in the legislative process. The phenomena Sherlock describes—a powerful executive and the cumbersome and corrupt nature of legislative procedures—are a long-term feature of the legal and political landscape.

While the military is no longer in the legislature, it remains an important, but often less appreciated, institution in constitutional developments in Indonesia, often posing a direct challenge to constitutional democracy. The primary contribution of the next chapter by Marcus Mietzner is one of legal and political history: to explain how and why the military at first opposed the initial 1945 Constitution, only to later shift to a position of support for and defence of the Constitution. Mietzner's chapter reveals how the military is partly behind the contemporary calls to return to the initial 1945 Constitution, which poses a real threat to the future of constitutional democracy.

The constitutional amendments of 1999–2002 reformed the role of the military and the police and reaffirmed the rights of a person accused of a crime. In Chapter 4, Fachrizal Afandi and Adriaan Bedner interrogate the substance of these changes and ask whether the rule of law is upheld in terms of how the police and prosecutors conduct criminal investigations and trials. They argue that the police and public prosecution have developed practices to circumvent the constitutional rights of the accused. A prime example is that police detain an accused using the terminology of 'securing', that is, securing an accused person in their possession. The police contrast the idea of 'securing' with 'arrest' in order to circumvent the constitutional rights of an accused. Afandi and Bedner also show how the prosecution are perceived to be subordinate to the executive and the police, while the police imagine themselves as a fourth branch of government. Afandi and Bednar suggest that the state remains an authoritarian regime because it continues to use security forces for political ends. Their chapter reminds us that formal constitutional amendment may only be the beginning of steps towards constitutional democracy and may not enhance the rule of law if not institutionalized through the core institutions of the state such as criminal justice agencies.

In Chapter 5, Rachael Diprose focuses on the challenges of decentralization. Decentralization has been a big part of the country's contemporary trajectory. This means that provincial and local government authorities are important to the story of constitutional democracy in Indonesia. Diprose considers how the balance has been struck between district, provincial, and central powers in terms of natural resources and how that balance has changed and been disputed over time.

Turning to the courts, Dian Rositawati focuses her chapter on the Judicial Commission. The Judicial Commission is designed as an independent body, that is, independent from both the executive and the judiciary, which means that the Supreme Court was not given a representative on the Commission. In response, the Supreme

Court has set itself in opposition to the Judicial Commission. An unusual decision in 2016 by the Constitutional Court limited the powers of the Judicial Commission, effectively reducing its ability to ensure accountability. The shared supervisory powers of the Supreme Court and the Judicial Commission, as expressed in regulation, are somewhat illusory as the Supreme Court has the upper hand with the power to review any such regulations. The alert reader may also notice that in Indonesia, the Supreme Court accepts applications from the judicial association (often led by judges of the Supreme Court itself), a conflict of interest for the Supreme Court. Further, some Constitutional Court decisions have gone against the Judicial Commission. However, in 2018, the Constitutional Court reaffirmed the power of the Commission in the selection process by deciding that the Commission was only required to put forward one candidate per vacancy. Overall, the Supreme Court claims an expanded concept of judicial independence that limits the role of the Judicial Commission and its ability to ensure judicial accountability.

The next two chapters focus on legal and political issues raised by elections, which have been the hallmark of the past two decades of constitutional democracy. In their chapter, Adhy Aman and Dirk Tomsa argue that constitutional design has deferred key electoral details to legislation and this has left the electoral framework open to potential abuse by the legislature of the day. There have been major changes to the electoral rules before every national election. Debate over legislative changes to electoral laws has been fierce and often influenced by the larger political parties. Despite this, Aman and Tomsa argue that the independent bodies tasked with upholding electoral integrity and the Constitution (the Electoral Commission and Election Supervision Body) have performed well under difficult conditions.

Although not anticipated by the Constitution, the Election Supervision Body (commonly known by the acronym *Bawaslu*) is an example of an institution that has become crucial to protecting constitutional democracy, as the chapter by Fritz Siregar demonstrates. Since 1998, as electoral practices developed, the need arose for an election supervision body, that is, an independent agency that can monitor and receive complaints about the Election Commission itself up until election day. *Bawaslu* has grown enormously in its role and in public reputation in recent years. The ongoing dispute over which institution should have the power to resolve electoral disputes presents a potential opportunity for *Bawaslu* to expand its mandate and powers. The Constitutional Court currently has the power to resolve electoral disputes, but consideration is being given to other models for such dispute resolution. Fritz discusses the design options being considered and comparative models available. One option is to establish a new Election Court or to empower *Bawaslu* to adjudicate cases as a specialized court. This goes to the debate about the role and function of specialized courts and to what extent such courts can be used to bypass issues of corruption inherent in the general courts (Crouch 2019). In previous work, I have suggested that while the numerous specialized courts are a striking feature of Indonesia's post-1998 judicial reform landscape, the relative success of these institutions (and how success is understood) lies in the details, such as whether they are independent from the executive and general judiciary, its level of resources, and the relationship between the new court and the executive (Crouch 2019). From a review of various models, Fritz suggests that an independent electoral court, rather than a specialized court under the jurisdiction of the Supreme Court, would be a preferred model for electoral dispute reform in Indonesia.

The second part of the book focuses on the protection of rights and the role that the Constitutional Court has played in building and maintaining constitutional democracy (Mietzner 2010). Like many constitutional courts around the world with wide standing rules, the Indonesian Constitutional Court plays a key role in determining cases involving constitutional rights, although its approach has changed over time and has at times been conservative and strategic (Butt 2012). Andrew Rosser's chapter argues that social rights litigation in Indonesia has typically been collective in orientation, with non-government organizations (NGOs) the central driver of this action, and that social rights litigation has had a real impact on policy outcomes. With a specific focus on health and education. Rosser suggests that the primary goal of social rights litigation by NGOs has been policy driven and aimed to confront reforms that would privatize public services and in doing so risk empowering predatory bureaucratic and business actors. Rosser suggests that overall, from 1998 to 2015, social rights litigation had an impact on public policy. Yet he is conscious that with the decline of democracy, this may not be the case in the future. Rosser shows that many of the conditions that enabled such social rights litigation and policy change in the past are changing, and this may limit social rights litigation in the future.

In a separate chapter, Stefanus Hendrianto (Hendri) weighs in on the debate on whether and how the Constitutional Court has contributed to informal constitutional change. Hendri suggests that the Court has intentionally engaged in informal constitutional change. He describes Indonesia's constitutional amendment culture as one that combines aspects of both flexibility and rigidity. Hendri offers four case studies of informal constitutional amendment: on elections; the economy; the bill of rights; and religion. One of the most high-profile examples of informal constitutional amendment is the decision of the Court that the legislative and presidential elections must be held simultaneously, despite the absence of any such explicit requirement in the Constitution. The idea of informal constitutional amendment is relatively underexplored in the Indonesian context and this chapter opens up this debate.

Yance Arizona's chapter explores the rights of indigenous peoples. The debate over recognition of indigenous people's rights to culture, language, and land, among others, has experienced significant revival in Indonesia over the past decade. Yance Arizona shows how the idea of indigeneity and rights for indigenous people have been a part of constitution-making processes since 1945 and examines its contemporary manifestation. Yance suggests that since independence there have been six stages in the constitutional recognition, or lack thereof, of indigeneity in Indonesia. Post-1999, the sixth and current stage Yance identifies is when the constitutional amendment process enhanced indigenous rights by providing for specific recognition of the status of special regions and of adat law communities (Art 18D). Several regions including Yogyakarta, Papua, West Papua, and Aceh have special recognition. However, similar to the past, the recognition clause is limited in scope because traditional political institutions and customary land rights cannot be contrary to certain national interests, laws, and regulations.

The constitutional right to religious freedom and permissible state limitations on that right have been the subject of much contention in Indonesia. One of the reasons is that the Constitution departs from international practice and includes reference to 're-ligious values' as a permissible basis for the state to limit the right to religious freedom. The concept of religious values as a limit on the right to religious freedom allows the courts to engage in a form of judicial deference to recognised religious author-ities (Crouch 2016). The limit of religious values has been used by the Constitutional Court to justify upholding laws that in practice are used to target religious minorities and those perceived to deviate from orthodox Islamic teachings (Crouch 2013). In their chapter, Ahmad Rofii and Nadirsyah Hosen explain the debate leading up to the amendment of the 1945 Constitution and how the idea of religious values came to be inserted into the limitations clause. There was debate about whether this was even ne-cessary, and constitution-makers had no clear consensus about what religious values might mean. Rofii and Hosen illustrate how the Constitutional Court has approached the task of interpreting religious values in at least four different ways through two case studies: the Blasphemy Law and the Zakat Management Law. Overall, they point to a lack of clarity in how the Court is interpreting the idea of religious values.

The chapter by Abdurrahman Satrio addresses the Constitutional Court's de-cision on the issue of LGBT rights and same-sex relations. The court case that prompted discussion on this issue was distinctly anti-rights—the applicant sought to argue that adult same-sex relations should be criminalized under the Penal Code. In their argument, the petitioners referred to the idea that religious values can be used as a legitimate constitutional limitation on rights (see Rofii and Hosen, this volume). Satrio finds that the Court failed to unequivocally declare that any ef-fort to criminalize same-sex relations was unconstitutional nor did it go further to offer an interpretation of the Constitution in support of LGBT rights. Nevertheless, in the context of Indonesia, Satrio suggests that the Court's approach was a stra-tegic move. The Court deferred to the legislature in what Satrio suggests was a kind of weak-form review. The Court suggested any such proposal was for the legislature to consider as part of attempts to revise the penal code. There have been many at-tempts to reform the penal code, but no such attempts have ever been successful. Satrio suggests that, on one reading, this was an implicit way for the Constitutional Court to protect LGBT rights without having to explicitly decide the case in a way that may risk backlash from conservative groups.

The final chapter by Mark Cammack offers a reflection on the jurisprudence and achievements of the Constitutional Court through an examination of the idea of legal certainty. Cammack explores the nebulous concept of legal certainty and how it has been deployed by the Court. He firstly takes us through various comparative uses and understandings of the term, from international, regional, and domestic usages, in civil law and common law systems. The idea of legal certainty has come to be a catch-all argument before Indonesia's Constitutional Court, a way to ensure a petition is heard before the bench. Cammack suggests that under the cover of legal certainty, the Court has been able to hear constitutional cases on a wide range of laws. Through an analysis of a range of cases, he demonstrates that there are no limits to the scope of legal cer-tainty. This wide jurisdiction for the Court, Cammack suggests, is one means by which the Court makes up for the shortcomings of the Supreme Court. This finding is con-sistent with other scholarship that suggests specialized courts are used to circumvent problems in the general courts (Crouch 2019).

It has been twenty years since the conclusion of the constitutional amendment process, resulting in the amended 1945 Constitution. The chapters in this volume reflect on the progress in favour of constitutional democracy during this time, as well as the setbacks and future threats and challenges. While all authors acknowledge progress made, assessments vary on how far there has been decline in constitutional democracy, and how far it may decline further.

* * *

The purpose of this chapter has been to explore the case of Indonesia through the idea of transformational authoritarian constitutions. I show that debates in Indonesia about the nature and scope of constitutional democracy and its relationship to liberalism and human rights, go back to the 1940s. These debates on constitutional democracy run through three interim or transitional constitutions: the initial 1945 Constitution; the 1949 Provisional Constitution, and the 1950 Provisional Constitution. In 1959, the Constituent Assembly's efforts to design a permanent constitution were overruled by Soekarno who controversially claimed to use his executive power to reinstate the initial 1945 Constitution. Later, under several decades of Soeharto's New Order authoritarian regime, the designation of the initial 1945 Constitution as sacred and the promotion of Pancasila democracy were strategies to resist calls for constitutional change and target those calling for democratic reform. Underlying both Soekarno's and Soeharto's rules was Soepomo's idea of integralism, a convenient justification for authoritarian rule.

The major political shift in 1998 created space for constitution-making, resulting in the amended 1945 Constitution as a transformational authoritarian constitution. The 1945 Constitution was formerly a constitution used under authoritarian rule and to further illiberal ends. Constitution-makers transformed the Constitution through amendment to foster constitutional democracy. The authoritarian constitution facilitated a powerful and unlimited executive; an undemocratic legislature; subordinate courts; the absence of protection for rights; a highly centralized governance system; and the ideology of integralism. In contrast, the amended 1945 Constitution was transformational in five main ways. It transformed a powerful and unlimited president to a president appointed by the people with reduced powers and with a maximum term limit; it transformed a weak and coopted legislature into a representative legislature; it transformed a subordinate judicial system into one independent of the executive and with a new Constitutional Court tasked with upholding the bill of rights. Further, there was a transformation from centralization to decentralization, and from an ideology of integralism to constitutional democracy.

The precise nature of constitutional democracy, and the shape and scope of its relationship to liberalism and human rights, has been the subject of debate ever since. I suggest that in 2019 the first period of the amended Constitution came to an end, and the second period has been marked by the persistent threat of constitutional amendment that could see the return to aspects of the initial 1945 Constitution and authoritarianism. Indonesia certainly illustrates the possibilities of a transformational authoritarian constitution. Yet it also demonstrates the potential limits of a transformational authoritarian constitution. Such constitutions may be open to abuse by critics who prefer the initial constitution and the authoritarianism it facilitated. The initial authoritarian constitution is a constitutional touchstone in debates on constitutional reform and leaves open the risk of reversion to the former authoritarian constitution. This suggests that transformational authoritarian constitutions may be limited in time, as it delays and defers, but does not necessarily solve, fundamental issues about the role and powers of the state.

The cases of Indonesia and Chile show the temporal ability of such constitutions to resolve constitutional debates and the contrasting directions such constitutions may go. In the direction of constitutional democracy, Chile has initiated a new constitution-making process to finally replace the transformational authoritarian Constitution of 1980. In contrast, Indonesia risks commencing a constitutional amendment process that may take it back to authoritarian rule under the initial 1945 Constitution. At the time of publication, calls to return to the 1945 Constitution remained, but it is uncertain if such calls will be realized. This volume is offered in the shadow of that uncertainty, conscious of the potentially fragile, or at least highly contested, future for the transformational authoritarian constitution and the constitutional democracy it seeks to facilitate.

References

Antara News (2017) 'BJ Habibie: Indonesia perlu miliki GBHN' 22 August, https://www.antaranews.com/berita/648205/bj-habibie-indonesia-perlu-miliki-gbhn.

Aspinall, Edward and Ward Berenschot (2019) *Elections, Clientelism, and the State in Indonesia.* New York: Cambridge University Press.

Aspinall, Edward (2015) 'Oligarchic Populism: Prabowo Subianto's Challenge to Indonesian Democracy' 99 *Indonesia* 1.

Bedner, Adriaan (2017) 'The Need for Realism: Ideals and Practise in Indonesia's Constitutional History in M Adams, A Meuwese, and E Hirsch Ballin (eds) *Constitutionalism and the Rule of Law: Bridging Idealism and Realism.* Cambridge: Cambridge University Press. pp 159–194.

Bourchier, David (2015) *Illiberal Democracy in Indonesia: The Ideology of the Family State.* New York: Routledge.

Bourchier, David M (2019) 'Two Decades of Ideological Contestation in Indonesia: From Democratic Cosmopolitanism to Religious Nationalism' 49(5) *Journal of Contemporary Asia* 713–733.

Burns, Peter (2004) *The Leiden Legacy: Concepts of Law in Indonesia.* Leiden: KITLV Press.

Butt, Simon (2012) 'Indonesia's Constitutional Court: Conservative Activist or Strategic Operator?' in Bjoern Dressel (ed) *The Judicialization of Politics in Asia.* New York: Routledge. pp 98–116.

Butt, Simon (2015) *The Constitutional Court and Democracy in Indonesia.* Leiden: Brill.

Butt, Simon, Melissa Crouch, and Ros Dixon (2016) 'The First Decade of Indonesia's Constitutional Court' 16(2) *Australian Journal of Asian Law* 1–7.

Butt, Simon and Tim Lindsey (2012) *The Constitution of Indonesia.* Oxford: Hart Publishing.

Crouch, Melissa (2013) *Law and Religion in Indonesia: Conflict and the Courts in West Java.* London, New York: Routledge.

Crouch, Melissa (2016) 'Constitutionalism, Islam and the Practise of Religious Deference: The Case of the Indonesian Constitutional Court' 16(2) *Australian Journal of Asian Law* 1–15.

Crouch, Melissa (2019) 'The Judicial Reform Landscape in Indonesia: Innovation, Specialisation and the Legacy of Dan S Lev' in Melissa Crouch (ed) *The Politics of Court Reform: Judicial Change and Legal Culture in Indonesia*. New York: Cambridge University Press. pp 1–32.

Crouch, Melissa (2020) 'Constitutional Touchstones: Peace Processes, Federalism and Constitution-making in Myanmar' 18(4) *International Journal of Constitutional Law* 1350–1372.

Crouch, Melissa (2021) 'The Promise and Paradox of Women in the Judiciary in Indonesia' in Melissa Crouch (ed) *Women and the Judiciary in the Asia-Pacific*. New York: Cambridge University Press. pp 149–177.

Diprose, Rachael, Dave McRae, and Vedi Hadiz (2019) 'Two Decades of Reformasi in Indonesia: An Illiberal Turn?' 49(5) *Journal of Contemporary Asia* 691–712.

Drooglever, Pieter J (1997) 'The Genesis of the Indonesian Constitution of 1949' 153(1) *Bijdragen tot de Taal-, Land- en Volkenkunde* 65–84.

Elson, Robert E (2013) 'Two Failed Attempts to Islamize the Indonesian Constitution' 28(3) *Sojourn* 379–437.

Feith, Herbert (2007) *The Decline of Constitutional Democracy in Indonesia*. first published 1962. Cornell University Press. Jakarta, Indonesia: Equinox Press.

Fealy, Greg and Edward Aspinall (eds) (2010) *Suharto's New Order and its Legacy: Essays in Honour of Harold Crouch*. ANU Press: Canberra.

Ginsburg, Tom (2020) 'Transformational Authoritarian Constitutions: The Case of Chile' in T Ginsburg and A Huq (eds) *From Parchment to Practise: Implementing New Constitutions*. New York: Cambridge University Press. pp 239–262.

Ginsburg, Tom and Aziz Huq (2020) 'Introduction: From Parchment to Practise' in T Ginsburg and A Huq (eds) *From Parchment to Practise: Implementing New Constitutions*. New York: Cambridge University Press. pp 1–28.

Indrayana, Denny (2008) *Indonesian Constitutional Reform 1999-2002: An Evaluation of Constitution-making in Transition*. Jakarta: Kompas Book Publishing.

Ihsanuddin (2016) 'Ingin Hidupkan GBHN, Megawati Pastikan Tak Ada Kepentingan Dirinya atau PDI-P' *Kompas*, 12 January, <https://nasional.kompas.com/read/2016/01/12/15153011/ Ingin.Hidupkan.GBHN.Megawati.Pastikan.Tak.Ada.Kepentingan.Dirinya.atau.PDI-P>.

Klare, Karl E (1998) 'Legal Culture and Transformative Constitutionalism' 14 *South African Journal on Human Rights* 146.

Kusuma, AB (2004) *Lahirnya Undang-undang Dasar 1945: Memuat Salinan Dokumen Otentik Badan Oentoek Menyelidiki Oesaha-2 Persiapan Kemerdekaan*. Depok: Badan Penerbit Fakultas Hukum Universitas Indonesia.

Lev, Daniel S (1965) 'The Politics of Judicial Development in Indonesia' vii, 2 (Jan) *Comparative Studies in Society & History* 173–199.

Lev, Daniel S (1978) 'Judicial Authority and the Struggle for an Indonesian Rechtsstaat' 13(1) (Fall/Winter) *Law & Society Review* 37.

Lev, Daniel S (2009) *The Transition to Guided Democracy: Indonesian Politics 1957-1959. Jakarta*. First published 1966, Cornell Southeast Asia Program Publications. Indonesia: Equinox Publishing.

Lindsey, Tim (2006) 'Indonesian Constitutional Reform: Muddling Towards Democracy' 6 *Singapore Journal of International and Comparative Law* 244–301.

Lubis, Todung Mulya (1994) *In Search of Human Rights: Legal Political Dilemmas of Indonesia's New Order 1966-1990*. First printed 1993. Jakarta: PT Gramedia Pustaka Utana, SPES Foundation.

Mietzner, Marcus (2010) 'Political Conflict Resolution and Democratic Consolidation in Indonesia: The Role of the Constitutional Court' *Journal of East Asian Studies* 10. Mietzner,

Marcus (2015) *Reinventing Asian Populism: Jokowi's Rise, Democracy, and Political Contestation in Indonesia*. Policy Studies No 72. Honolulu: East-West Centre.

Mietzner, Marcus (2018) 'Fighting Illiberalism with Illiberalism: Islamic Populist and Democratic Deconsolidation in Indonesia' 21(2) *Pacific Affairs* 261.

Morfit, Michael (1981) 'Pancasila: The Indonesian State Ideology According to the New Order Government' 21(8) *Asian Survey* 838.

Nasution, Adnan Buyung (1992) *The Aspiration for Constitutional Government in Indonesia: A Socio Legal Study of the Indonesian Konstituante 1956 – 1959*. Jakarta: Pustaka Sinar Harapan.

Nasution, Adnan Buyung (2011) *Towards Constitutional Democracy in Indonesia*. Papers on Southeast Asian Constitutionalism, the University of Melbourne.

Power, Thomas P (2018) 'Jokowi's Authoritarian Turn and Indonesia's Democratic Decline' 54(3) *Bulletin of Indonesian Economic Studies* 307–338.

Razak, Imanuddin (2016) 'View Point: GBHN and the Assurance of Sustainable Development' *Jakarta Post*, 17 January, https://www.thejakartapost.com/news/2016/01/17/view-point-gbhn-and-assurance-sustainable-development.html.

Setiawan, Ken (2019) 'The Human Rights Courts: Embedding Impunity' in Melissa Crouch (ed) *The Politics of Court Reform: Judicial Change and Legal Culture in Indonesia*. New York: Cambridge University Press. pp 287–310.

Tate, C Neal and Torbjorn Vallinder (eds) (1995) *The Global Expansion of Judicial Power*. New York: New York University Press.

Teitel, Ruti (2000) *Transitional Justice*. New York: Oxford University Press.

Tempo (2014) 'Habibie: Kembailkan GBHN', *Tempo.com*, 26 March, Jakarta https://nasional.tempo.co/read/565577/habibie-kembalikan-gbhn.

PART 1
LEGAL AND POLITICAL FOUNDATIONS AND INSTITUTIONS

2

The Consequences of Halfway Constitutional Reform

Problems of Lawmaking in Indonesia's Parliament

Stephen Sherlock

Introduction

Legislatures are, by definition, law-making institutions. It is conventionally expected in a democracy that a parliament will have the full power to pass, amend, or reject draft legislation. Of course, in Westminster and other parliamentary systems, the location of executive government inside the legislature may compromise the powers of the parliament in practice, but the constitutional authority to pass bills into law still resides with the parliament. In presidential systems, with a clearer separation of executive and legislative branches of government, legislatures generally have a formidable array of powers in the legislative process, in both theory and practice. It may be the case that most legislation is initiated and drafted by the executive—and consultation between the two branches may be close and continuous—but ultimately the authority to decide on the fate of legislation is the sole prerogative of the legislature.

In Indonesia, however, this is not the case. This chapter argues that the common perception that the 1999–2002 constitutional reforms transferred full law-making power from the president to the parliament is misplaced. In reality, the reforms only went halfway. While the amended Constitution clearly describes a presidential system, it does not grant sole legislative authority to the parliament. Instead, the power to make laws is shared between the parliament and the president, and all draft legislation must have the joint agreement of both branches of government before it can become law. To make matters worse, these constitutional provisions have been interpreted not only to mean that the president must give final assent to legislation, but that his/her representatives must be present and involved in every step of the legislative process, from developing legislative priorities through to deliberations on each clause of a bill. Executive government has veto power over every key decision in the lawmaking process, from planning to promulgation.

The chapter argues that the Constitution's clauses on law-making, and the way it has been applied in practice, are at the heart of the problems with Indonesia's legislative process, especially the issue of poor legislative productivity. We need to go beyond the widespread perception that the problem is caused by laws becoming stuck in the mire of an unproductive parliament and look more deeply into the issue. Of course, these matters cannot be separated from the problematic behaviour of political actors

Stephen Sherlock, *The Consequences of Halfway Constitutional Reform* In: *Constitutional Democracy in Indonesia*. Edited by: Melissa Crouch, Oxford University Press. © Stephen Sherlock, 2023. DOI: 10.1093/oso/9780192870681.003.0002

in parliament, as I have argued previously. These, in turn, reflect the transactional and corrupted nature of Indonesian politics in general (Aspinall and Sukmajati 2016). But to the extent that there are institutional issues involved, we need to develop a more complete picture of the context within which the parliament operates, in this case the constitutional context.

The development of this argument unfolds in three main parts. In part I, I set the scene by introducing the main features of Indonesia's parliament, outlining the changes made to the structure and authority of legislative bodies in the first three constitutional amendments. This is followed by a review of existing literature on the parliament, noting how limited it is compared to other aspects of Indonesian politics and describing its key themes. Part II addresses the contention that the constitutional reforms swung power too far in favour of the parliament and created a 'legislative-heavy' system, showing that, on the contrary, the provision for 'joint agreement' on laws between parliament and president meant that the transfer of power went only halfway. This is elaborated by showing how the parliament's rules of procedure deeply embed executive government in the legislative process. Part III shows how joint deliberation of the DPR and government on draft legislation creates a de facto or 'silent' presidential veto and greatly complicates the legislative process, contributing to the infamous delays in passing laws. Two case studies on legislation in the early 2000s demonstrated how the government's ability to exercise its veto out of public view at a procedural level made it more effective in practice. A further three case studies from the last decade have shown that cumbersome parliamentary procedures, developed to implement the requirement for 'joint agreement', are at the root of blockages in the passage of laws. This is particularly so when executive government agencies are unable to agree to produce a single government position on the content of legislation. Finally, chaos in law-making has only been exacerbated when successive presidents have used regulations in lieu of law, revealing their apparent incapacity to control and coordinate their ministers and creating the absurd situation where the president invalidates legislation he had only just agreed to.

The Parliament and Indonesia's Constitution

The amended 1945 Constitution provides for two institutions with a role in legislation at the national level: the People's Representative Council (*Dewan Perwakilan Rakyat*, DPR) (Arts 19–22) and the Regional Representative Council (*Dewan Perwakilan Daerah*, DPD) (Art 22C&D). Because of the existence of these two chambers, Indonesia's parliament is sometimes described as bicameral, but it is in effect unicameral. This is because the only chamber with the authority to pass, amend, or reject draft legislation is the DPR—the Constitution is unambiguous in stating that 'the DPR holds the power to make laws' (Art 20(1)). The DPD has only advisory powers and can draft laws on a range of issues related to regional affairs, but such draft laws must be submitted to the DPR for passage into law (Art 22D(1)) (Sherlock 2005). The Constitution also provides for a People's Consultative Council or MPR (*Majelis Permusyawarahan Rakyat*), a body which combines the members of the DPR and MPR.

In the original 1945 Constitution, the MPR sat at the apex of the system, 'exercising in full' the sovereignty of the people (Art 1), holding the power to elect the president and to draft 'broad outlines of state policy'. Following the amendments of 1999–2002, however, the MPR has no legislative role (except reviewing the Constitution), with its main function now being to ceremonially inaugurate the president. Because of the DPR's exclusive powers over the passage of laws and independent oversight over the executive, the term 'parliament' used in this chapter can be taken to mean the DPR.

The Constitution also provides for regional assemblies known as Regional Houses of Representatives or DPRD (*Dewan Perwakilan Rakyat Daerah*) (Art 18(3)). While these are legislative bodies in a broad sense, it needs to be emphasized that they do not draft laws (*undang-undang*) but can only make regional regulations (*peraturan daerah*) that sit below laws in the Indonesian hierarchy of legislation (Art 18(6)). The procedures for the operation of regional government are made by laws passed by the DPR (Art 18(7)).

Constitutional Reform and the Parliament

Following the collapse of President Suharto's New Order regime in 1998 and the constitutional amendments of 1999–2002, the parliament was amongst the first targets for change. Horowitz described the reform process as a 'game of inches'; incremental changes over a 'protracted' period rather than a single revision or rewriting of the document (2013: 89). But the reformers were 'determined to reverse the presidential supremacy of the previous four decades' (2013: 93) and considered a crucial first step to be to shift law-making power away from the president (where it had resided in the original Constitution) to the DPR. This and limiting the president to two terms in office were the crucial changes in the first round of reform in 1999. Thus, as mentioned above, Article 20(1) placed legislative power in the hands of the DPR and gave individual DPR members the 'right to put forward draft laws' (Art 21). The crucial caveat—the main focus of this chapter—is that laws would be made with the 'joint agreement' of the president (Art 20(2)).

Other reforms to legislative systems were left to the second and third rounds of amendments in 2000 and 2001. These included the creation of the DPD and DPRDs and the redefinition of the role and authority of the MPR. The 2002 reforms also defined the functions of the DPR as 'legislation, budget and oversight' (Art 20A(1)). In order to strengthen the DPR's power of oversight over the president, the reforms provided the parliament with the right of interpellation, to conduct inquiries, to put questions, to present its findings and opinions, and to put forward proposals to the executive (Art 20A). An important further change that was very prominent at the time, but which is increasingly being forgotten today, was the abolition of military representation in the DPR, with the entire chamber to be fully chosen by popular election (Art 19(1)). Candidates for the DPR were to be nominated by political parties, while those for the DPD would be non-party individuals (Art 22E).

Literature on the Indonesian Parliament

The literature on Indonesia's legislature is limited when compared to the extensive scholarly attention given to other elements of the Constitution and other political institutions. Intensive studies on the political parties competing for parliamentary representation and on the electoral processes leading to the composition of parliament have produced a very impressive body of work (eg Aspinall and Sukmajati 2016; Mietzner 2013; Tomsa 2008), but there appears to be much less interest in the operations of the legislature and its members after they have been elected. This was understandable during the New Order, when the parliament was a hand-picked body that rubber-stamped law-making decisions made by the president and which did not exercise any meaningful oversight over the executive branch. But in the post-New Order era, when the parliament has become an important centre of power, the scholarly coverage of the legislature remains something of a lacuna in the study of Indonesia's Constitution and politics.

Nevertheless, there is a body of scholarly international and Indonesian literature on the parliament. On the New Order parliament, Suryadinata (1987) drew attention to the fact that while the legislature was a rubber stamp it was nonetheless as the site of contention between various factions in the military's parliamentary representatives during the drafting of certain laws that affected the material interests of elite groups. Similarly, an unpublished doctoral thesis by Datta (2002) provided insights into the extent and limits of debate within the highly controlled parliament of the Suharto era. The transition to democracy and the immediate post-1998 period was examined by Ziegenhain (2005, 2008) who argued that the parliament played a decisive role in facilitating changes that established a democratic framework during the pivotal first years after the fall of the Suharto regime, but that its effective powers were eclipsed by the executive once the constitutional arrangements were put in place (Ziegenhain 2008: 8).

Scholarship on the post-*reformasi* parliament has primarily revolved around two broad themes. The first theme has been the interaction between the newly empowered legislature and executive government since the constitutional reforms, and the second has focused on whether the internal procedures and modes of operation in parliament—most of which are Suharto-era legacies—have facilitated or hindered the emergence of a democratic, representative institution.

On the first, responding to the contention that the constitutional amendments of 1999–2002 had shifted Indonesia from an 'executive-heavy' system to a 'legislative-heavy' system, Kawamura (2010) and Sherlock (2011, 2015) largely concurred in arguing that this change has not occurred, and that the question of the respective power of the two branches of government could not be answered purely in terms of constitutional law. It had to be placed in the context of political party dynamics, the 'rainbow cabinet' strategies used by successive presidents, as well as characteristics of internal decision-making processes in the parliament.

On the second theme, a number of scholars have sought to understand the interaction between political parties and leaders and parliamentary procedure, and its wider implications for Indonesian democracy. Decision-making and competition amongst power players within the parliament must take place within the bounds of inherited and basically unreformed internal organs and systems, but in the course of applying, making use of, and manipulating those systems, the players are gradually imbedding certain interpretations, practices, and political culture. Kawamura (2011), for example, has seen consensus-based decision-making (*musyawarah-mufakat*) in parliament mainly as an impediment to efficiency, while Sherlock (2012) has argued that the procedure is not only inefficient but gives a monopoly on decision-making power to party leaders, to the exclusion of ordinary members of parliament and to the detriment of public consultation and accountability. Sherlock (2003, 2007, 2009, 2011, 2018b) also extended the critique to a wide range of other elements of the way power and decision-making operates in the parliament, most of which are products of the Sukarno and Suharto periods and reflect the limited extent of the 1999–2002 constitutional reforms to the legislature. Adihputri (2015a, 2015b) also emphasized the importance of internal procedures and culture within parliament as impediments to the development of a democratic legislature, concluding that 'for the break with the authoritarian order to be fully realized, parliamentary procedures and practices need to be reformed'. The systems in need of reform included not only systems created under the New Order regime, but also legacies of the Dutch colonial era (Adihputri 2014). Indonesian language analysis by parliamentary staff (Katharina 2007; Bako et al 2008) has also concentrated on issues of parliamentary procedure, particularly in the context of proposals for reform. Some legal commentary and work on legal theory in lawmaking has also touched on issues of parliamentary procedure (eg Setiadi 2004; Febriansyah 2016; Prasetyaningsih 2017).

There is also a corpus of work taking the discussion beyond the confines of the parliamentary precinct into wider societal issues. Sherlock (2018b) has shown that the behaviour of politicians in parliament is influenced by a wider structure of political and economic incentives and pressures created by the electoral system, voter behaviour, and the character of political parties in Indonesia. Prihatini (2019a, 2019b) similarly draws linkages between the challenges faced by women contesting parliamentary elections and their experience as legislators, examining 'not only what hinders women winning elective office but also which women win and what happens once they get into parliament'. Djadijono (2007) analysed the implications of political parties' legislative power to 'recall' or dismiss their representative for the quality of parliamentary performance. Lay (2017) has examined the development of engagement with parliamentary processes by civil society organizations (CSOs). To this we should also add the literature on parliamentary public engagement produced by CSOs, some of it ephemeral and polemical, but some with a more substantial analytical character (eg Formappi 2005; Riskiyono 2016), including *Jurnal Pemilu dan Demokrasi* published by the Association for Elections and Democracy (*Perludem*) and bulletins from the Centre for Law and Policy Studies (*PSHK*). Some of this work delves quite deeply into the operations of the DPR, reflecting the fact that, from time to time, CSO input has had a significant impact on the content of individual pieces of legislation.

DPR's Legislative Powers and the President

The following discussion analyses the effects of the 1999 constitutional amendment, which changed the apportionment of law-making power between the president and the parliament, giving them a shared role in the legislative process. It shows how this halfway reform has given executive government an effective veto over legislation and produced a cumbersome and ineffective law-making system.

A 'Legislative-Heavy' Political System?

The 1999 constitutional amendment transferred law-making authority from its old site in the presidential palace to the DPR building. There was agreement between popular and elite reform advocates that such a change was of primary importance for correcting the excessive power of the presidency during the New Order. But discussion about the performance of the DPR since the amendments has seen some apparent regret about the change. Predictably, the DPR has become increasingly assertive in Indonesia's governance, and this has given birth to a discourse about the parliament becoming too powerful vis-à-vis the executive branch of government. According to this theory, the dominance of the president during the Suharto era represented an 'executive-heavy' system in which executive agencies wielded excessive power. But today, it is contended, the balance has swung too far in the other direction, upsetting 'checks and balances' and leading to a 'legislative-heavy' system. The argument first appeared in non-governmental organization (NGO) and media circles as part of a critique of corruption amongst legislators (Detiknews 2008; Formappi 2005; Susanti 2007), and has become accepted wisdom in much commentary (Republika 2014). It has also gained credence in scholarly literature, with Kawamura, for instance, concluding that 'the Indonesian presidential system after the introduction of institutional reforms is relatively "weak" and comparatively "legislative-heavy"' (2010: 48).

There are at least two problems with such analyses. First, they are an indication that many in the Indonesian political class have still not grasped the meaning of the constitutional amendments. Proponents of the idea of a problematic, 'legislative-heavy' system usually argue that since Indonesia has presidential (as opposed to parliamentary) government, the DPR should not be playing such an assertive role and is impinging on executive prerogatives. But accusations that the DPR is trying to impose a 'parliamentary system' betray ignorance of the fact that the new constitutional amendments eliminated the confusingly semi-parliamentary features of the old arrangements. The more clearly defined presidential system post-amendment inevitably made the DPR more likely to exercise its independent mandate. In most presidential systems, the separation of powers makes the parliament very strong, as a cursory examination of the immense power of the US Congress would illustrate.

Second, and much more important, the idea that constitutional reforms have excessively empowered the DPR obscures the reality that the transfer of law-making powers from the president to the DPR was not all that it appeared to be. Although there was indeed an important change in the balance of power between the two branches of government, the legislative power conferred on the parliament was partial and ambiguous, and moved only halfway towards transferring the locus of power. The apparently profound change foreshadowed in Article 20(1) was compromised by the following clause, which stated that laws would be made through 'joint agreement' (*persetujuan bersama*) between the president and the DPR (Art 20(2)). So in fact the DPR was not given the sole authority to make laws at all but had to share that role with the president.

In the excitement about the first amendment, the implications of this provision were not fully appreciated by most analysts. An international observer of the amendment debates, Andrew Ellis, was amongst the few to note at the time that the 'real transfer of power was not as significant as many imagined' (2007:24). Indeed, one member of the MPR committee drafting the constitutional reforms later came to realize the effect of the provision when he became a law-maker in the DPR and expressed his 'regret that we didn't take this issue seriously' during the reform debate.[1] The extent to which the significance of the issue has been fully appreciated by legal and political scholars is mixed. The leading constitutional analyst and former Constitutional Court judge, Jimly Asshiddiqie, reportedly described the provision as a 'peculiarity' of Indonesia's system of government (Republika 2014). One scholar produced a largely unnoticed article proposing the provision be amended to take away the need for presidential approval while still allowing for the president to be involved in deliberations (Elwan 2018: 444). There was a brief flurry of media interest in the issue at the end of 2014 when it appeared newly elected President Joko Widodo might be facing a hostile parliamentary majority led by Widodo's presidential opponent, Subianto Prabowo, but this disappeared along with the fading away of Prabowo's short-lived coalition (Wiyanti 2014; Republika 2014). While the literature on the constitutional reforms notes the changes to the DPR's law-making powers, it does not consider the implications for law-making and politics (Lindsey 2002; Indrayana 2008; Butt and Lindsey 2012). Horowitz states simply that the first amendment 'gave legislative power to the DPR' (2013: 93), with no apparent awareness of the effect of the 'joint agreement' clause. He gave more attention to debates about the authority of the largely powerless DPD (2013: 124ff) and the role of the MPR (2013: 93–94), while misleadingly describing the new arrangements as a 'three-house legislature' (2013: 106 and 159).

Joint Agreement on Legislation: How the Process Works

There are profound and wide-ranging implications for law-making in the constitutional reform that requires that the president agree to all legislation. Before detailing these implications, we need to look at how the legislative process is structured in practice to enable 'joint agreement'. Rather than law-making being interpreted as the business of legislators and their parties—as is normally the case in a separation of powers system—the demands of Article 20(2) are taken to mean that legislative drafting and debate must directly involve executive government from start to finish. The instrument to implement this joint process is the National Legislative Programme

---

[1] Interview with Djoko Susilo, DPR member, Jakarta, 18 November 2005.

(*Prolegnas*), published at the start of each five-year term of the DPR and president, in which both sides list the legislation that they have agreed should be passed during that term. Responsibility for drafting each bill is assigned to either the government, the DPR, or (in the case of matters related to regional affairs) the DPD. Each year, an annual list is also published, setting out priority legislation for that year.

Once action on a particular bill on the annual programme has begun, the DPR rules of procedure (*tata tertib*) prescribe that deliberations take the form of a dialogue between the relevant DPR committee and the respective minister, regardless of whether the draft of the legislation is the responsibility of the government or the DPR. Both sides must be present in every meeting for the process to proceed. Ministers conventionally attend the opening committee meetings and in subsequent meetings they are often represented by senior ministry officials, especially at lower-level subcommittee meetings. At the initial meetings both the party caucus (*fraksi*) leaders and government representatives present their respective general views on the draft legislation.

The real heart of the discussion is then a series of debates over a 'list of issues' (*Daftar Inventarisasi Masalah—DIM*) which is an inventory of all the matters on which the government and each party have differing opinions—usually insertions or deletions of clauses or amendments to their wording. Each of the matters on the list (by convention each item is called 'a *DIM*') is debated in turn and one by one the matters are eliminated until every item has been resolved and agreement is said to have been achieved. The draft is then finalized in various technical sub-committees, to be scheduled at an upcoming plenary session of the DPR where it will be formally passed and prepared for presentation to the president for signature. Passage through the plenary is almost always a formality, taken by general acclamation. Only in very exceptional cases has there been real debate in the plenary.

It is important to stress that at every stage in this process decisions are not made by majority vote but by consensus or unanimous consent (*musyawarah-mufakat*). The procedure purportedly derives from traditional Javanese village practices and was introduced into the national political stage during Sukarno's Guided Democracy, adopted by Suharto and, in Kawamura's view was 'used for repressive purposes' by both regimes (Kawamura 2011: 6, cf Ward 2010). This system is not just a convention or accepted practice but is formally prescribed as the preferable method by the DPR rules of procedure, which state that majority votes should only be resorted to if agreement is not possible through unanimous consent. But this does not mean that every individual member must agree on every decision, but rather that party caucus leaders—usually in backroom lobby meetings—reach agreement amongst themselves and then declare that unanimity has been achieved. The system is thus effectively a vote by party leaders, where each caucus has a veto but where the unspoken understanding is that caucus leaders will go along with the majority position for the sake of public unanimity.[2]

---

[2] On occasions, where one or more party caucuses have continued to dissent, they have staged a walk-out of the plenary rather than provide their consent to unanimity. This was implicitly an abstention, but the vote was still recorded as having been achieved through unanimous agreement (*mufakat*) because no-one still in the meeting expressed disagreement. On other occasions individual members have publicly disagreed with a decision, but only in the media not during the formal process.

In addition to the normal channel for law-making through DPR-government deliberations in the parliament, the president's legislative power is also boosted by extra power to make laws without reference to the DPR. The Constitution states that the president can make regulations in lieu of law (*Perppu*) 'on matters of pressing urgency' (Art 22). This article was part of the original version of the Constitution and was not removed during the amendment process because it was considered that the president should be able to respond quickly during emergencies and produce regulations that had the force of law. But the Constitution does not define the circumstances that constitute an emergency and, in practice, the president has the power to decide when it is appropriate to use this mechanism. The parliament has a post facto role in the regulations because it must be approved by the DPR in its next session. But the regulations cannot be amended, only accepted or rejected by the DPR. If rejected, a regulation ceases to have effect, if accepted it becomes a normal statute.

Problems in Law-making: A Constitutional Issue

The DPR has been the subject of repeated opprobrium since the end of the New Order for what critics see as its poor performance in producing legislation. Every year since 1998, the numerical targets for legislation listed on the national legislative programme have never been achieved, and every year this situation draws scorn from the media and is the starting point for civil society criticism. Commentators in non-government, media, and activist circles routinely dismiss the parliament as unproductive, obstructionist, overshadowed by executive power, and more representative of narrow partisan interests than those of the people, with its members portrayed as lazy, self-interested, and corrupt (eg Formappi 2005).

There are clearly problems with the legislative process and its apparent incapacity to keep up with the needs of government. But rather than focusing exclusively on the failings of the DPR, as is the conventional line of attack, in this chapter I argue that there are broader issues at stake that originate from the Constitution's definition of the legislative process as a joint government–DPR undertaking. I have highlighted six important elements of the legislative process that will be considered in this section. These elements are all either defined in the Constitution or are necessitated by constitutional provisions and interact with them. The first element—joint DPR–presidential agreement on legislation—is the key to everything else. The other elements are the government's effective veto at all stages of the legislative process, the national legislative programme, the use of DIMs as the basis for discussion, and decision-making through unanimous consent rather than voting. Finally, there is the power of the president in an emergency, as he/she defines it, to make regulations with the force of law, with the proviso that they are later endorsed by the legislature.

Joint Deliberation and the President's 'Silent Veto'

The most important implication of the requirement that the government be involved in every stage of law-making is that the executive has an effective veto on legislation.

Some commentary has argued that the president has no power of veto—as it would be understood in the US presidential system—because the reformed Constitution provides that draft legislation becomes law within thirty days of its passage through the DPR, regardless of whether or not it has been signed by the president (Laksmana 2009). But in practice, the provision for 'joint agreement' means that a US-style presidential veto has no relevance in the Indonesian system. The amended Constitution gives the president or his/her ministers the power to prevent the passage of legislation or to force amendments at any stage during the process of deliberation. As Kawamura has pointed out, 'the parliament cannot proceed to final voting … [on a bill] as long as it fails to acquire presidential approval' (2010: 13). Therefore, by definition, 'when a bill is passed in parliament, the president has already approved [it]' (ibid) and the thirty-day rule is a mere formality. Jimly Asshiddiqie is quoted as saying that 'it's true that there is no phrase veto [in the Constitution] but it can be called a veto' (Wiyanti 2014). The power has been called a 'silent veto' by members of the DPR because it happens largely outside media and public view during committee debate and therefore can be exercised with minimal political risk to the government. One CSO activist described it as a 'veto at the front' (*veto depan*)—a veto that operates well before legislation is formally submitted to the president for his/her signature (Republika 2014).

Paradoxically, the fact that the government's ability to override the will of the parliament appears to be merely procedural makes it more potent in practical political terms and, as will be shown below, it has been frequently exercised. It has rarely been the case that the government has openly rejected a legislative proposal from the DPR because it has such an array of other procedural weapons in its armoury. For example, if the government has responsibility for drafting a particular bill, discussions can be stalled indefinitely if the responsible ministry fails to compose a draft of the legislation or delays sending it the DPR. If the DPR has responsibility for a bill, but the government delays naming its minister to join deliberations with the counterpart DPR committee, proceedings cannot begin. Similarly, if a government ministry has been nominated, but its representative, either the minister or an official, does not attend any particular meeting, the meeting cannot be convened.

Let us examine some instances where legislation has been stopped because of such actions by the government. An early example shows that post-amendment presidents were unlikely to surrender either law-making or other roles despite the 1999 reforms strengthening the DPR. In 2003, the DPR initiated legislation that would specify the number of government ministries a presidential administration should have and that would require DPR approval for its creation or abolition. The legislation would have removed a great deal of presidential discretion, with constitutional specialist and State Secretary Yusril Mahendra arguing that it intruded into the prerogatives of executive government (*Jakarta Post* 2005, 2007).[3] Unsurprisingly, the proposal was met with strident criticism in executive government circles and was opposed by the Megawati

---

[3] 'Ministry bill to eliminate presidential prerogative' *Jakarta Post*, 12 September 2005; 'House to go ahead with state ministries governance bill' *Jakarta Post*, 10 March 2007.

administration. Passage of the legislation therefore inevitably became blocked, but not because the two sides were arguing their respective cases inside the DPR committee, but because the government had taken the simple expedient of declining to name a counterpart minister, thus preventing parliamentary processes from going ahead. The bill remained on the legislative programme for the rest of the five-year term, but deliberations went no further. The draft was placed on the legislative programme again after the 2004 elections, but the legislation sat largely undeliberated until early 2007 when the DPR decided to revive it. The bill was eventually passed in 2008, and while the DPR managed to retain some of its planned influence over the structure of executive government, the predominance of the president's authority was affirmed when most of the key provisions in the first draft of the legislation were, one by one, surrendered by the parliament (*Jakarta Post* 2008).

The power of the veto was again forcefully demonstrated in 2004 when the DPR attempted to call a showdown and defy the president's legislative authority in the case of the Batam free trade zone legislation. The DPR had initiated legislation in 2001 to declare a free trade zone in certain areas around Batam in the province of Riau to take advantage of the region's proximity to Singapore. The government, however, took issue with various aspects of the DPR's draft legislation and refused to agree to the legislation. Characteristically, the initial tactics of the government, under President Megawati, was not to debate the issue in parliament with members of the responsible DPR committee, but just to hold off designating which minister or ministers would be responsible for parliamentary deliberations.

Any progress on the bill was stalled until the first half of 2004 when the government took action to resolve the issue following pressure from investors seeking to have legal certainty before the DPR was dissolved at the end of September 2004, after the elections in April. But, once again, rather than negotiate the points of differences with the parliamentary committee, the government unilaterally drafted its own version of the legislation and submitted it to the DPR for agreement. This was contrary to the agreement in the national legislative programme that drafting of the Batam FTZ legislation was to be the responsibility of the DPR. The Minister for Industry and Trade, Rini Suwani, was assigned to take lead responsibility for the government side (*Jakarta Post* 2004a). Predictably the DPR refused to agree to the government's draft and the House was faced with the extraordinary situation of two competing bills before the responsible committee on the same issue. A meeting of the committee was convened for 7 September to discuss the impasse with government ministers but, to the infuriation of the DPR members, Suwani and the other ministers failed to attend. Following this repeat of the government's now-familiar tactic to increase pressure on the DPR, the chair of the DPR, Surya Dharma Ali, threatened to defy the government and pass the legislation regardless of the ministers' failure to negotiate an agreement (*Jakarta Post* 2004b).

In an atmosphere of showdown, the ministers did attend a committee meeting, at which it was decided that, in the absence of agreement, the legislation would have to be indefinitely deferred until the issue could be resolved by the new DPR to be inaugurated in October. In a sudden move, however, committee leaders took the matter to a plenary session of the House that evening, which agreed to their proposal that the parliament should pass the legislation even though the constitutionally required presidential agreement had not been received. With the plenary session declaring the legislation passed, the DPR secretariat proceeded with normal formalities and sent the legislation to the State Secretariat for it to be assigned a number and promulgated as law.

It is not clear whether the DPR really intended to test the government's power to veto legislation or, as some thought, was acting out of pique at the government's actions in issuing a rival draft and effectively boycotting a meeting with the DPR committee. In any case, there was little chance that the parliament could win on the issue, as subsequent events showed. The Minister for Law, Yusril Mahendra, quickly declared that the DPR's passage of the legislation was invalid because it had not fulfilled the constitutional requirement of presidential agreement (Tempo 2004). The full machinery of executive government authority was then mobilized to nullify the DPR's draft, with the State Secretariat refusing to issue a number for the document, without which it could not be operationalized. Next, the head of Batam's tax office stated his refusal to accept the DPR draft as law 'in line with the central government's policy', clearly expressing his attitude to the parliament with the reported statement that 'whatever the House says, finally, it's the government which takes the action' (*Jakarta Post* 2004d). Any possibility that the DPR might be able to take judicial action was effectively quashed by the statement by the head of the Constitutional Court that the government had 'strong grounds for filing a complaint with the Constitutional Court'. In fact, the DPR took no further action, its draft did not become law, and the proposed law effectively lapsed with the dissolution of the 1999–2004 DPR. The result was that the power of the president and his/her ministers to procedurally veto any legislation during the process of deliberation with the DPR was affirmed and solidified.

As mentioned above, the national legislative programme repeatedly makes the DPR a butt of ridicule for perceived under-performance. However it is rarely appreciated that the document is not simply a product of the parliament but is, in theory, a planning instrument used to coordinate the roles of both the president and the legislature in the law-making process. In practice, the programme is essentially a wish-list of all the legislation that each government ministry would like to have passed, together with those in the sights of each DPR policy committee. Representatives from the DPR's legislation committee and the Ministry of Law then meet to decide which bills will make it to the official list. The five-year legislative programme is of little value as a guide to what the joint law-makers will do, given the realities of government and the appearance of unexpected issues over such an extended period. And, in practice, appearing on the annual programme does not actually mean a particular bill will receive any special priority, but merely reflects the fact that unless it is on the programme it cannot be debated. Whether a particular bill is debated and whether it is completed within their allotted annual period (which they are frequently not), depends not on prioritization in the legislative programme, but entirely on political negotiations between the various sides in the debate, namely the DPR caucus leaders in the DPR and the various ministries with a stake in the legislation. The result is that the DPR is never able to pass even a significant proportion of the legislation on the list.

'When We are Ready, They are not Ready': Joint Deliberation and the Problem of Coordination

We have seen that Article 20(2) of the Constitution has given the president an effective or 'silent' veto over legislation, a power which has been used by the government to get its way during disputes with the parliament and which was reaffirmed during the DPR's rather ineffectual challenge to it in 2004. But the implications of the provision for the legislative process do not always involve a conscious attempt by the government to frustrate the will of the parliament. Long delays in the passage of legislation through the DPR can often stem from ineffective coordination between the parliament and the executive, as well as lack of coordination amongst various parts of the government. The biggest impact of joint deliberations is that it complicates the law-making process and, thereby, multiplies the effects of already dysfunctional processes within both executive government and the parliament (Sherlock 2015). In the words of a veteran and vocal DPR member, Djoko Susilo, the provision is an impediment to law-making because it required two branches of government to synchronize. In his words 'when we [the DPR] are ready they [the executive] are not ready, when they are ready we are not ready' (interview with author 18 November 2005).

The following are examples of delayed passage of legislation caused by uncoordinated and sometimes conflicting views of multiple state institutions, as well as disagreement about the wording of draft legislation between an executive agency and a parliamentary committee. In all cases, it is the parliament that becomes the target of criticism. The cumbersome reality of reaching agreement between two branches of government in a separation of powers system is rarely appreciated and the DPR is seen as the source of the problem.

In the case of the civil service law (Law 5/2014), there was a protracted four-year passage through the DPR because of the lack of a single agreed position on the part of the president and his ministers. In 2009, the DPR drafted legislation on civil service reform aiming to bring about major changes to personnel management in the bureaucracy. The proposal was the initiative of a number of former ministers elected to the DPR who saw their new legislative role as an opportunity to challenge the power of entrenched officials who had frustrated their efforts for reform while they were ministers. It required some effort for the initiators to get all the key players in the DPR to support the idea—the DPR leadership, heads of party caucuses, and head of the relevant committee—but this was eventually achieved, and a draft was officially accepted by the DPR as proposed legislation. If the DPR had the power to deliberate independently—without the involvement of government representatives—the draft might have expeditiously passed through the parliamentary system and become law. This was not to be, however, because the legislation encountered strong opposition from officials in the Ministry of Home Affairs who led the government side of the joint deliberations. The Ministry proposed changes (DIMs) that would have greatly weakened the law's powers. The proposed changes were quickly rejected by the DPR committee members, but because of the procedural requirement for unanimous consent (*mufakat*), the deadlock between representatives of the two branches of government meant that deliberations were frozen. The impasse was not broken until many months later when it was brought to the attention of President Yudhoyono. With the intervention of the president, the Home Affairs Ministry returned to negotiations with the DPR and a compromise was reached on the contentious clauses—a compromise which conceded most of contentious issues in favour of Home Affairs. The whole affair demonstrated, firstly, the power of the executive to get its way over the parliament through its effective veto and, secondly, that delays in the passage of legislation are frequently caused by the incapacity of government ministers and senior officials to present a single coordinated position during negotiations with the DPR. In this case, a blockage was overcome only because the president personally stepped in.[4]

A similar situation developed over the deliberations on revisions to the anti-terrorism law (Law 15/2003) from 2016 to 2018. With concerns about a rising threat of domestic terrorism in Indonesia, amendments to the law had been debated in the DPR from early 2016 but were at a standstill for two years because of disagreements about clauses defining terrorism. As usual, the failure to pass the law was blamed on the 'notoriously sluggish parliament' (Asianchronicler 2018), but the actual sticking point was that two executive government bodies were refusing to move on a point that each saw as of fundamental importance to its institutional authority. The police (*Polri*) were named in the existing legislation as having sole responsibility to deal with acts of domestic terrorism and were resisting claims by the military (*TNI*) that terrorism should be defined in such a way as to give the military a role (BBC Indonesia 2017). In the words of the chair of the DPR committee, there was a 'hot potato' (*bola panas*) in the hands of the government—not the DPR—which had brought the process to a standstill (BBC Indonesia 2018). It was not until a particularly horrific act of domestic terrorism in 2018, focusing domestic and international attention on the issue, that President Joko Widodo intervened and put forward a compromise position that allowed the law to be passed. Once again, only presidential authority could overcome a dispute between government institutions which was preventing the passage of a law.

The case of amendments to the law on migrant workers (Law 39/2004) in 2018 repeated the story of uncoordinated government, while also demonstrating the clumsiness of the procedure of resolving differences through the production of contending lists of issues (DIMs). The first draft of the amendments was produced by a DPR committee and accepted by the plenary as a DPR initiative. Once the government had named its responsible ministries, the next stage was for each ministry and each party caucus to submit DIMs on matters where they wanted amendments to the initial draft. According to the chair of the committee responsible for the legislation, this produced an inventory of over 900 DIMs from government because there were three government agencies (Ministry of Foreign Affairs, the migrant workers agency, and the Manpower Ministry) that 'did not speak with one voice' (interview with Dede Yusuf 1 May 2014). In other words, there were 900 issues where, one by one, unanimous consent would have to be reached. The committee chair took the view that no substantial progress would be made if standard procedure were followed, so he conducted negotiations to reduce the differences to the ten major issues and to eliminate the great majority of the DIMs. Even then these negotiations took six months. Eventually all the

---

[4] This version of events is based on a number of interviews by the author with key actors in government and parliament in 2014, together with the account by Mietzner (2014).

differences were resolved and a final version passed, but only because the prescribed systems of decision-making were circumvented.

Regulations in Lieu of Law: The President's Ultimate Weapon?

The discussion so far has demonstrated the capacity of the president and his/her ministers to determine the content of legislation and to veto parliamentary decisions, and how joint DPR-government deliberations can complicate the law-making process. But despite the formidable legislative powers already available to the president, incumbents of the office since 1998 have increasingly circumvented the parliament and resorted to the additional power of regulations in lieu of law (*perppu*) that the Constitution specifies should be used only in emergencies. The following section shows that while some *perppu* have been used for their express purpose, they have also been used to avoid debate with the parliament and as an instrument to enforce the president's will against opposition from within state institutions. I also show that the *perppu* mechanism has been used in ways that lay bare the lack of coherence and coordination amongst government agencies, the problem that has repeatedly destabilized the process of law-making.

The most prominent example of what could be an appropriate resort to a *perppu* was its use by the Yudhoyono administration in response to the 2004 tsunami in Aceh. Such a disaster clearly justified the rapid creation of a legal framework to organize relief and was arguably what the constitutional drafters had in mind when they created the *perppu* mechanism. A similar assessment could not, however, be made of the *perppu* issued as a way out of the imbroglio over the Batam free-trade zone. As discussed above, the government had vetoed the DPR's legislation in 2004 at the end of the 1999–2004 parliamentary term. When disagreements with the DPR once again loomed in the following term, the government moved to effectively circumvent the authority of the DPR by issuing a *perppu* stating that the zone could be created through government regulation rather than by law. The contention that a largely administrative measure which had lain unresolved for several years required emergency measures had little credibility, but this is what the government was implicitly claiming by its actions. In the case of the anti-terrorism law, the Widodo administration did not issue a *perppu* but threatened to do so in a move that was clearly aimed to put pressure on the various sides debating the stalled legislation to resolve the deadlock before the government intervened unilaterally.

Finally, the *perppu* mechanism has been used in ways that do not actually make sense in constitutional terms and which have revealed serious dysfunction in successive presidential administrations. Presidents SBY and Jokowi have both issued *perppu* to overturn the effect of legislation already passed by the DPR. In 2014, after the DPR passed legislation (Law 22/2014) which would have abolished the popular election of regional government heads, SBY issued a *perppu* which reversed the change. In 2018, the Jokowi administration promulgated a *perppu* to countermand legislation passed by the DPR which would have introduced certain changes to the internal procedures and organs of the parliament (Sherlock 2018a). But such measures created the bizarre situation where the president issued regulations to nullify legislation that he had only shortly before jointly agreed with the parliament to pass into law. In accordance with the Constitution, these proposed laws could not have become law unless they had received presidential agreement.

There are two possible explanations for what occurred in these cases. The first was that the president was not made aware of the law and its implications by the minister leading the deliberations in the DPR. The second was that the president knew of the legislation but wanted some way to reverse his decision following political backlash to the law. Both scenarios uncover serious shortcomings in the machinery of government. The relevant minister clearly had a responsibility to apprise the president of what he/she was doing in parliament and to provide advice about the political implications, while the president had a responsibility to keep abreast of developments and direct his ministers accordingly. If both actors allowed matters to proceed without mutual consultation, they were either negligent or were effectively in breach of their constitutional duties, or both. It could also be argued that the president's personal advisers were remiss in carrying out their role of protecting the president from political risk.

In fact, these events were symptoms of the lack of coordination between state institutions, ministers, and senior officials that we have seen has had such negative effects on the legislative process. We have cited multiple examples of where agencies have held up legislative deliberations because they were defending the perceived interests of a particular part of government rather than developing a single government position before going into discussions with the parliament. That such a lack of policy coherence could continue through the entire law-making process and put the president in the position of having to overturn his/her own legislation was an indictment of institutional weaknesses, and particularly unfortunate when the legislative branch was routinely targeted for blame.

Conclusion

This chapter has argued that the problematic nature of Indonesia's law-making processes is entwined with the allocation of equal legislative powers to the parliament and the president in the amended Constitution. It is well known that the political culture of the DPR is still riven with the legacies of authoritarianism and that transactional politics and corruption are rife. But it is less often appreciated that institutional factors such as constitutional provisions—and the way they are interpreted—greatly complicate the situation and are critically important for understanding why it so hard to make law in Indonesia. The way constitutional powers have been implemented in practice has created endless possibilities for blockages because the DPR's rules of procedure deeply embed the executive branch in the legislative process. Laws cannot be finalized until both the president and the parliament agree on every clause, leading to lengthy and cumbersome procedures (such as the debating of DIMs) and the delay of decisions until the achievement of unanimity.

While the DPR is usually blamed for the slow passage of legislation, both the executive and legislative branches must in fact bear responsibility. It is politically convenient for the government to have the parliament perceived to be the main problem, but this perception can only be created because there is a general lack of understanding amongst the political class and public about the operation of the re-formed Constitution.

Indeed there is abundant evidence that the composers of the 1999–2002 constitutional reforms did not fully appreciate the implications of their decision to go only halfway towards displacing the presidency from its pre-reform role as law-maker. Even a well-functioning parliament would encounter difficulties in making the post-reform legislative system work efficiently. Since the reality is that since the executive branch as well as the legislature exhibit deep systemic problems, chaos in law-making is likely to be a fixture of Indonesian politics.

References

Adihputri, Ratih (2014) 'The Dutch Legacy in the Indonesian Parliament' 2(2) *Political Sciences and Public Affairs*

Adihputri, Ratih (2015a) 'Political Culture in the Indonesian Parliament: Analysing Parliamentary Debates on the Regional Parliaments 1999-2009', unpublished PhD thesis, University of Jyväskylä.

Adihputri, Ratih (2015b) 'Parliamentary reforms through parliamentary procedure: A lesson-learnt from the Indonesian parliament', Paper submitted to the 12th Workshop of Parliamentary Scholars and Parliamentarians, Wroxton College, Oxfordshire, 25–26 July 2015, https://ww.wroxtonworkshop.org, accessed March 2020.

Asianchronicler (2018) 'Under attack, Indonesia trades liberty for security', 26 May.

Aspinall, Edward and Sukmajati, Mada (2016) *Electoral Dynamics in Indonesia: Money Politics, Patronage and Clientelism at the Grassroots*. Singapore: NUS Press.

Bako, R et al. (2008) *Kajian terhadap Peraturan Tata Tertib DPR RI*. Pusat Pengkajian (Studies on the rules of procedures, DPR Ri), Pusat Pengolahan Data dan Informasi Sekretariat Jenderal DPR RI, Jakarta.

BBC Indonesia (2017) 'Pegiat HAM tolak 'pelibatan langsung TNI' dalam menindak terorisme' (Human rights activists reject 'direct military involvement' in cracking down on terrorism'), 1 June, https://www.bbc.com/indonesia/indonesia-40104073.

BBC Indonesia (2018) 'DPR sahkan revisi UU Terorisme, Perppu tak lagi diperlukan' (DPR passes revision of terrorism law: regulation in lieu of law no longer needed), 25 May, https://www.bbc.com/indonesia/indonesia-44248953.

Butt, Simon and Tim Lindsey (2012) *The Constitution of Indonesia: A Contextual Analysis*. Oxford and Portland, Oregon: Bloomsbury Publishing.

Datta, Indraneel (2002) 'Parliamentary Politics in Soeharto's Indonesia 1987–98', unpublished PhD thesis, School of Oriental & African Studies, University of London.

Detiknews (2008) 'Era *legislative* heavy, DPR cenderung korupsi' [Legislative-heavy era, DPR is prone to corruption], detikNews, 25 April, http://www.detiknews.com/read/2008/04/25/152820/929540/10/era-legislative-heavy-dpr-cenderung-korupsi.

Djadijono, M (2007) 'Fraksi, *Recalling* Dan Performance Wakil Rakyat' (Party Caucus, Recalling and the Performance of the People's Representatives) 36(2) *Analisis CSIS*.

Ellis, Andrew (2002) 'The Indonesian Constitutional Transition: Conservatism or Fundamental Change?' 2002(6) *Singapore Journal of International & Comparative Law* 116–153.

Ellis, Andrew (2007) 'Indonesia's Constitutional Change Reviewed' in Ross McLeod and Andrew MacIntyre (eds) *Indonesia: Democracy and the Promise of Good Governance*. Singapore: ISEAS, 21–40.

Elwan, La Ode Muhammad (2018) 'Reconstrues Legislation: The Effectiveness of Presidential Veto in Government System in Indonesia Based on the State of the Republic of Indonesia 1945 Constitution' 2(2) *Halu Oleo Law Review*.

Formappi (2005) *Lembaga Perwakilan Rakyat di Indonesia: Studi dan Analisis Sebelum* dan *Setelah Perubahan UUD 1945* (People's representative institutions in Indonesia: Study and analysis before and after amendments to the 1945 constitution). Jakarta: Formappi.

Febriansyah, Ferry Irawan (2016) 'Konsep pembentukan peraturan perundang-undangan di Indonesia' (Concepts of the drafting of legislation in Indonesia) 12(3) *Perspektif* 220–225..

Horowitz, Donald (2013) *Constitutional Change and Democracy in Indonesia*. Cambridge: Cambridge University Press.

Indrayana, Denny (2008) *Indonesian* Constitutional *Reform 1999–2002*. Jakarta: Kompas Book Publishing.

Jakarta Post (2004a) 'Batam bills leave *Govt*, House split', 7 August, https://jawawa.id/newsitem/batam-bills-leave-govt-house-split-1447893297.

Jakarta Post (2004b) 'House threatens to endorse FTZ bill without govt consent', 8 September.

Jakarta Post (2004c) 'Govt told to seek review of Batam free trade bill', 21 September.

Jakarta Post (2004d) 'Batam Tax Office Ignores House's "Law"', 24 September.

Jakarta Post (2005) 'Ministry bill to eliminate *presidential* prerogative', 12 September.

Jakarta Post (2007) 'House to go ahead with state ministries governance bill', 10 March.

Jakarta Post (2008) 'House passes state ministry bill', 22 October.

Katharina, Riris (2007) *Pemetaan masalah parlemen ditinjau dari peraturan tata tertib DPR: Rekomendasi perbaikan kinerja DPR melalui revisi tata tertib,* (Mapping parliamentary problems by review of the DPR rules of procedure: Recommendations to improve DPR performance through revision of procedures). Jakarta: Forum Politisi-Friedrich Naumann Stiftung.

Kawamura (2010) 'Is the Indonesian president strong or weak?', *IDE Discussion Paper* no 235.

Kawamura (2011) 'Consensus and democracy in Indonesia: Musyawarah-mufakat revisited', *IDE Discussion Paper* no 308.

Laksmana, Evan A (2009) 'New house, new rules'. Jakarta: Centre for Strategic and International Studies. 24 October.

Mietzner, Marcus (2014) 'The president, the 'deep state' and policymaking in post-Suharto Indonesia: a case study of the deliberations on the Civil Service Act'. Report for the Partnership on Governance Reform (Kemitraan), Jakarta.

Lay, Cornelis (2017) 'Political Linkages between CSOs and Parliament in Indonesia: A Case Study of Political Linkages in Drafting the Aceh Governance Law' 25(1) *Asian Journal of Political Science* 1–24.

Lindsey, Tim (2002) 'Indonesian Constitutional Reform: Muddling towards Democracy' 2002(6) *Singapore Journal of International and Comparative Law* 244-301.

Mietzner, Marcus (2013) *Money, Power and Ideology: Political Parties in Post-Authoritarian Indonesia*. Singapore: NUS Press.

Prasetyaningsih, Rahayu (2017) 'Menakar kekuasaan presiden dalam pembentukan peraturan perundang-undangan menerut undang-undang dasar 1945' (Measuring presidential legislative powers under the 1945 constitution) 4(2) *Padjadjaran Jurnal Ilmu Hukum* 263-280. https//.doi.org/10.22304/pjih.v4n2.a3 (accessed 28 august 2022).

Prihatini, Ella (2019a) 'Challenges to Equal Representation: Female Deputies in the Indonesian National Parliament', unpublished PhD thesis, University of Western Australia.

Prihatini, Ella (2019b) 'Explaining Gender Gaps in Indonesian Legislative Committees' 2019 *Parliamentary Affairs* 1-24.

Republika (2014) 'Jurus veto untuk presiden baru', (Veto stance for the new president) 14 October, https://www.republika.co.id/berita/koran/teraju/14/10/14/ndfotp-jurus-veto-untuk-presiden-baru.

Riskiyono, Joko (2016) *Pengaruh partisipasi publik dalam pembentukan undang-undang: Telaah atas* pembentukan *undang-udang penyelenggara pemilu* (Influence of public participation in the legislative drafting: Review on the drafting of the law on election management). Jakarta: Association for Elections and Democracy (Perludem).

Setiadi, Wicipto (2004) 'Makna persetujuan bersama dalam pembentukan undang-undang serta penandatangan oleh presiden atas rancangan undang-undang yang telah mendapat persetujuan bersama' (Meaning of joint agreement in legislative drafting and the president's signing of draft laws that have been jointly agreed) 1(2) *Jurnal Legislasi Indonesia* 21-26.

Sherlock, Stephen (2003) *Struggling to Change: The Indonesian Parliament in an Era of Reformasi*. Canberra: Centre for Democratic Institutions.

Sherlock, Stephen (2005) 'Indonesia's Regional Assembly: Democracy, Representation and the Regions', CDI Policy Papers 2005/1. Canberra: Centre for Democratic Institutions.

Sherlock, Stephen (2007) 'The Indonesian Parliament after Two Elections: What has Really Changed?' CDI Policy Papers 2007/2. Canberra: Centre for Democratic Institutions.

Sherlock, Stephen (2009) 'Parties and Decision-Making in *the* Indonesian Parliament: The Case of the Anti-Pornography Bill' 10(2) *Australian Journal of Asian Law* 159-183.

Sherlock, Stephen (2011) 'People's Forum or Chamber of Cronies?: The Parliament in Indonesia's Decade of Democracy' in Edward Aspinall and Marcus Mietzner (eds) *Problems of Democratisation in Indonesia*. Singapore: ISEAS, pp 160-180.

Sherlock, Stephen (2012) 'Made by Consensus and Committee: Parties and Policy in the Indonesian Parliament' 20(4) *Southeast Asia Research* 551–68.

Sherlock, Stephen (2015) 'A Balancing Act: Relations between State Institutions under Yudhoyono' in Edward Aspinall and Marcus Mietzner (eds) *The Yudhoyono Presidency: Indonesia's Decade of Stability and Stagnation*. Singapore: Institute for Southeast Asian Affairs, pp 93-113.

Sherlock, Stephen (2018a) 'Jokowi should share the blame for the MD3 shambles', *New Mandala*, http://www.newmandala.org/jokowi-shares-blame-md3-debacle.

Sherlock, Stephen (2018b) *What Makes Politicians Behave the Way They Do?: Political Economy of Parliamentary Representation in Indonesia*. Jakarta: MAMPU Program.

Susanti, Bivitri (2007) *Menyoal Kompetisi Politik dalam Proses Legislasi di Indonesia* [The Question of Political Competition in the Legislative Process in Indonesia]. Jakarta: Pusat Studi Hukum dan Kebijakan (PSHK).

Suryadinata, Leo (1987) 'Politics in Indonesian Parliament, 1966-85' 15(1) *Southeast Asian Journal of Social Science*.

Tempo (2004) 'RUU FTZ batam batal menjadi undang-undang' (Draft bill on Batam FTZ cancelled as law) *Tempo.com*, 23 September, https://bisnis.tempo.co/read/48449/ruu-ftz-batam-batal-menjadi-undang-undang.

Tomsa, Dirk (2008) *Party Politics and Democratisation in Indonesia: Golkar in the Post-Suharto Era*. London & New York: Routledge.

Ward, Ken (2010) 'Soeharto's Javanese Pancasila' in Edward Aspinall and Greg Fealy (eds) *Soeharto's New Order and its Legacy: Essays in Honour of Harold Crouch*. Canberra: ANU Press, 27-38.

Wiyanto, Sri (2014) 'Adakah hak veto presiden dalam sistem ketatanegaraan?' (Is there a presidential veto in the system of state institutions?), *Merdeka*, 10 October, https://www.merdeka.com/politik/adakah-hak-veto-presiden-dalam-sistem-ketatanegaraan.html.

Ziegenhain, Patrick (2005) 'The Indonesian Parliament and its Impact on Democratic Consolidation', in Jurgen Ruland, Clemens Jurgenmayer, Michael Nelson, and P Ziegenhain (eds) *Parliaments and Political Change in Southeast Asia: A Comparative Study of India, Indonesia, the Philippines, South Korea and Thailand*. Singapore: Institute of South East Asian Studies, pp 33-52.

Ziegenhain, Patrick (2008) *The Indonesian Parliament and Democratisation*. Singapore: Institute of South East Asian Studies.

3

Defending the Constitution, But Which One? The Indonesian Military, Constitutional Change, and Political Contestation, 1945–2020

Marcus Mietzner

Introduction

In October 2019, the association of retired army officers held a seminar in Yogyakarta to discuss its position on the Constitution. At the meeting, the former Army Chief of Staff Agustadi Sasongko Purnomo (2007–2009) and the former Deputy Army Chief of Staff Kiki Syahnakri (2000–2002) spoke for many of their fellow retired officers when they declared that the current Constitution violated the principles of the original 1945 Constitution. Most importantly, they claimed that direct presidential elections were not in line with the idea of indirect representation enshrined in the 1945 Constitution, and that the downgrading of the People's Consultative Assembly (*Majelis Permusyawaratan Rakyat*, MPR) from the country's highest lawmaking body to a marginal forum with limited functions was in opposition to the spirit of the nation's initial constitutional drafters (Gatra 2019). Therefore, the attendees demanded, Indonesia needed to return to the original 1945 Constitution; in effect, that was equivalent to calling for the restoration of the authoritarian polities under Sukarno (1959–1965) and Suharto (1966–1998), which had used the 1945 version of the Constitution as the legal basis for their repressive rule.

The event in Yogyakarta reflected the general ambivalence of many officers in the Indonesian National Military (*Tentara Nasional Indonesia*, TNI) towards the Constitution. On the one hand, TNI has traditionally defended the Constitution as a cornerstone of its mission and *raison d'être*. But on the other hand, it has been very selective about which version of the Constitution it is willing to defend: since 1959, it has defended the original document of the 1945 Constitution. By contrast, the temporary Constitutions in place between 1945 and 1959 as well as the post-1998 amended Constitution have been met either with open rejection or grudging acquiescence. In the post-Suharto polity, many officers refrain from openly opposing the amended Constitution while still in active service but speak out after retirement. Officers who assumed a post-military career in politics are often particularly vocal in their calls for a return to the 1945 Constitution. In addition to the examples mentioned above, the former TNI commander Djoko Santoso (2007–2010) publicly suggested the

Marcus Mietzner, *Defending the Constitution, But Which One? The Indonesian Military, Constitutional Change, and Political Contestation, 1945–2020* In: *Constitutional Democracy in Indonesia.* Edited by: Melissa Crouch, Oxford University Press.
© Marcus Mietzner, 2023. DOI: 10.1093/oso/9780192870681.003.0003

restoration of the 1945 version of the Constitution (Waspada 2018), and Prabowo Subianto, Suharto's former son-in-law and a senior officer during the latter's regime, made this demand the platform of his 2014 and 2019 campaigns.

Why do many military officers feel so attached to the original 1945 Constitution, despite the fact that almost no military representative was involved in drafting it and the document gave no specific privileges to the armed forces? Why, on the other hand, is it so difficult for the officer corps to come to terms with the existing constitutional amendments, the drafting of which had seen TNI participation through its own MPR faction? This chapter traces the origins of this apparent contradiction, arguing that many in the officer corps came to endorse the 1945 version of the Constitution because of its extreme vagueness, which opened opportunities for TNI's institutionalized political representation. Both the detailed temporary Constitutions of the immediate post-1945 period and the amended Constitution after Suharto's fall were too specific for the TNI—the detailed regulation of political processes limited the military's room to manoeuvre.

The chapter develops these arguments in four steps. It first portrays the initial opposition of the officer corps towards the Constitutions of the 1940s and 1950s. In the second section, it highlights the evolution of TNI's strong support for the 1945 version of the Constitution in the second half of the 1950s, and how it benefitted from its implementation by two successive authoritarian regimes between 1959 and 1998. The third section explains TNI's involvement in, and response to, the four rounds of constitutional amendments after Suharto's fall. In the fourth section, the chapter shows how TNI's opposition to the amendments slowly but steadily penetrated the civilian sphere as well. From this process, new civilian-led initiatives to restore the two elements of the original 1945 Constitution mentioned by the TNI retirees above have emerged: namely, indirect presidential elections, and the role of the MPR as the country's supreme political institution. Thus, the military's ambivalent attitude towards the post-authoritarian Constitution spilled over into other arenas, forming a significant threat to the sustainability of the democratic system.

TNI and Indonesia's Post-1945 Constitutions

In TNI's doctrinal writings and mission statements, 'defending the state ideology Pancasila, the Constitution and the unitary state' has emerged as a ubiquitous mantra (Larantuka News 2019). But the armed forces' fierce commitment to defending the Constitution is, in fact, a relatively new attitude—and a selective one at that. TNI's 'discovery' of its role as constitutional guardian dates to 1959, when then President Sukarno declared the return to the 1945 Constitution and the establishment of his autocratic Guided Democracy regime. In that regime, TNI was given significant institutional privileges, which the vagueness of the 1945 Constitution made possible and legitimized.

Prior to that, TNI's relationship with the post-1945 Constitutions was more chequered. To begin with, there were hardly any military officers involved in the drafting of the 1945 Constitution. This was despite the fact that at the time of drafting in mid-1945, Indonesian officers previously active in the Royal Netherlands East Indies Army

(*Koninklijk Nederlands Indisch Leger*, KNIL) and the Japanese militia Defenders of the Fatherland (*Pembela Tanah Air*, PETA) were already juggling to position themselves for the post-colonial period. The institutions in charge of drafting the Constitution, the Investigating Committee for Preparatory Work for Indonesian Independence (*Badan Penyelidik Usaha Persiapan Kemerdekaan Indonesia*, BPUPKI) and the Preparatory Board for Indonesian Independence (*Panitia Persiapan Kemerdekaan Indonesia*, PPKI), were made up almost exclusively of nationalist leaders, religious figures, and intellectuals. There were only two members of these bodies who had links to PETA: Abdul Kadir and Kasman Singodimejo. But the latter discontinued his military career immediately after independence in August 1945 and became a politician, occupying various positions in cabinet and parliament. Thus, the bodies that produced the 1945 Constitution were overwhelmingly civilian—a circumstance that did little to convince military figures that they had to hold the Constitution in particularly high regard as far as accepting orders from civilian authorities was concerned.

Against this background, the slowly emerging military—a chaotic amalgamation of KNIL, PETA, and local paramilitary elements—frequently violated constitutional orders. For instance, Article 10 of the Constitution stipulated that the president held the highest authority over the army, air force, and navy, but TNI showed its dislike for this regulation by strategically disregarding it. After the first TNI commander appointed by President Sukarno, Soeprijadi, mysteriously disappeared, the military elite proceeded to elect its own leader (Cribb 1991: 19; McFarling 1996: 37). Sudirman won this vote in November 1945, and although Sukarno later officially confirmed him, TNI's independent leadership election set the tone for much of the interaction between the civilian and military elites during the war against the Dutch between 1945 and 1949. Most importantly, many civilian leaders viewed negotiations with the Dutch as inevitable, causing the military to develop a deep disdain for what it perceived as weak and unprincipled civilian leadership. The armed forces, by contrast, cultivated an image of military heroism that stood up to the Dutch even in times of great adversity (and even though TNI was winning very few battles against them).

The military's polite ignorance of the president's superiority enshrined in the 1945 Constitution extended into the quasi-parliamentary regime put in place in late 1945. While the 1945 Constitution remained formally in place, it was in effect superseded by Vice-Presidential Decree No 10, issued on 16 October 1945. According to this decree, legislative power moved from the president to a newly appointed transitional parliament. Subsequently, the post of prime minister was created—no reference had been made to such a position in the 1945 Constitution. Based on this new arrangement, cabinet reported to the transitional parliament and the prime minister supported by it, while Sukarno remained president but had to accept a significant reduction of his real powers. Importantly for the military, this meant that a new (civilian) defence minister backed by the legislature was appointed and claimed superiority over the armed forces.

Thus, between late 1945 and late 1949, a constitutional arrangement was in place that provided for a semi-parliamentary system without nominally basing it on a new constitution. While the military found this confusing arrangement ideologically unappealing, it offered the opportunity to circumvent both Sukarno, who was still head of state, and the cabinet, the new seat of effective power. Hence, the military openly opposed the new defence minister, Amir Syarifuddin, who tried to put a civilian control structure (modelled along the 'political officers' customary in communist regimes) above the top brass (Anderson 1972: 370–371). At the same time, the armed forces also undermined Prime Minister Syahrir—indeed, in June 1946 military leaders played a key role in his kidnapping. According to Robert Elson (2001: 18), Sudirman himself had given his blessings for this action. The government moved against the main plotters and achieved Syahrir's release, but left Sudirman untouched. Sukarno did not fare much better: Sudirman rejected Sukarno's decision in December 1948 to have himself captured by the Dutch (rather than joining Sudirman in the guerrilla war), and he opposed the ceasefire proposed by the government to facilitate the Round Table Conference in Den Haag in the second half of 1949. Sukarno had to threaten to resign to convince Sudirman to adhere to the ceasefire order given by civilian authorities.

In short, while Indonesia's early military leaders formally acknowledged the 1945 Constitution, they actively sabotaged one of its key stipulations: that is, the authority of the civilian president (and the institutions exercising legislative and executive functions in his name after November 1945) to direct and control the armed forces. Civilian actors in charge of overseeing the military were often ignored at best or intimidated at worst, with officers' keen to demonstrate and consolidate their institutional autonomy from civilian control bodies. At that time, the 1945 Constitution was—in the eyes of many military leaders—the embodiment of civilian hubris: written by civilians to concentrate power in the hands of civilians, with no regard for the special interests of the military.

If TNI was unenthusiastic about the 1945 Constitution (and the related Vice-Presidential Decree of 1945), it was openly hostile to its two successor Constitutions. The Round Table Conference in Den Haag agreed that the newly independent state would be a federation, and so the Federated Republic of Indonesia (Republik Indonesia Serikat, RIS) was established in December 1949 and completed its Constitution in January 1950. The military viewed this outcome as confirmation of its scepticism towards the prowess of civilian leadership—and of its belief that the Dutch got the deal they wanted because of the ceasefire that the military had so fiercely opposed. The federation had indeed been a Dutch idea, clearly designed to fragment Indonesia and weaken Sukarno's Republic. In this case, however, Sukarno agreed with the military: he too wanted to disband the RIS as quickly as possible and therefore undermined it from the very beginning. The RIS eventually collapsed in August 1950, and its Constitution with it (Bourchier 2015: 95).

Apart from the fact that the RIS was a Dutch brainchild, the military also found very little in terms of substance that it liked in the 1950 Constitution. Articles 179 to 184 regulated in some detail the subordination of the armed forces to the civilian government. The president remained the military's highest commander; even lower-ranking officers were to be appointed by the president; the government was in charge of all defence affairs; and approval by parliament was needed to declare a state of war. There were also no privileges for the armed forces: no appointed seats in the parliament or the senate; no acknowledgment of the military's special status; and no extraordinary rights. Worse still, the 1950 Constitution stipulated the creation of a Constitutional Assembly that would be formed in order to debate a more permanent Constitution. In that Assembly, the military would again have no representatives—only elected members of parliament and the senate had membership rights (there were to be special elections to elect additional parliamentarians to the Assembly). Hence, the military not only disliked the 1950 Constitution, it was also irked at the fact that under the existing rules, it would have no role in writing the next, more long-term Constitution.

But the breakdown of the RIS brought no relief to the armed forces. On the contrary, the successor Constitution—the Provisional Constitution of 1950 (*Undang-Undang Dasar Sementara* 1950, UUDS 1950)—shifted the polity even further towards parliamentarism than the 1945 Vice-Presidential Decree had done. Parliament became the institutionalized power centre, and prime ministers ran day-to-day government. While nominally the president appointed ministers, in reality he had to select those proposed by a prime minister who had a majority in the legislature. Moreover, the UUDS 1950 had adopted the stipulations on the armed forces from the RIS Constitution (now Arts 124 to 129), thus confirming full civilian control over the armed forces. As in the RIS Constitution, the UUDS 1950 also handed no privileges to the armed forces, and it too envisaged a Constitutional Assembly without the participation of the military. Not surprisingly, then, the military elite felt marginalized from the post-1950 polity based on the UUDS. Civilian parties took turns in running government and sharing the patronage spoils, while the officer corps had to submit to cumbersome mechanisms of executive and legislative oversight. For a military that believed that it had single-handedly won independence, this was unacceptable.

The military did not only quietly grumble about what it viewed as an unfair state of affairs. After organizing demonstrations that called for the dissolution of parliament and the cessation of civilian interference in military affairs, the army leadership under General AH Nasution ordered tanks to surround the palace on 17 October 1952 (Sundhaussen 1982). In a tense meeting with Sukarno, key generals demanded that the president dissolve parliament—a right that they claimed was based on the UUDS 1950. Sukarno refused, however, and the affair backfired for the military officers involved in it. Instead of removing the political system that it so despised, the military had managed to manoeuvre itself even further to the political margins. It was only in this situation of increasing desperation that the military took a second look at the 1945 Constitution and began to lobby for its restoration.

Restoring the 1945 Constitution

While TNI had not been a strong supporter of the 1945 Constitution, the three subsequent constitutional arrangements made the officer corps warm up to the original document. This was because of the increasingly apparent contrasts between the 1945 Constitution and its successors. The 1945 Constitution had positioned the president as supreme commander of the armed forces, but the Vice-Presidential Decree No 10, the RIS Constitution, and the UUDS 1950 had set out much more detailed limitations of the military's role and power. Most significantly, the RIS Constitution and the UUDS 1950 closed the door to military representation in parliament and in the planned Constitutional Assembly. All members of these bodies had to be elected (with the exception of some representatives of ethnic minorities), making it impossible for the military to be recognized as a group worthy of special representation. The 1945 Constitution, on the other hand, allowed (in Art 2) for MPR representation of special groups (*golongan*), which could potentially include the military. Moreover, Article 19 set out such broad guidelines for the establishment of the legislature that even a fully appointed parliament was achievable, making it possible for military representatives to be appointed without contesting an election. In other words, a potential restoration of the 1945 Constitution promised to re-open opportunities for military participation in politics that the RIS Constitution and the UUDS 1950 had shut down.

The military lobbied for the re-introduction of the 1945 Constitution in several ways. First, it established its own political party in 1954, with the goal of participating in the 1955 elections (Kahin 2012: 125). The party was named League of Supporters of Indonesian Independence (*Ikatan Pendukung Kemerdekaan Indonesia*, IPKI), with Nasution playing a key role in its founding (Feith 1962: 405). IPKI demanded a return to the 'spirit' of 1945, including the Constitution of that year. Its calls were moderate at the beginning but grew more determined after the government ruled that any military officers running as IPKI candidates in the 1955 elections would have to resign from active service beforehand. The party only gained 1.4 per cent of the vote, which IPKI and military leaders blamed on the government's restriction of TNI candidacies, and which further alienated the armed forces from the democratic system. In the eyes of many military officers, IPKI's failure in the 1955 election removed any illusion that the military could operate in the parliamentary system, and the party as well as the TNI elite began to push harder for the restoration of the 1945 Constitution as a result.

A second TNI strategy to lobby for the revival of the 1945 Constitution involved searching for likeminded allies. Most key political parties had other ideas for a new Constitution—ranging from an Islamist state to a nationalist-corporatist polity—and thus were not overly receptive to the notion of simply returning to the 1945 document (Nasution 1992). But there was one leading actor who felt about the post-1945 Constitutions in a way that was strikingly similar to TNI's position: Sukarno, the largely ceremonial president. Just like TNI, Sukarno felt marginalized, aggrieved that his role as Indonesia's preeminent nationalist figure, founding president, and wartime leader was not appreciated by the current Constitution and the parties working within it. As explained above, there had been many tensions between Sukarno and the military, and the gulf between them remained wide. But they were united in their rejection of the status quo—and in their belief that returning to the 1945 Constitution could be the ideal solution to their troubles.

The military's third approach to preparing the ground for the return of the 1945 Constitution was the creation of a new doctrinal framework that was compatible with such a move. Once again, Nasution was the key player in this regard. In a major speech in 1958, Nasution introduced the idea of the Middle Way (*Jalan Tengah*) between a military takeover on the one hand and fully civilian rule on the other. Making his argument at a time of serial military coups in the Middle East, Africa, and Latin America, Nasution asserted that the Indonesian military did not want to take over government like so many of its counterparts in other developing countries had done—but that it wanted to have a political role of some sort. In describing the situation, he likened TNI to a volcano, which would eventually erupt if politicians continued to insist on putting a lid on it (Supriyatmono 1994: 114). In Nasution's view, the 1945

Constitution allowed sufficient space to implement this Middle Way vision—that is, a polity in which the military could sit in all relevant institutions (concretely, parliament and the MPR), but in which the civilian president and other parties remained prominent (Turner 2018: 185).

The efforts of the armed forces paid off in July 1959, when Sukarno—with the support of the military—declared the return to the 1945 Constitution. The failure of the Constitutional Assembly (which had been in session since 1956) to agree on a new document; growing regional conflicts; and general dissatisfaction with the political parties provided Sukarno and the generals with the pretext they needed to push through this restoration, which was constitutionally questionable. Sukarno subsequently established his autocratic Guided Democracy regime, in which the military played a significant role. In 1960, Sukarno dissolved the old, elected parliament and replaced it with a fully appointed legislature—in line with the vague stipulations in the 1945 Constitution. For the first time since independence, the military received representation as a special group, or *golongan*: it obtained 35 of the 283 seats (Pringgodigdo 1973: 267). This made it the third-largest faction in the parliament, after the Indonesian Nationalist Party (*Partai Nasional Indonesia*, PNI) and the *Nahdlatul Ulama* (NU). Nasution's plan to secure a political role for the military via the 1945 Constitution had worked.

It was in this period that the military's strong commitment to Indonesia's Constitution became part of its doctrinal rhetoric. Finally, the military had a Constitution, and an interpretation of that Constitution, that gave it privileges and thus was worth preserving. In contrast to previous Constitutions and arrangements that the military viewed as civilian products designed to keep the military away from politics, the re-introduced 1945 Constitution—with its new positioning of the armed forces as a *golongan*—was something the military believed in. Hence, from 1960 onwards, the 'protection of Pancasila and the Constitution of 1945' developed into the well-known TNI mantra that became one of its trademarks. Of course, the addition of '1945' to the name of the Constitution was not only a matter of formal correctness (as this was indeed its official title), it also signaled that the 1945 Constitution was the only constitution TNI was willing to defend, and that a change in Constitution would not automatically generate the same loyalty. For the armed forces, the Constitution was now much more than the legal foundation of the state it had pledged to protect—it was the basis for its own institutional privileges and power.

While Sukarno had moulded the 1945 Constitution in a way that the military's interests were accommodated, this constitutional engineering was brought to an entirely new level once a military general came to power in 1966. The armed forces' rise to government followed the slow but steady unravelling of the balance between Sukarno, TNI, and the Indonesian Communist Party (*Partai Komunis Indonesia*, PKI), which peaked in a botched pro-communist coup attempt in October 1965. Suharto, then a two-star general, emerged as the military's new leader amidst the ensuing chaos, and established himself in the presidency in a long period of transition between 1966 and 1968. While his regime, the New Order, was keen to dismantle almost everything related to Sukarno's 'Old Order', it left the 1945 Constitution in place. Suharto knew that the 1945 Constitution gave aspiring autocrats maximum flexibility in developing a regime tailored to their personal needs—and the needs of their supporting institutions, such as the military. In this spirit, he further increased the military's representation in the parliament—first to 45 seats in 1966 and then to 75 seats in 1971 and to 100 seats in 1987. As the military had additional members in the MPR, it commanded at times a third of all seats there—not coincidentally, that was the percentage needed to prevent a change of the Constitution (Lembaga Pemilihan Umum 1982: 19).

Even more importantly, Suharto used the gaping loopholes in the 1945 Constitution to create an electoral system that guaranteed his routine re-appointment by the MPR. Article 6(2) of the 1945 Constitution stated that the president was to be elected by the MPR, but Article 2 was very vague on how the MPR needed to be constituted. In addition to the members of parliament, the MPR contained 'delegates from the regions and from special groups'—no reference was made to how the latter were to be selected, and what their numbers had to be. Of course, Suharto took this to mean that it was he, as the president, who could appoint these delegates and determine their numbers. For the 1988, 1993, and 1998 MPR sessions, Suharto set membership at 1,000, with 500 delegates directly appointed by him. Since the parliament also included 100 appointed military members loyal to him, Suharto already had a majority of 600 MPR members in each session before the election even began. This did not mean that the remaining 400 'elected' members of parliament were independent—they were obliged to obtain security clearances from the military before they could run for office. Thus, Suharto had masterfully translated the 1945 Constitution into an autocratic election mechanism that left no room for unwanted surprises.

Although there were tensions between Suharto and the military in the later periods of the New Order (Honna 2003), the armed forces unswervingly stuck to the regime—and to their 'defending Pancasila and the 1945 Constitution' chant. References to the protection of the 1945 Constitution were typically deployed to legitimize the repression of regime opponents, which in turn served to sustain the political status quo. For instance, the then military commander, Maraden Panggabean cited the 1945 Constitution in a speech at parliament when justifying the repression of the 1974 student movement (Dewan Perwakilan Rakyat 1977: 127). Hence, under the New Order, the military used the 1945 Constitution as an all-purpose instrument to fend off challenges to its privileges and to discourage public discussion on possible revisions to (let alone the full replacement of) the Constitution. At the end of Suharto's rule, the 1945 Constitution was so deeply engrained in the psyche of many officers that any notion of constitutional change seemed heretic to them. This was ironic given how long the military had taken to endorse defending the incumbent Constitution as one of its core tasks. Suharto's fall in 1998 would shatter the military's hard-won identification with the existing Constitution and open a new round of uncertainty in which the armed forces had to come to terms with a Constitution it did not favour.

TNI and Post-Suharto Amendments

Suharto's resignation in May 1998, following an economic meltdown, mass demonstrations, and splits within the ruling elite (Aspinall 2005), came as both a relief and a shock to the military. On the one hand, Suharto had increasingly (mis)used the military as his palace guard, while handing benefits to his family and an inner circle of business cronies. Indeed, at the end it was the military that tapped him on the shoulder and explained that it would be impossible to defend him against the rising protests—Suharto resigned just hours later. But while Suharto's departure solved one problem for the military, it created a host of others. There had been discontent in the military over the way Suharto treated them in his later years, but there was still a more fundamental awareness that the armed forces drew significant privileges from his rule. These included access to patronage resources for senior generals, but also Suharto's protection of the 1945 Constitution that was the basis for the military's political representation in parliament and the MPR. All of this was now thrown into question, as it was certain that democratization would be accompanied by calls to revise the Constitution.

Facing these pressures, TNI decided to agree to constitutional amendments, but wanted to limit their scope and impact. In this spirit, TNI raised few objections to the first amendments made during the MPR session in October 1999. At the heart of these amendments was the new presidential term limit, which allowed for only one re-election. For TNI, this was not only acceptable but desirable, given that the military too had eventually fallen out with long-time autocrats Sukarno (who had been declared president for life by the MPR in 1963) and Suharto (who had been re-appointed seven times by the same body). The other constitutional changes were relatively minor in character and did not touch on the military's institutional interests. Most crucially, the principle of *golongan* being eligible for appointment to the MPR and parliament remained intact. For the military, the real fight to hold on to its political representation took place outside of the constitutional arena: under the leadership of Susilo Bambang Yudhoyono, the armed forces negotiated with legislators over the size of the military and police faction in the first post-Suharto parliament to be elected in June 1999. After tense discussions, in the course of which some parliamentarians insisted that TNI give up all of its delegates, it was agreed to halve the number of national military and police parliamentarians from seventy-five to thirty-eight, and to fix their numbers in regional parliaments at 10 per cent (Alagappa 2001: 483).

But while the 1999 amendments allowed TNI to continue its pledge to loyally defend the existing Constitution, this commitment began to weaken with the 2000 amendments. In that year's MPR session, Article 19(1) of the Constitution was changed to stipulate that all members of parliament had to be democratically elected. This removed the basis upon which Sukarno had appointed the 1960 legislature, including military MPs, and Suharto had installed a succession of military factions during his rule. In practice, this meant that the military would lose its national and local MPs by 2004. As consolation, the representation of *golongan* in the MPR was sustained for the time being, giving the military the impression that it could continue to claim representation in the MPR. This impression was strengthened by a separate MPR decree that stipulated that the military would leave the parliament by 2004 and the MPR 'by 2009 at the latest'. The military took this to mean that it had another nine years in the MPR—which appeared like a reasonably long timeframe and thus helped to mitigate the sense of panic that the forced departure from the parliament had initially triggered.

One year later, however, the military's sense of alarm was reignited. In the third round of amendments in 2001, the MPR decided to replace the election of the president by the MPR with a direct, popular vote. This meant that even if the military were allowed to stay in the MPR until 2009, as it believed it would, it would have very little influence there. For the military, holding on to MPR seats was important because in the past such seats translated into crucial votes in the presidential election. In 1999, the TNI votes in the MPR had been at the centre of the candidates' lobbying efforts, and the military was subsequently rewarded with cabinet posts (Mietzner 2000: 52–54). By removing the presidential vote in the MPR, the military's political weight was much reduced. In addition, the 2001 amendments introduced a Constitutional Court, which had the task—among others—to adjudicate in conflicts between state agencies. This role had thus far been played informally by the military, with rival civilian forces lobbying the armed forces for support and offering rewards in return. With direct presidential elections taking away the military's role as a power broker in the MPR, and the Constitutional Court assuming the function as a political referee previously carried out by the TNI, the officer corps felt that this was no longer 'its' 1945 Constitution. Instead, it was a new constitution that, in the eyes of many officers, misleadingly held on to its original name.

Accordingly, officers began to push for a cancellation of the existing amendments and a return to the original 1945 document. Mirroring Nasution's campaign in the early 1950s, they argued that especially the third round of amendments violated the spirit of the 1945 Constitution, and that therefore the sanctity of the original text had to be restored. As the MPR prepared for the fourth and final round of amendments in 2002, this 'return to the 1945 Constitution' demand became the official stance of the TNI leadership. In a joint statement by the TNI commander and the police chief on 30 July 2002 (two days before the beginning of the MPR session which was to finalize the amendments), the heads of Indonesia's security forces presented the civilian elite with two options. First, should there be no agreement on the fourth round of amendments, then all previous amendments should be cancelled and the original 1945 Constitution re-introduced until the 2004 elections—after which the process of amendments should begin from scratch. Second, should the fourth round of amendments be agreed upon, they should only be in place until the 2004 elections, after which a new Constitutional Commission should work on a new Constitution (TNI 2002). In either of these scenarios, the military wanted to rescind the amendments achieved since 1999 and have a new chance of restoring its old privileges.

In its initiative, the military felt emboldened by events in the previous year. In 2001, TNI had played a key role in removing President Abdurrahman Wahid from office amidst intense political conflict. As Wahid struggled against the parliament's impeachment initiative, the military decided the outcome of the conflict by siding with Wahid's opponents and voting against him in the MPR. Believing that the new power holders (President Megawati Sukarnoputri and other leaders who had initiated Wahid's removal) owed them for this intervention in the power struggle, military leaders apparently calculated that their stance on the amendments would carry significant weight. However, much to their disappointment, they found that it did not. The civilian elite collectively ignored the military's demand and finalized the constitutional amendments after intense but orderly debates. As a final insult, a new stipulation was introduced that removed the *golongan* from MPR membership, effectively ending TNI's presence there by 2004—and not in 2009, as envisaged and promised in the plan made in 2000.

In order to hand a face-saving concession to the military, the MPR agreed to the establishment of a Constitutional Commission. While this *appeared* like a substantial move, in reality it was not. The MPR decree that created the Commission described the body's task as 'studying' changes to the Constitution—without saying whether this meant researching the character of the changes already made or proposing new amendments. MPR leaders and civil society figures alike dismissed the Commission as a toothless tiger from the beginning (Liputan6 2002), and they were proven right: the Commission submitted its recommendation to the MPR in 2004 and was subsequently dissolved without a substantive discussion (Tempo 2007). None of its proposals was translated into a concrete amendment.

Immediately after the 2002 MPR session, TNI saw the need to issue a lengthy statement to clarify its view on the constitutional amendments. Until today, it remains the most comprehensive and clearest expression of TNI's open ambivalence towards the post-Suharto Constitution. In the statement, the military reaffirmed its view that the 1945 Constitution was the product of a 'mature' process of consideration among the founding fathers, and that it captured Indonesia's pluralist spirit as embodied in the state ideology, Pancasila. The only weakness of this document, TNI suggested, was that its brevity led to the possibility of multiple interpretations of its content. Accordingly, the task of the post-1998 amendments, in TNI's view, was simply to 'give clarity about the political system and avoid multiple interpretations' while 'consistently defending the foundational values of the proclamation of 17 August 1945' (TNI 2002). In what followed, the armed forces left no doubt that it viewed this post-1998 attempt at coming up with clarifying amendments as a failure. Describing the amendments as 'inconsistent', 'very dangerous for the stability and balance' of the nation, 'not comprehensive', and the product of 'short-term' and 'group-specific interests', the military painted a devastating picture of the Constitution it had the duty of defending.

While the military emphasized that it 'supported' the result of the 2002 MPR session, it nevertheless questioned its legitimacy. TNI highlighted the need for the Constitutional Commission to deliver a

> draft of the 1945 Constitution that can truly lead the Indonesian nation to a more democratic and modern life in the framework of the Unitary State of the Republic of Indonesia, in line with the values enshrined in the opening of the 1945 Constitution.

TNI also demanded a draft that will obtain 'the legitimacy and the largest-possible support from the entire Indonesian people'. The implication of this demand was that the current Constitution lacked these features. Against this background, the military's continued pledge to protect the '1945 Constitution' became a word game with a deeply political meaning: on the one hand, it formally fulfilled the military's obligation to defend the incumbent Constitution (as even the amended Constitution was still referred to as the 1945 Constitution); on the other hand, it subtly gave voice to the military's preference for the original document over the post-amendment version.

Constitutionally, therefore, the post-1998 military has been thrown back to a place where it had been in the 1950s: it has to serve a Constitution that gives it no privileges, and that it is keen to remove sooner rather than later. Yet there are significant differences to that period too. To begin with, the post-Suharto military may have lost many of the politico-economic benefits it received under the autocracies of Sukarno und Suharto, but it is not as marginalized as the armed forces in the early 1950s. Retired military officers are frequently invited into cabinet; the armed forces retain a high level of institutional autonomy; and its officers continue to enjoy impunity for a series of past and present human rights violations (Mietzner 2018a). Thus, the pressure on TNI to work towards the removal of the unloved Constitution is today much lower than it was in the 1950s when Nasution wanted an institutionalized role for the military in politics at all costs. As it turned out, the post-2002 military did not even have to run its own campaign on reviving the 1945 Constitution. Almost twenty years after the amendments were completed, some sections of the civilian elite itself became embittered with many of these changes and began to lobby for a partial restoration of the 1945 Constitution.

Military and Civilian Opposition to the 2002 Amendments

After its scathing criticism of the 2002 amendments, TNI subsequently became more indirect and subtle in voicing its stance on the Constitution. As indicated above, the military relied on the ambivalence inherent in its routine pledges of loyalty to 'Pancasila and the 1945 Constitution', assuming that audiences understood that its core allegiance was to the original 1945 document. One of the most skilful operators of this strategy of constitutional dog whistling was Gatot Nurmantyo, the TNI commander between 2015 and 2017. He made sure that his formal speeches included at least one reference to TNI's loyalty towards the '1945 Constitution', but otherwise did not hold back with his view that the current political system was incompatible with the values enshrined in that document. In a major speech in June 2017 (which took on themes he had talked about for some time), Gatot claimed that the incumbent democratic polity was not in line with Pancasila's fourth pillar, namely decision-making by consultation until a consensus is reached (Merdeka 2017). Instead, he pointed out, contemporary Indonesian democracy reached decisions by voting—which the constitutional amendments had anchored as a key democratic principle for the post-2002 regime. He finished his speech with a rousing 'I am willing to be shot for saying that Indonesian democracy is currently not in line with Pancasila. [...] That's how it is'.

Gatot's strategy, therefore, was to circumvent the thorny issue of TNI's duty to protect the existing Constitution by highlighting the current polity's violation of Pancasila, rather than openly critiquing the post-amendment Constitution. But Gatot's confidence that his target audiences would connect his attack on democratic voting with broader criticisms of the Constitution was well placed. Even before the June 2017 speech, a group of campaigners for the revival of the 1945 Constitution recognized that they had an ally in Gatot. In November 2015, the group, calling itself the Movement to Save the Unitary State of the Indonesian Republic (*Gerakan Selamatkan NKRI*), stated that 'we wanted to write a letter to the TNI commander, but we opted not to as the Commander is already aware that democracy in Indonesia is aberrant'. The group, which included the former TNI commander Djoko Santoso, then called for a return to the original 1945 Constitution (Detik 2015). A wide range of other civilians attached themselves to Gatot's agenda too. For instance, Dahlan Watihellu, who ran for the position of chair of the influential Islamic Student Association (*Himpunan Mahasiswa Islam*, HMI) in 2015, issued a glowing endorsement of Gatot, calling his critique 'very true' and demanding the restoration of the 1945 Constitution (Kobar 2015).

After Gatot's removal as TNI commander in December 2017, the military's public rhetoric on the constitutional status quo was toned down somewhat. But the military could afford to take a step back in this regard as the theme of restoring at least parts of the original 1945 Constitution had already taken roots in the civilian sphere as well. In fact, the main advocates for re-opening the constitutional debate and rectifying some of the previous amendments' 'excesses' were now affiliated with the civilian mainstream—and not, as in the past, only with military elements or nationalist associations at the political margins. In March 2018, for instance, Megawati Sukarnoputri—still chair of the ruling Indonesian Democratic Party of Struggle (*Partai Demokrasi Indonesia Perjuangan*, PDI-P)—came forward with her proposal to restore the so-called Broad Outlines of State Policy (*Garis-Garis Besar Haluan Negara*, GBHN). The GBHN had been regulated in Article 3 of the original 1945 Constitution and had been a key instrument of policy planning under the Suharto regime. Issued by the MPR every five years, it set out principles that all subordinated policy levels needed to adhere to. After the end of the New Order, the GBHN were removed from the Constitution in 2001.

Megawati had in the past often spoken about her disdain for decision-making by voting in parliament and the MPR, long before Gatot had raised the same critique in his speeches. But her routine complaints had generally been dismissed as the musings of Sukarno's daughter, reflecting her nostalgic attachment to the past. This impression was strengthened by the fact that until 2018 there had been no concrete proposal by her party to restore parts of the 1945 Constitution. After her March 2018 speech, however, the party took systematic steps to push her proposal. At the August 2019 congress of PDI-P in Bali, the re-introduction of the GBHN was a key topic, and it was included in the party's policy recommendations. The reason for this demand, the party claimed, was the supposed lack of consistency in the government's long-term policy since the abolition of the GBHN (BeritaSatu 2019). In Megawati's and PDI-P's view, the frequent changes in the presidency made it impossible to implement a development plan that went beyond just short-term reactions to day-to-day needs in the field. Megawati's proposal received much applause from other civilian actors, including the incumbent MPR chair as well as politicians vying for this position in the upcoming term. In fact, candidates for the MPR chair lobbied Megawati for her support by promising that they would help re-introduce the GBHN if elected (Liputan6 2019).

Arguably, Megawati's sudden initiative to re-introduce the GBHN, after having been inactive on the issue for sixteen years, was more tactical than ideological in nature. While she was nominally the chair of the 'ruling' party because President Joko Widodo (or 'Jokowi') was a member of PDI-P, her ability to control Jokowi was severely limited. Jokowi had turned out to be a much more autonomous actor than Megawati had envisaged. Worse still for Megawati, the prospect that a core PDI-P cadre (such as her daughter Puan Maharani) would become president in the future looked rather slim. At the same time, PDI-P had finished first in three out of the five post-Suharto legislative elections, and thus was more likely to be the largest faction in the MPR rather than having one of its own cadres in the presidency. With the potentially re-introduced GBHN, PDI-P would be able to set state policy that any president had to abide by—whether this was a president only loosely tied to PDI-P or one not associated with the party at all. Clearly, this was the way Jokowi understood Megawati's move, and in uncharacteristically clear language, he rejected it as an undue attempt to impose limitations on his presidential autonomy (Tempo 2019). Undeterred, Megawati insisted on maintaining her position.

While the military avoided taking a public stance on the GBHN controversy, it was widely accepted that the officer corps had a particular affinity towards these MPR guidelines. Wiranto, the last TNI commander in the New Order and now a leading politician, and Prabowo Subianto, Suharto's former son-in-law, senior New Order general, and later Jokowi's rival in the 2014 and 2019 elections, had gone on record long before Megawati to support the re-introduction of the GBHN. Wiranto had done so explicitly by highlighting the role of the GBHN as a corrective towards a 'democratic culture' brought in from other, presumably Western countries (Liputan6 2019). Although the relevance of the GBHN for the military was somewhat reduced by the fact that the generals were no longer represented in the MPR, the notion that state policy would be made in backroom deals between a few hundred MPR members rather than a democratically elected president was perfectly in line with traditional corporatist thinking within the officer corps. This was even more so as the potential revival of long-term development plans opened the possibility of revisiting other constitutional issues, including that of military representation in the MPR and other political institutions.

The speculation that the GBHN issue only served as an entry point for much broader attempts to change the Constitution was confirmed in November 2019 by the new MPR chairman Bambang Soesatyo. In re-activating an MPR body to study constitutional changes that had been created in 2015, Soesatyo made it clear that all options were on the table. He listed these options as: first, returning to the original 1945 Constitution 'in line with the Presidential Decree of 5 July 1959'; second, a fifth round of constitutional amendments; third, the cancellation of all four previous rounds of amendments and the writing of an entirely new Constitution; fourth, a limited amendment only focusing on re-introducing the GBHN; and fifth, leaving the current Constitution in place (Detik 2019). In other words, the new MPR leadership echoed many of the proposals the military had made in 2002: from the return to the 1945 document to going back to the constitutional drawing board.

There are two main reasons why civilian elites began to adapt the constitutional critiques made by the military almost two decades earlier. First, for many party elites, there were too many outsiders taking advantage of the system that leaders of established parties had put together in 2002. Indeed, since the amendments, not a single traditional party politician had won the presidency (concretely, since the first post-amendment, direct ballot in 2004). Yudhoyono triumphed in 2004 and 2009 as a retired military officer and cabinet minister, having cobbled together his Democrat Party in a hurry to meet registration requirements. Subsequently, Jokowi did not even bother to found his own party, using PDI-P as a vehicle to prevail in 2014 and 2019 but caring very little about its institutional development. Many of the candidates positioning themselves for the 2024 elections are also independents emerging from outside the party system: for instance, Anies Baswedan, the governor of Jakarta; Ridwan Kamil, the governor of West Java; and Sandiaga Uno, a businessman and failed vice-presidential candidate in 2019. Thus, popular non-party figures have turned out to be the main beneficiaries of the 2002 amendments—rather than the parties that designed them (Aspinall 2015).

Not coincidentally, then, the push for reviving elements of the 1945 Constitution (by either limiting presidential authority or abolishing direct presidential elections) has come from unpopular establishment figures who had lost to outsiders in presidential contests: Megawati, who lost in 2004 and 2009; Surya Paloh, who first failed to win the Golkar nomination and then to secure a candidacy through his own Nasdem party; Wiranto, who lost in 2004 and 2009; the leader of the PKB party, Muhaimin Iskandar, who had failed to get the vice-presidential nomination in 2019; and Prabowo, who—although an outsider himself—was defeated by the political upstart Jokowi in the 2014 and 2019 contests. In short, these elite figures felt a sense of alienation similar to that of Sukarno in the 1950s, and resorting to key elements of the 1945 Constitution appeared like a tested and realistic option to them. As in the 1950s, these marginalized civilian leaders could count on similar sentiments being held in the military—whether in the vocal community of retired officers or the more restrained active brass.

The second reason for the frustration of many civilian leaders with the post-2002 Constitution has been the increasing political costs associated with it. The introduction of direct presidential elections in 2004 and the beginning of direct local executive elections in 2005 (which had not been mandated, but inspired by the constitutional amendments) led to a massive explosion in campaign costs. This spike in political expenses intensified further with the switch to an open-party list system in 2009. This system forced candidates to compete with nominees from their own party, leading many of them to engage in vote buying (Muhtadi 2019). While this change was not the direct result of the constitutional amendments, it was ordered by the Constitutional Court—which argued that the previous, semi-open list system violated the amended Constitution. Thus, although civilian elites continue to reap benefits from the status quo through their extensive access to patronage resources, that access has come at an increasing cost. Moreover, as at the presidential level, established party politicians have been exceedingly losing out to popular and wealthy outsiders in legislative elections: the rate of parliamentary incumbency losses has been consistently around 50 per cent, with newcomers often outspending incumbents (Kompas 2019).

For the military, this constellation has a big advantage: it does not have to take the lead role in agitating against the amended Constitution in the way it did in the 1950s. At this stage, it can sit back and watch the events unfold, with retired military leaders giving a voice to the thinking within the armed forces and civilian politicians saying many of the things about the Constitution that the TNI leadership had controversially expressed in 2002. In all of these developments, the TNI can be certain of one thing: eventually, there will be new amendments to the post-2002 Constitution, and whatever their scope will be, they are unlikely to be disadvantageous to the armed forces. Given the current climate of increasing politico-ideological illiberalism (Mietzner 2018b), any fresh amendments by the MPR are set to move the Constitution closer to the corporatist spirit of the 1945 document, rather than further away from it. If and when that happens, the military is certain to feel vindicated—its 2002 re-commendations on the Constitution will have at least partially prevailed, albeit with a twenty-year delay.

Conclusion: TNI, the Constitution and Democracy

What, then, has the role of the military been in shaping Indonesia's Constitutions and their democratic quality? Despite TNI's obvious prominence in upholding autocratic interpretations of the 1945 Constitution between the 1950s and 1990s, the answer is more complex that it may initially seem. As demonstrated in this chapter, the military had almost no say in the drafting of the original 1945 Constitution; in the Vice-Presidential Decree No 10 of 1945 that introduced semi-parliamentarism; in the 1950 Constitution of the RIS; and the UUDS 1950. It did play a limited role in the amendments to the 1945 Constitution made between 1999 and 2002, but its input was mostly ignored. There were only two political contexts in which the military had strong influence on the outcome of constitutional developments. First, whenever the interests of the military and anti-democratic elites met, the impact on Indonesian democracy has been devastating. When Sukarno and TNI bundled their discontents over the UUDS 1950 to undermine the incumbent democratic system, they were able to jointly re-introduce the 1945 Constitution and establish autocracy. Similarly, TNI's opposition towards the 2002 amendments only became relevant when it was shared, in the late 2010s, by key civilian forces. Thus, military opposition towards democratic Constitutions is effective only if it aligns with comparable streams in the civilian sphere.

Second, military influence on constitutional amendments has been formidable whenever the level of repression in politics was high. Such repression handed a key role to the military, and it used this role to exploit and shape the Constitution. Suharto's use of the 1945 Constitution to erect an authoritarian regime tailored to his interests (and to that of the military) was only made possible by the takeover of 1966, the subsequent brutal purge of all leftist groups, and the tight socio-political controls accompanying the establishment of the New Order. Unlike in the 1950s, no civilian consent was necessary to enforce an utterly autocratic interpretation of the Constitution—the latter was presented as a fait accompli and imposed unilaterally. It was only in the later years of the New Order, when Suharto's relationship with the armed forces became increasingly strained, that he tried to gain the approval of major civilian groups for his continued rule—and for the ongoing autocratic interpretation of the 1945 Constitution. To that end, Suharto integrated Muslim groups, technocrats, and business leaders into his regime. Ultimately, his rule collapsed when the approval of these civilian actors was no longer forthcoming, and the military too was ready to move on from Suharto's tired government.

While TNI's impact on constitutional change has thus been dependent on civilian collaboration or rare direct military intervention, the armed forces' attitude towards existing Constitutions has negatively influenced Indonesia's democratic culture in another, more subtle way. A key function of any military is the politically disinterested protection of its country's democratically installed Constitution. In TNI's case, however, this protection has been selective and qualified. During the war against the Dutch, the military often operated outside of the constitutional chain of command. Afterwards, it opposed the RIS and UUDS arrangements—both legitimate Constitutions. In the early 2000s too, the military stated that it preferred the 1945 Constitution to the amended document. In combination, these episodes have raised continuous questions about the commitment of the military to the defence of the democratic constitutional order should it come under attack. By routinely referring to the '1945 Constitution' as the one it feels obliged to defend, the military has deliberately left the question of its real loyalties open. Only twice in its history, it seems, did the military feel that it served the 'right' Constitution: under Sukarno and Suharto, when the original version of the 1945 Constitution was in place. Given the current discussions on reviving at least parts of this Constitution, the military may soon be in the same position again.

References

Alagappa, Muthiah (2001) 'Conclusion' in Muthiah Alagappa (ed), *Coercion and Governance: The Declining Political Role of the Military in Asia*. Stanford: Stanford University Press. pp 433–498.

Anderson, Benedict R O'G (1972) *Java in a Time of Revolution. Occupation and Resistance, 1944–1946*. Ithaca, New York: Cornell University Press.

Aspinall, Edward (2005) *Opposing Suharto: Compromise, Resistance and Regime Change in Indonesia*. Stanford: Stanford University Press.

Aspinall, Edward (2015) 'Oligarchic Populism: Prabowo Subianto's Challenge to Indonesian Democracy' 99 *Indonesia* 1–28.

BeritaSatu (2019) 'PDIP Ingin MPR Jadi Lembaga Tertinggi dan Hidupkan GBHN', 11 August.

Bourchier, David (2015) *Illiberal Democracy in Indonesia: The Ideology of the Family State*. London: Routledge.

Cribb, Robert (1991) *Gangsters and Revolutionaries: The Jakarta People's Militia and the Indonesian Revolution, 1945–1949*. Sydney: Allen & Unwin.

Detik (2015) 'Gerakan Selamatkan NKRI: Kembalikan Pancasila dan UUD 1945', 12 November.

Detik (2019) 'Bamsoet Sebut Perubahan Konstitusi Bisa Mengantar Babak Baru Bangsa', 5 November.

Dewan Perwakilan Rakyat (1977) *Dewan Perwakilan Rakyat, Periode 1971-1977*. Jakarta: Sekretariat Jenderal DPR.

Elson, Robert E (2001) *Suharto: A Political Biography*. Cambridge: Cambridge University Press.

Feith, Herbert (1962) *The Decline of Constitutional Democracy in Indonesia*. Ithaca, New York: Cornell University Press.

Gatra (2019) 'Purnawirawan TNI AD: Pilpres Tak Sesuai UUD 1945 & Pancasila', 29 October.

Honna, Jun (2003) *Military Politics and Democratization in Indonesia*. London: RoutledgeCurzon.

Kahin, Audrey R (2012) *Islam, Nationalism and Democracy: A Political Biography of Mohammad Natsir*. Singapore: NUS Press.

Kobar (2015) 'Menanggapi Statement Panglima TNI, Bakal Calon Kandidat Ketum PB HMI Angkat Bicara', 10 October.

Kompas (2019) 'Anggota DPR Terpilih Terdiri dari 50,26 Persen 'Wajah Lama', 80,52 Persen Laki-laki', 4 September.

Larantuka News (2019) 'Siaga Pemilu, Panglima TNI Pastikan Pancasila, UUD 1945, NKRI Harga Mati', 9 April.

Lembaga Pemilihan Umum (1982) *Memperkenalkan Anggota-Anggota Dewan Perwakilan Rakyat Hasil Pemilihan Umum 1982*. Jakarta: Lembaga Pemilihan Umum.

Liputan6 (2002) 'Komisi Konstitusi yang Tiada Arti', 12 August.

Liputan6 (2013) 'Setuju GBHN Dihidupkan, Prabowo: Agar Demokrasi Tak Carut Marut', 17 December.

Liputan6 (2019) 'Bambang Soesatyo Ketua MPR, Agenda PDIP Mengamandemen UUD 1945 Bakal Mulus?', 5 October.

McFarling, Ian (1996) *The Dual Function of the Indonesian Armed Forces: Military Politics in Indonesia*. Canberra: Australian Defence Studies Centre.

Merdeka (2017) 'Setuju Panglima TNI, Ketua MPR Sebut Demokrasi RI Kebablasan', 5 June.

Mietzner, Marcus (2000) 'The 1999 General Session: Wahid, Megawati and the Fight for the Presidency' in Chris Manning and Peter Van Diermen (eds) *Indonesia in Transition: Social Aspects of Reformasi and Crisis*. Singapore: Institute of Southeast Asian Studies. pp 39–57.

Mietzner, Marcus (2018a) 'The Indonesian Armed Forces, Coalitional Presidentialism, and Democratization' in Robert W Hefner (ed) *Routledge Handbook of Contemporary Indonesia*. London and New York: Routledge. pp 140–150.

Mietzner, Marcus (2018b) 'Fighting Illiberalism with Illiberalism: Islamist Populism and Democratic Deconsolidation in Indonesia' 91(2) *Pacific Affairs* 261–282.

Muhtadi, Burhanuddin (2019) *Vote Buying in Indonesia: The Mechanics of Electoral Bribery*. Singapore: Palgrave McMillan.

Nasution, Adnan Buyung (1992) *The Aspiration for Constitutional Government in Indonesia: A Socio-Legal Study of the Indonesian Konstituante, 1956–1959*. Jakarta: Pustaka Sinar Harapan.

Pringgodigdo, AG (1973) *Ensiklopedi Umum*. Yogyakarta: Penerbit Kanisius.

Sundhaussen, Ulf (1982) *The Road to Power: Indonesian Military Politics, 1945–1967*. Kuala Lumpur: Oxford University Press.

Supriyatmono, Hendri (1994) *Nasution, Dwifungsi ABRI dan Kontribusi ke Arah Reformasi Politik*. Surakarta and Yogyakarta: Sebelas Maret University Press.

Tempo (2007) 'Komisi Konstitusi Minta Kajiannya Digunakan untuk Perbaikan Konstitusi', 22 February.

Tempo (2019) 'Beda Dengan PDIP, Jokowi Isyaratkan Tolak Amandemen UUD 1945', 15 August.

TNI (2002) 'Sikap TNI-Polri Terhadap Perubahan Keempat UUD 1945 Pada ST MPR 2002'. Jakarta: Mabes TNI.

Turner, Barry (2018) *A. H. Nasution and Indonesia's Elites: 'People's Resistance' in the War of Independence and Postwar Politics*. London: Lexington Books.

Waspada (2018) 'Mantan Panglima TNI: Kembali ke UUD 1945 Yang Asli', 8 January.

4

Between Upholding the Rule of Law and Maintaining Security

Criminal Justice Actors in Indonesia's Constitution

Fachrizal Afandi and Adriaan Bedner

Introduction

Until now, we have secured 33 people. We secure them, we don't arrest them!

(Nana Sudjana, the Metro Jakarta Chief of Police) (CNN 2020)[1]

(To the police) 'Please stop using the term "securing", because it is not known (in the code of criminal procedure). Securing (in practice) does not relate to security since police officers often beat (suspects), and do not give them access to a lawyer.'

(Nelson Nikodemus, LBH Jakarta Legal Aid Activist)
(Tempo 2020, BBC 2020)[2]

These quotes are typical of current public debates in Indonesia concerning police treatment of persons who are involved in demonstrations against the government. According to observers, the police often use excessive violence against protesters and prevent them from seeking the protection of the law by 'securing' instead of officially arresting them (Prayogo 2019: 14–19; BBC 2019). The police prefer the former ('securing'), because Article 19 of the Code of Criminal Procedure (KUHAP) only allows them to arrest and detain someone for twenty-four hours. Longer detention requires more paperwork and is only allowed if the criminal offence is serious (Art 21).[3] The term 'securing' is not mentioned in any regulation and the police therefore have no legal basis for 'securing' a suspect; they simply assume that using this term relieves them from their duties under KUHAP and allows them to keep persons in custody indefinitely. Until the present, only a few cases of 'securing' have been taken to court, but judges have been reluctant to condemn the practice as unlawful (YLBHI 2021). This is a clear sign that many judges are inclined to side with the police and prosecutors. In several pre-trial proceedings where judges had to consider the lawfulness of an 'arrest',

---

[1] 'Sampai saat ini ada sekitar 33 orang yang kami amankan. Ini kami amankan, bukan kami tangkap'.
[2] 'Polisi berhentilah pakai istilah "amankan", karena itu tidak dikenal. Dan seringkali malah tidak "aman" karena dipukul, tidak boleh hubungi siapa-siapa, tidak dikasih akses pengacara'.
[3] For the sake of clarity: the police do *not* need a prosecutorial or judicial order.

Fachrizal Afandi and Adriaan Bedner, *Between Upholding the Rule of Law and Maintaining Security* In: *Constitutional Democracy in Indonesia*. Edited by: Melissa Crouch, Oxford University Press. © Fachrizal Afandi and Adriaan Bedner, 2023.
DOI: 10.1093/oso/9780192870681.003.0004

they also appeared reluctant to interfere and preferred to dismiss the claim on account of formal pretexts (Eddyono et al 2014: 6).[4]

These practices indicate that the constitutional amendment process between 1999 and 2002 did not change criminal procedure in the way one might have expected. The introduction of a human rights catalogue into the Constitution suggests that criminal procedure would henceforth be governed by the principles of legality and due process. However, it takes more than legislative changes to achieve the rule of law. As we will argue in this chapter, Indonesia's constitutional amendments failed to change the mode of operation of the police and the public prosecutor, as well as the institutional structures, procedures, and ideology that underpin it. While some effective reforms have taken place within the judiciary (Rositawati 2019: 245–246; Afandi 2021: 112–113), this has not yet promoted greater accountability of the police and prosecutors. In essence, the situation today is similar to Soeharto's New Order, when the police were part of the military, and when police and public prosecutors followed the army's example in pursuing the single overriding objective of regime preservation.[5]

This chapter provides an analysis of the authority, tasks, and mode of operation of police and public prosecutors in post-New Order Indonesia's criminal justice system. Its point of departure is the amendments to the Constitution and the attempt to alter the character of the criminal justice system as it had developed under previous authoritarian regimes. Nonetheless, as already indicated in this introduction, the values underlying the present system still emphasize crime control and maintaining public order rather than due process. Criminal law continues to serve primarily as a means of strengthening state control over society and achieving high rates of arrest, prosecution, conviction, and incarceration (Afandi 2021: 165). How successful the system has been in this respect is demonstrated by the staggering rise of the number of prisoners and the overcrowding of prisons.[6] Moreover, criminal justice actors have remained an instrument of the government to secure its political interests. In this respect, Indonesia has continued to look more like an authoritarian state than a state under the rule of law.

The first part of the chapter discusses the different constitutional provisions on security, defence, judicial power, and human rights in the Constitutions that have been in place since Indonesia became independent. We focus on how these constitutional regimes have influenced the state institutions involved in the criminal law process—in particular the police and the Prosecution Service—how these have changed over time and how they operate in practice. The next section examines how these criminal justice actors have continued to rely on a security approach in performing their tasks. We will argue that despite the separation between the police and the military, the former has retained the characteristics of a military organization. The Prosecution Service has to a large extent followed these examples. Its emphasis on hierarchy, its

---

[4] A good example is the recent judgment by the South Jakarta District Court brought by Ravio Parta (Tirto 2020).

[5] The military via the Operational Command for the Restoration of Security and Discipline (*Komando Operasi Pemulihan Keamanan dan Ketertiban*, KOPKAMTIB) supervised all of the criminal justice actors including the police, prosecutors, and judges (Lolo 2008; Afandi, 2021).

[6] From 2011 to 2014 the number of inmates rose from 136,145, to 167,136 (Ditjenpas 2014).

preference for military style uniforms,[7] and its training of new staff[8] are far removed from what one would expect of a magisterial organization.

The military nature of the main organisations involved in criminal justice promotes an authoritarian approach. We will subsequently look at criminal procedure, how it has remained unchanged, and how human rights have had little or no influence on it. And finally we discuss the dominant position of the police in the criminal justice system, their competition with the military, and their resistance to supervision by prosecutors and judges. In our conclusion we bring together our main findings and offer a single suggestion for bringing criminal procedure more in line with the rule of law.

Constitutional Arrangements Concerning Criminal Justice

Since Indonesia became independent in 1945, it has had four constitutions. All of these constitutions were compromises between different political ideologies, of which the most important were liberalism, integralism, socialism, and Islamism.[9] Although the traces of these four major currents in Indonesian political thought can be perceived in each constitution, liberalism and integralism have alternated as the dominant ones (Bedner 2017: 291).

Indonesia's first constitution was drafted at the end of the Japanese occupation. It was dominated by an integralist perspective on the state, putting the community above the individual, and tending towards totalitarianism (Logemann 1962). The 1945 Constitution was virtually devoid of rule-of-law guarantees: it did not contain a human rights catalogue, held no provisions on due process, and provided no explicit protection for the independence of the judiciary. Indonesia's second constitution was adopted about four years later, at the end of the Revolution when the Netherlands was forced to abandon its attempts at regaining control of its former colony. This 1949 Federal Constitution was drafted during the negotiations between the Indonesian Republic and the Dutch government. Although it was replaced in 1950 by the so-called Provisional Constitution, the liberal nature of the 1949 Constitution was preserved. These constitutions share similarities in that they included human rights catalogues (Arts 7–34), held specific provisions on due process (Arts 11–17), and prohibited the government from interfering with the judiciary (Art 103).[10] This meant that from

---

[7] High-ranking prosecutors use stars as their insignia, middle-ranking prosecutors use gold jasmine buds, and officers use gold bars, all of which are copied from the military (Afandi 2021: 78).

[8] Candidates must learn military marching and get physical training from army instructors. They are also taught how to give a military salute to seniors, as well as being required to conduct morning and afternoon parades (Afandi 2021: 95).

[9] For a slightly different categorization, see Bourchier and Hadiz 2003.

[10] These included: freedom from torture or cruel, inhuman or degrading treatment, or punishment (Art 11); protection from unlawful arrests and detentions (Art 12); equality before the law (Art 13); presumption of innocence (Art 14); the prohibition of criminal punishment, such as any deprivation or punishment of a guilty party which would result in the loss of civil rights (Art 15); a ban on home searches without a legal basis (Art 16); and the protection of privacy (Art 17). Apart from these provisions, Art 7(4) of the 1950 Constitution empowered the judiciary to control and supervise coercive measures applied by police and prosecutors during criminal investigation and proceedings.

1950 until 1959 Indonesia's constitutional system provided explicit guarantees to citizens who were subject to criminal investigation and prosecution.

Despite the volatile political situation, most of the time the criminal justice system operated in line with these provisions (cf Feith 2007: 320; Lev 2007: 238).[11] What was remarkable about this situation was that the criminal code of procedure in place did not support the constitutional clauses on due process. Instead of making the former Netherlands-Indies Code of Criminal Procedure for Europeans applicable to all Indonesians, the Indonesian legislator chose to uphold the Revised Indonesian Regulation (*Herziene Indonesisch Reglement*, HIR), the procedural code applied to Indonesians during colonial times. The HIR was much more repressive in nature than the *Reglement op de Strafvordering* used for Europeans as it contained few due process clauses (Lev 2000: 75). However, during the 1950s the Indonesian Prosecution Service used the due process clauses from the *Reglement op de Strafvordering* as a supplement to the HIR. They could do this on the basis of Emergency Law 1/1951, which stated that the HIR was a *guideline* for criminal cases only. This opened up the possibility for the use of other sources as well (Afandi 2019: 89).

The question then is why the Prosecution Service apparently preferred to follow the stricter rules of the *Reglement op de Strafvordering* rather than take advantage of the discretion provided for in the HIR. The answer to this question presumably lies in the way the Prosecution Service perceived themselves and the image they liked to present to the outside world. In the 1950s, the Prosecution Service was part of the magistracy, which was a key institutional feature of the criminal justice system. Emergency Law 1/1951 placed the Prosecution Service on an equal footing with the judiciary, thus emphasizing its status and independence (Art 5).[12] It granted public prosecutors the same position as originally held by the *Officieren van Justitie*, who in the colonial era were responsible for prosecuting Europeans. These *Officieren* held a much higher status than the 'lowly' *Djaksa*, who were mere civil servants prosecuting Indonesians in criminal cases (Afandi 2021: 48).

The magisterial identity of the prosecutor made it difficult for the government to intervene in the prosecution process for political reasons.[13] The best-known case demonstrating the Prosecution Service's independence was the one against Minister of Justice Djody Gondokusumo (1953–1955). Although administratively the Prosecution Service fell under his department, he could not stop the prosecutor from bringing charges of corruption against him, which ultimately led to his conviction in the criminal court (Yahya 2004).[14]

---

[11] So far, little research has been done on criminal law practice during this period, so our account is based on the few sources we have, which are rather general in nature.

[12] Law 7/1947 on the structure of the Supreme Court and the Supreme Prosecution Office and Law 19/1948 dealt with the structure and jurisdiction of the judiciary and the Prosecution Service.

[13] Like in other civil law inquisitorial systems, the Indonesian public prosecutors were judicial officers. Even if in some countries the public prosecution service is also part of the executive, they have a higher degree of independence than common officials. Even while they are bound by policies of the Prosecution Service, they have discretion in deciding which cases to prosecute and how to prosecute them (Luna and Wade 2012).

[14] This does not mean that there was no political intervention in criminal processes at all. A notorious case in point—although never fully cleared—is the trial of the Dutch men Schmidt and Jungschläger, who were accused of rebellion against the Indonesian Republic. However, it looks as if in this case not only the public prosecutor but also the judge was unduly influenced (Goran 1957). A contradictory contemporary

Part of their magisterial function and even more important in the everyday practice of criminal justice was the Prosecution Service's supervisory role in criminal investigations by the police. This role was explicitly mentioned in the HIR (Art 38). The police could only perform searches and confiscate goods following a search after they had obtained permission from the district court. This request had to be made by the public prosecutor (Art 42 jo. 77 HIR). The police also had to report to the public prosecutor when they made arrests and imposed temporary detention for crimes carrying a sentence of five years' imprisonment or more (Art 71(2) HIR). The public prosecutor decided whether such detention ought to be applied, and s/he could order the police to prolong it by up to twenty days. The police had to ask permission from the prosecutor for an extension. In case of further extensions, the prosecutor needed to ask permission from the Chief of the District Court (Art 83(c)(4) HIR).

The relationship between the prosecutor and police was also important in the proceedings of criminal investigations. These were led by the prosecutor, with the police officer involved having the status of assistant-magistrate (*hulp magistraat*). This mechanism required collaboration between the police and the prosecutor, and ensured the police observed the due process clauses in the Constitution. Finally, it shielded the police—at least to a degree—from political intervention by the government (Afandi 2021: 51).

Another feature of the system under the 1950 Constitution was that members of the military who were charged with a criminal offence went to trial in the same courts as ordinary citizens. The indictment was moreover made by 'ordinary' public prosecutors (Art 27 of Law 5/1950).[15] The Chief Prosecutor served simultaneously as Chief Military Prosecutor.[16] In this capacity, he also held the authority to supervise the military police, which was the only institution separate from the civilian criminal law system. The absence of separate military courts and prosecutors during the 1950s no doubt contributed to the arrest, prosecution, and conviction of a number of high-ranking military officers for serious crimes such as smuggling, corruption, desertion, and insurrection (Yahya 2004: 197–206).

However, during this period, the military's rise to political power gradually limited the authority of civilian criminal justice actors in prosecuting crimes by the military. The rise of the military was evident through the passage of two emergency laws.[17] The latter's Article 6(4) gave the military commander the power to take over a criminal investigation if the case involved a military officer (Yahya 2004: 57).

---

evaluation is Ubani 1957. For a thorough (and highly critical) account of the trials (in Dutch), see Hoegen 2020: 130–229.

[15] The Prosecution Service could use the HIR and Wetboek van Strafvordering (Code of Criminal Procedure or SV) procedures when prosecuting the military. See Art 1 of Law 8/1946.

[16] See Government Regulation S.4/1948, on military titular rank. The Chief Prosecutor's rank was Army Lieutenant General.

[17] Emergency Law 1/1958 on Criminal Procedure for the Military Courts and Law 74/1957 on the State of Emergency. Officially the latter is called '*Pencabutan* "Regeling PO De Staat Van Oorlog En Beleg" *dan Penetapan Keadaan Bahaya*' ('Revocation of the "Regulation regarding the State of War and Siege" and of the Determination of the State of Emergency'). It was enacted because of the rapid deterioration of the economic situation and armed rebellions aimed at secession in West Sumatra and South Sulawesi.

The military's dislike of the liberal 1950 Constitution, which prevented it from being involved in civilian politics, led the military to lobby for the re-enactment of the 1945 Constitution. Supported by the stalemate in the deliberations about a new constitution in the Constituent Assembly, the military convinced President Soekarno to dissolve the Assembly and restore the 1945 Constitution with its lack of civil rights, checks, and balances (Lev 1963: 355–356; Said 2002: 33–34).[18]

This absence of constitutional checks and balances, and of any guarantees for civil and political rights in the 1945 Constitution, came to play an important role in the deterioration of the criminal justice system. Under Soekarno's Guided Democracy, the police and the Prosecution Service became formally subject to the president, who had the legal right to interfere in judicial proceedings.[19] Formally speaking, this provision was the all-time low in the development of the rule of law in Indonesia. However, in practice, matters would become even worse during the New Order. The presidential prerogative to interfere in judicial proceedings was removed, but the appointment of judges and prosecutors became highly politicized and in this manner Soeharto ultimately found a more effective way to control the legal process (Pompe 2005: 171–173). In other words, both regimes could intervene at will in criminal procedure to further their political interests (Lolo 2008: 77–89; Afandi 2021: 72), but the New Order inflicted more fundamental damage to the institutions concerned. One of the results was that in their verdicts many judges started to uncritically follow the indictment made by the public prosecutor (Afandi 2021: 152–155).

Another important development under the New Order regime concerned the military's rise to power in civilian affairs. The military's position was legitimized through the so-called dual function doctrine (*dwifungsi*). Appealing to national cultural and historical values, *dwifungsi* created a military structure parallel to and intertwined with the 'civilian' government. *Dwifungsi* supported the appointment of military officers (active or retired) to government posts and reserved a number of seats for them in parliament (Honna 1999).

The militarization of the state also extended to the criminal justice system. The Soeharto regime maintained Soekarno's measure to remove the police from the Department of Home Affairs and to make them a branch of the Indonesian military. They officially became one of the four Armed Forces of the Indonesian Republic (*Angkatan Bersenjata Republik Indonesia*, ABRI).[20] The new government also turned the Prosecution Service into a military-style bureaucracy. Military influence further extended through appointments in the Prosecution Service. Most chief prosecutors during the New Order were active or retired military officers (Afandi 2021: 58).[21] This

---

[18] The irony was that the Constituent Assembly had agreed to include a bill of rights, democratic government, and other checks and balances in its draft but could not agree what the official foundation of the state should be (Pancasila or Islam) (Nasution 1992: 388–401).

[19] Law 19/1964 on the Judiciary (Art 19) held that the president could intervene in the judicial process, for 'the interest of the revolution, the honour of the State and the People, or a pressing societal interest'. These concepts were not further defined. Law 13/1965 on the General Courts and the Supreme Court (Art 23) elaborated the procedure of intervention.

[20] The integration of the police into the military structure—operationally, politically, and administratively—meant that it fell under the Minister of Security and Defence. This position was occupied by the highest commander of the military.

[21] During the New Order, two chief justices, Mudjono and Ali Said, also had a background in the military.

period of more than thirty years of military influence had a profound impact on the structure, values, and attitude of both the police and the Prosecution Service. It produced a system that championed a strongly hierarchical, security-oriented approach to law enforcement and criminal proceedings (cf Bull and Stratta 1995; Meliala 2001).

As the 1945 Constitution contained neither provisions on human rights nor on judicial independence, the New Order regime had ample space to use the criminal justice system for political purposes without having to fear legal challenges. The vague constitutional provisions on national defence together with the *dwifungsi* doctrine allowed the regime to involve the military in safeguarding domestic security and controlling the criminal justice system. The military used their power through the secret service known by the acronym KOPKAMTIB. The KOPKAMTIB could take over criminal cases from the police and the Prosecution Service. From 1981, the new Code of Criminal Procedure (*Kitab Undang-Undang Hukum Acara Pidana*, KUHAP) strengthened the military's power by reducing the supervisory power of prosecutors and judges over the police during the investigation.

The Code adopted the military idea of the 'unity of command'.[22] It also introduced the principle of 'built-in control', which means that the leadership has full control over its investigators and prosecutors (Harahap 2007: 79). As a consequence, police officers cannot make any independent decisions in investigations prior to permission from their superiors, and public prosecutors are bound by tight guidelines and their superior's decisions in bringing charges and filing appeals against judicial rulings. The KUHAP also allows the police to conduct investigations without involving or notifying the public prosecutor, and to apply coercive measures, such as pre-trial detentions and foreclosure, without supervision from the prosecutor or the judiciary (Arts 16–49). As a result, prosecutors have no means to check whether an investigation is properly conducted. This may cause problems during the trial, because prosecutors lack the information needed to defend their indictment against claims by the defendant that the police have transgressed their powers during the investigation (Tirto 2018).

Post-Soeharto: Continuing the Security Approach

After Soeharto was forced to step down in 1998, the People's Consultative Assembly (*Majelis Perwkilan Rakyat*, MPR) started a process to amend the 1945 Constitution. The changes were so sweeping that it would be more appropriate to speak of a new constitution than mere amendments. One of the amended Constitution's key features was that the military had to give up its institutional engagement in politics and its responsibility for internal security. This task was assigned to the police, who were no longer part of the armed forces. The relevant Article 30 reads as follows:

1) Every citizen shall have the right and duty to participate in the defence and security of the state.

---

[22] The unity of command principle emphasizes a single command for each unit and limits interference from other parties in the supervision and control of unit members. The army believes that supervision and control from other institutions, without the permission of the officers in command, will interfere with the preparation of military operations (Zen and Sirait 2006: 12).

2) The defence and security of the state shall be conducted through the total people's defence and security system, with the Indonesian National Military (TNI) and the Indonesian National Police (POLRI) as the main forces, and the people as the supporting force.

3) The Indonesian National Military, consisting of the Army, Navy and Air Force, as an instrument of the state have the duty to defend, protect, and maintain the integrity and sovereignty of the state.

4) POLRI, as the instrument of the state that maintains public order and security, have the duty to protect, guard, and serve the people, and to enforce the law.

5) The structure and status of TNI and POLRI, the authority relationships between TNI and POLRI in performing their respective duties, the conditions concerning the participation of citizens in the defence and security of the state, and other matters related to defence and security, shall be regulated by law.

Even a superficial reading of these clauses indicates that the boundary between military and civilian rule is not watertight. It continues the 'total people's defence and security system'[23] which was part of the *dwifungsi* doctrine that justified the army's involvement in civilian politics during the New Order. Moreover, it gives the military responsibility for maintaining the integrity of the state, which potentially includes actions against 'subversion'.[24] Nonetheless, the amendment reinforced the position of the police and promoted them to the same level as the military. The police now have their own constitutional authority regarding law enforcement.

Although the police are no longer part of the military, in 2002 the new Police Law upheld its military nature. Most police tasks and powers in the law were copied from the regulations concerning the military's function of maintaining security during the New Order. It is therefore unsurprising that the police have continued to apply a repressive security approach in criminal investigations instead of one that is in conformity with the rule of law (cf Widjajanto 2004: 135–136).[25]

One problematic aspect of Article 30(4) is that the police tend to mix up their task of law enforcement with the objective of maintaining public order and security. As the Constitution does not regulate the relationship between the police, the Prosecution Service, and the judiciary, the police have continued their autonomous role in law enforcement as before 1998, with little external oversight. On one hand, this is logical because the 1981 Code of Criminal Procedure (KUHAP) is still in place. But it is

---

[23] Known in Indonesia as SISHANKAMRATA, this acronym stands for *Sistem Pertanahan Dan Keamanan Rakyat Semesta*.

[24] One example is the Navy's role as the main law enforcer throughout the Indonesian territorial waters. Article 9(b) of Law 34/2004 on the Military retained this power based on the SISHANKAMRATA doctrine. A more specific legal basis for such enforcement is not only found in older laws, such as Law 5/1983 on the Indonesian Exclusive Economic Zone and Law 6/1996 on the Indonesian Waters, but also in the more recent Law 17/2008 on Shipping.

[25] This military-like hierarchy extends to the way the police operate (just as the Prosecution Service). A police investigator can only make an arrest or detain a suspect following an order from the police leadership (Arts 18 and 20 of KUHAP). Article 15 of the National Police Chief Regulation PERKAP 6/2019 also reinforces the organization's hierarchy by imposing the obligation on the investigator to submit an investigation plan to the police leadership. Without approval no one can start an investigation.

important to note that the police believe they are in the lead in the criminal justice process to maintain public order and security.[26]

In contrast to the police and the judiciary, the Prosecution Service have gained nothing from the constitutional amendments. To their frustration, the Constitution does not even mention them. In 2017, the Prosecution Service organized a national seminar in Bandung to publicly present their case for constitutional recognition. In his opening speech, Chief Prosecutor Prasetyo complained about the ambivalent position of the Prosecution Service, which is only implicitly mentioned in Article 24(3) as 'other bodies whose function is related to the judiciary'. In his words:

> An implicit reference like this certainly feels unclear and does not provide a sufficiently strong basis for the Prosecutorial Institution in the constitutional structure to perform their task, function and role, commensurate with their central place in the process of enforcing the law and which is no less important compared with other law enforcers, including the courts themselves.

In a relatively short speech, Prasetyo made this argument five times (Kejaksaan 2017).

This speech conveys a deeply felt frustration in the Prosecution Service that they are not taken seriously by other state agencies. Whether this is caused by a lack of constitutional recognition is a matter for discussion, but there is indeed overwhelming evidence that to a large extent the Prosecution Service have remained subordinate to the executive and the police.

All governments since 1998 have indeed continued to treat the Prosecution Service as no more than a part of the executive, just as during the New Order. This has several implications. Unlike the appointment of the Chief of Police, where the President needs the approval from Parliament, the Chief Prosecutor is appointed and dismissed without any involvement from other state institutions. The Chief Prosecutor is a member of the cabinet, who—like other cabinet members—can be replaced any time and at will by the president. Given its strongly hierarchical nature as an institution— which we will discuss below—the Prosecution Service has therefore remained a tool in the service of the president.[27]

The Prosecution Service perceives its relations with the police as even more problematic. We already mentioned their limited role in supervising police investigations.[28] Another frustration is that compared to the police[29] and the court, the Prosecution

---

[26] In its consideration and explanation KUHAP mentions the '*Wawasan Nusantara*' doctrine. This doctrine promotes an integralist perspective on the state and sets public order and legal certainty as goals of law enforcement. More surprisingly, the MPR adopted a resolution in 2000 (TAP MPR NO VII/MPR/2000) that also speaks of the role of the police as promoting the 'Wawasan Nusantara' and maintaining the security of social order.

[27] A notable example is when Chief Prosecutor Soedjono C Atmonegoro told President Habibie that the Prosecution Service would investigate the corruption committed by Soeharto and his family. A day later Habibie dismissed him. Another example is when former State Secretary Yusril Ihza Mahendra witnessed Prosecutor General Hendarman Supandji coming to President Susilo Bambang Yudhoyono to receive directions concerning a prosecution decision to investigate a particular corruption case (Afandi 2019: 94).

[28] For more details, see (Afandi 2021: 169–172).

[29] During Jokowi's presidency, the police have gained the biggest budget among criminal justice institutions. Many observers argue that the police now is politically the most powerful civilian institution (*Republika* 2019).

Service receives the smallest budget (Afandi 2021: 105). All district prosecution offices handle more criminal cases than their budget allows.[30] In some cases, the police even provide a budget to the public prosecutor for taking on particular cases,[31] which gives them the opportunity to pressure prosecutors, forcing the latter to accept their investigation file (BeritaSatu 2015; AJNN 2017). This threatens to reduce the function of public prosecutors to that of a postman, shuttling cases between the police and the court (Afandi 2019).

Taken together, their position as part of the executive, their reliance on the police, their hierarchical nature, and their military culture have turned the Prosecution Service into the perfect tool for upholding the authoritarian nature of criminal procedure in Indonesia. Individual public prosecutors have to serve their superior's interests and reinforce the regime's values to maintain political stability. The security approach to governance, typical for authoritarian criminal law systems, rates political stability much higher than human rights protection.

Moreover, criminal law has become an increasingly important policy tool for the government. Between 1998 and 2014, Indonesia enacted 563 laws, 154 of which contained criminal law provisions. These 154 laws include 716 new criminal offences. Most of these offences are regulatory offences, which is an indication of the state's reliance on criminal law to ensure citizens comply with its rules (Akbari 2015: 41). Moreover, the already mentioned overcrowding of prisons shows that the government is more than willing to put them to use.

Human Rights and Criminal Procedure

This trend towards authoritarianism has not been slowed by the human rights catalogue included in the amended Constitution, nor by the Human Rights Law (39/ 1999), which carries two articles specifically concerned with due process (18 and 19) that are not included in the Constitution. In fact, it seems as if human rights have become a kind of policy field in itself instead of a set of rules and principles that operates throughout the legal system. This may be a side effect of the post-1998 reforms to establish special guardian institutions for promoting human rights and protecting citizens against the state. Next to the National Human Rights Commission (*Komnas HAM*) that pre-dated the 1998 reforms, these guardian institutions include the Ombudsman, the Commission for the Prosecution Service (*Komisi Kejaksaan* or *KomJak*), the National Police Commission (*Komisi Nasional Kepolisian* or *KomPolNas*), the Judicial Commission (*Komisi Yudisial*), and the Witness and Victims Protection Agency (*Lembaga Perlindungan Saksi dan Korban*, LPSK). The latter four agencies have been established with the explicit purpose of promoting the proper

---

[30] In 2015, for instance, the Malang District Prosecution Office prosecuted 406 criminal cases when they only have the budget for 350 cases.

[31] Personal communication from a prosecutor in Jakarta, 2015. He confessed that, in some narcotics cases, if the prosecutor believes that evidence provided by the police is insufficient, the police chief can reassure the prosecutor that they will assist in the trial and provide a budget to support the prosecutor's work. This budget can be used to invite an expert witness or to keep the prosecutor and his family secure during the trial process.

functioning of the Prosecution Service, the judiciary, and the police, including their compliance with human rights. However, they are viewed with suspicion by the organizations they must supervise, and they moreover lack sufficient powers. The commissions for the Prosecution Service and the police have advisory powers only, and their recommendations can be safely ignored (Afandi 2021: 104–105, 140).

The most powerful actor among these guardian institutions involved in human rights protection is the National Human Rights Commission. *Komnas HAM* monitors and investigates human rights violations in any field in which they occur, including criminal justice (Crouch 2013). However, the Commission seems reluctant to become involved in promoting due process, which it considers to be covered already by *KomJak* and *KomPolNas*. For example, in 1999, the Commission declined the invitation by the Minister of Law and Human Rights to become involved in the revision of the Code of Criminal Procedure (Setiawan 2013: 90–92).

Another obstacle to extending the influence of human rights in the criminal process is that the Code of Criminal Procedure has not been amended. As already mentioned, the New Order designed the Code to strengthen the control of the military on criminal procedure and its provisions offer few guarantees for proper treatment of those suspected of having committed a criminal offence. Some of its shortcomings have been addressed in other regulations but to little avail. A good example is National Police Chief Regulation 8/2009, which was issued to ensure the observance of human rights during the investigation.[32] A key problem in implementing this regulation is the absence of an independent, effective, and impartial mechanism for examining complaints. This has fostered a climate of impunity for perpetrators of torture and other forms of ill-treatment during the police investigation (Amnesty International 2015: 39). As reported by legal aid activists and some researchers, despite this regulation, the police show little understanding of human rights and are happy to preserve the military legacy they inherited from the New Order (Tim Penelitian dan Dokumentasi LBH Jakarta 2015: 38). They believe that the presumption of innocence only applies during the trial in court, and not during the investigation. This means that the police presume that a suspect is guilty unless proven otherwise. They attach great importance to a confession, which can serve as key evidence in court. This provides an explanation for the many reports about police investigators who use force—including physical torture—to obtain a confession from a suspect (Gunawan et al 2012; Amnesty International 2015).

Presently, complaints about unlawful coercive measures during criminal investigations or ill-treatment by the police can only be addressed through what is referred to as the pre-trial hearing mechanism. This is a procedure in which a victim of unlawful treatment by the police or the prosecutor can bring a complaint to the district court before the case against him or her has started. A single judge decides on the claim and there is no appeal (Arts 77–83 KUHAP). However, because the pre-trial judge

---

[32] It contains 164 articles, which promote due process and human rights protection. For instance, Art 7 requires police officers to understand international conventions related to human rights such as the International Covenant on Civil and Political Rights (ICCPR), the Convention against Torture and the Convention on the Elimination of All Forms of Discrimination Against Women (CEDAW). Furthermore, the police are prohibited from conducting unlawful arrests and detention, torturing suspects, and committing other human rights violations during the criminal investigation (Art 11).

has limited time for examining the case,[33] in practice s/he tends to examine coercive measures only for their administrative correctness, without addressing the substance of the matter. As a result, pre-trial judges rarely decide that coercive measures are invalid (Supriyadi et al 2014).

A good example is the case in 2020 of Domiri, a key witness in a land conflict between peasants and a palm oil plantation company in Jambi. The police abducted Domiri during a break in a court hearing in Jambi District Court. They never summoned him and never labelled him officially as a suspect, initially saying that they 'secured' him. Only after lawyers from the Indonesian legal aid institution (YLBHI) called it an ordinary kidnapping, did the police state that it was a lawful arrest since they held an arrest warrant from the Head of Police of Jambi District (Setiawan, Putra, and Sari 2020: 81–83). When the case came up for a pre-trial hearing, the judge swept aside the plaintiff's argument that the arrest had interfered with the trial witness examination, even if the court had not been able to hear the testimony of Domiri (7/Pid.Pra/2019/PN Jmb, 25–27). The judge also ignored concerns that the police had not notified the court or asked for permission from the court's chairman to arrest the witness during the trial on the court's premises (18–20). One lawyer from YLBHI felt that the court sided with the police because the judge was intimidated by the presence of a massive police force in the court, which according to the police was needed to provide security during the hearing. Other lawyers from YLBHI were harassed because they initiated a pre-trial hearing.[34]

There has been no progress on improving due process in pre-trial hearings and Parliament showed little interest in amending KUHAP, so legal activists and lawyers have started looking for alternative ways to improve the Code. The most promising so far has been the Constitutional Court, although the record is mixed. Between 2003 and 2019, YLBHI and other civil society organizations (CSOs) submitted at least sixty-four petitions for constitutional review of KUHAP. Most of these cases referred to Article 28D(1) as the ground for review. This article reads as follows:

> Each person has the right to recognition, security, protection and certainty under the law that shall be just and treat everybody as equal before the law.

This is the constitutional clause that comes closest to guaranteeing due process, but it is far less specific than the due process clauses in the human rights law. From the sixty-four petitions it received the Constitutional Court upheld eleven, but only two of these rulings expanded the protection of suspects.[35] The first decision held that the

---

[33] A pre-trial judge examines an application and decides within ten days of the application being submitted (Arts 78 and 82(1) of KUHAP).

[34] Personal Communication from a legal activist, 4 January 2021.

[35] The other ones were the following; (1) Decision 65/PUU-VIII/2010 expanded the definition of the witness; (2) Decision 65/PUU-IX/2011 repealed the appellate procedure for the pre-trial hearing; (3) Decision 98/PUU-X/2012 allowed victims and NGOs to examine the dismissal of a criminal case in the pre-trial hearing; (4) Decision 114/PUU-X/2012 allowed appeal for cassation concerning decisions to acquit a suspect; (5) Decision 34/PUU-XI/2013 removed the restrictions in Art 268(3) KUHAP to limit a revision of a judgment by the Supreme Court to only once; (6) Decision 130/PUU-XIII/2015 put the obligation on an investigator to send a notification to the prosecutor no later than seven days after s/he started the investigation; (7) Decision 102/PUU-XIII/2015 stated that the pre-trial hearing can only be annulled when the trial is commenced before the pre-trial judge has had a chance to decide the case; (8) Decision 33/PUU-XIV/

word 'immediately' in Article 18(3) of KUHAP means that investigators must send a copy of the warrant to the suspect's family within seven days of the start of detention.[36] The second decision expanded the scope of pre-trial jurisdiction by extending it from arrest and detention to all coercive measures applied during the investigation, as well as to the process of labelling someone as a suspect.[37]

The Court thus did not provide the arena reformers were looking for, but in 2012 it went even one step beyond when in a judgment it further compromised the rights of accused in criminal trials rather than upholding them. The Court expressed its support for the Supreme Court practice to allow the public prosecutor to file an appeal for cassation against an acquittal by a lower court. This practice directly contradicts Article 244 of KUHAP, which only gives the right to appeal for cassation to the accused (Afandi 2021: 201–202). In an unparalleled argument the justices held that granting this power to the public prosecutor would not adversely affect the accused, because the Supreme Court could always decide to uphold the decision of the lower court.[38]

In summary, the Constitutional Court has played a very limited role in promoting due process in the criminal justice system and in one case even undermined the statutory rights of the accused in a criminal trial. To achieve genuine change, the KUHAP needs to be amended, something the Constitutional Court sometimes cannot and sometimes does not want to do.

The True Masters of the Crime Scene: The Police

As already discussed above, one of the most important constitutional amendments was the separation of the police from the military. Subsequently, a debate arose as to whether the police should become part of the executive. Although the police no longer automatically fell under the Minister of Defence, the latter saw good reason to keep them under his authority. He argued that the police would continue performing tasks related to state security; moreover, their position was defined in Article 30 of the Constitution, the same article that regulated the military. This proposal was resisted by the Chief Prosecutor. He saw an opportunity to return the police to the supervision of the Prosecution Service in criminal investigations as had been the situation before 1981. The third contender was the Minister of Home Affairs, who held that the police

---

2016 limited the application for review to those found guilty and his/her beneficiaries (heirs) and prohibited the prosecutor from filing a review (*Peninjauan Kembali*, PK); (9) Decision 103/PUU-XIV/2016 simplified the criminal court decision format in the appellate stage.

[36] Decision 3/PUU-XI/2013.
[37] Decision 21/PUU-XII/2014. This decision was controversial at the time because the consequence of the decision was that the Corruption Eradication Commission (*Komisi Pemberantasan Korupsi*, KPK) had to repeal its decision labelling Police General Budi Gunawan as a corruption suspect. During the pre-trial hearing, the KPK argued that such decisions fell outside of the scope of the pre-trial. However, NGOs such as the Institute for Criminal Justice Reform applauded the judgment for its wider importance. (ICJR 2015).
[38] Decision 114/PUU-XII/2012, in particular pp 28–29. One justice (Harjono) expressed a dissenting opinion, regarding the Supreme Court practice as a violation of the protection of the defendant's human rights. Harjono argued that the Supreme Court practice is not a basis for considering Art 244 of KUHAP as a violation of the Constitution (pp 31–35).

should come under his authority because of the role they play in maintaining order and security.

In the end, the police were positioned directly under the authority of the president. Originally a temporary measure, in 2002 this arrangement was made permanent in the Law on the Police (2/2002). From the perspective of the police, this had several advantages. It raised their institutional status and gave them considerable autonomy because the president has little time for supervision. Hence, policy and decision-making is mainly in the hands of the police leadership. This includes all decisions concerning the use of the police budget as well as managing off-budget income (Baker 2015a: 127).

In this debate, the police also relied on an ideological justification to support their autonomy. Referring to Dutch colonial law professor Van Vollenhoven's Catur Praja theory (Rajab 2003), the police argued that it is the fourth branch of state power and therefore entitled to an independent position within the state structure. They deploy the same theory to contend that they should take the lead in criminal justice. This view finds support with Indonesian constitutional law scholars who believe that Van Vollenhoven's Catur Praja theory indeed distinguishes between four branches of state power: the executive, the legislature, the judiciary, and the police. It would thus expand Montesquieu's idea of a separation of powers with a fourth branch (Asshiddiqie 2006; Utrecht 1986).[39]

Of all state agencies in Indonesia, probably no one has gained as much wealth, prestige, and power from their new position as the police. Between 2001 and 2020, the police budget increased from 5,3 trillion rupiah (Baker 2013: 137) to 104,7 trillion (Kementerian Keuangan 2020). However, the official budget is far outweighed by the funds the police secure for themselves from collusion with businessmen and running protection rackets for criminal activities such as gambling, prostitution, and trade in narcotics. Although nobody—not even the police themselves—know exactly how much money is involved, it certainly exceeds their official budget.[40] Liberated from the dominance of the military, the police have used their position to the full to assume a bigger portion of the shadow economy that keeps the state going (Baker 2013: 145–148).

The justification for such off-budget funding is that the official police budget is insufficient to cover the cost of their operations. While this may be true, Jacqui Baker has argued that it is the police themselves who have played an active role in maintaining this situation. She has pointed at the mismanagement of the official budget, most of which is allocated to the national police headquarters in Jakarta whose haphazard and slow disbursement prevents effective budgeting and planning at the district and subdistrict levels. This situation offers the police maximum leeway in doing whatever

---

[39] Ironically, this justification relies on a misinterpretation. Van Vollenhoven never talked about state *branches*, but about state *functions*. According to Van Vollenhoven the four state functions can be exercised by different branches at the same time, which is exactly the opposite of what the Indonesian police maintain. For example, the judiciary can simultaneously exercise its function to adjudicate a case, administer its bureaucracy, and issue regulations. Similarly, the executive can also issue regulations, solve cases, and police society (Vollenhoven 1934: 104–125). What Van Vollenhoven is doing here is bringing some realism to constitutional law. Also note that in the Netherlands his argument was later referred to in support of bringing the Dutch police under the Minister of Justice instead of Home Affairs (Stellinga 1950: 191).

[40] A report by researchers from Universitas Indonesia published in 2003 and based on interviews with officers at provincial and district level mentions figures from 60 to 95 per cent (Baker 2013: 140).

they like with the funds at their disposal, without being held to account. There is no legal restraint, the only limits being the informal rules of the moral economy of the police themselves (Baker 2013: 139–140; Baker 2015b: 320–323, 327–329). According to Baker, the fragmentation of power in the state has led to increasing independence of police units at lower levels of the organisation. It has also promoted the advancement of entrepreneurial police officers who manage to pay themselves for the expenditure of their department (Baker 2013: 141-142; Baker 2015b: 326-327). The police have also been successful in expanding their role in the government. Following the amendment of the Constitution, they have managed to fill several government positions held by military officers during the New Order with members of the police force.[41]

One reason the police have been able to extend their independence is that, during his ten years in office (2004–2014), President Yudhoyono never implemented the 'second-generation' reforms needed to promote democratic oversight and account-ability of the police. At heart a conservative, Yudhoyono stimulated professional-ization and modernization of the force through increasing their budget, promoting specialization, and promoting other 'technical' changes. However, he did little to make them more accountable (Baker 2015a: 115–116). The secrecy and lack of data con-cerning the police budget and how it is being spent make it extremely difficult for the National Audit Office (*Badan Pemeriksa Keuangan*, BPK) to conduct a proper audit (Harun 2007; Dwiputrianti 2011: 147 referred to in Baker 2015a: 122).[42] Even more importantly, by leaving the off-budget economy of the police in place and allowing it to grow, Yudhoyono relinquished the single most important tool to bring the po-lice within the accountability structures of the legal state (Baker 2012: 118–119, 124; Mietzner 2009).

Another feature of the police's organization reinforcing their autonomy are the em-ployment regulations they retained from the thirty-two years they were part of the military. Unlike the Prosecution Service, the police are not subject to civil service rules and can determine their own salary grades and other staffing rules. Former National Police Chief Awaludin Djamin even made a public statement that the police reform has changed its 'surface' into a civilian organization, but that the police have main-tained their core military characteristics (Djamin 2011: 15; cf Baker 2015b, 320).

Indeed, the police have also maintained the strictly hierarchical chain of command that runs through the organization. This means that investigations into police mis-conduct are subject to the same limitations as those into the military's. It leaves it en-tirely up to the police leadership to take disciplinary measures or start proceedings against their own personnel. According to civil society organizations, this regularly leads to impunity of police officers who have committed grave criminal offences (Tim Penelitian dan Dokumentasi LBH Jakarta 2015; Amnesty International 2009).

Because they report directly to the president, the police do not fall under the regular scrutiny of a minister, which leaves the National Police Commission as the

---

[41] Examples are the Director General of Immigration in the Ministry of Law and Human Rights and sev-eral Director Generals at the Ministry of Transportation. President Jokowi also appointed a former Vice National Police Chairman as Minister of Civil Servants and Bureaucratic Reform. See (Tirto 2018).

[42] In 2005, the Audit Office mentioned that only three out of the thirty-one regional police stations had ever submitted data to the Office (Baker 2013: 125–126).

sole external supervisory body. Because it reports to the president, the National Police Commission can exercise considerable influence. However, it has no powers of investigation, and among its nine members are three ministers (Home Affairs, Defence, and Justice and Human Rights) as well as three (currently two) retired police officers. Hence, the composition of the Commission compromises its independence. In the seven years of its existence the National Police Commission has never made any serious effort to address the many problems of the police nor has it tried to address the abuses of power by the police.

Of course, the military have not given up their turf to the police without resistance. In particular the competition for off-budget funds has reinforced the tension between the two (Mietzner 2009: 363; Crouch 2017: 469). The years of transition following 1998 saw frequent confrontations between the military and the police when the police tried to take over businesses affiliated with the military such as protection rackets for gambling and prostitution (Honna 2006). At present a degree of stability has been achieved, but matters have not been settled once and for all, which is reflected in occasional incidents.[43]

Conversely, the military have attempted to make a comeback in criminal justice by reasserting their dominance in the field of counter-terrorism. Deploying the government's slogan of the 'war on terror', the military claim their particular expertise warrants their involvement. This is a logical outcome of the government's reliance on a security rather than a criminal justice approach (Haripin, Anindya, and Priamarizki 2020).

The military can also muster legal support for their role in domestic security. The law on the military stipulates that they have two main functions; military operations (*operasi militer*) and military operations other than war (*operasi militer selain perang*).[44] This provides a justification for addressing contemporary domestic security challenges such as terrorism, transnational crimes involving drugs, arms and human trafficking, maritime piracy, and separatist movements—fields in which the police would prefer to have a monopoly (Haripin 2020: 8).

In 2018, the military also succeeded in reinforcing their position in the new Anti-Terrorism Law (5/2018), as Article 43I stipulates that counter-terrorism falls under 'military operations other than war'. The law delegates the technical details to a presidential regulation. At the time of writing, the draft presidential regulation has elicited many critical comments. Civil society organizations voice their concerns about the expansion of the military's role, in particular their authority to initiate counter-terrorism operations without the involvement of any other criminal justice actors (KOMPAS 2020).

In summary, the amendments to the Constitution have reinforced the position of the police, who are no doubt today the most powerful actor in criminal law. However, this position remains contested. At present, the police have most to fear from the military, as the tensions over the jurisdiction and authority between police and military have continued. The amendments to the Constitution ensure the continued role of the military in security affairs. This has led to political tensions and will remain an issue for controversy. The military may well at some point attempt to regain their authority

---

[43] For instance an attack by military on a police station in East Jakarta (Jakarta Globe 2020).
[44] Article 7 of Law 34/2004 on the Military.

over the police, as during the New Order. The Prosecution Service present far less of a challenge, but they will certainly try whatever they can to regain their original key position in criminal investigation. Their major objective is to have the KUHAP revised.

Conclusion

This chapter has demonstrated how the post-1998 constitutional amendments have failed to dismantle the authoritarian character of Indonesia's criminal justice system. Suspects and defendants have few rights, the institutional mechanisms to uphold these rights are weak, and the police prefer to ignore them. This is a worrying situation given that Indonesia, like many other countries, increasingly relies on criminal law to regulate society.

There are several explanations for the continuity we see with the previous authoritarian regime. When we look at legislation, the main problem is that the New Order's Criminal Code of Procedure (KUHAP) is still in place. During the early years of *Reformasi*, reformers did not prioritize criminal procedure and it seems that at present the window of opportunity has closed. The result is that the police have continued to dominate investigations, without much magisterial oversight. Public prosecutors still shuttle cases from the police to the court without exerting influence over the investigation process, and courts are reluctant to evaluate police measures taken during investigations.

This state of affairs contrasts sharply with the expectations raised by the inclusion of a human rights catalogue in Indonesia's Constitution. One might have expected that these rights would have made a difference to the criminal justice system. However, the constitutional clause that should guarantee due process is too general in nature and the Constitutional Court has been averse to reviewing provisions from the KUHAP. Other institutions charged with implementing human rights, such as the National Human Rights Commission, have not been seriously involved in criminal justice reform. As a result, there has been no 'mainstreaming' of human rights into criminal procedure.[45]

Another part of the explanation can be found in the institutional structures charged with criminal law enforcement. A major change introduced through constitutional amendment has been the separation of the police from the military. Pushing the military out of criminal law has promoted the transparency and legality of criminal procedure, but only to a limited extent. The police—who now are the most powerful actor in the criminal justice system—almost equal the military in neglecting standards of professionalism and integrity promoting the rule of law. They have retained their authoritarian character and are deeply involved in so-called off-budget financing mechanisms. These liberate them from formal control and from a need for effective planning. It keeps them engaged in collusion as well as in the criminal transactions they are supposed to investigate. The main interest of the police is to keep the situation as it is, which is to remain free from procedural limitations and supervision. The

---

[45] We do not even refer to the many violations of human rights in substantive criminal law, for instance clauses circumscribing freedom of expression. See, for instance, Setiawan 2020.

preference for 'securing' people instead of 'arresting' them, which we mentioned at the start of this chapter, is a typical example.

The Prosecution Service are unable to provide a counterbalance against the police. As they cannot exercise any formal control over the police, they lack the legal authority to align criminal procedure with the demands of due process. As a member of the Presidential Cabinet, the Chief Prosecutor is moreover subject to direct political influence on prosecution policy and decisions. But worse than that, the Prosecution Service are as militarized as the police, in their hierarchy, their uniforms, and their training, and like the police they have become highly dependent on off-budget financing. This has dragged them into the same institutional quagmire.

The last major actor in the criminal justice system are the courts. Most efforts at institutional reform post-1998 were aimed at the judiciary and although many observers are rather sceptical, we hold that some achievements have been made. However, in the field of criminal procedure, the courts do not play much of a role. They have generally failed to support due process through the pre-trial procedure, and in their judgments they have continued to rely heavily on the indictment, showing few signs of independent thought or concern for due process. In short, the judiciary have not returned to the inquisitorial role they had before they were made subservient to the New Order regime.

The final part of the explanation for the continued authoritarian character of Indonesia's criminal justice system concerns ideology. Its main feature is a continuous preoccupation with security, which is typical of authoritarian regimes. This dominance of the security approach is supported by the primacy of the police in the criminal process and their lack of accountability. The main concerns of the police are security and crime fighting, not upholding due process. Their promotion of rule of law notwithstanding, the constitutional amendments have retained the concept of a 'total people's defence and security system' and assigned a commensurate special role to the police and the military. They have not invested the institutions constituting the magistracy with sufficient powers to control the police; courts and prosecutors only play second fiddle.

We should add that global changes have also contributed to the ascendancy of the security approach. The global war on terrorism and the global war on drugs have prompted the Indonesian government to give wide powers to the police. Growing populism has likewise promoted the use of criminal law as a tool of regulation, leading to a rapid expansion of criminal clauses and an increasing reliance on criminal law actors for realizing policy goals. Even in the field of civil law we see that business disputes are now frequently translated into criminal offences.[46]

For all the reasons discussed, we are not too optimistic about a reorientation of criminal procedure on the rule of law in the near future. But if we were to start somewhere, it would be with revising the KUHAP and reinforcing the position of the Prosecution Service vis-à-vis the police.

---

[46] See for instance Kouwagam 2020: 131.

References

Afandi, Fachrizal (2019) 'The Indonesian Prosecution Service at Work: The Justice System Postman' in Melissa Crouch (ed) *The Politics of Court Reform Judicial Change and Legal Culture in Indonesia*. Cambridge: Cambridge University Press, 86-106.

Afandi, Fachrizal (2021) *Maintaining Order: Public Prosecutors in Post-Authoritarian Countries, the Case of Indonesia*. Leiden: Leiden University.

AJNN Kapolres Sabang Ajak Duel Kasi Pidum Kejari Sabang (The Sub-District Head of Police Invites the Head of the Prosecution Service in Sabang to a Duel), https://www.ajnn.net/news/ajak-duel-kasi-pidum-kejari-yara-kapolres-sabang-arogan/index.html, accessed 26 August 2022.

Akbari, Anugerah Rizki (2015) *Potret Kriminalisasi Pasca Reformasi Dan Urgensi Reklasifikasi Tindak Pidana Di Indonesia*. Edited by Supriyadi Widodo Eddyono. Jakarta: Institute for Criminal Justice Reform.

Amnesty Internasional. (2009) 'Urusan Yang Belum Selesai: Akuntabilitas Polisi Di Indonesia'.

Amnesty International (2015) 'Flawed Justice: Unfair Trials and the Death Penalty in Indonesia', https://www.amnesty.org/en/documents/asa21/2434/2015/en/, accessed 26 August 2022.

Asshiddiqie, Jimly (2006) PENGANTAR ILMU HUKUM TATA NEGARA JILID I. Jakarta: Sekretariat Jenderal dan Kepaniteraan Mahkamah Konstitusi, https://dkpp.go.id/wp-content/uploads/2018/11/pengantar_ilmu_hukum_tata_negara.pdf.pdf, accessed 26 August 2022.

BBCNews-Indonesia (2019) Penangkapan mahasiswa pasca demo di DPR disebut 'melanggar KUHAP' dan 'bentuk teror untuk meredam aksi', https://www.bbc.com/indonesia/indone sia-49871301, accessed 3 October 2020.

Berita Satu (2015) 'Petinggi Polda Maluku ancam tembak Jaksa' ('A high District Police Officer threatens to shoot a Public Prosecutor'), https://www.beritasatu.com/nasional/287332/petin ggi-polda- maluku-ancam-tembak-jaksa, accessed 26 August 2022.

Bedner, Adriaan (2017) 'The Need for Realism: Ideals and Practice in Indonesia's Constitutional History' in Maurice Adams, Anne Meuwese, and Ernst Hirsch Ballin (eds) *Constitutionalism and the Rule of Law: Bridging Idealism and Realism*. Cambridge: Cambridge University Press, 159--94.

Bourchier, David and Vedi R Hadiz (eds) (2003) *Indonesian Politics and Society: A Reader*. London: Routledge Curzon.

Baker, Jacqui (2012) 'The Rise of Polri: Democratisation and the Political Economy of Security in Indonesia'. London: London School of Economics and Political Science.

Baker, Jacqui (2013) 'The Parman Economy: Post-Authoritarian Shifts in the Off-Budget Economy of Indonesia's Security Institutions' 96 *Indonesia* 123–150.

Baker, Jacqui (2015a). 'Professionalism without Reform: The Security Sector under Yudhoyono' in Aspinall, Edward, Mietzner, Marcus, and Dirk Tomsa (eds) *The Yudhoyono Presidency: Indonesia's Decade of Stability and Stagnation*. Singapore: Institute of Southeast Asian Studies, 114–135.

Baker, Jacqui (2015b) 'The Rhizome State: Democratizing Indonesia's Off-Budget Economy' 47(2) *Critical Asian Studies* 309–336.

Bull, David and Erica Stratta (1995) 'Police-Community Consultative Committees: A Response to Paramilitary Policing?' 31(3) *Journal of Sociology* 67–82.

Crouch, Melissa (2013) 'Asian Legal Transplants and Lessons on the Rule of Law: National Human Rights Commissions in Indonesia and Myanmar' 5(2) *Hague Journal of the Rule of Law* 146–177.

Crouch, Melissa (2017) 'The Expansion of Emergency Powers: Social Conflict and the Military in Indonesia' 41(3) *Asian Studies Review* 459–475.

CNN-Indonesia (2020) 'Polisi Ciduk 33 Orang Demo Jokowi: Diamankan, bukan Ditangkap', https://www.cnnindonesia.com/nasional/20201020165353-12-560615/polisi-ciduk-33-orang-demo-jokowi-diamankan-bukan-ditangkap, accessed 1 October 2020.

Ditjenpas (2014) 'Over-crowded di Lapas/Rutan, sampai kapan?', http://ditjenpas.go.id/over-crowded-di-lapasrutan-sampai-kapan-bagian-1, accessed 5 January 2021.

Djamin, Awaloeddin (2011) *Sistem Administrasi Kepolisian Negara Republik Indonesia.* Jakarta: yayasan Pengembangan Kajian Ilmu Kepolisian.

Dwiputriati, S. (2011) 'Effectiveness of Public Sector and Audit Reports in Indonesia', PhD thesis, Crawford School of Economics and Government, Australian National University, Canberra.

Eddyono, Supriyadi W et al (2014) *Praperadilan Di Indonesia: Teori, Sejarah Dan Praktiknya.* Edited by Anggara. Jakarta: ICJR.

Feith, Herbert (2007) *The Decline of Constitutional Democracy in Indonesia.* Jakarta: Equinox Publishing.

Goran, AJ (1957) 'The Trial of Schmidt in Indonesia' 29(3) *The Australian Quarterly* 53–60.

Gunawan, Ricky et al (2012) 'Membongkar Praktik Pelanggaran Hak Tersangka Di Tingkat Penyidikan', https://lbhmasyarakat.org/wp-content/uploads/2016/04/Dokumentasi-Pela nggaran-Hak-Tersangka-Kasus-Narkotika-LBH-Masyarakat-2012.pdf, last accessed on 26 August 2022.

Haripin, Muhamad (2020) *Civil-Military Relations in Indonesia: The Politics of Military Operations Other than War.* Abingdon, Oxon: Routledge.

Haripin, Muhamad, Chaula Rininta Anindya, and Adhi Priamarizki (2020) 'The Politics of Counter-Terrorism in Post-Authoritarian States: Indonesia's Experience, 1998–2018' *Defense and Security Analysis* 36(3) 1–25.

Harahap, Yahya (2007) *Pembahasan Permasalahan Dan Penerapan KUHAP (Penyidikan Dan Penuntutan).* Jakarta: Sinar Grafika.

Harun, Harun (2007) 'Obstacles to Public Sector Accounting Reform in Indonesia' *Bulletin of Indonesian Economic Studies* 43(3), 365–375.

Hoegen, Ernestine (2020) *Een strijdbaar bestaan: Mieke Bouman en de Indonesische strafprocessen.* Amsterdam: Spectrum.

Honna, Jun (1999) 'Military Doctrines and Democratic Transition: A Comparative Perspective on Indonesia's Dual Function and Latin American National Security Doctrines', http://hdl. handle.net/1885/15280, accessed 26 August 2022.

Honna, Jun (2006) 'Local Civil-Military Relations during the First Phase of Democratic Transition, 1999-2004: A Comparison of West, Central and East Java' 82(October) *Indonesia* 75–96.

ICJR, *ICJR Apresiasi Putusan MK yang memperluas objek praperadilan*, https://icjr.or.id/icjr-apresiasi-putusan-mk-yang-memperluas-objek-praperadilan/, accessed 26 August 2022.

Jakarta Globe (2020) 'Army Chief Apologizes after Soldiers Attack Police Station' https://jakar taglobe.id/news/army-chief-apologizes-after-soldiers-attack-police-station/, accessed 12 July 2021.

Kejaksaan RI, Pidato Jaksa Agung Republik Indonesia (2017) 'Posisi Kejaksaan Dalam Amandemen Kelima Undang-undang Dasar Negara R.I tahun 1945', https://www.kejaksaan. go.id/pidato.php?idu=1&id=204&hal=2, accessed 12 December 2020.

Kementerian Keuangan (2020) Financial Notes and State Budget of 2020, https://web.kemen keu.go.id/media/16834/buku-ii-nota-keuangan-beserta-apbn-ta-2021.pdf, accessed 12 December 2020.

Kompas (2020) 'Pro dan Kontra Pelibatan TNI dalam Pemberantasan Terorisme' 11 August, https://nasional.kompas.com/read/2020/08/11/09512211/pro-dan-kontra-pelibatan-tni-dalam-pemberantasan-terorisme?page=all, accessed 26 August 2022.

Kouwagam, Santy (2020) 'How Lawyers Win Lands Conflicts', PhD thesis, Leiden University.

Lev, Daniel S (2000) *Legal Evolution and Political Authority in Indonesia*. The Hague: Kluwer Law International.

Lev, Daniel S (2007) 'Judicial Institutions and Legal Culture in Indonesia' in Claire Holt (ed) *Culture and Politics in Indonesia*. Jakarta/Kuala Lumpur: Equinox Publishing, 246–318.

Lev, Daniel S (1963) 'The Political Role of the Army in Indonesia' 36(4) *Pacific Affairs* 349.

Logemann, Johann HA (1962) *Nieuwe gegevens over het ontstaan van de Indonesische grondwet van 1945*. Amsterdam: Noord-Hollandsche Uitg. Mij.

Lolo, Ferdinand Tandi Andi (2008) *The Prosecutorial Corruption During the New Order Regime Case Study: The Prosecution Service of the Republic Indonesia*. PhD-thesis, University of Auckland.

Luna, Erik and Marianne Wade (2012) *The Prosecutor in Transnational Perspective*. Oxford: Oxford University Press.

Meliala, Adrianus (2001) 'Police as Military: Indonesia's Experience' 24 *International Journal of Police Strategies and Management* 420–431.

Mietzner, Marcus (2009) *Military Politics, Islam, and the State in Indonesia: From Turbulent Transition to Democratic Consolidation*. Singapore: Institute of Southeast Asian Studies.

Nasution, Adnan B (1992) *The Aspiration for Constitutional Government in Indonesia: A Socio-Legal Study of the Indonesian Konstituante, 1956–1959*. Jakarta: Pustaka Sinar Harapan.

Pompe, Sebastiaan (2005) *The Indonesian Supreme Court A Study of Institutional Collapse*. Ithaca, New York: Cornell University Press, Cornell Southeast Asia Program Publications.

Prayogo, Daywin (2019) *Hadiah Kayu Untuk Para Demonstran*. Jakarta.

Republika (2019) 'Pengamat sebut Indonesia berpotensi jadi negara polisi', 18 September, https://nasional.republika.co.id/berita/py033w409/pengamat-sebut-indonesia-berpotensi-jadi-negara-polisi, accessed 26 August 2022.

Rajab, Untung S (2003) *Kedudukan Dan Fungsi Polisi Republik Indonesia Dalam Sistem Ketatanegaraan (Berdasarkan UUD 1945)*. Cet. 1. Bandung: Utomo.

Rositawati, Dian (2019) 'Judicial Governance Judicial Independence under the One Roof System', PhD thesis, Tilburg University.

Said, Salim. (2002) *Tumbuh Dan Tumbangnya Dwifungsi: Perkembangan Pemikiran Politik Militer Indonesia 1958-2000*. Cet. 1. Jakarta: Aksara Karunia.

Setiawan, Ken Marijtje Prahari. (2013) 'Promoting Human Rights: National Human Rights Commissions in Indonesia and Malaysia', PhD thesis, Leiden University.

Setiawan, Ken Marijtje Prahari (2020). 'A state of Surveillance? Freedom of Expression under the Jokowi Presidency' in T Power and E Warburton (eds) *Democracy in Indonesia: From Stagnation to Regression?* Singapore: ISEAS-Yusof Ishak Institute. 254–276.

Stellinga, JR (1950) *De grondwet systematisch gerangschikt*. Edited by CW de Vries. Zwolle: Tjeenk Willink.

Tempo (2020) 'Penangkapan Peserta Demo, LBH Jakarta: Polisi, Berhenti Pakai Istilah Amankan', https://metro.tempo.co/read/1398184/penangkapan-peserta-demo-lbh-jakarta-polisi-berhenti-pakai-istilah-amankan, accessed 1 October 2020.

Tim Penelitian dan Dokumentasi LBH Jakarta (2015) 'Hukum Untuk Manusia Atau Manusia Untuk Hukum? Catatan Akhir Tahun Refleksi Hukum Dan HAM Indonesia 2015' Jakarta.

Tirto.id (2020) 'Praperadilan Ravio Patra: Bagaimana Penangkapan Ilegal Jadi Legal' (The Pretrial hearing of Ravio Patra case: How an Illegal Arrest Became Legal, https://tirto.id/praperadilan-ravio-patra-bagaimana-penangkapan-ilegal-jadi-legal-fQWd, accessed 28 November 2020.

Tirto.id (2019) 'Polisi: Kami Akui Ada Kasus Salah Tangkap' (Police: 'We confess that there have been cases of false arrest'), https://tirto.id/polisi-kami-akui-ada-kasus-salah-tangkap-cKi8, accessed 17 November 2019.

Tirto.id (2018) 'Bintang Berjatuhan dari Trunojoyo' (Stars have fallen from Trunojoyo), https://tirto.id/bintang-berjatuh-dari-trunojoyo-9eU, accessed 7 November 2018.

Ubani, B (1957) 'Indonesian Trial' 29(4) *Australian Quarterly* 98–103.

Utrecht, Ernst (1986) *Pengantar Hukum Administrasi Negara Indonesia*. Surabaya: Penerbit Pustaka Tinta Mas.

Vollenhoven, C Van (1934) *Staatsrecht Overzee*. Leiden-Amsterdam: El E. Stenfert Kroese's Uitgevers-Maatschappij N.V.

Widjajanto, Andi (2004) *Reformasi Sektor Keamanan Indonesia*. Jakarta: Pro Patria.

Yahya, Iip D (2004) *Mengadili Menteri Memeriksa Perwira Jaksa Agung Soeprapto Dan Penegakan Hukum Di Indonesia Periode 1950-1959*. Jakarta: PT.

YLBH (2021) *Praktik Penahanan Di Indonesia*. Jakarta: YLBHI.

Gramedia Pustaka Utama.Zen, A Patra M, and Hendrik Dikson Sirait (eds) (2006) 'Balik Arah Ke Era Kegelapan?: Nota Atas 3 RUU Disektor Keamanan (RUU Peradilan Militer, RUU Rahasia Negara, Dan RUU KUHP'. Jakarta: YLBHI dan Kemitraan.

Constitutional Court Decisions

Decision 65/PUU-VIII/2010.
Decision 65/PUU-IX/2011.
Decision 98/PUU-X/2012.
Decision 114/PUU-X/2012.
Decision 3/PUU-XI/2013.
Decision 34/PUU-XI/2013.
Decision 21/PUU-XII/2014.
Decision 130/PUU-XIII/2015.
Decision 102/PUU-XIII/2015.
Decision 33/PUU-XIV/2016.
Decision 103/PUU-XIV/2016.

5

Striking the Right Balance

Winding Back Indonesia's 'Big Bang' Decentralization

Rachael Diprose

Introduction

Age-old state-building debates have centred on how to structure the institutions of the state to balance power between competing interests nationally, and between the centre and the periphery, with an emphasis on minimizing the potential for conflict and secession (see, eg, Lijphart 1977; Horowitz 1991). The literature has also long been concerned with the ways that devolving powers from the centre might alleviate inter-group and regional tensions by providing autonomy to subnational segments (eg Kymlicka 1998; Hechter 2000; Brancati 2006; Suberu 2009; Selway and Templeman 2012; Pierskalla and Sacks 2017). These debates have been no less important in Indonesia, from the time of independence when a federal state structure was considered but rejected by young nationalists,[1] to pushes for greater autonomy for Indonesia's regions at various points in its post-independence history (Schiller 1955).

Indeed, historically, when grievances with the central government emerged in Indonesia—especially complaints that central government policy responses were ineffectual in some regions, or favoured particular regions or groups above others—they were accompanied by strengthened local patriotism and demands for greater autonomy for the regions outside Java (Legge 1961: 487). In the extreme, such dissatisfaction manifested in regional rebellions and separatist insurgencies (Harvey 1977: 7; Legge 1961: 13; Diprose 2009). Legge (1961: 231) argues that the very motto of the Republic, 'Unity in Diversity' (*Bhinneka Tunggal Ika*), recognizes the strength of regional awareness and the presence of distinct societies in the regions of Indonesia. However, the discourse at the central level, even in contemporary times, has often painted these local patriotisms as a source of inter-ethnic conflict and a threat to national integration. They can, however, also be considered as subnational groups mobilizing on the basis of dissatisfaction with centralized governance.[2]

---

[1] At independence there was much resistance to fully establishing a federal structure as the basis of the Constitution. At the beginning of the war of independence (1945–1949), the Dutch created the Federal State of East Indonesia in an effort to suppress the nationalist movement and split its power base. Some young nationalists thus rejected federalism, perceiving it was a Dutch strategy to circumvent the nationalist struggle by denying it full support from ethnic groups across the archipelago (Said 2006; Schiller 1955).

[2] See, eg, *Republika Online* (13 August 2001) 'Wapres: Masalah Disintegrasi, Insya Allah, Dapat Diatasi' (Vice President: The Problem of Disintegration, By the Will of God, Can be Overcome), https://www.republika.co.id; Syaukani et al (2001) 'Otonomi Daerah dan Integrasi Nasional' (Regional Autonomy and National Integration).

Rachael Diprose, *Striking the Right Balance* In: *Constitutional Democracy in Indonesia*. Edited by: Melissa Crouch, Oxford University Press. © Rachael Diprose, 2023. DOI: 10.1093/oso/9780192870681.003.0005

After years of demands for greater regional autonomy, with the end of Suharto's authoritarian New Order government in 1998, Indonesia went on to achieve significant political and institutional reforms over the next two decades. Four sets of amendments to the 1945 Constitution facilitated the enactment of Indonesia's 1999 decentralization laws and other democratic reforms. These initial decentralization laws transferred significant fiscal and political authority to districts and municipalities, going some way to addressing subnational political demands for greater political and fiscal autonomy that had beleaguered Indonesia's central administration since the 1950s. Meanwhile, some of the more technocratic promises of decentralization have indeed manifested, in the form of pockets of policy innovation suited to Indonesia's varied local contexts, with services also more accessible locally in some cases (Diprose, McRae, and Hadiz 2019b). However, the extent to which service delivery has been customized to meet the vast and varied needs of the communities across the archipelago has been uneven (Pierskalla and Sacks 2017; Zhang and McRae 2015).

While the new centre-periphery bargain that was struck has mitigated some past centre-periphery struggles, it has also presented new challenges and in some cases new forms of contestation between actors competing to control or influence Indonesia's subnational political economy, especially in the resource sector, which is the focus of this chapter. The substantial increase in the scale of actors vying for subnational power and influence has introduced complexities to resolving disputes over resource access and control, and has seen larger numbers of subnational actors pursuing predatory rent-seeking practices (Benda-Beckmann and Benda-Beckman 2013; Eilenberg 2014; Peluso and Lund 2012) that were the hallmark of the narrower set of powerful actors in Suharto's authoritarian administration (Robison and Hadiz 2004). Indeed, centre–periphery tensions over controlling licensing authority in particular, have become increasingly acute.

This chapter provides an overview of the changes that have been introduced with decentralization and the challenges that have emerged specifically in the extractive industries. Exploring resource sector dynamics is particularly important in Indonesia, as pressures to increase natural resource extraction have increased alongside growth in the Indonesian population and economy, increased global demand for resources, and the deregulation of trade and opening up of markets that initially accompanied democratization. New limits to both trade and markets have, however, more recently been introduced in some sectors. The chapter also illustrates the centre-periphery struggles and subnational dynamics that have evolved over the past two decades by drawing on examples from Banyuwangi District in East Java Province, and from Bangka and Belitung Islands in Bangka Belitung Province. It explores the tensions that have emerged in each of these resource-rich regions and the ways subnational governments have sought to maintain authority and influence while successive central administrations have sought to strengthen central powers over strategic resource sectors. The chapter demonstrates that the most recent iteration of the decentralization laws—the 2014 Local Governance Law—has wound back the licensing authority of district and municipal governments in the most lucrative resource sectors to favour the provincial level of government, which is the tier that lost out in the initial 'Big Bang' decentralization reforms. The question remains as to whether the emerging slow creep of recentralization strikes the right balance in Indonesia's centre-periphery and intra-periphery distribution of power and authority or whether demands for greater district authority will be met through policy reform in future.

Decentralization and Authority over Natural Resource Management in Indonesia

In 2001, Indonesia's initial decentralization laws—known as the Regional Autonomy Laws (Law 22/1999 on Local Government[3] and Law 25/1999 on The Fiscal Balance Between the Central Government and the Regions) were rolled out. A significant degree of political and fiscal authority was transferred to districts, bypassing provincial governments that were once the arm of the powerful New Order administration in Indonesia's regions. Through decentralization to the district level, and the district-splitting that resulted, Indonesia has created a greater degree of segmented autonomy.[4] Regional autonomy also created a space for the (re)establishment of local customs and traditional communities, institutions, and organizations. These groupings became entwined with local identity politics, claims to power and leadership, as well as management of local conflict and problem-solving mechanisms. Acciaioli (2001: 88) argues that the legislative changes:

> Open[ed] up a political space for the replacement of once nationally uniform institutions, local conduits of nationalist allegiance, by regionally variable organisations and procedures of governance that encode community aspirations in terms of adherence to local custom.

Revisions to the local governance laws later took place through Law 32/2004 on Local Administration and Law 33/2004 on the Fiscal Balance between the Central Government and the Regional Governments. These 2004 laws made some modifications and clarification of the initial laws, and together with other legislative changes also facilitated the direct popular elections of Indonesia's leaders from the president, down to governors, district heads and mayors, and village heads, challenging the prior authority of regional and central legislatures to make these appointments.

As Resosudarmo (2004: 111) highlights, at the time, it was argued that decentralization was good for natural resource management as it could incorporate 'local knowledge about the diverse resource base', and essentially the Regional Autonomy Laws stipulated 'the transfer of natural resource management authority to [subnational] regions, albeit with ambiguities and contradictions, and increase[d] the [subnational] regions' share of natural resource revenues'. The legislative changes saw districts

---

[3] Law 22/1999 devolved central government powers and responsibilities to local governments in all government administrative sectors except for security and defence, foreign policy, monetary and fiscal matters, justice, and religious affairs, without conditions and limitations. It also transferred functions, personnel, and assets from the central government to the provincial governments, as well as the district and the municipal governments.

[4] Eight new provinces were formed post-1999 to reach thirty-four, with the final province, North Kalimantan, added to the mix in 2012. Districts and municipalities proliferated from 292 in 1999 to 514 as of April 2017.

gaining significant authority to issue business and production licences and land use concessions, and to charge royalties (in the form of, eg, forest concession rights levies and other local taxes) in the extractive industries. That is, unless the forest or land concession area in question cross-cut district boundaries (in such cases, licences became the purview of the provincial government), or was of such a scale that the central government retained authority (greater than 50,000 hectares—especially in the forestry sector), or when large-scale concessions for forest use (*hak pengusahaan hutan*, HPH) and mining had been previously granted.

With the new-found revenue raising capacities for the first time in more than three decades, Indonesia's subnational regions could benefit significantly from the revenues of natural resource extraction that had previously been transferred to the centre. This resulted in an explosion in licences issued at a range of scales in the extractive industries leading to significant environmental degradation and depletion of the resource base (Resosudarmo 2004; McCarthy 2004; McCarthy 2010; McCarthy, Vel, and Affif 2012; McCarthy and Robinson 2016; Peluso and Lund, 2012; Eilenberg 2014). Meanwhile, the responsibility for management and financing of conservation areas was stipulated as a central government authority—encroachment on national parks and other conservation areas for logging and palm oil and other extraction continues to be of concern (KPA 2020; McCarthy and Robinson 2016).

At the same time, the reforms also increased the number of actors competing for subnational political office and seeking campaign funding, some of which was derived from companies in the resource sector seeking to shore up future networks to political actors for support for licences and permits. The decentralization of 'money politics' and patronage politics has been of concern to observers since the early years of the decentralization roll-out (eg Potter and Badcock 2001; Benda-Beckmann and Benda-Beckman 2013 among others) and in the ongoing clientelism that has become entrenched in the practice of gaining office at all levels (Aspinall and Sukmajati 2016).

As we can see and has been well documented, decentralization together with the other electoral reforms introduced, created new arenas to exercise power and increased subnational competition among individuals, customary and land-connected communities, domestic and international companies, and state actors to control the land and natural resource base. Further, using the example of land governance, Diprose, Kurniawan, and Macdonald (2019a) have highlighted how the inherent instability in Indonesia's politico-economic system has provided the space for international actors to influence domestic policymaking, particularly when they are able to establish coalitions with domestic actors. International and domestic companies are also able to influence subnational politico-economic dynamics by integrating social interests (such as smallholder farmers) into supply chains for palm oil, timber, and other extractive industries, while building coalitions with influential national and subnational political and economic actors (Diprose and Azca 2020).

The substantial increase in the scale of actors vying for subnational power and influence, however, has introduced complexities to resolving disputes over resource access and control. Indeed, centre–periphery tensions over licensing authority in particular have become increasingly acute. Writing in the early years of the implementation of the decentralization laws, McCarthy (2004) explains that decentralization introduced volatile socio-legal configurations and interacting national and subnational legal regimes that produced contradictory regulations and overlapping licences, particularly in the forestry, plantations, and land sectors. Competing actors sought to protect or advance their own interests by taking advantage of these inconsistencies, which initially benefited those subnational elites already accustomed to the entrenched patronage practices of the prior authoritarian regime.

The changes, however, also generated volatility. This has especially been the case when communities have sought to challenge others land claims or concessions for resource extraction, or when powerful actors have had competing claims. Examples include district officials or other subnational authorities seeking to challenge central government authority, which are discussed in the case studies below. They also include customary and village communities, which were better recognized under the decentralization laws, but their authority in the initial iteration of the laws remained unclear. The authority of villages (and *adat* (or customary) villages) has been further clarified through Law 6/2014 on Villages, in which villages hold origin rights (*hak asal usul*), defined as inherited rights and rights derived from community initiatives (rights to culture, community organizations, and land (Art 1)). These shared histories and identities of villages inform how villages are framed under the Law as autonomous and self-managing governmental entities, and Article 4 gives recognition and respect for villages existing prior to and after the formation of the Republic of Indonesia, and the diversity of these villages (Diprose et al 2020).

While such competition to control the resource base existed prior to the onset of democratization in 1999, access was tightly controlled by interests within or aligned with Suharto's authoritarian regime. During this time, it was not uncommon for central interests to override subnational interests, especially when subnational interests were in conflict with those of the influential actors at the centre—state-owned enterprises (SOEs), conglomerates, and the oligarchs wielded enormous power (Robison and Hadiz 2004). Under the 1967 Basic Forestry Law, all of Indonesia's forests were under central government authority, and any initial rights that provinces and districts had had to issue licences of small parcels of land (10,000 hectares and 5,000 hectares respectively) were revoked in 1970, when the forestry department set a new minimum concession size of 50,000 hectares. Suharto's government policies concentrated forest industries into a few large conglomerates, and logging concessions became a form of patronage bestowed to those supporting the interests of state elites (Resosudarmo 2004). Similar trends were found in other extractives industries such as oil and gas, coal, and minerals extraction (Diprose and Azca 2020). Much of Indonesia's land base was controlled by the central state, with few having the power or resources to challenge the authority of the military regime.

Customary claims on land have now gained greater validity following a ruling of the Constitutional Court. After receiving a petition from AMAN (the Alliance of Indigenous Peoples of the Indonesian Archipelago) seeking an amendment to the 1999 Forestry Law to recognize the land rights of custom-based communities located in forest areas, the Constitutional Court agreed to review Article 1(6), of the 1999 Law on Forestry, which stated 'Customary forests are state forests located in the areas of custom-based communities'. In 2013, the Constitutional Court ruled the wording invalid and contravening the Constitution, recognizing that customary land rights have equal status to state-managed land. In a 188-page verdict, the court rewrote Article

1(6) to read: 'Customary forests are forests located in the areas of custom-based communities.' The result is that customary forests are no longer a part of state forests and greater claims to land access and control on customary lands (where concessions already exist) can now be made (see also Arizona, this volume).

Contestation over Natural Resource Access and Control

Thus, decentralization and other politico-institutional reforms, have introduced new dimensions to the political economy of the resource sector and more widely in Indonesia, especially as new actors at the subnational level challenge the historically embedded patronage systems of land and resource allocation and control. It is unsurprising then that following the spate of communal, insurgent, and vigilante violence that escalated with the onset Indonesia's democratic transition and then subsided (Herriman 2012; Varshney Panggabean, and Tadjoeddin 2004), both protracted contestation over natural resources and governance disputes have emerged since that time as two of the most common forms of (often violent) conflict captured by Indonesia's National Violence Monitoring System (NVMS)[5] (Pierskalla and Sacks 2017). The NVMS captures conflicts with varied scales of violence. Resource conflicts[6] and governance conflicts[7] have persistently and frequently occurred since Indonesia decentralized, although the scale of violence per incident tends to be significantly smaller in comparison to the insurgencies and communal conflicts that Indonesia has previously experienced.

While these two forms of conflict have increased in frequency, Pierskalla and Sack's (2017) analysis of the NVMS data more broadly shows mixed results on the impact of decentralization on conflict in Indonesia. In line with Diprose's (2009) earlier province-specific findings, they find that the devolution of powers and the creation of new districts under decentralization has contributed in part to mitigating prior tensions (with centre-periphery disputes and widespread communal violence receding). Newly formed districts have lower rates of violent incidents overall, and as districts began to implement the direct elections of district leaders (rather than the appointment of the district head and deputy district head), those that had done so experienced lower levels of violence overall. However, once the direct elections of the leaders of provincial and district heads were implemented more widely, there have been higher levels of specific elections-related violence. Further, across Indonesia's thirty-four provinces, the evidence suggests that as the total revenue per capita (or wealth) rises, so too does the incidence of identity-related violence and violence in response

---

[5] This monitoring system draws on the systematic review of newspaper reports on conflict (violent and non-violent). The NVMS database captures data in the following categories: resource-related violence, governance-related violence, election and bureaucratic appointment-related violence, identity-related violence, separatism, popular justice, violence involved in law enforcement, and crime.

[6] In the NVMS, resource-related violence involves resource disputes including around land, mining, access to employment, salaries, and pollution.

[7] In the NVMS, governance-related violence involves responses to government policies or programmes (including public services, procurement/corruption, subsidies, region (province, district, village) splitting, and security forces).

to dissatisfaction with government service provision. Pierskalla and Sacks (2017: 221) argue, in line with the literature on inequalities (Stewart 2008; Cederman, Weidmann, and Gleditsch 2011; Tadjoeddin 2014), that 'when development is accompanied by rising expectations and inequitable access to services, conflicts may emerge'.

The Consortium for Agrarian Reform (*Konsorsium Pembaruan Agraria*, KPA) also specifically monitors land-related conflicts in Indonesia.[8] Its findings are also consistent with that of the NVMS data—conflict over land and resource access are widespread in Indonesia. Between 2015 and 2018, there were 1,771 agrarian conflict cases captured from KPA monitoring, in which more than 935,000 households were affected (KPA 2019). In 2020, the KPA documented 241 cases of agrarian conflicts in relation to plantations (122 cases with the majority related to palm oil plantations), forests (41), infrastructure development (30), property (20), mining (12), military facilities (11), coastal areas and small islands (3) and agribusiness (2). Most conflicts have tended to occur because of land grabs or dispossession, which positions local communities against the state, state-owned companies, or the private sector (Riggs et al 2016). Many cases have involved marginalized village communities, fishermen and farmers, and customary groups (*kelompok adat*) (KPA 2019, 2020). Many of the more violent conflicts tracked by the KPA have involved clashes with security forces protecting company concessions and property.

Even after the end of the New Order regime, large-scale projects have tended to be controlled by powerful actors (both state and non-state), who use their extensive state connections, including the security forces, to gain the tacit endorsement of state agencies for their activities, even if this means circumventing state regulations (McCarthy, Vel, and Afiff 2012). This is particularly the case in Indonesia's heavily resource-endowed peripheral 'frontier' regions and borderland where there are opportunities for capitalist resource exploitation and agricultural expansion—such as many of the provinces on the island of Sumatra, particularly in the northern areas such as Aceh, Riau and the Riau Islands, Jambi and other similar regions, and the outer islands of Sulawesi, Kalimantan, and Papua. In resource-endowed borderland regions in particular, all manner of commodities, people, goods, and services can flow across borders to take advantage of markets, resources, employment, and other opportunities, and to benefit from different regulatory regimes on either side of the border (see, eg, Diprose and Azca 2020).

Such regions in Indonesia tend to be particularly prone to unsustainable resource capture, land grabbing, and inequitable development (Eilenberg 2014; Peluso and Lund 2012). Indeed, the scholarship on frontiers and borderlands highlights that these regions are commonly considered to be sites of instability, conflict, and insecurity (Korf and Raeymaekers 2013; Goodhand 2008), especially given the vested interests in exploiting land and resource endowments. Large-scale land and resource exploitation has taken the form of fairly extensive and often unfettered primitive accumulation

---

[8] While the NVMS collects data through the systematic review of newspapers reporting on conflicts, KPA compiles data through its own monitoring of Indonesia's regions and is specific to land and natural resource conflicts. Identification of these conflicts by the KPA is undertaken via direct reports from victims; reports from the members of its networks, the results of its field visits, monitoring and investigations; data from its system that reports on responses to these conflicts; and from printed and online media reporting. It is helpful to draw on KPA data, as the NMVS data after 2014 is no longer publicly available.

in Indonesia over many years both prior to and following the implementation of decentralization (Peluso and Lund 2012; McCarthy and Cramb 2009). Revenues from natural resource extraction commonly buttress the state budget and fund development initiatives in lower and lower-middle income countries like Indonesia. At the same time, resource rents provide sources of licit and illicit rents for elites and their networks in return for favouring particular interests in land zoning, land and resource titling, and licences (McCarthy, Vel, and Afiff 2012; McCarthy 2004, 2009; Erman 2008). These are also the regions, particularly on the island of Sumatra, such as in Riau Province, but in many of the other borderlands and regions too, in which the KPA has tracked the most frequent agrarian conflicts.

Exploring cases of resource contestation in more detail provides a useful lens for illustrating the on-the-ground dynamics of resource conflicts in Indonesia's multi-level political order that involve both competing subnational and national interests in the extractive industries as well as continued centre-periphery struggles for power and authority in Indonesia. The cases discussed below illustrate competing and overlapping land use and claims for resource access in two Indonesian provinces—one where resource endowments have been more recently discovered (in the Banyuwangi region of East Java Province) and one where mining has long been undertaken (in Bangka Belitung Province). The discussion helps illustrate the complexities of challenging long-standing political settlements involving patron–client relations between the state, security forces, extractive companies, and social interests, and equally the challenges forging new arrangements to 'settle' contestation over resources in regions where new discoveries have opened up opportunities for actors to make claims to these resources.

Tin Mining in Bangka Belitung

Bangka and Belitung are two small islands (surrounded by tiny islets) that produce around 90 per cent of Indonesia's tin (Diprose et al 2022), and together constitute Bangka Belitung Province. The islands are situated off the coast directly north of Jakarta and off Sumatra to the east of Palembang (they were once a part of South Sumatra Province). When the new province was formed in 2000, it initially comprised the Bangka and Belitung Districts and the provincial capital of Pangkal Pinang. In 2003 these two districts 'blossomed' into many new districts to include the capital, Bangka, and Central, South, and West Bangka Districts, as well as Belitung and East Belitung Districts. This district-splitting reflected the wider phenomenon that dominated Indonesia's first decade after decentralization was introduced, in which new state offices, positions, and infrastructure were created along with the relevant high degree of authority under decentralization.

Arguably, tin is a global strategic mineral resource[9] given that it is essential as a solder for electronics, such as computers, mobile phones, and cars. Much of Indonesia's

---

[9] Strategic mineral resources, albeit an imprecise concept, are generally considered to be those minerals which are difficult to replace, often come predominantly from foreign sources, and are important to a country's economy and in particular its defence industry (Sutphin et al 1992).

tin is of a very high quality and is exported to meet international demand in areas that produce such commodities: in 2016, 95 per cent of Indonesia's tin was exported to countries in Asia (China, Singapore, Japan, Korea, and Taiwan) and to Europe (the United Kingdom, the Netherlands, France, Spain, and Italy) (PT Timah 2017). Indeed, its value to the Indonesian economy and state institutions has long been recognized: the New Order government designated the mineral as a strategic good. This meant that the security forces could be engaged to protect the resource and legitimately extract rents for these services. It also meant that the central state had greater powers to control mining activities and revenue flows and that securitized mining areas were relatively inaccessible to the general populace. Under the New Order, tin mining was controlled by the government department PN Tambang Timah—later reorganized as the SOE PT Timah[10] (Baldwin 1983)—which had the mining licence for the vast majority of the region's mineral area.

However, under pressure from the national government to increase the supply of tin and facing financial decline, PT Timah established partnerships with local companies to provide mining service/work contracts (*tambang kontrak karya*) to help mine tin; although they could not hold a concession for mining tin themselves (Erman 2008). Eighty-seven of these contracts were allocated to companies in Bangka Belitung, many of which were owned by Sino-Indonesians situated in or from Bangka (ibid), with their roots in the earlier migrant networks facilitated by the Dutch (Interviews 2017). In 1974, PT Timah also established the PT Koba Tin joint venture with the Australian Kajuara Mining Company, with PT Timah retaining a 25 per cent share of the joint venture (Baldwin 1983).

The mining service contracts allowed the tin extracted through small-scale illicit mining operations (particularly by artisanal miners) to be 'formalized' through procurement under the service contractors, who then on sold the tin to the large companies (Erman 2007, 2008). Erman (2008) details how tin smuggling through the nearby Riau islands to Singapore and in some cases Malaysia also thrived during the New Order period and beyond, often in coordination with the army and the navy, and the elaborate ways in which tin smugglers negotiated with custom officials, the navy, and bureaucrats in the tin smuggling trade. Thus, while the sector was dominated by the SOE PT Timah, artisanal mining and illicit tin exports also thrived. In other peripheral and border regions of Indonesia, similar patterns are evident, where informal cross-border trade of all manner of resources and goods have long thrived and are considered a common livelihood by local peoples—or the 'way things have always been done', such as in Riau and elsewhere (Diprose and Azca 2020; Eilenberg 2014).

---

[10] Initially, in 1976 what is now known as PT Timah was established as the full SOE PT Tambang Timah (Persero). In 1995, they sold 35 per cent, to public shareholders and listed the company on the Jakarta Stock Exchange. In 1998, it restructured to constitute the parent company PT Timah (Persero) Tbk with divested operations in a number of child companies, one of which was listed on the London Stock Exchange. In 2006, it cancelled its listing on the London Stock Exchange but remained listed on the Jakarta Stock Exchange. In 2014, it merged various operations including the parent company and the SOE PT Tambang Timah (which remained one of its divested interests) and became PT Timah as it is now known (PT Timah 2017).

Changing Interests in Indonesia's New Multi-Level Political Order

At the onset of democratization, tin was no longer recognized as a strategic commodity in Indonesia (Ministerial Decree 146/1999[11]), and this opened up the opportunity for tin mining to other interests. The early iteration of decentralization laws devolved the authority to grant some aspects of tin (and other mineral) mining licences to district governments. In response, the Indonesian Democratic Party of Struggle (PDI-P)-backed district head (who had beat contenders from the Golkar party that had once wielded significant influence in the region) introduced Bangka District Regulations 2 and 21/2001. These regulations allowed for a plethora of mining and tin sand export licences to be issued. Twenty-one enterprises took up mining and tin trade activities in the region in addition to PT Timah and the 75 per cent foreign-owned PT Koba Tin. Most of these twenty-one enterprises were owned by Sino-Indonesians situated in or from Bangka, and some had previously held the mining service/work contracts mentioned above with PT Timah under the New Order (Interviews 2016; Erman 2008). In effect, the district head—aligned with PDI-P that wielded significant power nationally at the time—drew these organizations, along with PT Koba Tin, into his coalition to counter the might of PT Timah.

With his new-found authority, the Bangka District Head also issued District Regulation 6/2001 on 'Unconventional Mining' (*Tambang Inkonvensional*), which recognized artisanal tin mining as a locally protected livelihood by the district government. Some of these artisanal tin miners had illicitly mined tin prior to decentralization, providing tin to the enterprises with mining service contracts mentioned above and to smuggling networks, but the number of artisanal tin miners grew significantly to some 130,000 by 2002 (Erman, 2008: 102). The Pangkal Pinang Mayor and the Belitung District Head in the province also quickly followed suit with their own similar regulations. Key in local public discourse at the time (an issue which continues today) was the degree to which the local populace had been locked out of the benefits of mining in the region, given that mining sites were heavily controlled by the military and operated by PT Timah and PT Koba Tin, and there were a restricted number of formal sector jobs available through these companies (Interviews 2017, 2019).

The district governments and the mayoralties across Bangka Belitung Province also increased the royalties and other levies charged to PT Timah for their large-scale mining activities in the region, bringing subnational authorities into conflict with the traditional large-scale mining interests. Other companies escaped some of these fees by accessing tin sands through the small-scale artisanal mining and middlemen.

Meanwhile, a number of investors also began to develop business interests in the region, particularly on Bangka Island. The larger firms sought first to collect tin from small-scale artisanal mining to onsell to larger companies; second, to organize artisanal miners; and third, through the later establishment of tin smelters discussed below. Many of the not-so-new twenty-one enterprises mentioned previously sought to consolidate their own interests and stopped providing services to PT Timah. They

---

[11] This decree further amends Ministerial Decree 558/1998 on General Provisions in the Export Sector.

became more directly involved in small-scale mining, sourcing tin from community mines that they could legally market and export through their own supply chain networks (Interviews 2017). These predominantly Bangka-Chinese middlemen also established a plethora of businesses related to mining. Thus, they acted as gatekeepers for securing and maintaining livelihoods in the region and 'formalizing' tin supply chains to the large companies. They offered better 'farm gate' prices to artisanal miners and cheaper tin to other companies than that which was proffered by PT Timah. They were also implicated in smuggling networks (Interviews, January 2017; Erman 2007).

Many were backed by what Erman (2007) describes as two of Indonesia's 'tin kings' who grew in prominence to have conglomerate interests in the early to mid 2000s. These influential businessmen were connected with (and had funded or established) many of the medium-sized mining service contracting companies mentioned above. They also had close military ties and political interests (funding campaigns and providing other benefits) both in Jakarta and in Bangka Belitung. Through their networks, they created jobs and other economic opportunities for many in the tin supply chain, including for artisanal miners, and provided social benefits to many communities from scholarships to other services for the poor (Erman 2007; Interviews 2018). As a result, the national tin company, PT Timah, lost a significant proportion of its market share and access to mining services, which saw its profits drop.

These changes also led to an expansion of international and local interests in extraction in Bangka Belitung. China's demand for tin was growing, which it was able to meet through its longstanding trade networks in the region—particularly given the growth in consumer interests in smart phones and other electronics produced in China requiring tin as the solder. Malaysian and Singaporean demands for tin were also able to be met through the licit and illicit trade flows—smuggling continued, drawing on the new upscaled flow of tin sands from small-scale mining and smelted tin (Erman 2007, 2008).

In 2002, the foreign investment component of the joint venture, PT Koba Tin, initially between PT Timah and the Australian Kajuara mining company, was acquired by the Malaysian Smelting Corporation Berhad (MSC)—a publicly listed company in Malaysia that competes with some of Indonesia's companies. Despite PT Timah being a partner, PT Koba Tin soon became its major competitor, also offering better prices to artisanal miners, setting up its own smelter plant on Bangka island, and it was closely connected to the network of smaller Bangka-Chinese mining and service companies.

While the dynamics and details are far more complicated than is presented here, the strategy of the local leadership to access the state for the benefit of subnational interests under decentralization was pursued with vigour, particularly by the Bangka District Head. As is discussed below, the district administrations in Bangka Belitung staved off efforts from the central government to informally wind back control of the tin sector to the centre, seeking legitimacy and popularity among local communities by creating livelihoods. The networks of private sector entrepreneurs were a part of this coalition of power and deeply connected with the district leadership, and helped to broker relationships between political, economic, and social interests. They also provided a means for local bureaucrats, often in competition but sometimes in cahoots with the local parliament, to garner popular support from voters. The competition for accessing tin mining subnationally was diffused, and through social inclusion (albeit with little attention to worker safety and the effects on the environment), the community-level violence seen in other parts of the archipelago was not seen in the province. However, together these subnational coalitions challenged central interests, particularly those of PT Timah and its patrons at the centre.

Violent Centre–Periphery Struggles

The new political economy for the region saw a proliferation of interested actors compete for primacy during the first decade of Indonesia's reform, and significant, sometimes violent contestation involving actors at the centre and in the Bangka Belitung region. While PT Timah was well connected to influential national interests (both bureaucrats and business conglomerates with ties to New Order oligarchies), during the early years of reform it had yet to fully reorganize to entrench their networks at the subnational level. However, the threat to PT Timah interests from declining profits brought about by the deregulation of tin licences and the levies charged by local governments, saw it lobby central government actors and the Governor to ban tin sand exports.

Drawing on a discourse of environmental damage and citing problems in tin smuggling (which was affecting tin prices) the Governor of the day, aligned with the opposition Golkar party (also the party of Suharto's authoritarian government), PT Timah, the Ministry of Mining and Energy, and the Ministry of Internal Affairs, complained to central authorities about the problems in the tin industry. Citing resource nationalism and social protection, eventually in 2002, the Minister of Trade and Industry outlawed the export of tin sands arguing that only tin in smelted form or tin bars could be exported, despite opposition from PDI-P-backed local politicians and local bureaucrats.

Meanwhile, during the struggle for authority, the Bangka District Head and his allies continued to pressure PT Timah to provide a share of ownership to the district, an effort which went on for some time but was unsuccessful. It also pushed for local people to be given senior roles in the company leadership based on the growing calls for 'local sons' (*putra daerah)* to reclaim local interests—a claim which was common across the archipelago at the time given the prior New Order practices of installing public and private sector actors in regions and in companies to represent the interests of the centre (Diprose 2002). The campaign was successful and a Bangka person was installed as the Director of PT Timah (Erman 2007). Further, in response to the re-regulation of tin sands export, six months later in January 2003, the district government found a way around the Minister's decree. The Bangka District Head:

> Issued Inter-Region Trading Licenses, or SIPAD (Surat Izin Perdagangan Antar Daerah), through District Regulation No. 20/2003 … Basically, it gave tin exporters the opportunity to trade in tin between regions, provided that the exporters had mining concession areas and sent the tin sand to another region where there was a tin smelting company. Exporters must also pay a tax on each kilogram of tin sand traded between regions. A total of 98 SIPAD were issued by the local Industry, Trade,

Cooperatives, and Investment Service (Dinas Perindustrian Perdagangan Koperasi dan Penanaman Modal, Indagkopem). (Erman 2007: 186)

In response to the new trading licenses, tin sand trade resumed, despite protests from Golkar and parties aligned provincially and in the district. Many smelting plants were also established in Bangka Belitung to export tin bars. This included smelting plants established by one of the 'tin kings' and PT Koba Tin. They were able to legalize the tin sands collected by artisanal miners and prepare these for export in ways which were inaccessible to PT Timah. The SIPAD licences provided a loophole for some of the (contested) interpretations of central regulations.

Again, PT Timah lobbied central actors and a centre–periphery power struggle ensued about the legality of district regulations and some of the tin smelting licenses (and whether the district had authority to issue these licences). The centre argued that many of the tin mining activities in Bangka Belitung were not permitted under their interpretation of the 1967 Mining Law and other regulations which sought to restrict the export of 'raw' materials. But mining in the district continued until, in October 2006, PT Timah through its national coalition of powerful actors won the day. Under instruction from the then President Susilo Bambang Yudhoyono, the national police and a detachment of the counterterrorism squad (Densus 88) were dispatched to Bangka Belitung to force the closure of three smelting enterprises and eighty-four units of 'Unconventional Mining'. They also captured a ship carrying ninety-three containers of tin bars owned by these three smelting companies, which were deemed to be illegal.

This action had violent local consequences. Company managers were detained, including the manager of the PT Koba Tin-owned smelting operation (Erman 2008). Five hundred tin workers and artisanal miners held a protest at the regional police station, crowds dispersed and re-formed, and a riot ensued. A few days later 2,000 people from across the districts protested in the provincial capital and managed to enter the Governor's office. Police responded with open fire during which six people were wounded and others were arrested. Around the same time, the residence of the Pangkal Pinang Mayor was 'terrorized' by unknown assailants (likely associated with the PT Timah coalition for his support of the artisanal miners). However, PT Timah had seen its main opposition reduced in economic power and influence, and it regained control of tin mining in the region.

Winding Back Control

Essentially, prior to 2006 the growing tensions saw two camps form: one that represented old (and more centralized) forces, and another representing new politico-economic forces. The Bangka District Head, along with other district heads in the region, sought local legitimacy and public authority by ensuring social interests were met. This was achieved predominantly by using the instruments of the state to recognize andlegalise the livelihoods of artisanal tin miners, and by accommodating local political and economic interests in the supply chain networks. They used this approach to gain power and to challenge the hegemony of PT Timah. Over a decade later, on

Belitung Island—where livelihoods have diversified after the departure of PT Timah's onshore mining operations in the late 1990s to encompass tourism and agriculture—local communities have refused to back potential candidates running in the district head elections unless they make a pact with communities that they will not support PT Timah's offshore mining activities, which are have begun to increasingly encroach on now popular tourism and fishing areas, despite the company having a current licence that was issued under the New Order (Interviews 2019; Diprose et al 2022).

On Bangka Island where PT Timah operations continue, however, ultimately the old conglomerate and political interests aligned with PT Timah won the day, with the central state using force in 2006 to close down smelters, which had an impact on the ways poor artisanal miners could access livelihoods. The centre, through a number of strategies, has used its interpretation of legislation and other instruments of the state, including security forces, to regain most of its control of the tin industry in the province, although the district can still charge various levies on companies.

It has achieved this by, first, in 2009, passing the Law on Mineral and Coal Industries (4/2009). Winanti and Diprose (2020) explain that the new law marked a shift in policy frameworks from what was emerging as a liberal, market-based approach to foreign direct investment (FDI), towards resource nationalism through which significant rules were introduced to ensure local content in mining operations that have significant FDI. Unprocessed minerals could no longer be exported and needed to be first smelted domestically, as a way of adding value and also to more officially outlaw illicit mineral exports. Between 2009 and 2020, more than twenty government regulations and ministerial regulations (particularly from the Ministry of Energy and Natural Resources) were introduced to operationalize the 2009 law (Winanti and Diprose, 2020). To justify the central state's efforts to strengthen control over the Indonesian natural resource base, President Yudhoyono's ruling coalition returned to Article 33 of the Indonesian Constitution, which specifies that the land, the water, and all the natural resources 'shall be under the powers of the state and shall be used for the most significant benefit of the people'. The administration also proposed to comply with the Constitution by shifting control of resource production to the state through SOEs during election campaigning (Winanti and Diprose, 2020: 7). While the swing back to a more nationalist orientation has been most apparent in the mining sector, especially in the ways the government has moved to renegotiate contracts with foreign mining companies, it has also apparent in a range of other sectors including finance (Abraham 2017), education (Rosser 2015), shipping (Dick 2008), health (Rosser 2017), and electricity (Jarvis 2012).

Second, in 2013, the central government did not renew the MSC's work contract that operationalized PT Koba Tin's operations. The company is no longer in operation in the region (MSC 2017) and PT Timah now faces reduced competition from the large-scale operator.[12] With depleted reserves on Belitung Island (it had ceased large-scale

---

[12] It is alleged that the work contract was abolished to help address issues with the Indonesia's falling tin exports and the plummeting price of tin (both considered to have resulted from rampant smuggling), given that in nearby Malaysia and Singapore the export of processed tin was growing and this was likely sourced (both illicitly and licitly) from Bangka Belitung's tin deposits, (Interviews 2017). Despite Singapore having no tin deposits of its own, it had an established smelting company (Erman 2008). More officially, the Indonesian government—as a part of a wider promotion of resource nationalism (eg through a proposal

operations there in the late 1990s), PT Timah has since scaled up its offshore mining operations in the region. In the absence of significant alternative livelihoods, particularly on Bangka Island, artisanal mining continues to operate, sometimes using unsafe practices. Further, a recent push into highly prized rare earth mining for PT Timah and other companies has signalled ongoing dependence on an extractive economy in the region (Interviews 2020; Lubis and Cahyafitri 2015).

Third, further revisions were made to regional autonomy through Law 23/2014 on Local Governance (revised in Law 9/2015). To settle the battle for licensing control, the revisions have given significant licensing authority (on larger scales) to provinces in strategic resource sectors such as mining, fisheries, and plantations, winding back the scale of the licences that can be issued by districts. Learning from the past, when the provincial governments were the arm of the central government in the regions, it is yet to be seen how local development will fare.

Fourth, a series of clamp-down measures was further supported by a succession of Trade Ministerial Decrees on Tin Exports issued in 2014, 2015, and 2018,[13] which guide implementation of the Mining Law. The latest decree (53/2018) requires companies to declare the sources of their tin ores, significantly increasing central government control over supply chains. The new export regulations make it exceedingly difficult for local smelters to export tin legally—only very few companies, such as PT Timah and PT Refined Bangka Tin, have been able to meet the regulatory and supply chain verification requirements (Taylor 2015).[14] PT Timah has been a major beneficiary of the most recent requirements for verification of sources, since it is one of the only companies with the requisite scale, know-how, and administrative capacity to comply with these requirements while also maintaining competitive tin prices.

With central interests wrestling back control, there has been little overt conflict since this time on Bangka Island. However, tensions continue, as do struggles between the tourism/fishing and the offshore mining industry on Belitung Island (Diprose et al 2022). That is not to say that all key issues—particularly related to environmental degradation, livelihoods, and safe work practices—have been wholly addressed. Rather, the local political economy has again reconfigured in what Meagher (2012) would call a corrosive form of more predatory rule. The space to contest large-scale interests or challenge the centrally endorsed patronage networks has narrowed. Local actors have now reorganized to take advantage of the somewhat illiberal 'resettled political

to limit the foreign ownership of Indonesia's mines to 49 per cent)— argued that Koba Tin was not contributing enough revenue to the national economy (http://www.reuters.com/article/kobatin-indonesia-idUSL3N0HF27N20130919).

[13] Ministry of Trade Regulations 44/M-DAG/PER/7/2014 on Tin Exports, 33/M-DAG/PER/5/2015 on Tin Exports (Amendment of regulation 44/2014) and 53/2018 (2nd amendment of Regulation 44/2014 and 33/2018). The Ministry of Energy and Mineral Resources controls large-scale mining licences and issues Clear and Clean (C&C) Status certification of companies (to demonstrate that they have met a number of regulatory requirements) so they are then able to apply for export permits.

[14] Under the regulations, companies seeking export certification are required to have a Competent Person Indonesia (CPI), who prepares a report on the source verification and mechanisms used. The CPI must be certified by a professional association such as the Indonesian Association of Mining Experts Indonesia (PERHAPI), or the Indonesian Geologists (IAGI). The CPI report must be verified by an independent body—either Sucofindo or Surveyor Indonesia. In practice, few companies are able to fulfil these requirements.

settlement' that is controlled by PT Timah and others involved in smelting (cf Diprose and Azca 2020). The supply of tin by artisanal miners has reverted to prior practices of selling tin to middlemen who control many aspects of the tin supply chain and who on-sell the tin illicitly collected by artisanal miners to tin smelters and PT Timah to supplement their large-scale mining.

Gold Mining in Banyuwangi

In contrast, different forms of protest and tensions are ongoing in relation to gold mining of more recently discovered deposits in Banyuwangi District in East Java Province, where mining is also in direct competition with other land uses such as the national park (and related tourism) and agriculture. In Bangka District, most social interests were wholly aligned behind the district head, whereas in Banyuwangi, the former district head (whose second term ended in 2020) was not able to satisfy all factions of social interests and unrest has grown over the new mine in Tumpang Pitu. Banyuwangi is the easternmost district on the island of Java. The region has become increasingly accessible since the airport was built with central government funding, following serious lobbying undertaken by well-connected central government parliamentarians from Banyuwangi.

New gold deposits were not discovered in and around the conservation forest in Banyuwangi District and neighbouring Jember in East Java Province (near the Java Sea) until the late twentieth century. Significant gold exploration and the establishment of the mine predominantly scaled up alongside the introduction of democratic reforms and decentralization—interests controlling the local political economy in the region were thus not as entrenched as in Bangka Belitung where tin mining has taken place for well over a century.

In 1991, the first exploration licence in the region was granted to PT Gamasiantara (Golden Eagle Indonesia). Activities were then continued by Korea Toosun Holdings until 1997, and then by Golden Valley Mines from 1997 onwards, with Placer Dome (1999–2000) and the Hakman Group JV later becoming involved.[15] Exploration revealed that the area had one of the biggest untapped gold deposits in the world. The exploration licence of the Hakman Group was cancelled in 2006 under instruction from the then District Head Ratna Ani Lestari. Rights were later granted to Indo Multi Niaga (IMN) in 2006 (formerly PT Indo Multi Cipta), which had an Australian company (Intrepid) providing investment funds.

When IMN sold its exploration licence to Merdeka Copper Gold, the Australian-owned Intrepid group objected, given it had already invested heavily in exploration activities. It took the both the IMN and the central government to international arbitration and eventually gained compensation of US $80 million from Merdeka Copper Gold in 2015.[16] The central government complained that many of the challenges that

[15] Putri Akmal, https://news.detik.com/berita/d-3173240/kata-bupati-anas-soal-kronologi-izin-tamb ang-emas-tumpang-pitu-banyuwangi.
[16] There were many contested dimensions of this process involving international, national, and subnational actors, which are not discussed here.

had emerged in relation to Banyuwangi gold mining licensing arrangements, as well as other local contestation, were triggered by district government decisions and that its hands were tied in resolving these disputes given Indonesia's decentralized structures. One central government advisor explained in an interview in 2018, that this was one of the reasons the central government was keen to wind back authority from provinces, so that it could better resolve emerging disputes.

Alongside the changing licensing arrangements, a number of business licences were also granted in the area to provide mining services and small-scale mining in the area, as was the case in Bangka Belitung with the onset of decentralization. These include PT Hakman Platina Metalindo, PT Jember Metal, and Banyuwangi Minerals. However, in the wider community there were splits between those who did and did not support the development of a large-scale mine in the forests of Meru Betiri in Banyuwangi and there have been periodic protests, some of which have turned violent, in the region over the past decade or so.

Winding Back Control

The area where the gold deposits were identified were already designated as forest protection areas (*hutan lindung*) in the Meru Betiri national park, which prohibits mining and other extraction activities. Thus, a staged process of land rezoning was undertaken to meet the strategic interests of central actors and eventually accommodate mining activities. In 2013, despite protests from local civil society groups, the conservation area was rezoned as production forest by the Minister of Forestry, which would accommodate a variety of activities not possible in forest protection areas. Authority to control activities in the rezoned production forest area was granted to the state-owned Indonesian forestry company, PT Perhutani, which at the time was almost bankrupt. Helping to address its financial problems, PT Perhutani then rented the land in the old conservation area to Merdeka Copper Gold and its three subsidiaries (Bumi Sukses Indo—BSI, Cinta Bumi Sukses Indo—CBSI, and Damai Sukses Indo—DSI) for mining activities. DSI and CBSI already had exploration licenses (*Izin Usaha Pertambangan*—note this is a permit not a contract) and in 2013, BSI was also granted an exploration licence. Mining activities commenced only recently in February 2017 under the auspices of BSI.

A number of tensions arose alongside the rezoning process, even prior to the commencement of gold extraction. The new Banyuwangi District Head, Azwar Anas, elected in 2010 with backing from the PDI-P party (the party dominating much of this part of East Java), did not originally support mining in the region given the issues already experienced involving IMN and Merdeka Copper Gold (and tensions within Merdeka Copper Gold itself—issues not discussed here). In his first term, the new district head sought a moratorium on mining in the region, recognizing it was not popular among many residents living next to the mining site, especially in Pesanggaran Subdistrict. However, as licences had already been granted by the prior district head in coordination with the central government, the new district head had limited options. His response was simply to clarify his position—there would be no new licences permitted but he could not do much about existing licences. While the new district head was quite popular overall, achieving some 88 per cent of the vote in his second term, some interviewees argued that he oscillated on his policy positions, with one stating in 2017 that 'his position is sometimes confusing – he puts the food in his mouth but does not don't swallow it' (Interviews 2017). He was less popular, however, in Pesanggaran Subdistrict where the mine site is situated, compared with other parts of the district.

Other groups that have tended not to support BSI activities at the Tumpang Pitu mine include those in the subdistrict whose agricultural livelihoods will or have been affected directly by mining activities and from environmental risks posed by mining. Indeed, students, environmental activists, farmers, fishermen, and NGOs protested when the Social and Environmental Impact Assessment (AMDAL) was signed in May 2008, which effectively helped progress approvals for activities. Artisanal miners who operate illicitly in the forests of PT Perhutani, which has been ongoing since the early 2000s, have also tended not to support the mine (Interviews 2017). Some interviewees explained that these artisanal miners have been supported by some of the community leaders in the subdistrict and the military, in particular the Navy, who gain illicit fees from protecting their illicit mining activities and the gold transport routes. By 2010, the number of artisanal miners had grown to some 12,000 people, particularly through migrating prospectors. Interviewees (2018) stated that BSI have encouraged the state to arrest these miners, which has fuelled further tensions between artisanal miners and community members and BSI.

Competing Interests and Outbreaks of Violence

The tensions above saw a riot break out in 2011 when BSI tried to clear out the artisanal prospectors, with three BSI offices burned down. The elite police forces, the provincial Mobile Brigade (Brimob), responded with force and three people were shot. Brimob also shot artisanal miners in the subdistrict in a different incident in July 2011. Several demonstrations took place over the following years involving thousands of people, and a riot broke out again in 2015.

In response to these kinds of incidents, the district head tried to establish ways to share mining opportunities (requesting a greater share for the district in the ownership of BSI) and to diversify livelihoods. In 2014, he developed a tourism programme in the district to mitigate the impact of the future large-scale mining activities and to create alternative livelihoods for the artisanal miners and others in the Pesanggaran Subdistrict. The location he chose to develop tourism was situated in and around the remaining part of the national park where fishing and artisanal mining also overlap, and part of which was controlled by PT Perhutani. However, as tourism activities scaled up, tensions emerged when PT Perhutani refused to share the revenues from the tourism park fees (Interviews 2018).

In 2015, a meeting was facilitated by the District Security Council (made up of civil servants and the security forces) between the artisanal miners, tourism interests, and BSI, to try and resolve the tensions, but this was unsuccessful in finding a compromise. At one point the regional police chief allegedly said the community had displayed no ethics in this meeting, and participants reported this back to villagers in Pesanggaran

Subdistrict, fuelling further tensions that day. The district head tried to host a meeting that evening with the community in the midst of the tensions in the subdistrict, bringing with him Muspida (the District Security Council) and Muspika (the Subdistrict Security Council) representatives, and an influential local Islamic leader from *Nadhatul Ulama* (NU), which is a powerful Muslim organization in the region and nationally. However, community members maintained that all of these interests were aligned to support the mine, including NU, and that the district head only invited people who were pro-BSI and supported the district head's tourism policy. Invitations to the meeting were issued through formal channels in the subdistrict government, indicating a degree of elitism. Some were excluded from being invited at all, including some of those who had been instrumental in mobilizing support for the anti-mining cause. Subsequently the appeal failed, and riots continued the next day.

During the riots, the villagers again burned down BSI offices and clashed with Brimob. Four people were shot and six were arrested. Not long after this, in 2016, the Minster of Mining and Energy declared mining in the area a Strategic Asset (RI 651 K/30/MEM/2016), meaning, as discussed earlier, that security forces (in this case the police) provide security for the mine site and legitimately charge fees for services, as was the case for tin under the New Order. But this has not been sufficient to hold back social unrest—in March 2017 protesters blocked heavy equipment to commence mining at the Tumpang Pitu mining site.

By 2018, those opposing the mine perceived that the district head, the mining company, the police, the powerful religious organisation (NU), and those with jobs in the mine were all aligned, and were also supported by PT Perhutani, which had the benefits from tourism nearby. In contrast, social interests—predominantly poor artisanal miners, farmers, and fishermen—especially in the Pesanggaran Subdistrict, with the support of activists, students, and civil society organizations (and the alleged tacit support of Navy officials that benefit from protecting artisanal mining) have continued to oppose the mine. Various forms of protest have continued to 2021. In contrast to Bangka District in Bangka Belitung Province in which the coalition between district authorities, networks of companies and entrepreneurs, and other influential actors were able to deliver on livelihoods and other opportunities to meet social interests— both at the onset of 'Big Bang' decentralization and as district powers were wound back—there is yet to be a political settlement that is able to bridge both social interests and more powerful politico-economic interests in Banyuwangi. It is evident that if powerful politico-economic coalitions are perceived to ignore or only accommodate the social interests of some sections of the community, or to meet elite interests and to ignore wider inequalities, they will not garner public support. This also leaves communities vulnerable to alignment with predatory interests.

Conclusion

Decentralization introduced a new multi-level political order including 'multiple, even mutually contradictory, institutions in which various structural powers are inscribed' (Lund 2006). While the devolution of powers went some way to mitigating prior centre–periphery tensions, global, centrifugal, and centripetal forces have become more entwined in Indonesia's decentred, multi-level governance regime. This has changed power dynamics and created new arenas of contestation and sometimes (albeit small-scale) violent conflict subnationally, particularly in relation to highly prized resource and land access. There are acute difficulties in managing contestation in resource-rich regions when there are overlapping or competing claims to access and control land and resources, where authority is contested between the centre and the periphery, and where there are competing uses of the land and the sea that create alternatives for community livelihoods and businesses. We see this in the case studies discussed above and in the wider data tracing conflict incidence.

The increased the scale of interests that seek to contest power and exercise influence in subnational environments include the more licit state interests concerned with governance arrangements, revenue generation, redistribution, and institution strengthening, as well as the more predatory state and private interests concerned with gaining resource rents by both licit and illicit means. It also includes social interests seeking to ensure they have access to livelihoods and incomes and to influence norms around socio-economic and environmental rights and access. The changes have also provided the opportunity for international interests to bypass the centre and seek direct influence over subnational actors.

Yet, the case analysis shows there is no easy fix for contestation over resources through regulation or force: extreme centralization generated contestation historically, as has decentralization more recently. Meanwhile, the more recent changes to the regulatory environment that include the partial winding back of some district powers has also produced different subnational effects.

In Bangka Belitung—the case with the long history of mining over centuries— decentralization threatened but did not entirely unravel the long-established power base of influential national interests, including those of PT Timah and other national actors with strong networks of subnational patronage. In the districts of Bangka Island in particular, through the use of force (itself a source of violence) and government legislation and regulations, the slow winding back of district powers has eased centre– periphery tensions in the tin sector by re-accommodating both predatory and other interests that were under threat, and returning the sector's political economy to a (somewhat modified) status quo in which large companies wield significant influence, but now districts do gain a larger share of the revenues. Yet, despite appropriating the discourse of social and environmental protection, central actors have garnered only partial public authority and support subnationally, especially given that in several instances force has been used by security forces to uphold central interests.

Drawing on the case analysis, under decentralization it seems that subnational leaders (or coalitions of subnational actors) use local legislation and other instruments of the state and draw on networks that connect social interests with political and economic interests to seek public legitimacy, exercise authority, and endeavour to create stability. The succession of district heads and governments in Bangka District and the other districts in Bangka Island, in coalition with other subnational actors, have tended to have greater legitimacy because they were early movers in utilizing their new regulatory authority for the benefit of the district, and they have continued to deliver on the local social, political and economic contract. Although this is within a local economy that is almost entirely reliant on tin—there are few competing livelihoods and economic sectors in this region that might challenge the subnational politico-economic status quo. At the same time, building the legitimacy of the subnational leaders in the Bangka Island districts has not entirely involved 'a genuine transformation of regulatory authority or offered local populations a preferable alternative to the prior situation of neglectful or predatory rule' (cf Meagher 2012: 1073). While communities can now access resource-related artisanal mining livelihoods that were once restricted, they are still dependent on both predatory and other patrons to sell tin and access welfare. Many are still poor and working conditions are dangerous.

In other regions discussed above, similar strategies have been used by district leaders. However, there are different challenges posed by competing sectors and their influential backers, as well as the extent to which district interests are at odds with those of the centre. The districts in Belitung Island continue to be embroiled in a battle between tourism and offshore mining, but artisanal onshore mining in the old PT Timah pits has long been recognized in local legislation, and as with Bangka Island, the centre has not sought to override this recognition. However, in Banyuwangi, where mining is a more recent development, the winding back of some district powers has constrained the options of district leaders to use local regulations that might override the centre and satisfy social interests. The networks established by local leaders have not managed to connect to all prominent social interests and we see varied degrees of satisfaction and dissatisfaction among Banyuwangi's multiple publics.

The analysis illustrates the ways different nodes of power are brought into closer proximity or become intertwined in democratizing multi-level governance contexts in relation to the resource sector: the economic power of large extractive industries funded by international and domestic interests, the political power of state regulators at both national and subnational levels, and the social mobilization of power of the wider population through advocacy groups and, in some cases, through more predatory types of networks. Tensions emerge when interests are not aligned, and these nodes of power collide and are made more complicated by overlapping or competing claims for licences or tenure. Brokering these nodes of power through creating assemblages that connect the interests of the central and subnational state, the market, and social needs is an important part of creating a new, stable political order in such multi-level contexts, whether or not such order displays the tenets of liberal democratic norms.

While the Bangka District case shows the tensions and instability that characterized the first decade of decentralization and other reforms have not re-emerged as most actors gain from the present politico-economic settlement, the situation is more complicated in other districts where there are competing sectors and factional splits between coalitions of influential actors, and especially when these networks extend to the centre. In Banyuwangi District, where economic, political, and social interests do not entirely align, and central government interests to support the development of the mine have seemingly won the day, protests and other actions continue in the face of overriding central government regulations and police action to protect the development of the mine. Even a popular district head has been unable to constrain tensions, particularly given some community groups perceive that socio-economic justice is yet to be achieved. It is evident from these cases that suppressing or sidelining social interests creates risks for continued contestation—in Banyuwangi and the districts of

Belitung Island, the subnational political settlement has been unable to fully accommodate both the interests of different social forces in these regions, as well as those of the market, and the state at the centre and subnationally.

As we can see, getting the balance of power and authority right is challenging where Indonesia's strategic sectors are concerned, especially the extractive industries, as resource sectors have long been sites of struggles for authority, power, and influence, whether between the centre and the periphery or among subnational actors. Indonesia is not alone in facing such challenges given the lucrative stakes of land and resource access. Lessons from history elucidate the risks of extreme recentralization in these sectors, particularly if subnational regions receive few benefits. Contemporary lessons also illustrate the importance of creating inclusive subnational bargains and taking competing political economies into account to manage tensions in situations where there is greater segmented autonomy.

References

Abraham, Thomas Kutty (2018) 'Indonesia's Nationalism', https://www.bloomberg.com/quickt ake/indonesias-nationalism, accessed 3 December 2021.

Acciaioli, Greg (2001) 'Grounds of Conflict, Idioms of Harmony: Custom, Religion, and Nationalism in Violence Avoidance at the Lindu Plain, Central Sulawesi' 72 *Indonesia* 81–114.

Aspinall, Edward and Mada Sukmajati (eds) (2016). *Electoral Dynamics in Indonesia: Money Politics, Patronage and Clientelism at the Grassroots*. Singapore: NUS Press.

Baldwin, William L. (1983) *The World Tin Market: Political Pricing and Economic Competition*. Durham NC: Duke University Press.

Benda-Beckmann, Franz and Benda-Beckmann, Keebet (2013) *Political and Legal Transformations of an Indonesian Polity: The Nagari from Colonisation to Decentralization*. Cambridge: Cambridge University Press.

Brancati, Dawn (2006) 'Decentralization: Fuelling the Fire or Dampening the Flames of Ethnic Conflict and Secessionism?' 60 *International Organization* 651–685.

Cederman, Lars-Erik, Weidmann, Nils B., and Gleditsch, Kristian Skrede (2011). 'Horizontal Inequalities and Ethnonationalist Civil War: A Global Comparison' 105(3) *American Political Science Review* 478–495.

Dick, Howard (2008) 'The 2008 Shipping Law: Deregulation or Re-regulation' 44(93) *Bulletin of Indonesian Economic Studies* 383–406.

Diprose, Rachael (2002) 'Putra Daerah: Identity, Grievances and Collective Action', BA Honours thesis, University of New South Wales.

Diprose, Rachael (2009) Decentralization, Horizontal Inequalities and Conflict Management in Indonesia 8(1) *Ethnopolitics* 107–134.

Diprose, Rachael, Kurniawan, Nanang Indra, and Macdonald, Kate (2019a) 'Transnational Policy Influence and the Politics of Legitimation' 32 *Governance* 223–240, doi: 10.1111/gove.12370.

Diprose, Rachael, McRae, Dave, and Hadiz, Vedi R. (2019b) 'Two Decades of *Reformasi*: Indonesia and its Illiberal Turn' 49(5) *Journal of Contemporary Asia* 691–712, doi: 10.1080/00472336.2019.1637922.

Diprose, Rachael et al (2022). 'Regulating Sustainable Minerals in Electronics Supply Chains: Local Power Struggles and the 'Hidden costs' of Global Supply Chain Governance' 29(3) *Review of International Political Economy*, 792-817.

Diprose, Rachael and Azca, Muhammad Najib (2020) 'Conflict Management in Indonesia's Post-authoritarian Democracy: Resource Contestation, Power Dynamics and Brokerage' 20(1) *Conflict, Security and Development* 191-221.

Diprose, Rachael et al (2020). 'Women's Collective Action and the Village Law: How Women are Driving Change and Shaping Pathways for Gender-inclusive Development in Rural Indonesia', University of Melbourne, Universitas Gadjah Mada and MAMPU. www.mampu.bappenas.or.id and https://www.demisetara.org. doi: 10.46580/124326.

Eilenberg, Michael (2014) *At the Edges of States: Dynamics of State Formation in the Indonesian Borderlands*. Leiden: Brill.

Erman, Erwiza (2007). 'Deregulation of the Tin Trade and Creation of a Local Shadow State; A Bangka Case Study' in Schulte Nordholt, Henk, and van Klinken, Gerry (eds) *Renegotiating Boundaries: Local Politics in Post-Suharto Indonesia*. Leiden: KITLV Press. pp 177–202.

Erman, Erwiza (2008). 'Rethinking Legal and Illegal Economy: A Case Study of Tin Mining in Bangka Island' 37 *Southeast Asia: History and Culture* 91–111.

Goodhand, Jonathan (2008). 'War, Peace and the Places In Between: Why Borderlands are Central' in Pugh, Michael, Cooper, Neil, and Turner, Mandy (eds) *Whose Peace? Critical Perspectives on the Political Economy of Peacebuilding*. London: Palgrave. pp 225–244.

Harvey, Barbara S. (1977). *Permesta: Half a Rebellion*. Cornell Modern Indonesia Project, Southeast Asia Program, Ithaca, New York: Cornell University Press.

Hechter, Michael (2000) *Containing Nationalism*. Oxford: Oxford University Press.

Herriman, Nicholas (2012) *The Entangled State: Sorcery, State Control, and Violence in Indonesia*. New Haven: Yale University Southeast Asia Studies.

Horowitz, Donald L. (1991) *A Democratic South Africa? Constitutional Engineering in a Divided Society*. Berkeley: University of California Press.

Jarvis, Darryl S.L. (2012). 'The Regulatory State in Developing Countries: Can it Exist and Do We Want It? The Case of the Indonesian Power Sector' 42(3) *Journal of Contemporary Asia* 464–492.

Konsorsium Pembaruan Agraria (KPA) (2019). *Catatan Akhir Tahun 2018*. Jakarta: Konsorsium Pembaruan Agraria.

Konsorsium Pembaruan Agraria (KPA) (2020) *Catatan Akhir Tahun 2018*. Jakarta: Konsorsium Pembaruan Agraria.

Korf, Benedikt and Raeymaekers, Timothy (eds) (2013). *Violence on the Margins: States, Conflict and Borderlands*. New York: Palgrave Macmillan.

Kymlicka, Will (1998) 'Is Federalism a Viable Alternative to Secession?' in Lehning, Percy B. (ed) *Theories of Secession*. New York: Routledge, 121-160.

Legge, John David (1961) *Central Authority and Regional Autonomy in Indonesia: A Study in Local Administration, 1950-1960*. Ithaca: Cornell University Press.

Lijphart, Arend (1977) *Democracy in Plural Societies: A Comparative Exploration*. New Haven: Yale University Press.

Lubis, Anggi M. and Cahyafitri, Raras (2015) 'Timah to Start Mass Production of Rare Earth in Two Years', *Jakarta Post*, October 23, https://www.thejakartapost.com/news/2015/10/23/timah-start-mass-production-rare-earth-two-years.html, accessed 3 December 2021.

Lund, Christian (2006) 'Twilight Institutions: An Introduction' 37 *Development and Change* 673–684.

McCarthy, John F. (2004) 'Changing to Gray: Decentralization and the Emergence of Volatile Socio-legal Configurations in Central Kalimantan, Indonesia' 32(7) *World Development* 1199–1223.

McCarthy, John F. (2010) 'The Limits of Legality: State, Governance and Resource Control in Indonesia' in Aspinall, Edward Aspinall and van Klinken, Gerry (eds) *The State and Illegality in Indonesia*. Leiden: Brill, 87–106.

McCarthy, John F. and Cramb, R.A. (2009). 'Policy Narratives, Landholder Engagement, and Oil Palm Expansion on the Malaysian and Indonesian Frontiers' 175(2) *Geographical Journal* 112–123.

McCarthy, John F., Vel, Jacqueline A.C., and Afiff, Suraya (2012) 'Trajectories of Land Acquisition and Enclosure: Development Schemes, Virtual Land Grabs, and Free Acquisitions in Indonesia's Outer Islands' 39(2) *Journal of Peasant Studies* 521–549.

McCarthy, John F. and Robinson, Kathryn (eds) (2016). *Land and Development in Indonesia: Searching for the People's Sovereignty*. Singapore: ISEAS-Yusof Ishak Institute.

Meagher, Kate (2012). 'The Strength of Weak States? Non-State Security Forces and Hybrid Governance in Africa' 43(5) *Development and Change* 1073–1101.

MSC (2017) 'MSC: A Global Integrated Tin Mining and Smelting Group', http://www.msmelt.com/abt_hist.htm, accessed 3 December 2021.

Peluso, Nancy and Lund, Christian (eds) (2012) *New Frontiers of Land Control*. London: Taylor and Francis.

Pierskalla, Jan H. and Sacks, Audrey (2017) 'Unpacking the Effects of Decentralised Governance on Routine Violence: Lessons from Indonesia' 90 *World Development* 213–228.

Potter, Lesley and Badcock, Simon (2001). *The Effects of Indonesia's Decentralisation on Forest and Estate Crops in Riau Province: Case Studies of the Original Districts of Kampar and Indragiri Hulu*. Bogor, Indonesia: Centre for International Forestry Research.

PT Timah (2017) 2016 Annual Report. https://www.timah.com/v3/ina/laporan-laporan-tahunan/, accessed 3 December 2021.

PT Timah (2017) History of PT Timah. https://www.timah.com/v3/ina/tentang-kami-sejarah/, accessed 18 November 2020.

Republika (2017) Gubernur Babel Moratorium Izin Tambang Timah. *Republika*. http://nasional.republika.co.id/berita/nasional/daerah/17/08/19/ouxhrt384-gubernur-babel-moratorium-izin-tambang-timah, accessed 3 December 2021.

Resosudarmo, Ida Aju Pradnja (2004) 'Closer to People and Trees: Will Decentralisation Work for the People and the Forests of Indonesia? 16(1) *European Journal of Development Research* 110–132.

Riggs, Rebbeca Anne, et al (2016) 'Forest Tenure and Conflict in Indonesia: Contested Rights in Rempek Village, Lombok' 57 *Land Use Policy* 241–249, doi: 10.1016/j.landusepol.2016.06.002.

Robison, Richard and Hadiz, Vedi R. (2004). *Reorganising Power in Indonesia: The Politics of Oligarchy in the Age of Markets*. New York: Routledge.

Rosser, Andrew (2015) 'Law and the Realisation of Human Rights: Insights from Indonesia's Education Sector' 39(2) *Asian Studies Review* 194–212.

Rosser, Andrew (2017) *Litigating the Right to Health: Courts, Politics and Justice in Indonesia*. Honolulu: East West Center.

Said, Salim (2006) *Soeharto's Armed Forces: Problems of Civil Military Relations in Indonesia*. Jakarta: Pustaka Sinar Harapan.

Schiller, Arthur A. (1955) *The Formation of Federal Indonesia 1945-1949*. The Hague: W van Hoeve.

Selway, Joel and Templeman, Kharis (2012) 'The Myth of Consociationalism? Conflict Reduction in Divided Societies' 45(12) *Comparative Political Studies* 1542–1571.

Stewart, Frances (ed) (2008) *Horizontal Inequalities and Conflict: Understanding Group Violence in Multiethnic Societies, with a foreword by Kofi Annan*. London: Palgrave.

Suberu, Rotimi T. (2009). 'Federalism in Africa: The Nigerian Experience in Comparative Perspective' 8(1) *Ethnopolitics* 67–86.

Sutphin, David M., Subin, Andrew E., and Reed, Bruce L. (1992) *International Strategic Minerals Inventory Summary Report: Tin. U.S. Geological Survey Circular 930-J*. Collingdale: Dianne Publishing.

Tadjoeddin, Mohammad Zulfan (2014) *Explaining Collective Violence in Contemporary Indonesia*. Basingstoke: Palgrave Macmillan.

Taylor, Michael (2015,) 'Three Indonesian Firms Meet New Export Rules for Industry', *Jakarta Globe*, October 30, https://jakartaglobe.id/context/three-indonesian-tin-firms-meet-new-export-rules-industry/, accessed 3 December 2021.

Varshney, Ashutosh, Panggabean, Rizal and Tadjoeddin, Mohammad Zulfan (2004) 'Patterns of Collective Violence in Indonesia (1990–2003)'. Jakarta: United Nations Support Facility for Indonesian Recovery Working Papers No 04/03.

Winanti, Poppy S. and Diprose, Rachael (2020) 'Reordering the Extractive Political Settlement: Resource Nationalism, Domestic Ownership and Transnational Bargains in Indonesia' 7(4) *The Extractive Industries and Society* 1534–1546.

Zhang, Diane and McRae, Dave (2015) *Policy Diffusion: The Replication of Jamkesda and Bosda*. AIPD, http://www.ksi-indonesia.org/en/news/detail/aipd-publication---policy-diffusion-a-four-district-study-of-the-replication-of-health-insurance-jamkesda-and-bosda-in-indonesia.

6

Building Walls Rather than Bridges

The Judicial Commission vs the Supreme
Court in Indonesia

Dian Rositawati[1]

Introduction

The establishment of a judicial council or judicial commission is one example of an initiative to both strengthen independence and accountability of the judiciary, while also mitigating the effect of bureaucratization in the judiciary. Each judicial council is designed in slightly different ways with different powers, ranging from managing court personnel and resources to supervising and disciplining judges. Judicial councils are expected to break institutional bottlenecks and provide a better approach to judicial reform (Hammergren 2002). However, as demonstrated in various countries, the creation of the council is no guarantee that problems will be resolved. The issue of the relationship and tension between judicial councils and the courts is a reality around the world.

In Indonesia, the amendments to the 1945 Constitution established a Judicial Commission. This was a response to the introduction of a one roof system, which gave the Supreme Court the power to administer all the courts. The introduction of the Judicial Commission aimed to strengthen the accountability of the judiciary. In 2004, as soon as the Commission was established, the first conflict between the Commission and the judiciary emerged and has continued ever since. Prolonged conflict between these two institutions has led to the failure of the external function of supervision and accountability of the judges and the judiciary, but also impacts the public whose demands for judicial integrity go unmet.

This chapter aims to investigate the problems that hinder the success of the Judicial Commission as an accountability mechanism of the judiciary enshrined in the Constitution. This chapter traces the historical background of the establishment of the Commission, the formulation of the legal framework that determine the design of the Commission, and the functioning of the Commission by looking at the debates that took place in various conflicts between the Commission and the courts.

---

[1] This chapter draws on the author's PhD dissertation of Tilburg University, the Netherlands, entitled 'Judicial Governance in Indonesia: Judicial Independence under the One Roof System'.

Dian Rositawati, *Building Walls Rather than Bridges* In: *Constitutional Democracy in Indonesia*. Edited by: Melissa Crouch, Oxford University Press. © Dian Rositawati, 2023. DOI: 10.1093/oso/9780192870681.003.0006

The Role of a Judicial Commission

Different countries have come up with diverse approaches on how to strengthen the independence of the judiciary from government intervention while at the same time maintaining professionalism through better court management. One of the approaches is by establishing a judicial commission or judicial council. Transferring a considerable degree of judicial administration power from the government to the judicial councils has been one the preferred alternatives in countries around the world, beginning in 1946 in France and followed by more than 100 countries (Hammergren 2002). But ever since the introduction of the idea, there is increasing debate in terms of how far a judicial council can contribute to a more efficient and effective judiciary while at the same time serving to foster greater independence of the judiciary (Hammergren 2002). The establishment of a judicial council also brings about changes in the model of responsibility arrangement, which causes shifts in the constitutional balance of power (Voerman 1999).

The trend of establishing a judicial council is particularly widespread in European countries and Latin American countries as part of judicial reform movements. Each country places different functions in the council, but some of these councils are responsible for handling supportive functions of the judiciary including, but not limited to, court budget, selection, personnel management, supervision, training, and education. Based on research of various judicial councils in the Europe, Wim Voerman distinguishes two models of judicial councils: the Southern European model and the North European model. The Southern European councils are mostly established by the constitution and have typical functions with regards to the appointment and promotion, training and disciplinary powers of court members, either by giving advice or by exercising the power itself (Voerman 2003). The North European councils possess different characteristics. Rather than focusing on the career of judges, this latter model focuses on court administration, including case management, promotion of legal uniformity, court budgeting and planning, and the distribution and allocation of resources, which aim to enhance the efficiency and effectiveness of the judicial organization (Voerman 2003). The Southern European councils are to be found in Italy, Spain, France, and Belgium, whereas the Northern European councils are established in Sweden, Ireland, Netherlands, and Denmark (Voerman 2003).

Although the models provided by Voerman are based on his research of the judicial councils in Europe, these two models represent general characteristics of judicial councils around the world. However, Voerman also suggests that every council is unique because it is the product of the diverging political and cultural development in each legal system that is rooted in the historical and social context within each country (Voerman 2003).

The Establishment of the Judicial Commission in Indonesia

A Brief History

The idea of the judicial council or commission in Indonesia evolved since it was first introduced. In 1968, the initial form of the council, called the Council of Judge's

Research and Consideration (*Majelis Penelitian dan Pertimbangan Hakim*, MPPH), was proposed during the drafting of a law on judicial power. The draft law established a council that had responsibilities for a broad range of judicial management aspects including the selection, transfer, and promotion, and the supervision of ethics and conduct of judges.[2] However the MPPH was proposed not as an 'independent commission' but as a consultative forum for the government and the judiciary, to decide matters related to judicial administration. Seno Adji, the chief justice at the time, proposed that the MPPH should be composed of the chief justice, the minister of justice, senior justices, representatives of the Indonesian Judges Association (IKAHI), and a representative of the advocates association.[3] Along with the proposal from the Supreme Court, parliament also proposed that there should be a representative from the legislature and public prosecutors (Yusuf 2008: 214–216). Despite the debate, this proposal of the MPPH as envisaged by the Bill was withdrawn and the MPPH was not mentioned in Law 14/1970 (Pompe 2005: 110).

In 1998, the discussion on the importance of a judicial commission re-appeared during the preparation to introduce the one roof system, which transferred the authority over court administration from the executive to the Supreme Court. In 1999, a similar design was proposed by the Integrated Team of the Government[4] during the preparation of the one roof system and was referred to as the Judges Honorary Board (*Dewan Kehormatan Hakim*, DKH). According to the team, the DKH should be given the function of providing binding recommendations to the Supreme Court on selection, transfer, and promotion of judges, and to supervise quality, integrity, conduct, and ethics of judges (Kantor Menteri Negara 1999: 46). The proposal for the MPPH and the separate proposal for the DKH resembled the Southern European commission model, which has a distinctive function related to appointment, transfer, and disciplinary power (Voerman 2003). The suggested composition of the proposed DKH was more mixed compared to the proposed MPPH. The DKH would have included active judges, practitioners, academics, and other elements (Kantor Menteri Negara 1999: 46), while the previously proposed MPPH was dominated by the representatives of the Supreme Court and the Justice Department.

Since the idea of the commission was first introduced in 1968, from discussions on the bill on judiciary power in the 1970s to the preparation of the one roof system thirty years later in 1998, the motive for the introduction of a Judicial Commission was always to promote accountability and protect the integrity of judges. The Integrated Team suggested the establishment of an independent body, a Judicial Commission, that should respond to the issues of an additional workload for the Supreme Court and

---

[2] Article 32(1) of Bill of Law 14/1970: The MPPH shall consider and make final decision on advice or recommendations pertaining to the appointment, advancement, transfer, dismissal, and official measures/sanction of judges, which will be advanced by both the chairman of the Supreme Court and the Minister of Justice.

[3] Official statement of the Government on the discussion of the Bill on Judicial Power and Bill on the Arrangement, Power and Procedural Law of the Supreme Court, during the plenary session of Parliament (DPR-GR 1971: 38–39).

[4] The integrated team was formed through Presidential Decree 21/1999 and revised by Presidential Decree 42/1999 on the Integrated Team to Assess the Implementation of the MPR Decree 42/1999 concerning the Strict Separation of Judicial Functions from the Executive. The members of the team were made up of some of the best lawyers, professors, and justices in Indonesia at that time.

the potential abuse of power by the Supreme Court (Nasution 1999). This proposal derived from the realization that the workload of the Supreme Court would significantly increase after the introduction of the one roof system. Therefore they suggest the establishment of an Honorary Board as a check and balance mechanism to the Supreme Court and to reduce the burden of the Supreme Court particularly in the management and oversight of judges, including supervision, recommendations for promotion and transfer of judges, as well as the development and enforcement of a code of conduct for judges (Kantor Menteri Negara 1999: 48, 51).

Following the proposal of the Team, in 1999, the idea was included in the discussion to amend the Law on Judicial Power. The Elucidation of Law 35/1999 mentioned the term 'the Honorary Board of Judges' which later became the foundation of the establishment of the Judicial Commission. The general Elucidation of the law states the importance of establishing the Honorary Board of Judges to create checks and balances, with the tasks of supervising the conduct of judges and drafting a code of ethics (code of conduct) for the judges, as well as providing recommendations on recruitment, promotion, and transfer of judges.[5]

Although the principal characteristic of the commission was the same for the MPPH and DKH, the final design agreed upon during the amendment of the 1945 Constitution was slightly different. The discussion during the constitutional amendment process indicated that the legislature viewed the judiciary from a legal traditional perspective. The judiciary is understood as a professional organization where the judge is the centre of attention (Fix-Fierro 2003), rather than understanding courts as complex organizations in which the issue of management is also central (Heydebrand 1977; Mohr 1976). Member of the House of Representatives, Hamdan Zoelva, a representative of the Crescent Star political party (*Fraksi Partai Bulan Bintang*, FPBB) and Zein Badjeber, of the United Development political party (*Fraksi Partai Persatuan Pembangunan*, FPPP), argued for the importance of an honorary board of judges, the forerunner of the Judicial Commission in Indonesia (Mahkamah Konstitusi 2010: 65–66):

> The performance of the Supreme Court lies not in the Supreme Court, but in their judges. Therefore, it is necessary to establish an honorary board of judges and to incorporate it in the Constitution, which constitutes from the different elements, including judges, lawyers, as well as among those who actually have high integrity. They are the one who will review the performance of a judge, and recommend the dismissal of a judge.[6]

During the discussion on the Amendment of the 1945 Constitution, the Supreme Court also supported the need to establish the Honorary Council or Judicial Committee to conduct external supervision on the ethics and conduct of judges (Mahkamah Konstitusi 2010: 86–90). In 2003, the Supreme Court drafted the academic draft that would accompany the law and designed the powers and authority of

---

[5] General Elucidation, Law 35/1999.
[6] Hamdan Zoelva and Zein Badjeber, prominent members of the House of Representatives, shared the same arguments (Mahkamah Konstitusi 2010: 65, 66, 70).

the Judicial Commission.[7] This academic draft mentions concerns about the Supreme Court's growing judicial power; that the court was considered not prepared to conduct all of its duties; and that a Judicial Commission was therefore needed (Mahkamah Agung Republik Indonesia 2004: 13–14).

Composition and Power of the Judicial Commission

In 2001, the Judicial Commission was introduced in the Third Amendment of the 1945 Constitution, which stipulates that the Commission should be independent and given the authority to select justices of the Supreme Court and to maintain and enforce the honour, dignity, and the conduct of judges. The Constitution mandated that the institution should be independent. Although the principal characteristic of the commission remained the same with MPPH and DKH, the final design agreed upon during the Amendment of the 1945 Constitution was slightly different. According to Article 24B of the Third Amendment of the 1945 Constitution: 'The Judicial Commission is independent and has the authority to propose the appointment of justices and other authority in order to maintain and uphold the honour, integrity and behaviour of judges.'

The reference to this body as an independent commission means that there are no representatives of the Supreme Court sitting in the Commission. The Commission is comprised of seven commissioners according to Law 22/2004 on Judicial Commission. In the discussion on the Bill of Judicial Commission most of the members of parliament, as well as public opinion, supported the argument that the membership of judges would be contrary to the principle of independence and might interfere with the objectivity of the commission in the execution of its duties (Sekretariat Jenderal Komisi Yudisial 2013: 86–90, 103–104). Furthermore there was an intention to balance the power of the judiciary by establishing a commission comprised of representatives of different stakeholders outside the judiciary (Sekretariat Jenderal Komisi Yudisial 2013: 97). Based on these considerations, according to Law 22/2004, the composition of the Judicial Commission comprises former judges, legal practitioners, law academics, and society members.[8] The composition of all non-judicial members, and a minority of former judges, was intended to secure its neutrality against the judiciary.

Article 24B(1) of the Third Amendment of the 1945 Constitution also mentions that '… the other authority in order to maintain and uphold the honour, nobility and behaviour of judges'. However the translation of the 'other authority' in Law 22/2004 was narrower than the authority of the DKH, which covers a broad range of judicial management aspects including selection, supervision, transfer, and promotion, although it should be noted the proposed design of the DKH involved members of the judiciary. The primary task of the Commission according to Law 22/2004 is to conduct supervision over judges, and later the amendment of the law added the authority to conduct

---

[7] This document was published by the Mahkamah Agung Republik Indonesia, entitled 'Academic Draft and Bill on Judicial Commission'.

[8] Article 6(3) of Law 22/2004.

selection of judges.[9] The authority of supervision attributed to the Commission by the law is limited to providing recommendations on a disciplinary sanction to the Supreme Court. The commission can only impose one kind of sanction that is binding in nature, namely, a written reprimand. The other two forms of sanction that are more serious—'suspension' and 'termination'—are to be decided by the Supreme Court based on the recommendation of the Commission.

In conducting the supervisory function, the law provides that the role of the Commission is as an external supervisor, while the Supreme Court has the power to do internal supervision (Art 32A(1) and (2), Law 3/2009). The terms of internal and external supervision are not clearly defined in the law. The term 'internal supervision' refers to the supervisory function conducted by a unit of the judiciary or the Supreme Court, while the term 'external supervision' refers to the supervisory function conducted by an agency outside the Supreme Court or the Judicial Commission. According to Law 18/2011, the Judicial Commission together with the Supreme Court is also responsible for the selection of judge candidates. Again, there are overlapping functions between these two institutions, which require the two institutions to work together. The dynamic relationship between the Supreme Court and the Judicial Commission will be discussed in the next section.

Conflicts Between the Judicial Commission and the Supreme Court

In August 2005, the Judicial Commission was established, and its commissioners were elected. Soon after this, in December, a conflict between the Commission and the Supreme Court arose. In the middle of tension between the Anti-Corruption Commission and the Supreme Court in a suspect corruption case involving Probosutedjo (the half brother of former President Soeharto), the new commission intervened by investigating some judges and court staff. Chief Justice Bagir Manan ignored a summons from the Judicial Commission to undergo questioning regarding his alleged involvement in this case.[10]

In January 2006, the Judicial Commission intended to evaluate the performance of all forty-nine Supreme Court's justices and remove those found to be crooked or lacking integrity, in a move supported by President Yudhoyono. During a meeting with President Yudhoyono, the Commission proposed that the president issue a Government Regulation in Lieu of Law (known as 'perpu') to give a legal basis for the evaluation of Supreme Court justices. However, this proposed plan faced strong resistance from the justices of the Supreme Court. 'I doubt the replacement regulations will go ahead', said Supreme Court Chief Justice Bagir Manan.[11] The Indonesian Judges Association (*Ikatan Hakim Indonesia*, IKAHI) also opposed the Commission's

---

[9] Article 14A of Law 49/2009; Art 13A of Law 50/2009; Art 14A of Law 51/2009.

[10] Bagir Manan was questioned in relation to a case involving the former President Soeharto's half-brother, Probosutedjo. KPK arrested Probosutedjo's lawyer and retired judge Harini Wiyoso who were caught red-handed carrying cash that was intended for Bagir Manan.

[11] *Tempo Magazine* 21/VI/24–30 January 2005.

proposal and claimed that the move was an insult to the Supreme Court and legislature because the current justices were selected by the legislature (Detik.com 2006). The legislature refused the proposal because it was considered against the law and might trigger conflict between state institutions. It asked the Commission to focus on the selection of new candidate judges of the Supreme Court.

In March 2006, the conflict intensified when the Judicial Commission compiled a list of thirteen 'problematic justices' (*hakim bermasalah*) and the list was published by the press. The Supreme Court claimed that the Commission had recklessly compiled the list without carrying out any formal investigations. The judges of the Supreme Court responded defensively by reporting the commissioners to the police. Justices Artidjo Alkostar and Harifin A Tumpa and several other justices had also prepared to file a case to the police.[12]

The Judicial Commission's decision to publish this list was followed by more actions by the Commission, and the relationship between these institutions deteriorated. Up until 2020, there have been three Commissioners—from 2005 to 2010, 2010 to 2015, and 2015 to 2020.[13] Conflicts between the Judicial Commission and Supreme Court have arisen in every generation of Commissioners. As explained earlier, this conflict was also caused by overlapping authority and differences in interpreting and exercising this authority, which will be explained in the sections below.

Conflict in the Supervision of Judges

In the area of supervision, the Supreme Court and the Judicial Commission have different interpretations on the scope of supervision authority. The Judicial Commission's first case was related to a court decision concerning a dispute over the mayoral election in Depok, West Java. Although the Supreme Court overruled the decision, the Judicial Commission then carried out its own investigation and determined that the West Java High Court was mistaken in imposing a sentence in its court decision. The Judicial Commission in its early cases seems to believe that its authority to supervise judges was not limited only to their behaviour but also to the content of their judicial decisions. The Supreme Court argues that what is considered as supervision of ethics and conduct does not include supervision over judicial decisions. However, the Judicial Commission believes that examining judicial decisions is part of investigating the misconduct of a judge. This difference of view has triggered conflict between these institutions. Later on, the Commission corrected its move in reviewing court decisions by indicating that a court decision is only an 'entrance' to investigate allegations of a judge's misconduct. But in practice it is difficult to distinguish whether the

---

[12] Justice Harifin A Tumpa (who later became chief justice and replaced Bagir Manan) and several other justices whose names were also included in the list, had also prepared to file a case to the police.

[13] There have been three generations of Commissioners, each of which lasted for five years. The first generation of Commissioners was led by Busyro Muqqodas and lasted from 2005 to 2010; the second generation lasted from 2010 to 2015 led, among others, by Suparman Marzuki; and the third generation lasted from 2015 to 2020 led, among others, by Jaja Ahmad Jayus.

examination of a court decision was carried out as a pre-examination of misconduct or to assess the substance of the decision itself.

In 2006, thirty-one justices of the Supreme Court applied to the Constitutional Court for judicial review of several articles in Law 22/2004 on the Judicial Commission. Upon that submission, the Constitutional Court decided that the provisions of the law that regulates the supervision function had created inconsistency in the interpretation of the object of supervision. The Constitutional Court further asserted that the absence of a code of conduct agreed to by the Supreme Court and the Judicial Commission had resulted in improper practice when the Judicial Commission investigated indications of judicial misconduct through evaluating their decisions.[14] Therefore, the Court concluded, the law needed to be amended.[15] This decision not only nullified the supervisory power of the Judicial Commission but also created a temporary vacuum over the external supervision function for five years until the enactment of Law 18/2011 to amend the Law 22/2004. To respond to the decision of the Constitutional Court, in 2009, the amendment of the Law on the Judiciary clearly mentions that the implementation of the supervisory task by the Judicial Commission and the Supreme Court should not influence the independence of the judge in examining and deciding cases.[16]

In an effort to bridge communication and release tension between these two institutions, the Judicial Commission and the Supreme Court enacted regulations to implement its joint authority in the areas of supervision and also selection of judges.[17] Despite the enactment of these regulations, some judges still raised concerns that violations involving unprofessional conduct were often used by the Judicial Commission to recommend disciplinary sanctions for a judge in relation to deciding cases.[18] While the Supreme Court is one of the institutions that enacted this regulation, based on its power for judicial review of regulation under law, it can also declare the regulation null and void. In August 2011, the Supreme Court responded to a submission requesting a judicial review of the Joint Regulation on the Enforcement of the Code of Ethics and Code of Conduct of Judges.[19] The Supreme Court in its decision revoked eight points of the code of conduct of judges related to supervision of the professional aspects of

---

[14] Decision 005/PUU-IV/2006, p 187.

[15] In 2006, the Judicial Commission sought to secure 're-selection' of the entire Supreme Court justices, who viewed this idea as an attempt at collective dismissal. In response, thirty justices, including members of the leadership, filed a judicial review action before the Supreme Court seeking to severely restrict the powers of the Judicial Commission.

[16] Article 41 and Elucidation of Law 28/2009.

[17] Joint Regulation Chief Justice of the Supreme Court and Head of the Judicial Commission 047/KMA/SKB/IV/2009 and 02/SKB/P.KY/IV/2009 on the Guideline of the Enforcement of Code of Ethics and Code of Conduct of Judges; 01/PB/MA/IX/2012 and 01/PB/P.KY/09/2012 on Selection of Judges; 03/PB/MA/IX/2012 and 03/PB/P.KY/09/2012 on Joint Investigation; 04/PB/MA/IX/2012 and 04/PB/P.KY/09/2012 on Judges Honorary Board.

[18] Personal communications with a Supreme Court justice in April 2016 and a high court judge in October 2018.

[19] The judicial review was requested by a group of advocates, namely, Henry P Panggabean, Humala Simanjuntak, Lintong Siahaan, and Sarmanto Tambunan. Pangabean is a former justice of the Supreme Court. The Judicial Commission questioned the legal standing of the applicants because they were deemed not to have a direct interest in the regulation. However, the Supreme Court accepted the submission.

judges in deciding cases.[20] The decision of the Supreme Court clearly supported the interests of judges and the Supreme Court itself.

Conflict in the Selection of Judges

Conflicts between the Commission and the Supreme Court have arisen not only over the supervisory function but also over the authority to jointly conduct the selection of judicial candidates. This power to select judicial candidates is not regulated in the Judicial Commission Law 22/2004 and was only added later in Law 8/2004 on the Amendment of Law on the General Court, Law 3/2006 on the Amendment of Law on the Islamic Court, and Law 9/2004 on the Amendment of Law on the Administrative Court. Unfortunately, these laws do not clarify the powers shared by these two institutions. The Law on the General Court, for example, only mentions that: 'The selection process for the appointment of district court judges is carried out *jointly* by the Supreme Court and the Judicial Commission'[21] (emphasis added). A similar provision also appears in the amendment of law on the Islamic Court and the Administrative Court mentioned above.

In 2010, the unclear division of authority became an issue in relation to the selection of judges. The Supreme Court had undertaken a process of appointing new judges. One of the Commissioners claimed that the outcome of the selection process was unconstitutional because it did not include the Judicial Commission.[22] Again, following the conflict between these two institutions, in 2015 the IKAHI submitted a judicial review petition to the Constitutional Court. In contrast to the previous Constitutional Court's ruling which overturned the article on supervision but at the same time requested amendment of the law in relation to the supervision mechanism, the Constitutional Court nullified the authority of the Judicial Commission to select candidate judges on the grounds that this provision interferes with the independence of judges because it might cause the Supreme Court to become dependent on the Commission.[23] This is an unwarranted consideration because involvement of other institutions outside the judiciary in the selection of judges is a common process in other countries and such a mechanism does not necessarily influence judicial independence.

---

[20] Supreme Court Decision 36 P/HUM/2011. The panel of judges was led by Justice Paulus Effendi and the members of the panel included Justice Ahmad Sukardja, Justice Rehngena Purba, Justice Takdir Rahmadi, and Justice Supandi.

[21] Article 14A of Law 49/2009.

[22] The Supreme Court stated that it had tried to involve the Commission in the selection process, and initial discussions had been conducted, but it was not properly followed up before the commissioners' term of office ended and they were replaced by new commissioners. Then, a year after the selection, the Judicial Commission stated that the 2010 selection result was unconstitutional because the Supreme Court did not involve the Commission.

[23] Decision 43/PUU-XIII/2015.

Conflict in the Selection of Supreme Court Justices

One of the most significant powers of the Judicial Commission that is clearly stated in Article 24A(3) of the Third Amendment of the 1945 Constitution is to select justices of the Supreme Court. Although the wording in the Constitution and legal frameworks are clear on this matter, conflict in its implementation still arose. There are at least two issues in the selection of Supreme Court justice: first is the inter-branch relationship between the Supreme Court and the legislature, as well as with the Judicial Commission; and the second one is on the composition and requirement of career and non-career judicial candidates (see generally Crouch 2019).

In 2007, the Commission conducted the first selection of Supreme Court justices. Law 22/2004 on the Judicial Commission and Law 3/2009 on the Supreme Court requires the Commission to provide three times the number of available vacancies. In practice, the Commission has difficulty being able to meet the number of candidates to submit to the legislature. Almost every year, from 2006 to 2012, the Judicial Commission had never been able to meet the requirement that the number of candidates be three times the number of vacancies in a single selection process (Komisi Yudisial 2012). Furthermore the legislature often returned the list of candidates already submitted by the Judicial Commission and asked the Commission to repeat the selection process and add more candidates to meet the number of vacancies in the Supreme Court.

In this process there are at least two sources of conflict with the Supreme Court. First, there were many career judges who failed in the nomination process in the Judicial Commission and this caused dissatisfaction among the judges. Second, the emergence of dissatisfaction among several justices mostly came from career backgrounds, due to the lack of experience and legal knowledge in examining cases from several non-career judges chosen by the Judicial Commission. Furthermore, the appointment of Gayus Lumbun as justice, despite his political party background,[24] also raised concerns for several justices and Supreme Court leaders over the risk of politicization of the Supreme Court.[25] The source of the conflict with the legislature came from, among others, the frequent return of the candidate list from the legislature to the Commission on the grounds that the number of candidates did not meet the quota. In addition, the decision-making process in the legislature through the 're-selection' process that repeats the stages carried out by the Judicial Commission is also considered to reflect distrust of the Judicial Commission selection results.

In 2012, three law faculties with legal counsel from representatives of various legal non-governmental organizations (NGOs) closely connected with the Judicial Commission[26] filed a lawsuit for judicial review of the Law on the Supreme Court and the Law on Judicial Power which regulates the selection of justices. The Constitutional

---

[24] Gayus Lumbun was a former Member of Parliament from the Indonesian Democratic Party of Struggle (*Partai Demokrasi Indonesia Perjuangan*, PDIP).

[25] Personal interview with former Supreme Court's leadership and justices.

[26] The NGOs that represented the lawsuits include, among others, the Indonesia Corruption Watch (ICW), Indonesia Legal Roundtable (ILR), Jakarta Legal Aid (LBH Jakarta), Indonesia Legal Aid Foundation (YLBHI), and Transparency International Indonesia (TII).

Court ruled that the meaning of 'election' in Article 8(2)–(4) concerning the Supreme Court shall be amended or should be read with the meaning of 'approval'. In the decision, the Constitutional Court also stated that the requirement to have three candidate justices for each position was no longer binding, and the Commission shall submit one candidate for one vacant position. The Constitutional Court decision changes the role of the legislature from selecting candidates to approving (or disapproving) one candidate. Although the Judicial Commission welcomed this ruling, it also invited dissatisfaction on members of parliament (Detik 2017) and had an unexpected impact on the selection of the Supreme Court justices. Although most of the time parliament approves the majority of the candidates submitted by the Judicial Commission, there were times when parliament rejected all or almost all of the names on the candidate list.[27]

In 2016, the tension between career and non-career justices culminated when two judges[28] filed a judicial review on Law 3/2009 on the Supreme Court to the Constitutional Court on the requirement for a non-career candidate to apply as a justice of the Supreme Court. The Constitutional Court ruled that a candidate of Supreme Court justice from the non-career path only fulfils the requirements if he or she has legal expertise in a particular field.[29] Furthermore, the Constitutional Court held that the needs of justices from the non-career path shall be determined based on the needs of the Supreme Court. The Constitutional Court's decision basically returned to the situation under Supreme Court Law 14/1985, where non-career judges were only recruited based on need as determined by the Supreme Court. The Constitutional Court's decision triggered concerns from the Judicial Commission who argued that this arrangement would limit the opportunities of judicial candidates from non-career paths, and the risk that the Supreme Court would only prioritize judges from career paths. However, after 2000, the selection of the Supreme Court justices in fact produced sixteen justices of which a majority (nine) were non-career judges. The selection was based on the provisions of Law 14/1985, which stated that the selection of Supreme Court justices is based on a career system and is a closed system, but in certain cases it is also possible to appoint justices from non-career backgrounds.

Conflict in the Power of Court Administration

The Judicial Commission has pushed for an extended role in court administration and management. This effort to extend the scope of its authority is derived from the unclear interpretation of Article 24B of the Constitution which states '... other authority in order to maintain and uphold the honour, dignity and behaviour of judges'. From 2010 to 2015, the second generation of commissioners advocated for an additional role in court budgeting by interpreting the mandate of the Constitution 'to uphold the

---

[27] According to the Judicial Commission Annual Reports from 2012 to 2019, parliament approved three out of five candidates in 2019, while in 2018 they approved two out of five candidates, and in 2019 they rejected all the candidates on the list.

[28] The petition was submitted by Binsar Gultom, a judge from Central Jakarta District Court, and Lilik Mulyadi, a high court judge from Medan High Court.

[29] Constitutional Court Decision No 53/PUU-XIV/2016.

dignity of judges' to include the guarantee of budget sufficiency for judges. The former commissioner of the Judicial Commission interprets 'other authority' as the authority in the area of judge administration, including in the transfer and promotion system.[30] From 2015 to 2020, the third generation of commissioners proposed the concept of 'shared responsibility' as a criticism of the autonomy of the Supreme Court under the one roof system. There was debate over the bill on the judiciary. In 2016, the Judicial Commission even published their own version of the bill's Academic Draft as a way of expressing their views on this matter. The Commission proposed that the judges' administrative authority ought to be shared with the Judicial Commission, including the selection of judges, transfer, and promotion, as well as the supervision and disciplinary functions. The Supreme Court, on the other hand, saw this as an attack on the idea of the one roof system. In reaction to the aspirations of the Judicial Commission with regard to the improvement of judicial administration, the Supreme Court tends to be defensive and reluctant to engage in discussion, for example by repeating the phrase '*satu atap harga mati*' or 'one roof system or die'. This has aggravated the situation between the two institutions and efforts to improve the justice administration system.

An Explanation for the Conflict

The idea of having a judicial commission was added to the Constitution as a response to legal practitioners and civil society who cautioned against giving courts such seemingly boundless independence from the executive. Law 35/1999, which officially introduced the one roof system, mentions in its Elucidation the need to strengthen checks and balances of the judiciary by the introduction of the Judges Honorary Board, later referred to as the Judicial Commission. However, in practice the Judicial Commission has not been able to achieve the goal of its establishment. A former commissioner and an active commissioner also acknowledge the inability of the Commission to achieve its goals for several reasons including, among others, the limited scope of authority of the Commission.[31]

This chapter has identified several problems that hindered the success of the Judicial Commission as an accountability mechanism for the one roof system: first is the organizational design problem; second is the composition of the commissioners; third is the difference in the interpretation of the authority of the Commission; and last is the more technical aspect related to the practice of communication between the Commission and the Court.

The first problem is the design of the Judicial Commission. The issues of judicial corruption, the integrity of judges, and degrading public trust towards the judiciary dominated the debate over the introduction of the one roof system that gave the courts independence from the executive. Furthermore, the focus of judicial reform at the time was more on the issue of institutional independence by liberating the judiciary

---

[30] Interview with former Commissioner and Head of the Judicial Commission, 15 January 2019.
[31] Interviews with former Head and Commissioner of the Judicial Commission, 15 January 2019 and the current Commissioner of the Judicial Commission, 18 May 2018.

from the intervention of the executive. These considerations influenced the creation and introduction of the Judicial Commission. However, the issue that was overlooked in the one roof system was organizational questions arising as a consequence of the transfer of court administration powers from the executive, including judicial administration, resources, and budget.

The design of the Judicial Commission was influenced by classic views, which perceived the judicial organization as an organization of judges and judges as the centre of attention (Fix-Fierro 2003). In consequence, the performance of the Supreme Court lies with the judges, rather than with Supreme Court itself, and therefore an honorary board of judges (later named the Judicial Commission) is necessary (Mahkamah Konstitusi 2010: 65–66). The perspective of the centrality of judges in court organization influenced the design of the authority of the Judicial Commission, which is also focused on the judges, namely the supervision and the selection of judges. Problems in the original design of the Judicial Commission are reflected in the constitutional wording and the implementing law, which is poorly conceived and drafted. These problems concern the scope of authority, the unclear scope of jurisdiction caused by the overlapping authority with the Supreme Court, and the advisory powers of the Judicial Commission.

The second issue is related to the characteristic of the Judicial Commission as an independent organization, which is reflected in the composition of its commissioners. The aim was to create a neutral commission against the judiciary. But it has not been without problems. The pool of the Commission consists of non-judicial members, which weakens its relationship with the Supreme Court. As mentioned earlier, the composition of the Judicial Commission comprises former judges, legal practitioners, law academics, and society members.[32] Based on the conflicts that happened between the Commission and the Supreme Court, it seems that the presence of former judges as part of the Commission's members have not been able to bridge the communication gap and resolve the conflict between these institutions. Furthermore, not only is trust more difficult to build between the Court and the Commission, but there is also relatively limited knowledge and experience in the Judicial Commission of how to work best with the Supreme Court.

The third issue is the scope of authority of the Judicial Commission. Conflicts between the Commission and the Supreme Court have occurred in every generation of commissioners. The primary source of conflict arises from the authority of the Commission, whether from the interpretation of the existing authority or from the attempt of the Commission to broaden its authority. The debate over authority is due to different interpretations of the provision in the Constitution that states '… other authority in order to maintain and uphold the honour, dignity and behaviour of judges' (Art 24(b)). Furthermore, in the selection of judges and supervision, the law requires that it should be carried out 'jointly'[33] and 'in coordination'[34] by the Supreme Court and the Judicial Commission. But the law does not regulate and explain the meaning of the word 'jointly' and 'in coordination' at a practical level when there is overlapping

---

[32] Article 6(3) of Law 22/2004.
[33] Article 14A(2) of Law 49/2009; Art 13A(2) of Law 50/2009.
[34] Article 13C(1) of Law 49/2009; Art 12C(1) of Law 50/2009; Art 13C(1) of Law 51/2009.

authority. And lastly the laws do not provide a mechanism for resolving disagreements (if any) between these two institutions.

While the Judicial Commission has continuously sought to expand its authority, the Supreme Court has protectively guarded its powers under the one roof system and resisted efforts to ensure it is more accountable. The tensions and conflicts over the role and authority of the Judicial Commission hinder the Commission from being able to perform as an accountability mechanism of the one roof system. Furthermore, the long and unresolved tension between these two institutions has eroded the authority of the Commission.

The fourth issue is related to the communication practice between these two institutions, which exacerbated the conflicts. The problems of the original design and the debates over authority have affected the function of the Judicial Commission and its relationship with the Supreme Court. The Judicial Commission is a necessary counterweight to the enormous powers and autonomy of the judiciary after the introduction of the one roof system. Its role, which demands diplomatic subtlety, is hard to realize in an environment marked with high expectations (Pompe 2011). Fourteen years after its establishment, the Commission has not yet been able to reconcile its role and has remained in doubt about its position and authority. The Judicial Commission sometimes presents itself as the partner of the judiciary, but has often stood on the opposing side and pointed out its failures.

Some judges do agree that the role of the Judicial Commission in the supervision of judges' conduct is important as a balance to the internal supervision function of the Supreme Court, which is more subjective and influenced by the esprit de corps.[35] However, in conducting this function the Commission has a hard time balancing its repressive instincts while at the same time managing its image as a partner to the judiciary (Pompe 2011). Moreover, the Commission's desire to participate in eradicating corruption and being tough on corruption in the judiciary has received some support from the public but has also received criticism from judges and increased their distrust of the Commission. This has resulted in many of the Commission's recommendations not being taken seriously by the Supreme Court. On the one hand, the Judicial Commission revealed that the Supreme Court followed up only 15 per cent of its recommendations.[36] But on the other hand, the Supreme Court argued that the recommendations submitted by the Commission did not meet the evidence standards or were related to the judicial technical aspects (*aspek teknis yudisial*) of the Court's decision and therefore could not be followed up (Tirto.id 2019).

---

[35] Interview with a High Court Judge, 9 July 2018; Interview with a former parliament member 1999–2004, 7 April 2016.

[36] Judicial Commission's Official Release 06/Siaran Pers/AL/LI.04.01/3/2019 entitled 'Hanya 15 Persen Rekomendasi Sanksi KY Ditindaklanjuti MA pada 2016-2018', 1 March 2019, https://www.komisiyudis ial.go.id/frontend/pers_release_detail/103/hanya-persen-rekomendasi-sanksi-ky-yang-ditindaklanj uti-ma-pada.

Conclusion

The Judicial Commission has not yet been able to achieve the goal for which it was established, namely upholding the integrity of judges. The Commission desperately needs to reflect on its approach to conducting the supervision of judges and how best to manage the role it currently has. From the perspective of internal supervision, the centralized supervision mechanism of the Supreme Court does not have the capacity to supervise all courts and judges. This is not to mention the challenges of effective internal supervision created by problems of internal independence and individual independence as affected by the exercise of the centralized administrative power of the Supreme Court.

To be able to carry out its accountability function, the Judicial Commission as an institution supporting the function of the judiciary is required to play a constructive role as a partner of the Supreme Court. However, to carry out this kind of role the Judicial Commission needs to provide constructive support behind the scenes, where it proactively cooperates with the Supreme Court to improve the integrity and professionalism of judges while at the same time maintaining public trust in the judiciary.

From the wider perspective of the existence of the Judicial Commission as an accountability mechanism, the Judicial Commission has not been able to carry out its function effectively. This is caused by the inappropriate design of the Commission, resulting in a gap between the needs of the one roof system and the existing design of the Commission. Furthermore, the legal framework is also problematic, and the poor drafting created uncertainty as to how the Judicial Commission should position itself before the judiciary. This situation has only worsened with the shrinking authority of the Commission. Both problems, in turn, led to the erosion of trust between the Judicial Commission and the Supreme Court reflected in the continuing rivalry and conflict between these two institutions. However, this situation should not be interpreted as giving rise to the immediate need to expand the authority of Judicial Commission. Rather, this situation should be a reason to reflect on the design of the organization in relation to its political context.

Just like many other judicial councils or judicial commission in the world, Indonesia's Judicial Commission has also faced challenges. The introduction of the Judicial Commission was not a solution on its own. It is not a guarantee that the problem of judicial accountability and integrity will be solved. The discussion on how to strengthen judicial integrity and judicial accountability must not only focus on the issue of authority but should also discuss institutional problems and procedures and clarify the rule of the games between these two institutions. Hammergren mentioned that a council's success depends on factors such as understanding the problems to be resolved, the selection of appropriate solutions, and skill in implementing change. The Indonesian experience shows us both the potential and the limitations of this institution.

References

Bell, John (2006) *Judiciaries within Europe: A Comparative Review*. Cambridge: Cambridge University Press.

Crouch, Melissa (2019) 'The Judicial Reform Landscape in Indonesia: Innovation, Specialisation and the Legacy of Dan S Lev' in Melissa Crouch (ed) *The Politics of Court Reform: Judicial Change and Legal Culture in Indonesia*. Cambridge: Cambridge University Press. pp 1–32.

Detik.com (2017) 'Putusan MK tentang Seleksi Hakim Agung dinilai Rugikan DPR', 23 March 2017, https://news.detik.com/berita/d-3455401/putusan-mk-tentang-seleksi-hakim-agung-dinilai-rugikan-dpr, accessed 18 June 2020.

Detik.com (2006) 'IKAHI Tolak Mentah-mentah Seleksi Hakim', *Detik.com*, 6 January 2006, https://news.detik.com/berita/d-514193/ikahi-tolak-mentah-mentah-seleksi-ulang-hakim-agung, accessed 18 June 2020.

DPR-GR (1971) 'Undang-Undang tentang Ketentuan-Ketentuan Pokok Kekuasaan Kehakiman'. Jakarta: PT Intibuku Utama.

Fix-Fierro, Hector (2003) *Courts, Justice and Efficiency: A Socio-Legal Study of Economic Rationality in Adjudication*. Oregon: Hart Publishing.

Hammergren, Linn A (2002) *Do Judicial Council Further Judicial Reform? Lessons from Latin America*. Working Papers, Rule of Law Series, Democracy and Rule of Law Project, Carnegie Endowment for International Peace.

Heydebrand, Wolf V (1977) 'The Context of Public Bureaucracies: An Organizational Analysis of Federal District Courts' 11 *Law & Society Review* 759–821.

Kantor Menteri Negara (1999) 'Laporan Tim Kerja Terpadu Mengenai Pengkajian Pelaksanaan TAP MPR RI Nomor X/MPR/1998 Berkaitan dengan Pemisahan yang Tegas antar Fungsi-Fungsi Yudikatif dari Eksekutif. Jakarta: Koordinator Bidang Pengawasan Pembangunan dan Pendayagunaan Aparatur Negara Republik Indonesia.

Komisi Yudisial, Siaran Pers 06/Siaran Pers/AL/LI.04.01/3/2019 entitled 'Hanya 15 Persen Rekomendasi Sanksi KY Ditindaklanjuti MA pada 2016-2018', 1 March 2019, https://www.komisiyudisial.go.id/frontend/pers_release_detail/103/hanya-persen-rekomendasi-sanksi-ky-yang-ditindaklanjuti-ma-pada, accessed 20 May 2021.

Komisi Yudisial (2012) *Menjaga Keseimbangan Meneguhkan Kehormatan – Kiprah 7 Tahun Komisi Yudisial RI 2005-2012*. Jakarta: Pusat Data dan Layanan Informasi Komisi Yudisial. 26–32.

Mahkamah Agung Republik Indonesia (2004) *Naskah Akademis dan Rancangan Undang-Undang tentang Komisi Yudisial, Mahkamah Agung Republik Indonesi*a. Jakarta: Mahkamah Agung Republik Indonesia.

Mahkamah Konstitusi (2010) 'Naskah Komprehensif Perubahan Undang-Undang Dasar Negara Republik Indonesia Tahun 1945 (Latar Belakang, Proses dan Hasil Pembahasan 1999-2002), Buku VI Kekuasaan Kehakiman. Jakarta: Sekretariat Jenderal dan Kepaniteraan Mahkamah Konstitusi, revised edition.

Mohr, Lawrence B (1976) 'Organization, Decision and Court' 10 *Law & Society Review* Vol.10 No. 4 (Summer, 1976), pp 621–642.

Nasution, Adnan Buyung (1999) 'Urgensi Pemisahan Kekuasaan Kehakiman (Yudikatif) dari Kekuasaan Pemenrintah (Eksekutif)', *Himpunan Hasil Pengkajian Pelaksanaan TAP MPR-RI Nomor X/MPR/1998 Berkenaan dengan Pemisahan yang Tegas Antara Fungsi-Fungsi Yudikatif dari Eksekutif*. Edited by Tim Kerja Terpadu. Jakarta: Kantor Menteri Negera Koordinator Bidang Pengawasan Pembangunan dan Pendayagunaan Aparatur Negara Republik Indonesia, 122-126.

Pompe, Sebastiaan (2005) *The Indonesian Supreme Court: A Study of Institutional Collapse*. Ithaca, New York: South East Asia Program Publication, University of Cornell.

Pompe, Sebastiaan (2011) 'The Judge S case and Why Court Oversight Fails', *Jakarta Post*, June 13, http://www.thejakartapost.com/news/2011/06/13/the-judge-s-case-and-why-court-oversight-fails.html.

Rositawati, Dian (2019) 'Judicial Governance in Indonesia: Judicial Independence under the One Roof System', PhD thesis, Tilburg University.

Sekretariat Jenderal Komisi Yudisial (2013) *Risalah Pembentukan Komisi Yudisial: Cikal Bakal, Pelembagaan dan Dinamika Wewenang*. Republik Indonesia: Komisi Yudisial.

Tirto.id (2019) 'KY Sebut 130 Hakim Bermasalah, Ketua MA: Hanya 41 Rekomendasi KY', Tirto.id, 27 December, https://tirto.id/ky-sebut-130-hakim-bermasalah-ketua-ma-hanya-41-rekomendasi-ky-ephW.

Voermans, Wim (1999) 'Councils for the Judiciary in Europe' 8 *Tilburg Foreign Law Review* 121–134.

Voermans, Wim (2003) 'Councils for the Judiciary in Europe: Trends and Models', in Francisco Fernándes Segado (ed) *The Spanish Constitution in the European Constitutional Context*. pp 2133–2144.

Yusuf, Ahmad Mukhlis (2008) *Presiden RI Ke II Jenderal Besar HM Soeharto dalam Berita*. Jakarta: Antara Pustaka Utama.

Legislation

Law 14/1970 on the Judicial Power.

Law 14/1985 on the Supreme Court.

Law 2/1986 on the General Court.

Law 5/1986 on the Administrative Court.

Law 7/1989 on the Islamic Court.

Law 35/1999 on the Amendment of Law 14/1970 on the Judicial Power.

Law 4/2004 on the Judicial Power.

Law 5/2004 on the Amendment of Law 14/1985 on the Supreme Court.

Law 8/2004 on the Amendment of Law 2/1986 on the General Court.

Law 9/2004 on the Amendment of Law 5/1986 on the Administrative Court.

Law 22/2004 on the Judicial Commission.

Law 3/2006 on the Amendment of Law 7/1989 on the Islamic Court.

Law 3/2009 on the Second Amendment of Law 14/1970 on the Judicial Power.

Law 48/2009 on the Judicial Power.

Law 50/2009 on the Second Amendment of Law 7/1989 on the Islamic Court.

Law 51/2009 the Second Amendment of Law 5/1986 on the Administrative Court.

Law 18/2011 on the Amendment of Law 22/2004 on the Judicial Commission.

Regulations

Joint Regulation Chief Justice of the Supreme Court and Head of the Judicial Commission 047/KMA/SKB/IV/2009 and 02/SKB/P.KY/IV/2009 on the Guideline of the Enforcement of Code of Ethics and Code of Conduct of Judges.

Joint Regulation Chief Justice of the Supreme Court and Head of the Judicial Commission 047/KMA/SKB/IV/2009 and 02/SKB/P.KY/IV/2009 on the Guideline of the Enforcement of Code of Ethics and Code of Conduct of Judges.

Joint Regulation Chief Justice of the Supreme Court and Head of the Judicial Commission 01/PB/MA/IX/2012 and 01/PB/P.KY/09/2012 on Selection of Judges.

Joint Regulation Chief Justice of the Supreme Court and Head of the Judicial Commission 03/PB/MA/IX/2012 and 03/PB/P.KY/09/2012 on Joint Investigation; and 04/PB/MA/IX/2012 and 04/PB/P.KY/09/2012 on Judge Honorary Board.

Constitutional Court Decisions

Decision 005/PUU-IV/2006.
Decision 43/PUU-XIII/2015.
Decision 36 P/HUM/2011.

7

The Constitutional and Legislative Foundations of Indonesia's Electoral Regime

Adhy Aman and Dirk Tomsa

Introduction

Despite the crucial importance of elections for the functioning of representative democracy, the Indonesian Constitution does not contain detailed legal provisions about how the country's leaders are elected. Instead, it mainly provides foundational norms and institutions of the political system, while delegating details, such as the choice of the legislative and presidential electoral systems or the eligibility of contestants, to laws. This chapter outlines the evolution of the constitutional and legislative framework of elections in Indonesia to analyse how frequent changes to this framework have affected the conduct of elections and the trajectory of the political party system. Moreover, the chapter reflects on the roles of the General Election Commission (*Komisi Pemilihan Umum*, KPU) and the General Election Supervisory Agency (*Bawaslu*) in safeguarding the integrity of the electoral process in Indonesia, as mandated by the Constitution and by law, and affirmed by the Constitutional Court.

Overall, the chapter highlights that the constitutional provisions have provided flexibility for lawmakers to alter electoral institutions and processes through laws occasionally checked by the Constitutional Court as guardian of the Constitution. While this flexibility has advantages, the frequent changes to presidential and parliamentary elections pose enormous challenges for electoral management bodies, candidates, and voters. These problems include, among others, presidential nomination thresholds that have resulted in fewer candidates for voters to choose from and undermined the constitutional intent of a two-round presidential election system. Despite these challenges, Indonesia's electoral regime remains one of the most democratic in Southeast Asia, largely due to the checks and balances provided by the Honorary Council of General Election Organisers (DKPP) and *Bawaslu* that have ensured that the General Election Commission conducts elections in line with its constitutional mandate of being national, permanent, and independent.

The Constitution as the Basic Law on Elections

Indonesia has a presidential system of government. This system has its institutional origins in the country's first Constitution, which was drafted, somewhat hastily, in 1945, in the final days of the Japanese occupation. Against the background of the

Adhy Aman and Dirk Tomsa, *The Constitutional and Legislative Foundations of Indonesia's Electoral Regime* In: *Constitutional Democracy in Indonesia*. Edited by: Melissa Crouch, Oxford University Press. © Adhy Aman and Dirk Tomsa, 2023. DOI: 10.1093/oso/9780192870681.003.0007

colonial experience, presidentialism was the preferred choice for Indonesia's nation-alist leaders because the obvious alternative, parliamentarism, was deemed to be too closely associated with the Dutch colonial rulers. Nevertheless, the first Constitution did not enshrine a pure presidential system. Even though Article 4(1), stated un-equivocally that 'The President of the Republic of Indonesia shall hold the power of government in accordance with the Constitution', the highest state organ was in fact the People's Consultative Assembly (*Majelis Permusyawaratan Rakyat*, MPR), which among other responsibilities was granted the task of electing the president indir-ectly (UUD 1945 Awal, Art 6(2)). Direct elections, a hallmark of presidential systems around the world, did not feature in Indonesia's constitutional arrangements in 1945.

Generally, the 1945 Constitution was very modest in its provisions on elections. When it was first promulgated, the founding fathers had deliberately created a 'short and elastic' Constitution, intended to only provide 'basic provisions' and 'broad in-structions for the Central Government and other state institutions to implement statehood and social justice'. In a speech to the Committee for the Preparation of Indonesian Independence (*Panitia Persiapan Kemerdekaan Indonesia*, PPKI) on 18 August 1945, Indonesia's first president, Soekarno, declared that 'when we have [later] governed peacefully, we certainly will summon the *Majelis Permusyawaratan Rakyat* to create a more complete and perfect constitution' (Indrayana 2008). Eleven years later, after Indonesia had temporarily adopted two different constitutions (in 1949 and 1950), a Constitutional Assembly was finally convened to follow up on Soekarno's statement, but the assembly faltered due to irreconcilable differences between secular nationalists and Islamists over the role of religion in the state (Nasution 1992). In July 1959, Soekarno dissolved the assembly and reinstated the original 1945 Constitution, which would then remain in place unchanged until 1999.

This background is useful to understand why Indonesia's original Constitution, which still forms the basis of today's Constitution, was so simple and short. In fact, these key characteristics—'short and elastic'—remain part of the Constitution today, despite four rounds of amendments between 1999 and 2002. Indeed, the long and elab-orate Constitution for the Federal Republic of Indonesia (1949) and the subsequent 1950 Provisional Constitution left a lasting sour note for Indonesia's political elites. This is evident from the MPR's rejection of suggestions made by scholars after the end of the Soeharto era to replace the 1945 Constitution, instead of merely amending it. Moreover, the 1945 Constitution was still viewed by certain elements of society as a 'sa-cred document' (MKRI 2010a: 5–6), despite strong arguments put forward by Harun Al Rasyid (1998: 2–3) that even Soekarno never intended it to be a permanent consti-tution. This temporary nature was acknowledged by the MPR's Ad Hoc Committee III which was established in 1999 to oversee the review of the Constitution. In the end, the committee recommended to the MPR to merely amend the 1945 Constitution be-cause of its sacred nature and because the MPR did not have enough time on its hands to conduct a constitutional overhaul (MKRI 2010a: 142–143).

The simplicity and shortness of the 1945 Constitution is particularly evident when looking at its provisions concerning elections, including the new sections on elec-tions for president, the People's Representative Council (*Dewan Perwakilan Rakyat*, DPR), Regional People's Representative Council (*Dewan Perwakilan Rakyat Daerah*, DPRD), and the Regional Representatives Council (*Dewan Perwakilan Daerah*, DPD) as well as electoral management bodies. The need to include new provisions on elections into the post-*reformasi* 1945 Constitution was first expressed during the second meeting of the Working Body of the MPR on 6 October 1999 (MKRI 2010b: 508). It then took three more years of deliberations until all new sections relating to elections were formally adopted by the MPR.

Importantly, the amendments to the 1945 Constitution enshrined six principles that must be upheld by laws and regulations that govern general elections in Indonesia. Four of them already existed during the New Order, albeit not promulgated in the Constitution, while two more were added during *reformasi*. The first four (older) principles are: direct (*langsung*), public (*umum*), free (*bebas*), and secret (*rahasia*), while the two additional ones are honest (*jujur*) and fair (*adil*). During the MPR deliberations on the Fourth Amendment in August 2002, M Abduh Pardede of the United Development Party (PPP) declared that in a modern democracy, fairness should be explicitly included as a principle because in Indonesia's experience, the principle of free has always been put forward, but in the absence of fairness, freedom of choice has been designed to mislead (MKRI 2010b: 200). Similarly, in the eyes of Suwarno, a member of the Indonesian Democratic Party of Struggle (*Partai Demokrasi Indonesia-Perjuangan*, PDI-P), the principle of honesty was necessary to ensure that New Order-style rigged elections are not repeated (MKRI 2010b: 380).

Beyond the key principles, the amended 1945 Constitution contains the following provisions on elections:

- Election of the President and Vice-President in Article 6A(1)–(5)
- Election of DPR members in Article 19(1) *juncto* Article 2(1) and Article 22E(3)
- Election of DPD members in Article 22C(1) *juncto* Article 2(1), Article 22C(2), and Article 22E(4)
- Election of governors, regents, and mayors in Article 18(4)
- Election of DPRD members in Article 22E(2) and (3).

The amendments also added a new chapter on 'General Elections' (Chapter VIIB), which contains one article and six paragraphs. Significantly, most of the new sections are fairly short on detail, outlining broad principles rather than complex institutional arrangements. In that sense, the amended document still resembles the original version from 1945, even though the amendments have of course added many important reforms. But details about the exact nature of elections are few and far between.

Instead, the Constitution consciously delegates authority for more detailed and specific regulation of elections to laws.[1] Key examples of issues that remained unresolved in the Constitution and were left to regulation by law include nomination thresholds for parties and candidates, the exact format of the electoral system for legislative elections, the question whether local executive leaders shall be elected directly or indirectly, and the question whether or not all elections shall be held concurrently or

---

[1] This has been repeatedly enforced by the Constitutional Court through what it calls '*delegasi kewenangan terbuka*' (open delegation of authority)—see, eg, Decision 51-52-59/PUU-VI/2008 [3.17]

separately.[2] As will be shown below, this lack of constitutional detail on elections has meant that laws on the elections have changed before every election since 1999.

Constitutional and Legal Foundations of Presidential Elections

Although Indonesia's founding fathers favoured a presidential system of government, direct presidential elections were not included in the original 1945 Constitution. Rather, constitutional authority to elect the president was initially granted to the MPR, which acted as the highest state organ until the constitutional amendments of 1999–2002. Nevertheless, throughout his more than twenty years as Indonesia's first president, Soekarno was never elected, neither directly nor indirectly.

It was not before Soeharto took power in the aftermath of the 1965 mass killings that the indirect election system through the MPR was eventually used for the first time in 1968. Soeharto, however, did not allow any other candidate to run for president but himself, so the idea of an 'election' was little more than a 'useful fiction' (Liddle 1996). Following Soeharto's consolidation of power, this useful fiction was upheld throughout the authoritarian New Order era (1966–1998), where the MPR always 'acted by agreement reached through deliberation and consensus rather than the mechanism of voting' (Ellis 2007: 24). This consensus, of course, was never difficult to achieve as all MPR members were either handpicked by the president or at least approved by the regime via a rigid screening process. Unsurprisingly, Soeharto won all indirect presidential elections in the MPR between 1968 and 1998 unopposed and always successfully imposed his choice of vice-president on the MPR delegates.

In May 1998, just two months after he had been elected for his seventh consecutive five-year term, Soeharto was forced to resign in the face of a severe economic crisis and mass student protests (Forrester and May 1998). The end of the New Order, however, did not lead to the immediate abolition of the indirect election modus for the president. Interim president BJ Habibie, who as incumbent vice-president at the time of Soeharto's resignation had taken over the presidency in accordance with constitutional provisions, opted to first organize free elections for the DPR in June 1999 rather than convene a special committee to draft a new constitution. Once the new lower house was inaugurated, its elected members joined 38 representatives of the armed forces as well as 130 provincial delegates and 65 functional group representatives appointed by the General Election Commission to form a new MPR which was then, in October 1999, tasked to choose a new president through the same indirect election mechanism as in the New Order. The surprise winner of this election was Abdurrahman Wahid, an Islamic cleric and leader of a relatively small party in the House of Representatives (Mietzner 2009). As it turned out, this was the first and last time in the post-Soeharto era that a president would be elected through the MPR.

---

[2] This issue became pertinent when presidential elections were held concurrently with legislative elections for the first time in 2019 and when lawmakers decided on a road map to hold all local executive elections simultaneously by 2024 (MKRI 2010b: 545).

Wahid's election demonstrated that even though the MPR was now freed from the shackles of authoritarian presidential control, the existence of more than 200 appointed members and the indirect election mode for the president made a mockery of the public will. Megawati Soekarnoputri's PDI-P had clearly won the legislative election in June, yet the popular daughter of first president Soekarno was then denied the presidency by horse-trading party elites in the MPR (Mietzner 2009: 261–262). Only when Wahid was impeached by the House of Representatives over allegations of corruption and abuse of power in July 2001 did Megawati, who had been elected as vice-president in 1999, ascend to the presidency.

The controversial rise and demise of Abdurrahman Wahid prompted many lawmakers who had been tasked with revising the Constitution after the 1999 election to reconsider their views about the nature of Indonesia's political system. Constitutional amendments had begun during the 1999 MPR session in which Wahid was elected and continued a year later, but it was not before the third round of amendments in November 2001 that delegates eventually agreed to replace the indirect presidential election system through the MPR with direct presidential elections (Horowitz 2013). It took another year to finalize the exact wording for all relevant paragraphs of the revised Constitution, but eventually the new Article 6A read as follows:

(1) The President and the Vice President shall be elected as a pair by the people directly.
(2) Each pair for President and Vice President shall be proposed prior to general elections by a political party or by a coalition of political parties contesting the general elections.
(3) The pair of Presidential and Vice Presidential candidates that receives more than fifty percent of the vote from the total of votes in the general election with at least twenty percent of the vote in more than half of the total number of provinces in Indonesia, shall be installed as President and Vice President.
(4) In the event that no pair for Presidential and Vice Presidential candidates is elected, the two pairs of candidates who have received the first and second highest number of votes in the general election shall be submitted to direct election by the people and the pair that gets most of the votes shall be installed as President and Vice President.
(5) The procedure to organize the election for President and Vice President shall be further regulated by law.

Paragraph (1) requires the presidential and vice-presidential candidates to run together on the same ticket, similar to the United States. This differentiates Indonesia from the Philippines where the president and vice-president are elected separately, thus allowing the possibility for the elected president and vice-president to have opposing views and policies. The Duterte-Robredo administration was a good example of this, while Estrada-Arroyo more than a decade earlier was another.

Paragraph (2) provides a strong standing for political parties in Indonesia's political system. Parties, either individually or as a group, are the only entities authorized by the Constitution to nominate candidates for both president and vice-president. This constitutional feature was strengthened by the Constitutional Court in 2008 when it rejected a case that sought to allow individuals to run as independent candidates.[3]

The formula by which a candidate ticket is declared a winner is provided under Paragraph (3). To be inaugurated as president and vice-president, the winning ticket must obtain more than 50 per cent of the votes *and* at least 20 per cent of the total provincial votes in at least half of the provinces. This is a staggered formula, and it is intentionally so.[4] The first test is that the ticket should win a simple majority even if there were more than two candidate tickets. This consequently requires a run-off election if none of the tickets got the required majority as provided by Paragraph (4).

The fifth paragraph of Article 6A presents an example of what the Constitutional Court calls an 'open delegation of authority' by the Constitution to legislation. Basically, all other implementing regulations on presidential elections are hereby delegated to policy choices made by lawmakers 'as long as the chosen policies do not exceed the authority of lawmakers, do not constitute as an abuse of power, and are clearly not in conflict with the 1945 Constitution'.[5]

In addition to Article 6A, there were other important amendments, including the removal of the MPR as the highest state organ and the introduction of a presidential term limit of two five-year terms (Art 7). In addition, a new section on elections (Art 22E) stated not only that 'Every five years general elections are to be organized in a direct, public, free, secret, honest, and fair way' (Paragraph 1), but also that 'The general elections are organized to elect the members of the DPR, the DPD, *the President and the Vice President* [emphasis added] and the DPRD' (Paragraph 2). Thus, Indonesia had at last adopted the quintessential pillars of a conventional presidential system, in line with Lijphart's (1999: 117–118) criteria for presidentialism which include a single person executive, direct presidential elections, and a fixed-term chief executive who is not subject to the confidence of the legislature.

Lawmakers in charge of the constitutional reforms were driven by two main considerations. First, they were concerned about the very survival of the Indonesian nation-state after East Timor had been granted an independence referendum, separatist insurgencies in Aceh and Papua flared up, and ethnic and religious violence ripped through parts of Kalimantan, Sulawesi, and Maluku. To address these concerns in the constitutional design of the new presidential system, Paragraphs 1 and 3 of Article 6A were engineered to follow a centripetal logic which sought to ensure 'that only broadly supported, nationally oriented candidates would be elected to office' (Reilly 2007: 47).

Second, the constitutional reformers endeavoured to make sure that political parties, and especially the larger parties who dominated parliament after the 1999 election, would not be marginalized as political actors by the new focus on direct presidential elections (Sherlock 2004: 6). To that end, Article 6A(2) gave parties the prerogative to nominate presidential candidates. Independent candidatures, on the other hand, were not permitted. And while the Constitution did not specify how large a party would need to be in order to have the right to nominate a pair of candidates,

---

[3] Decision 56/PUU-VI/2008.

[4] MPR deliberation records shows that this idea was first proposed by the Political Expert Team (MKRI 2010b: 320).

[5] Decision 51-52-59/PUU-VI/2008 [3.17].

legislators used the opportunity provided by the need to draft a detailed election law—as mandated by Article 6A (5)—to restrict the number of potential candidates.

When the Law on the Election of the President and Vice President was passed in July 2003, it included a passage which stated that nominations of presidential candidates were limited to parties or coalitions of parties which received at least 5 per cent of the popular vote or 3 per cent of seats in the DPR (Art 101). Significantly, these figures were only 'transitional'; in Article 5(4), the law already indicated that these figures were to be raised. And so they were. From 2009 onwards, only parties or coalitions of parties that had won at least 25 per cent of the popular vote or 20 per cent of seats in the DPR could nominate candidates, so that it became imperative for small parties to build coalitions before they could consider nominating a presidential candidate (Crouch 2010: 66). Consequently, the number of candidate pairs noticeably dropped from five in 2004 to three in 2009 and two in 2014 and 2019 respectively as Table 7.1 below shows.

Constitutional and Legal Foundations of Parliamentary Elections

The key principles that shaped the design and evolution of the presidential election system—centripetalism and a desire to strengthen large political parties—have also been a hallmark of the reforms of the parliamentary election system after 1998. But in contrast to presidential elections, whose main features have remained largely intact since the constitutional amendments, parliamentary elections have undergone noteworthy changes over the years. Significantly, though, continued efforts by the larger parties to tweak the electoral rules in their favour have twice been thwarted by the Constitutional Court.

Legislative bodies in Indonesia exist at three different levels: national/central, provincial, and regency/city. At the national level, Indonesia adopts a bicameral system: the House of Representatives or *Dewan Perwakilan Rakyat* (DPR) is the more powerful lower house, while the upper house, only created via constitutional amendment in 2001, is called the Regional Representatives Council or *Dewan Perwakilan Daerah* (DPD). Members of both houses combine to form the MPR, whose functions comprise the authority to change or amend the constitution, to inaugurate the President and/or Vice-President, and to impeach the President and/or Vice-President. At the subnational level, every province, regency, and city has a regional parliament (*Dewan Perwakilan Rakyat Daerah*, DPRD) with the authority to promulgate regional regulations, to oversee the executive and to determine the annual budget for the region.

As mentioned above, the first legislative elections of the post-Soeharto era took place in June 1999, four months before the constitutional amendment process began. The electoral rules for this election were determined in tense negotiations between interim president Habibie and representatives of the three parties that held seats in the last New Order parliament, namely the former regime party Golkar and the two former opposition parties PPP and PDI (Shin 2012). The most consequential decision that was made in these early negotiations was to reject a reform proposal to introduce a plurality-based 'First Past the Post' system and rather retain the same kind of proportional representation system that had already been used during the state-engineered New Order elections from 1971 to 1997. Significantly, constitutional reformers did not revisit the electoral system during the amendment process from 1999 to 2002, so the Constitution refers to legislative elections only in very generic terms.

First, Section VII about the House of Representatives focuses mainly on the legislature's rights, power, and functions. Only Article 19(1) refers to elections, stating that 'The members of the DPR are elected through a general election'. Second, Section VIIA about the newly created DPD also primarily deals with the functional aspects of the new institution, while elections are only mentioned generically in Article 22C(1): 'The members of the DPD shall be elected from each province through a general election.' Despite the paucity of detail, it is important to note that these formulations in Articles 19 and 22C make it very clear that all members of the legislative bodies are to be elected through general elections, thus abolishing the original construct of some MPR members, including representatives of the military, being appointed by the president, as was the case during the New Order. Third, the new Section VIIB about general elections, which was added to the Constitution during the third round of amendments in 2001, mentions basic principles of democratic elections, but stays clear of any details about the electoral system:

(1) Every five years general elections are to be organized in a direct, public, free, secret, honest, and fair way.
(2) The general elections are organized to elect the members of the DPR, the DPD, the President and the Vice President and the DPRD.
(3) The participants in the general elections to elect the members of the DPR and of the DPRD are political parties.
(4) The participants in the general elections to elect the members of the DPD are individuals.
(5) The general elections shall be organized by a general elections commission that shall be national, permanent and independent in nature.
(6) Further provisions regarding the general elections are to be regulated by law.

Paragraphs (3) and (4) of the article are noteworthy for their information about who is allowed to compete in the elections for DPR and DPD. Paragraph (3), for instance, stipulates that contestants in DPR and DPRD elections are political parties. This directly blocks independent/individual candidates from running for DPR and DPRD seats in a non-partisan manner.[6] By contrast, Paragraph (4) sets 'individuals' as contestants in DPD elections. While this formulation clearly ruled out political parties as contestants, it led to confusion as to whether or not individual candidates could be affiliated with political parties. Some people contended that the DPD was meant only for individuals with no partisan affiliations whatsoever, while others interpreted this differently, arguing that individuals could very well have partisan loyalties, they were just not to be nominated by political parties as institutions. In 2008, the Constitutional Court resolved this debate when it decided that this Paragraph does not 'implicitly

---

[6] This was confirmed by the Constitutional Court through its Decision 56/PUU-VI/2008.

intend' for the contestants in the DPD elections to be non-partisan,[7] thus effectively allowing contestants who are close to political parties to run as long as they nominate themselves rather than be nominated by a political party as in DPR elections.

By delegating the finer details of the electoral system to legislation, as stipulated in Paragraph (6), the constitutional reformers granted the political parties represented in the DPR 'wide scope to influence their own future political fortunes' (Sherlock 2004: 5). Extraordinarily, the parties have interpreted this outcome of the constitutional reform process as a mandate to redesign the electoral framework ahead of every single national election that followed. New laws on general elections were passed in 2003, 2008, 2012, and 2017. In addition, new laws on political parties were crafted with similar frequency, in 2002, 2008, and 2011. Among the most important goals of this continued institutional engineering was the intention to build a nationwide party system and to reduce the number of parties.

First, in an effort to prevent the formation of regional or ethnic parties, all election and party laws have included requirements for parties to have local chapters and branches in a certain number of provinces and districts. These requirements became progressively stricter over the years. If in 1999, parties were only required to have regional chapters in 50 per cent of all provinces and 50 per cent of districts or municipalities in that province, by 2019 these figures had increased to 100 per cent of all provinces, 75 per cent of districts/municipalities in the province, and 50 per cent of subdistricts in the districts/municipalities (Law 7/2017 on General Elections, Article 173(2). Over time, these increased restrictions curbed the number of parties competing in national legislative elections from forty-eight in 1999 to sixteen in 2019.

Second, Indonesia's larger parties have continuously sought to use electoral institutions to stymy competition from smaller parties. In the first post-Soeharto election in 1999, the four largest parties won a combined vote share of nearly 80 per cent, but due to an ill-conceived *next election threshold* which allowed parties that failed to meet the 2 per cent benchmark to still enter parliament but not to compete in the next election, a total of twenty-one parties won at least one seat in parliament. In subsequent elections, the threshold was not only raised incrementally, reaching 4 per cent in the 2019 election, but in 2009 it was also transformed into a *parliamentary threshold* which barred parties that failed to clear the threshold from entering parliament. Thus, micro parties soon disappeared, but, as Table 7.1 shows, party system fragmentation has remained high nevertheless as the vote share of the larger parties slowly decreased due to dealignment, internal frictions within parties, and increasingly clientelistic voting patterns.

Significantly, the threshold regulation was never applied at the subnational level. Initially, this may have been intended as an appeasement of local concerns about the lack of regional-based parties. Thus, by not applying the threshold to the local level, parties that were particularly popular in specific regions could still get adequate representation in the provincial, municipal, and district parliaments. But it led to hyper-fragmentation in some of these parliaments, especially in Eastern Indonesia, where low levels of party institutionalization and the prevalence of clientelism helped small

---

[7] Decision 10/PUU-VI/2008 [3.24].

Table 7.1 Number of Presidential and Vice-presidential Candidates: Setiawan and Tomsa (2022: 47)

Election Year	Nomination Restriction	Number of Candidates	Winner
2004	5% of the vote or 3% of DPR seats	5	Susilo Bambang Yudhoyono
2009	25% of the vote or 20% of DPR seats	3	Susilo Bambang Yudhoyono
2014	25% of the vote or 20% of DPR seats	2	Joko Widodo
2019	25% of the vote or 20% of DPR seats *in the previous election* (presidential and parliamentary elections were held on the same day for the first time in 2019)	2	Joko Widodo

parties to win substantial numbers of seats (Tomsa 2014). After three consecutive elections had resulted in progressively higher fragmentation in many regions, national elites decided to extend the threshold regulation to the subnational level when they drafted the 2012 election law. But this revision was successfully challenged in the Constitutional Court, where eight out of nine judges declared that a threshold at the subnational level 'failed to accommodate, and even impeded, political aspirations across Indonesia's diverse regions' (Butt 2015: 197).

This was by no means the only time the Constitutional Court intervened in the DPR's electoral engineering efforts. It also invalidated attempts to exempt large parties from the KPU verification process and it rejected affirmative action provisions intended to increase female representation in political institutions. Moreover, in 2008 it ruled that important sections of the electoral law which regulated the allocation of seats to candidates in the partially open list proportional representation system were unconstitutional. For the court, the partially open list system used in 2004 gave political parties undue control over which candidates would eventually be elected to parliament, whereas the spirit of the electoral system was 'to elect a candidate who obtains the most number of votes instead of the highest ranking in the party list' (Hendrianto 2016: 102). Thus, where most candidates are elected based on their position on the party list rather than the number of votes they receive, so the court reasoned, neither the people's sovereignty, as mandated in Article 1 of the Constitution, nor the constitutional principle of justice, as mandated in Article 28D(1), could be maintained (Butt 2015: 207).

Following this decision by the Constitutional Court, Indonesia adopted a fully open list proportional representation system from 2009 onwards, even though the former chief justice of the Constitutional Court, Mahfud MD, later denied that this had been the court's intention (Tashandra 2017). The enormous implications of this electoral system change will be discussed in some detail below, but before moving to this discussion it is important to briefly outline the constitutional foundations of the third type of elections in Indonesia, namely elections for local executive leaders or *pilkada* (*pemilihan kepala daerah*).

Elections for Heads of Local Government (Pilkada)

In 2005, direct elections for governors, regents, and mayors were introduced 'as a by-product of the MPR's decision to introduce direct election for the presidency' (Crouch 2010: 113). Prior to that, the leaders of subnational governments had been elected indirectly through local parliaments. The switch to direct elections was intended to end the widespread practice of vote buying inside parliament and to open up new opportunities for enhanced citizen participation, competition, and accountability in local politics. Once again though, the regulatory framework for these elections was formalized in laws rather than in the constitution, even though local executive elections did receive considerable attention during the constitutional amendment process.

Indeed, the constitutional reformers in the post-*reformasi* MPR debated the inclusion of elections for the heads of local governments as part of general elections. Theo L Sambuaga from the Golkar Party, for example, was quite explicit in his support for all main executive positions to be directly elected by the people when he said the following at the 28th Meeting of the MPR's Ad Hoc Committee I on 8 March 2000:

> Indirect elections are also democratic [if] through democratic process. But direct elections has a stronger feel of people's representation, stronger feel of people's trust upon the person the mandate is given, whoever is elected President. Not only President, but also all political positions, President, Vice President, Governor, Regent [and] Mayor. (MKRI 2010b: 264)

Gregorius Seto Hariyanto of the Love the Nation Democratic Party (*Partai Demokrasi Kasih Bangsa*, PDKB) added at the same meeting that indirect elections of governors and regents, though legitimate, had attracted mass protests in certain regions (MKRI 2010b: 267). Another MPR member, Valina Singka Subekti of the Functional Group faction, believed the inclusion of directly elected governors and regents into Indonesian electoral practice would enhance the MPR's resolve for introducing direct presidential elections (MKRI 2010b: 312). All in all, support within the Ad hoc Committee for direct elections of local leaders was quite widespread and the committee came close to including these elections in Article 22E(2), which lists the types of direct elections sanctioned by the Constitution.

In the end, however, it was not included in that paragraph. Instead, a passage was inserted into Article 18(4), which merely stated that heads of regions are to be elected 'democratically'. Lukman Hakim Saifuddin from the PPP said that by leaving this out of Article 22E, it would provide liberty for lawmakers to decide whether heads of regions should be elected directly or indirectly (MKRI 2010b: 578), a statement that was seconded by Baharuddin Aritonang from the Golkar Party. And so, it was left to the government of the day to interpret the constitutional rules on general elections and draft a regional autonomy law that would outline the details of the electoral system.

Law 32/2004 on Regional Autonomy was passed in 2004 and it stated explicitly in Article 56(1) that heads of local government were to be elected democratically and directly. Moreover, it mandated that candidates had to run in pairs with a deputy and that the pairs had to be nominated by a party or a coalition of parties that had won at least 15 per cent of the vote or seats in the last local legislative election. Significantly, the mandatory nomination through parties was invalidated by the Constitutional Court in 2007 so that independent candidates were allowed to contest local executive elections from 2008 onwards. However, the revised regulations imposed a number of administrative hurdles on independent candidates so that parties have largely retained their monopoly on nominating candidates.

In a development that mirrored the evolution of the nomination requirements for presidential candidates, the threshold for gubernatorial, mayoral, or regent candidates seeking to obtain a nomination from a party or a coalition of parties was tightened in subsequent years as the regional autonomy law was revised. According to Law 1/2015, only parties that had won at least 25 per cent of the vote or 20 per cent of the seats in the local legislature were allowed to nominate candidates. Along with the onerous requirements for independent candidates to obtain large numbers of signatures from citizens in support of a candidature, the tightened nomination requirements led to a shrinking pool of candidates who had the resources to compete. In fact, between 2015 and 2018, the number of uncontested elections where voters only have the choice between endorsing or rejecting a sole contender rose from three in 2015 to nine in 2017 and sixteen in 2018 (Tomsa 2020: 20). As we shall see in the following section, this narrowing of electoral choices for Indonesia's citizens has also shaped the nature of presidential elections, with serious implications for the quality of Indonesian democracy.

Political Implications of the Institutional Framework

Despite the frequent changes to the institutional frameworks, elections are still widely regarded as a hallmark of Indonesian democracy. The voting process is generally free and fair, turnout is high, and violence low. Especially when compared to global and regional averages, Indonesia's democracy in general and its electoral framework in particular are performing well (IDEA 2022). And yet, since at least 2014 there are growing concerns that the frequent changes are not only failing to provide stability in electoral management, but that they are actually weakening rather than strengthening electoral integrity and, by extension, democratic quality in Indonesia. As a matter of fact, many broader assessments of Indonesian democracy in recent years have pointed to a worrying trend from stagnation to regression (Warburton and Aspinall 2019). And while many of the reasons for this regression are beyond the realm of institutional engineering and electoral politics, there are at least two developments in electoral system design—one pertaining to presidential elections and one to parliamentary elections—that have contributed to the decline in democratic quality in Indonesia.

First, the tightening of the presidential nomination threshold after the first successful direct election in 2004 narrowed the field of contenders in subsequent presidential elections and thereby contributed to growing polarization in Indonesia. As mentioned above, in the 2004 election, nominations of presidential candidates were limited to parties or coalitions of parties which received at least 5 per cent of the popular vote or 3 per cent of seats in the DPR. Subsequently, these thresholds were raised to 25 per cent of the popular vote or 20 per cent of seats in the DPR (see Table

7.1). In 2019, these thresholds were retained, even though presidential and parliamentary elections were held on the same day that year so that legislative election results could actually no longer be used to determine the coalitions for nominating a presidential candidate. As a way out, results from the 2014 election were used for that.

As Table 7.1 shows, since the introduction of the higher nomination threshold, Indonesian voters no longer enjoy great choice in presidential elections. In 2009, three candidates competed for the highest office, but in 2014 and 2019, the number of candidates declined to the bare minimum of two. This has not only reduced competition, it has also had major consequences for the nature of electoral campaigning and voter mobilization. With only one opponent to attack, campaign teams in 2014 and 2019 were much more antagonistic and aggressive in their strategies than in the previous polls in 2004 and 2009.

Significantly, the hostility was driven by somewhat different campaign narratives, yet they both had the same effect of growing polarization. In 2014, when Joko Widodo and Prabowo Subianto faced off for the first time, the main dividing line was a perceived difference in their attitudes to democracy. While Jokowi presented himself as a defender of the democratic reform narrative, Prabowo ran a populist and hyper-nationalist campaign with anti-democratic undertones (Tomsa 2018: 280). In 2019, by contrast, none of the two candidates stood for democratic reform ideals anymore, so the pattern of polarization shifted from politics to religion. As Prabowo embraced Islamist hardliners, Jokowi framed himself as the defender of the constitutional ideals of pluralism, as enshrined in the Pancasila. The somewhat different underlying drivers of polarization demonstrated that, as Mietzner (2019: 11) noted, polarization 'was not only a result of socio-demographic trends; it was also the consequence of an electoral system narrowing the choice of presidential nominees to two'.

Second, the integrity of parliamentary elections has suffered with the progressive shift from a closed list over a partially open list to a fully open list proportional representation system. The adoption of the open list system in 2009 effectively transformed legislative elections from party-dominated affairs into contests between individual candidates. Though parties are still the organizational vehicles that register with the General Election Commission (independent candidates are not allowed), all candidates on a party list are visible to the voter on the ballot paper and a seat won by a party in a given constituency will be allocated to the candidate with the highest number of

Table 7.2   Party System Fragmentation 1999–2019: Authors' own calculations based on media reports and election results published by the General Election Commission

	1999	2004	2009	2014	2019
Electoral/Parliamentary threshold	2%	2.5%	2.5%	3.5%	4%
Absolute number of legislative parties	21	16	9	10	9
Effective number of legislative parties	4.7	7.1	6.2	8.2	7.5
Vote share of the largest four parties	79.5	58.8	57.2	55.7	53.9

votes, regardless of that candidate's position on the list. In practice, this system turned candidates from the same party into direct rivals and incentivized more and more personalistic campaigns. As Aspinall and Sukmajati (2016: 33) wrote about the 2014 campaign, 'parties played a surprisingly minimal role in organizing most candidates' grassroots campaigns'.

As this electoral system is applied within a dysfunctional party funding framework which grants political parties only minimal state subsidies to fund their day-to-day operations (Mietzner 2015), parties usually leave all campaign-related costs to the candidates. And these costs are extensive as many candidates have resorted to increasingly excessive vote buying and other forms of money politics in order to distinguish themselves from other competitors (Muhtadi 2019). Significantly, this vote buying comes on top of numerous other expenses incurred by candidates including payments to the party to actually receive the nomination in the first place as well as fees for consultants, campaign managers, and brokers in charge of mobilizing clientelistic networks at the grassroots.

All in all, running for political office in Indonesia is now an extremely expensive undertaking. In 2019, candidates could expect to spend 1–2 billion rupiah (100,000–200,000 AUD) to finance a campaign for a DPR seat (Jatmiko 2018). In this environment, competent and experienced candidates who lack sufficient financial resources are increasingly excluded. Women in particular are struggling as they often lack the financial clout to fund their own campaigns (Prihatini 2019). Thus, the open party list system, while superficially increasing choice for voters and establishing a more direct connection between candidates and voters, has effectively transformed the electoral arena into a playground for wealthy male elites.

In sum, the institutional frameworks for both presidential and parliamentary elections have been altered so drastically from the initial framework in 1999 that Indonesian elections now display at least three worrying trends. First, presidential elections have fostered polarization as the number of candidates has decreased after nomination rules were tightened. Second, parliamentary elections have transformed into individualistic contests where vote buying is so rampant due to weak political finance regulations and enforcement that candidates from lower socio-economic backgrounds stand little chance of running for office. Third, without the safeguards of a 'level-playing-field-making' political finance framework, the system has failed women seeking better representation as the exclusionary effects of high campaign expenses outweigh other institutional incentives for improving female representation built into the electoral system, for example, quota for nominating female candidates. It is for these reasons that some observers have argued that despite the multitude of changes to the electoral system, yet another electoral reform is necessary in order to rectify the weaknesses that have crept into the system over the years (Mietzner 2019).

Safeguarding Electoral Integrity: Indonesia's Electoral Management Bodies

Such further reforms, however, seem unlikely at this stage because, as stated earlier, the broad parameters of Indonesia's electoral framework are intact and the current framework, including its various shortcomings, largely suits the interests of the country's political elite. To at least maintain current levels of electoral integrity, it is therefore of utmost importance that Indonesia's various electoral management bodies can continue to work independently and without interference from state actors. Over the years, the General Election Commission, the General Election Supervisory Agency (*Bawaslu*), and the Honorary Council of General Election Organizers (DKPP) have won widespread respect for their role in organizing Indonesia's complex electoral regime. This chapter will therefore conclude with a brief discussion of this trifecta and its embedment in Indonesia's constitutional and legal framework.

Of the three electoral management bodies tasked with organizing, implementing, and monitoring the lawful conduct of elections in Indonesia, only a general elections commission is mentioned in Article 22E(5) of the Constitution.

(5) The general elections shall be organized by a general elections commission that shall be national, permanent and independent in nature.

During the constitutional amendment deliberations, it was PDI-P who first suggested the inclusion of a constitutional provision that would guarantee the independence of election administration. The party proposed that 'general elections are conducted by a general elections commission that is permanent, national, independent, and whose members are competent and are not active members of political parties contesting in elections' (MKRI 2010b: 517). The provision on membership did not make it into the final wording, but it would later be significant in a Constitutional Court case in 2010.

The inclusion of the indefinite article 'a' prior to 'general elections commission' was also done on purpose by the MPR. In explaining the wording, Jakob Tobing, the Chairman of the MPR Ad Hoc Committee I, emphasized at the end of a committee meeting on 6 June 2000 that the Constitution was not intended to give the electoral management body a specific name, but rather to acknowledge the establishment of 'a' body to manage elections (MKRI 2010b: 528).

Moreover, the fact that the words 'general elections commission' are not written in title case suggests that the constitutional reformers did not intend it to necessarily be just one body. This is evident from the statement of Syarief Usman bin Yahya of the National Awakening Party (*Partai Kebangkitan Bangsa*, PKB) at the 5th Meeting of the MPR Working Body's Commission A on 13 August 2000, where he cited the need for the Constitution to allow some flexibility for lawmakers to determine the best institutional construct as time progresses (MKRI 2010b: 561). Indeed, the Constitutional Court later affirmed that a General Election Supervisory Agency (*Bawaslu*) may exist alongside the KPU. Crucially, both institutions are designed to be permanent, national, and independent bodies with the same function of administering elections as per Article 22E(5) down to the regency/city level.[8] That court ruling then gave lawmakers the confidence to establish the Election Organisers' Honorary Council through Law 15/2011 as a body tasked with handling breaches of the election organizers' ethics code.

---

[8] Decision 11/PUU-VIII/2010 and reinforced by Decision 48/PUU-XVII/2019.

The 'permanent' nature of the KPU and *Bawaslu* ensures the bodies remain in place in between elections. They are therefore not affected by changes in government or the timing of elections. Moreover, the 'national' nature of the commission means that it is responsible for all elections nationwide including, as was later affirmed by the Constitutional Court, elections for local executive leaders. While the attributes 'permanent' and 'national' were not controversial during the constitutional amendment process, the 'independent' nature of the commission was and has continued to be so. In 2011, lawmakers used the revisions to the general elections law (Law 15/2011) to remove the requirement for candidates for KPU membership to have resigned from membership of a political party five years prior to application as a candidate (as had been stipulated in the previous elections law, Law 22/2008). Somewhat audaciously, they replaced it with 'on the spot' resignation with no required lead time prior to application.

But the move by party elites drew widespread public criticism and consequently, some 136 institutions and individuals filed a petition to the Constitutional Court to test the constitutionality of such a provision, arguing it violated Article 22E(5) of the 1945 Constitution. The Constitutional Court ruled that the independent nature provided in the Constitution is closely linked to non-partisanship so that the general elections commission must not side with political parties or any election contestant. The possibility of 'on the spot' resignations prior to application for candidacy, so the court's explanation, may provide a legal opportunity for those loyal to political parties or other election contestants to become election organizers. Therefore, the provision under Law 15/2011 was declared unconstitutional.[9]

Conclusion

All in all, Indonesia's chosen path for designing the constitutional foundations of its electoral systems has provided exactly the kind of flexibility envisaged by the constitutional reformers in the early transition years, even though they may not have anticipated that lawmakers would revise the electoral laws before every single national election. In addition to the frequent and substantial changes to the national election laws, the legal framework for regional autonomy including local elections has also changed several times. As this chapter has shown, these frequent changes were a by-product of Indonesia's constitutional arrangements about elections, which outline several broad principles but few details. In fact, key constitutional provisions deliberately call for details about the conduct of elections to be regulated by law.

Political elites in the Indonesian government and parliament have progressively used this constitutional mandate to design an electoral regime that serves their interests. Over time, electoral choices for citizens have narrowed and aspiring candidates from lower socio-economic backgrounds, including many women, have found it increasingly difficult to compete in a system dominated by wealthy male elites. These

---

[9] Decision 81/PUU-IX/2011.

growing pains are reflected in increasingly pessimistic assessments of Indonesian democracy.

Some important checks and balances, however, remain in place to safeguard the integrity of elections. Notably, the Constitutional Court has played a significant role in checking the legality of certain legislative provisions. Although the evolution of the open list electoral system in the aftermath of the crucial 2008 ruling shows that the court's interventions can sometimes have unintended consequences, it is worth noting that since its establishment, the court has also issued many influential rulings that have curbed the ambitions of national elites to tighten the screws on electoral competition. Moreover, the trifecta of independent electoral management bodies has excelled at organizing Indonesian elections over the years. For future elections, it is imperative that these institutions retain their independence so that Indonesian elections at all levels will continue to follow the constitutional principles of direct, public, free, secret, honest, and fair.

References

Al Rasyid, Harun (1998) 'Relevansi UUD 1945 dalam Orde Reformasi' 10(5) *Jurnal Hukum* 1–8.

Aspinall, Edward and Sukmajati, Mada (eds) (2016), *Electoral Dynamics in Indonesia: Money Politics, Patronage and Clientelism at the Grassroots*. Singapore: NUS Press.

Butt, Simon (2015) *The Constitutional Court and Democracy in Indonesia*. Leiden/Boston: Brill.

Crouch, Harold (2010) *Political Reform in Indonesia after Soeharto*. Singapore: ISEAS.

Ellis, Andrew (2007) 'Indonesia's Constitutional Change Reviewed' in Ross H. McLeod and Andrew MacIntyre (eds) *Indonesia: Democracy and the Promise of Good Governance*. Singapore: ISEAS. pp. 21–40.

Forrester, Geoff and May, Ronald James (eds) (1998) *The Fall of Soeharto*. Bathurst: Crawford House.

Hendrianto, Stefanus (2016) 'The Curious Case of Quasi-Weak-Form Review: Judicial Review of Electoral Process in Indonesia' in Po Jen Yap (ed), *Judicial Review of Elections in Asia*. London and New York: Routledge. pp 95–114.

Horowitz, Donald L. (2013) *Constitutional Change and Democracy in Indonesia*. Cambridge: Cambridge University Press.

IDEA, International Institute for Democracy and Electoral Assistance (2022) *The Global State of Democratic Indices*, https://www.idea.int/gsod-indices/#/indices/compare-countries-regions, accessed 8 August 2022.

Indrayana, Denny (2008), *Indonesian Constitutional Reform 1999-2002: An Evaluation of Constitution-Making in Transition*. Jakarta: Kompas Book Publishing.

Jatmiko, Bambang Priyo (2018) 'Ingin Jadi Caleg, Berapa Miliar Dana Dibutuhkan?', *Kompas. com*, 1 August, https://ekonomi.kompas.com/read/2018/08/01/064607526/ingin-jadi-caleg-berapa-miliar-dana-dibutuhkan?page=all, accessed 31 December 2019.

Liddle, R William (1996) 'A Useful Fiction: Democratic Legitimation in New Order Indonesia' in RH Taylor (ed) *The Politics of Elections in Southeast Asia*. New York: Cambridge University Press. pp 34–60.

Lijphart, Arend (1999) *Patterns of Democracy*. New Haven and London: Yale University Press.

Mietzner, Marcus (2009) *Military Politics, Islam and the State in Indonesia: From Turbulent Transition to Democratic Consolidation*. Singapore: ISEAS.

Mietzner, Marcus (2015) 'Dysfunction by Design: Political Finance and Corruption in Indonesia' 46(4) *Critical Asian Studies* 587–610.

Mietzner, Marcus (2019) 'Indonesia's Electoral System: Why It Needs Reform'. Discussion paper, available at https://www.newmandala.org/indonesias-electoral-system/, accessed 9 August 2022.

MKRI, Secretariat General of the Constitutional Court of the Republic of Indonesia (2010a) '*Naskah Komprehensif Perubahan UUD 1945 Buku I*' (*Comprehensive Script of the 1945 Constitution Amendments Book I*). Jakarta: Mahkamah Konstitusi Republik Indonesia.

MKRI, Secretariat General of the Constitutional Court of the Republic of Indonesia (2010b) '*Naskah Komprehensif Perubahan UUD 1945 Buku V*' (*Comprehensive Script of the 1945 Constitution Amendments Book V*). Jakarta: Mahkamah Konstitusi Republik Indonesia.

Muhtadi, Burhanuddin (2019) *Vote Buying in Indonesia: The Mechanics of Electoral Bribery*. Houndmills, Basingstoke: PalgraveMacmillan.

Nasef, M Imam (2014) 'Studi Kritis Mengenai Kewenangan Dewan Kehormatan Penyelenggara Pemilu dalam Mengawal *Electoral Integrity* di Indonesia' (A Criticial Study on the Authority of the Election Organisers' Honorary Council in Safeguarding Electoral Integrity in Indonesia) 3(21) *IUS QUIA IUSTUM Law Journal* 378–401.

Nasution, Adnan Buyung (1992) *The Aspiration for Constitutional Government in Indonesia: A Socio-legal Study of the Indonesian Konstituante, 1956-1959*. Jakarta: Pustaka Sinar Harapan.

Prihatini, Ella S (2019) 'Women's Views and Experiences of Accessing National Parliament: Evidence from Indonesia' 74 *Women's Studies International Forum* 84–90.

Reilly, Benjamin (2007) 'Electoral and Political Party Reform' in Ross H McLeod and Andrew MacIntyre (eds) *Indonesia: Democracy and the Promise of Good Governance*. Singapore: ISEAS. pp 41–54.

Setiawan, Ken MP and Tomsa, Dirk (2022) *Politics in Contemporary Indonesia: Institutional Change, Policy Challenges and Democratic Decline*. London and New York: Routledge.

Sherlock, Stephen (2004) *The 2004 Indonesian Elections: How the System Works and what the Parties Stand For*. Canberra: Centre for Democratic Institutions.

Shin, Jae Hyeok (2012) 'Electoral System Choice and Parties in New Democracies' in Dirk Tomsa and Andreas Ufen (eds) *Party Politics in Southeast Asia: Clientelism and Electoral Competition in Indonesia, Thailand and the Philippines*. London and New York: Routledge. pp 101–118.

Tashandra, Nabilla (2017) 'Mahfud MD: Sistem Pemilu Terbuka dan Tertutup Tak Melanggar Konstitusi', *Kompas.com*, 18 January, https://nasional.kompas.com/read/2017/01/18/15192 861/mahfud.md.sistem.pemilu.terbuka.dan.tertutup.tak.melanggar.konstitusi, accessed 9 August 2022.

Tomsa, Dirk (2014) 'Party System Fragmentation in Indonesia: The Sub-National Dimension' 14(2) *Journal of East Asian Studies* 249–278.

Tomsa, Dirk (2018) 'Regime Resilience and Presidential Politics in Indonesia' 24(3) *Contemporary Politics* 266–285.

Tomsa, Dirk (2020) 'Public Opinion Polling and Post-truth Politics in Indonesia' 42(1) *Contemporary Southeast Asia* 1–27.

Warburton, Eve and Aspinall, Edward (2019) 'Explaining Indonesia's Democratic Regression: Structure, Agency and Popular Opinion' 41(2) *Contemporary Southeast Asia* 255–285.

8

Election Supervision in Indonesia

Options for Reforming the General Election Supervisory Agency

Fritz Siregar

Introduction

Holding elections that are democratic and that have integrity is a necessity for democracy and the rule of law. Elections are a link between the people and the government (Chillcote 2003: 23). Elections are the most tangible form of sovereignty in the hands of the people and the most concrete form of popular participation in the administration of the state (Setiadi 2008: 29). Elections are used as a parameter to judge whether a country is democratic (Sorensen 2003: 1). As stated by Powell (2000: 4), 'there is a widespread consensus that the presence of competitive elections, more than any other feature, identifies a contemporary nation-state as a democratic political system'.

An electoral management body is a vital part of a democratic state. Democratic elections require election administrators who act fairly, without violence and without intimidating candidates and voters (Pamungkas 2009: 12). An election requires a body with the power to administer the election in an impartial and independent manner (Ranawijaya 1983: 16–17), and these matters are often set out in a constitution.

In Indonesia, Article 22E(5) of the Constitution states that a permanent and independent national election commission is responsible for implementing elections (Butt and Lindsey 2012: 70). According to the law on elections,[1] the commission was named the General Election Commission (*Komisi Pemilihan Umum*, KPU). Other institutions involved in elections include the General Election Supervisory Agency or (*Badan Pengawas Pemilihan Umum, Bawaslu*) and the Honorary Election Ethics Council (*Dewan Kehormatan Penyelenggara Pemilu*, DKPP).[2] These three institutions (KPU, *Bawaslu*, and DKPP) work to ensure that elections are national, permanent, and independent (Asshiddiqie 2007: 787).[3]

---

[1] Law 12/2003 on General Elections for Members of the *Dewan Perwakilan Rakyat* (People's Representative Council or DPR), *Dewan Perwakilan Daerah* (Regional Representative Council or DPD), and *Dewan Perwakilan Rakyat Daerah* (Regional People's Representative Council or DPRD.

[2] Law 15/2011 on Election Administrators was later amended by Law 7/2017 on Election Law.

[3] 'National' means that these three institutions are formed as institutions with a national scope of work. 'Permanent' means that membership is continuous until the end of the term of office. Being 'independent' means that, when carrying out its main tasks and authority, it must not be intervened or influenced by other institutions.

Fritz Siregar, *Election Supervision in Indonesia* In: *Constitutional Democracy in Indonesia*. Edited by: Melissa Crouch, Oxford University Press. © Fritz Siregar, 2023. DOI: 10.1093/oso/9780192870681.003.0008

The idea of establishing an electoral court as a special court is not new in Indonesia (Crouch 2019).[4] The increase of the General Election Supervisory Agency's authority through the amendment of Law 7/2017 is considered to be one step towards creating the electoral court. However, the question remains as to what institutional design of an electoral court is best suited to Indonesia? Should it be formed by establishing a new institution, or by reforms to the authority of the General Election Supervisory Agency, as the existing election supervisory agency?

This chapter considers the options to transform Indonesia's General Election Supervisory Agency (*Bawaslu*) into a special electoral court. The chapter identifies two options. First, transforming the General Election Supervisory Agency into a special electoral court and integrating it as part of the judicial branch and Supreme Court. Second, establishing the special electoral court as an autonomous body and a semi-judicial institution. This chapter suggests that the first option is the most viable because the design of the Constitution does not allow judicial power outside of the Supreme Court and the Constitutional Court.

Election Management Bodies in Indonesia

During the New Order era, elections were the responsibility of the General Election Institute (*Lembaga Pemilihan Umum,* LPU). The existence of political parties was a mere rubber stamp (Santoso and Budhiati 2019: 116). Election supervision was carried out by a supervisory committee chaired by the attorney general, and election observers were not allowed (Santoso and Budhiati 2019).

After 1998 and the fall of President Soeharto, it was widely recognized that election management required major reform. The LPU was replaced by the KPU, which was established by Presidential Decree 16/1999. The KPU is a free and independent institution that reports to the president.[5] KPU membership consists of one representative from each political party participating in the election, as well as five government representatives, with voting rights distributed between party representatives and government representatives.

Election supervision is carried out by the Election Supervisory Committee (*Pengawas Pemilu* or *Panwaslu*). From the centre to the district level, Election Supervisory Committee membership includes judges and community leaders and does not involve government officials. The Election Supervisory Committee supervises all cycles of the holding of elections, resolves disputes arising in the holding of elections, and follows up on findings, disputes, and disagreement that cannot be resolved. It reports to law enforcement agencies.[6]

The Election Supervisory Committee does not have authority to decide disputes over election violations.[7] In resolving disputes, the Committee only acts as a mediator

---

[4] Law 10/2016 concerning Regional Head Election, Art 157 states 'to form a special judicial body to settle election result dispute'.

[5] Law 3/1999 on General Elections for Members of the DPR, DPD, and DPRDs.

[6] Article 26 of Law 3/1999.

[7] Law 3/1999 on General Elections for Members of DPR, DPD, and DPRDs.

whose decisions are not binding. Likewise, in dealing with election criminal acts, the Committee can only forward its findings of alleged criminal violations to law enforcement agencies without any authority to hold the police accountable for following up on the findings submitted by the Committee (Santoso and Budhiati 2019: 143). Despite these weaknesses, the Committee played a strategic role when the KPU failed to determine the results of the 1999 elections because political parties disputed the results[8] (Ma'shum 2001: ix). The Committee examined the objections raised by party representatives and found that the election results determined by the KPU were valid (Thoha 2014: 130).

In 2004, the general election management changed again after the constitutional amendment process.[9] This led to Law 12/2003 that established the KPU as the national, permanent, and independent electoral management body responsible for organising elections. The KPU submits reports to the president and parliament during election cycles (Gaffar 2013: 132). The KPU formed the Election Supervisory Committee, which is subordinate and therefore accountable to the KPU. The Election Supervisory Committee formed the Provincial Election Supervisory Committee, which is accountable to the Election Supervisory Committee, and the Provincial Election Supervisory Committee formed the District/City Election Supervisory Committee, which is accountable to the Provincial Election Supervisory Committee. The District/City Election Supervisory Committee formed the Sub-District Election Supervisory Committee, which is accountable to the District/City Election Supervisory Committee.

In terms of authority, the Election Supervisory Committee acts as a tool for law enforcement, even though it is also a bridge to authorized law enforcement agencies. This is because, in addition to the Election Supervisory Committee supervising the cycles of the election administration, it receives reports of election violations, verifies them, and forwards them to the relevant authority (Santoso and Budhiati 2019: 170). The Election Supervisory Committee's recommendations are limited to recommendations to the Election Commission, and the status of the recommendations is dependent on the Election Commission itself. The Election Supervisory Committee only has the authority to settle disputes that do not contain violations. The problem of authority ultimately has implications for the Election Supervisory Committee's imbalanced handling of both criminal and administrative violations. In the 2004 legislative elections, 3,153 election crime reports were handled by the Election Supervisory Committee. Only 2,413 were forwarded to the police, and of these, 1,022 were decided by the District Court. For administrative violations, out of 8,946 reports, 2,822 were handled by the Election Commission (Santoso and Budhiati 2019: 171–172).

In the lead up to the 2009 General Election, the various electoral management bodies were again reformed. A significant change involved filling the positions of Election Commission members using a selection team formed by the president. The

---

[8] The 1999 election was considered 'unique'. The reason is because of two different opinions about elections. Based on the Election Oversight Committee and international observers, the 1999 election was carried out democratically. Ironically, the KPU said (at the time it consisted of representatives of political parties) that the election was undemocratic and experienced many irregularities/irregularities.

[9] In accordance with the mandate of Art 22E(5) of the 1945 Constitution.

selection team's candidates were submitted to parliament to take the fit and proper test. In another significant change, the Election Supervisory Committee, which was previously ad hoc and part of the Election Commission, was transformed into an independent and permanent General Election Supervisory Agency (*Bawaslu*) at the national level. The provincial and district/city levels were still ad hoc, and the KPU played a role in the recruitment of Election Supervisory Committee members.

In 2010, the functions of the Election Commission and General Election Supervisory Agency were separated.[10] This decision arose from a judicial review case that was submitted by the General Election Supervisory Agency to the Constitutional Court. The General Election Supervisory Agency questioned the involvement of the General Election Commission in forming the Election Supervisory Committee in the regions. The General Election Supervisory Agency considered that the General Election Supervisory Agency had the authority to form the Election Supervisory Committee (Suswantoro 2016: 5). In making its decision, the Court stated that the recruitment mechanism of the Election Supervisory Committee members made them dependent on the General Election Commission.[11] Through this decision, the existence of the General Election Supervisory Agency was confirmed as an independent institution like the Election Commission, so the Election Commission and Election Supervisory Agency are equal. Both the Election Commission and Election Supervisory Agency are national, permanent, and independent election management bodies. This decision only applied after the 2009 General Election, and so did not apply to disputes from the 2009 election decided in 2010.

Before the 2014 elections, efforts were made to consolidate the electoral management bodies, including affirming the Election Commission as an independent institution. The Election Commission as a permanent and hierarchical institution has a large workload because it not only conducts elections at the national level, but also continues to coordinate and supervise the implementation of local elections at the regional level (Santoso and Budhiati 2019: 224). In terms of supervision, efforts were also made to strengthen the Election Supervisory Agency.[12] The Election Supervisory Agency is no longer subordinate to the Election Commission but has an equal status. Further, the Election Supervisory Agency was previously only responsible for settling disputes between election participants. The Election Supervisory Agency was given the authority to resolve disputes between election participants and the Election Commission.[13] In addition, the Election Supervisory Agency was given the authority to resolve disputes over Regional Head Elections (*Pilkada*).[14]

In 2011, the Ethics Council was created for at least two reasons.[15] First, there had been several cases involving corruption in elections, as well as other cases relating to the independence of the election organizer. Second, there was a problem regarding the ineffectiveness of the enforcement of ethical standards by the Election Commission and Election Supervisory Agency (Santoso and Budhiati 2019: 234). For these reasons,

---

[10] Decision 11/PUU-VIII/2010.
[11] Regulated in Law 22/2007 on Electoral Administrator.
[12] Based on Art 69(2) of Law 15/2011 on Election Administrator.
[13] Law 8/2012 on General Election for Members of the DPR, DPD, and DPRDs.
[14] Law 8/2015 on Regional Head Election (*Pilkada*).
[15] Law 15/2011 on Electoral Administrator.

it was necessary to form a separate institution that had the primary function of supervising the ethics of the electoral management bodies.

Before the 2019 elections, the law concerning electoral management bodies was revised again. The most visible change was a shift in the status, duties, and authority of the Election Commission, Election Supervisory Agency, and Ethics Council. The duties and authority of the Election Commission in solving administrative violations decreased, while the duties and authority of the Election Supervisory Agency increased. The accreditation of election observers, which was initially the authority of the Election Commission, was transferred to the Election Supervisory Agency. Further, the Election Supervisory Agency's duties and authority in electoral dispute settlement were strengthened. The Election Supervisory Agency is even the only electoral management body that is authorized to declare election violations which lead to disqualification of the presidential candidate.

Theoretical Framework on Election Supervision

In the design of electoral laws, the Election Supervisory Agency is authorized to supervise elections across Indonesia. The role of the Election Supervisory Agency is not only to supervise elections but also to act as an authorized institution to resolve election process disputes—both disputes between election participants and between participants and electoral management bodies.[16] This reinforces the Election Supervisory Agency's authority in carrying out its duties in the area of election supervision and law enforcement. The Election Supervisory Agency guarantees and supervises the process of conducting elections with integrity and in a democratic and dignified manner. The design of this body aims to realize the principles that underlie election supervision management more broadly.

Power obtained through periodic elections determines the government, advances the welfare of citizens through responsive policymaking, enables the dissemination of decision-making, and promotes active public participation (Pildes 2004). Therefore, democracy is a system of government that aims to serve the interests of the people. Citizens are involved in decision-making processes through their representatives. As a result, the objective of democracy is to maintain and establish the people's sovereignty. Strong argues that:

> by democracy in this sense, we, therefore, mean a system of government in which the majority of the grown members of the political community participate through a method of representation which secures that the government is ultimately responsible for its actions to that majority. In other words, the contemporary constitutional state must be based on a system of democratic representation which guarantees the sovereignty of the people (Strong 1961: 13).

---

[16] Law 7/2017 on Election Law.

In Strong's view, a democratic state is based on a system of democratic representation that guarantees the sovereignty of the people. The same opinion was held by Kelsen (1973: 284), who stated that 'democracy means that what is represented in the legal order of the State is identical with the wills of subjects'.

Based on the ideas proposed by Strong and Kelsen above, the existence of the Election Supervisory Agency is necessary to uphold people's sovereignty, which is central to democracy. The existence of the Election Supervisory Agency in supervising the management of elections is intended to strengthen democratic institutions. Elections are one of the most important processes in democracy. The importance of elections is illustrated by Hanan (2019: ix–x) who stated that 'it is difficult to imagine democracy without an election. It is also hard to imagine a quality democracy without a quality election'.

The Election Supervisory Agency encourages the implementation of elections that fulfil procedural and substantive requirements. There is a risk that activities in the electoral process have the potential to reduce the constitutional rights of citizens to vote and be elected, which can lead to disputes. To guarantee an honest and fair election, voters, those who participate in the election and the general public, need to be protected from irregularities such as fear, intimidation, bribery, fraud, and other practices (Santoso 2011, 29). The Election Supervisory Agency not only prevents, identifies, and fixes election irregularities, but it also sanctions perpetrators in line with international standards (International IDEA 2002, 93). The sanctions aim to protect all election stakeholders and the people as holders of sovereignty and also to uphold electoral justice.

Electoral Justice

The concept of electoral justice means that every party involved in an election, such as election participants, candidates, campaign teams, and community members, should not be disadvantaged or treated unfairly by the election organizer (Hidayat 2015: 3). The expression 'electoral justice' has various meanings. In a broad sense, it means ensuring that every action, procedure, and decision related to the electoral process is in line with the law. It also ensures that the enjoyment of electoral rights is protected and restored, which gives people who believe their electoral rights have been violated the ability to make a complaint and receive a hearing and an adjudication (International IDEA 2010: 9).

Electoral justice is not just about proceedings to enforce electoral rules; rather, it informs the design and conduct of electoral processes, and it influences the actions of all stakeholders. In addition to the influence of the law or the legal framework governing the electoral processes themselves, the electoral justice system is heavily influenced by the socio-cultural, historical, and political context. Hence, diverse electoral justice practices and systems exist in different national and regional contexts around the world. An electoral justice system needs to operate efficiently in a technical sense. It should also act effectively, which means independently and impartially, and it should promote justice as well as transparency, accessibility, inclusiveness, and equal opportunity (Junaidi, Maulana, and Rahmah 2020: 3).

Electoral justice mechanisms include all of the means that are in place to prevent electoral disputes, as well as the formal mechanisms for resolving them by institutional means and the informal mechanisms or alternative means for their resolution. In democracies, electoral justice plays a decisive role in ensuring the stability of the political system and adherence to the legal framework; thus, it also contributes to the consolidation of democratic governance. The role of electoral justice has become recognized as a crucial factor in all democracies, whether emerging or established. Electoral justice encompasses the means for preventing violations of the electoral legal framework, as well as those mechanisms that aimed at resolving electoral disputes that arise from the non-observance or breach of the law. In this regard, it includes both formal and informal mechanisms for electoral dispute resolution (Junaidi, Maulana, and Rahmah 2020: 9).

Electoral justice is not merely interpreted within procedural–formalistic limits (regulatory measures and the availability of complaint mechanisms). Electoral justice includes the prevention of electoral disputes, the resolution of electoral disputes, and the alternative electoral dispute resolutions. Electoral justice concerns equality between citizens, that is, equality in the nomination, voting, vote counting, and seat allocation of legislative bodies. It also ensures free and fair competition (Fahmi 2016: 170). Thus, electoral justice covers all aspects that affect how elections operate freely and equally. *Bawaslu* aims to realize free and equal elections in its position as an election supervisory agency.

Models of Electoral Dispute Resolution

Disputes arise at every general election. Disputes can occur between participants and the election organizer and between election participants. In addition, disputes may arise during various cycles of the election—for example, in relation to the candidacy and the results of the election itself. However, the emergence of a dispute or problem should not be considered a weakness of an electoral system but rather an important element that must exist. The existence of an effective dispute resolution mechanism is needed to maintain the legitimacy and integrity of an election. Petit (2000: 5) stated that 'challenges to election results, or the conduct of elections, should not be considered a weakness of the electoral system, but a sign of its resilience'.

When an electoral process functions well, the existence of an electoral justice system ensures that the rights of the people in the election are maintained and that mistakes do not occur. In contrast, when a fraud or violation occurs, the electoral justice system must be able to resolve and recover the losses that have been experienced. Therefore, from the perspective of human rights, an electoral justice system is not limited to resolving election disputes; rather, it protects citizens' political and voting rights. In this case, the electoral justice system not only protects basic political rights, such as the right to assemble, the right to vote, gender equality, freedom of association and affiliation, the right to security, and the right to engage in public activities, but also the rights of freedom of opinion, freedom of association, the right to information, and the right to submit complaints (Electoral Integrity Group no date: 3).

An electoral justice system is a mechanism provided by a country to guarantee and ensure that actions, stages, and decisions are in accordance with the existing legal framework, and to protect and restore the exercise of suffrage (International IDEA 2010: 9). In some contexts, it is regulated at the local, regional, and international levels. The electoral justice system is a key instrument of the rule of law and a guarantee of the implementation of democratic principles to safeguard freedom and justice in elections.

Similarly, electoral dispute resolution is a system to review legal electoral decisions or procedures (ACE Project 2012). The review can be conducted through judicial and political institutions. Election dispute resolution is needed to ensure real protection and effective law enforcement of citizens' right to vote and the right to be elected. Given the broad understanding of the dispute resolution mechanism above, I focus on the existence of an institution authorized to make decisions on electoral disputes that arise.

The existence of electoral dispute resolution mechanisms is closely related to the due process of law. Procedurally, the concept of due process of law requires a fair and proper process before making a decision that may be detrimental to the individual (Lim 2006: 5). Procedurally, the main objective of the due process of law is to ensure that the fact-finding process in dispute resolution also accommodates conflicting interests between the parties (Fleiner 2005: 20). Thus, the due process of law is not only about the existence of the mechanism, but also ensuring that the mechanism works properly and is fair.

At an international level, there are ten principles of electoral dispute resolution known as the Accra Guiding Principles on Electoral Justice (Ghana Principles) (*Bawaslu*-International IDEA 2018, 14). These principles include integrity, participative, in accordance with the law, impartial and fair, professional, independent, transparency, without violence, regularity, and reception. (Electoral Integrity Group no date: 4–11). There are also guidelines for the design and administration of electoral complaints adjudication systems (IFES, 2011: 16).

Electoral dispute settlement systems around the world are diverse because of the regulatory models and institutions involved. The electoral framework and administrative processes in the resolution of election disputes depend on the cultural, political, and legal traditions of each country. There is no single approach that can work for all countries (Dahl and Clegg 2011: 121).

In terms of the existence of electoral dispute resolution mechanisms, three main models of electoral dispute resolution are used in various parts of the world: resolutions by judicial institutions, resolutions by electoral institutions, and special institutions for electoral dispute resolution. In addition to these main models, countries use other mechanisms, such as dispute resolution through the parliament or constitutional council of the respective country.

The majority of countries around the world, amounting to 59 per cent, or as many as 132 countries, give the judiciary branch authority to settle election disputes. In contrast, 37 per cent, or as many as eighty-four countries, including Indonesia, implement dispute resolution using election management bodies. Around 12 per cent, or as many as twenty-seven countries, use special institutions for electoral dispute resolution. The rest—around 11 per cent, or as many as twenty-five countries—implement special mechanisms to resolve election disputes.

There are various electoral dispute resolution models around the world. ACE Project identifies five types: legislative model, judicial model, special judicial model, Constitutional Court model, and alternative dispute resolution (ADR) models (ACE Project 2012). Similarly, International IDEA identifies four types:[17] legislative; judiciary; election management body, which has judicial power; and ad hoc bodies, which are formed by involving international bodies or forming bodies as part of an internal unit that handles election dispute resolution at the national level (International IDEA 2010: 14). In this chapter I discuss five models of dispute resolution institution, drawing on the work of International IDEA and ACE research.

The Legislative Model

From a historical perspective, the legislative model departs from the principle of the separation of powers, which requires independence between the branches of government (Enriques 2010: 64). The legislative election dispute resolution model was formed as a mechanism to defend the legislature from the possibility of intervention by the executive. This model may be applied by a state that is not yet fully ready to adopt the concept of judicial election disputes (ACE Project 2012). In this model, the legislature is given the authority to determine election validation. In the context of the United States (US), this is known as the qualification or certification of elections[18] (Senate 2017).

However, there are currently no countries in the world that fully implement this model because of the potential for abuse. Almost all countries that implement this system still involve the judiciary in the election dispute resolution process (Orozco-Henríquez 2010: 15). For example, Articles 105 and 107 of the Lithuanian Constitution stipulate that the Constitutional Court has the authority to determine whether there are violations in the Lithuanian presidential and parliamentary elections. The Lithuanian parliament has the authority to give a final decision on decisions issued by the Constitutional Court (Enriques 2010: 66).

The Judicial Model

The judicial model, also known as the English model, gives the authority of dispute resolution to judges or judicial bodies of the first instance in the branch of judicial power to resolve election disputes. This model stems from the idea that judicial institutions are independent. Experts who support this model underlie the argument that

---

[17] International IDEA's classifications are based on the existence of the highest decision-making body assigned to dispute resolution in national legislative elections held in all democracies.

[18] In the US legislative election system, the certification of congress is an official document containing the name and term of office issued by parliament that gives rights and authority to members of the house of representatives or senate congress. Examples of certification of congress documents can be found at https://www.congress.gov/congressional-record/2017/1/3/senate-section/article/S1-4, accessed 9 August 2022.

the task of making decisions and imposing qualification sanctions in elections has a judicial element in them, so it must be carried out by the judiciary.

The model of resolution by the judiciary is a solution where there are many violations by the legislative or political body that has been entrusted to govern the electoral dispute resolution system (Orozco-Henríquez 2010: 15). Efforts to resolve election problems must be kept away from political interests or the political parties themselves, but they must be based on the rules and values of justice itself. International IDEA divides the settlement model by the judiciary into four groups: (1) general court, which is part of the judicial branch; (2) council or constitutional court; (3) administrative court; (4) special election court. Among these models, a dispute resolution system through a general court that is part of the judicial branch is the most commonly applied model. In designing such a system, it is necessary to consider the independence and credibility of the existing justice system—especially in new democracies or in countries that are in a period of democratic consolidation. If the justice system is not considered credible, not independent (although not proven true), or under the control of an executive or political party in government, the credibility of the electoral dispute resolution system will be lost. One country that implements election dispute resolution using this model is Australia.

In contrast, the administrative court model is a type of electoral dispute resolution system that is not widely used by countries. In this model, dispute resolution is carried out by the administrative court, which is both independent and part of the judicial branch that acts as the highest and final decision-maker. The application of this model can be found in two countries, namely Finland and Colombia.

The Settlement Model by a Special Election Court

This model was developed in Latin American countries by creating a special electoral dispute resolution agency tasked with settling election dispute processes and election results disputes. This institutional model can be part of a judicial or executive body and can function like a court of first instance or an appeal. The development of this model is drawn from Latin American countries. The model illustrates the development of democracy in the region, and the main strength of the model—dispute settlement by special institutions to settle election cases—is that dispute resolution can be carried out quickly, and the judge who acts has experience and familiarity with the issue and the law (Davis-Roberts 2009). Two main models of dispute resolution are used by this special institution: establishing an autonomous institution, and an institution that is part of the judiciary branch.

The first model is autonomous dispute resolution institutions that are special institutions formed by the constitution that are not part of the three main state branches (executive, legislative, and judicative). The formation of this model is the first stage in moving from a traditional dispute resolution model that is based on political discourse to a new justice system that is tasked with resolving disputes based on legal procedures. The formation of this autonomous institution is also a follow-up to integrating dispute settlement into the judicial branch. Institutional independence is important to ensure it is not affected by political influence. The benefit of this model is that it can prevent the judicial institution from political intervention.[19] One country that has been successful in implementing this model is Mexico[20] (Enriques 2010: 85). In 1996, reform of the Mexican constitution created an autonomous judicial institution, which has special jurisdiction to handle election-related cases with final decisions (Tribunal Electoral del Poder Judicial de la Federacion 2012: 3). According to a report by the Inter-American Commission on Human Rights (IACHR), the Mexican electoral judiciary has issued decisions that have significantly pushed Mexico to become a democratic country—for example, by imposing fines on several political parties that have been proven to have committed money politics (IACHR 2018: 101).

In addition to being an autonomous judiciary, some states have an independent dispute resolution authority to organize and administer the electoral process, hear disputes, and issue final decisions (International IDEA 2010: 17). There is a risk of abuse of authority in this model, especially if decisions made cannot be appealed or compared. The possibility of abuse of authority is greater if only one authority agency is appointed to hold elections while simultaneously resolving disputes that arise in elections: in this case, the electoral management body acts as the judge and the disputed party for the same case. The institutional model of the Election Supervisory Agency (*Bawaslu*) of the Republic of Indonesia provides an example of this model.

The second model is special electoral dispute resolution institutions that are part of the judicial branch as election-specific judicial institutions that have been created based on due process considerations (ACE Project 2012). This institution is still designed to be independent from other judicial bodies. This dispute resolution model starts from the idea that election disputes must be procedurally resolved in accordance with universal and fundamental binding principles. Some of these special courts are permanent. However, there are also temporary courts, which are formed only in relation to an upcoming election. If a country does not have a large number of election disputes, it may be sufficient to have temporary courts during the pre-election and post-election periods (International IDEA 2010: 16).

The Model of Dispute Resolution by the Constitutional Court

Electoral dispute resolution by a constitutional court is widely known as the Austrian model. Many constitutions in Europe that were formed after World War I followed the Weimar Constitution (1919) and the Austrian Constitution (1920) by giving the Constitutional Court the authority to resolve election disputes.[21] In the Austrian context, for example, the resolution of disputes in parliamentary elections, presidential

---

[19] In Latin American countries, special electoral justice institutions have been formed by sixteen of the nineteen countries in the region. Ten of the sixteen countries have established autonomous dispute resolution institutions, including Mexico, Costa Rica, Chile, Ecuador, El Salvador, Guatemala, Honduras, Panama, Peru, and Uruguay.

[20] In the investigative report, the Inter-American Commission on Human Rights reported that the elections in Mexico are among the most exciting in the region of Latin America.

[21] The Austrian Constitution gives authority to the Constitutional Court to resolve any disputes arising from the election of representative institutions at both the central and regional levels. This authority then developed to include all other democratic activities, such as the referendum since 1929 and the presidential election since 1931.

election, and other democratic matters such as referendums have long been the jurisdiction of the Constitutional Court. The Constitutional Court can even order a re-election (Enriques 2010: 70). With the inclusion of a Constitutional Court or tribunal in the electoral dispute resolution system, decisions about the validity of the electoral process are carried out by bodies that have explicit constitutional jurisdiction. In some countries, constitutional councils or courts are part of the judicial branch. Other countries, such as France, have an electoral dispute resolution system that combines the use of institution with administrative review and constitutional review authority with autonomous administrative agency.

Alternative Dispute Resolution Models and Ad Hoc Bodies

The alternative dispute resolution (ADR) model relies on dispute resolution other than settling disputes through a judiciary branch. This model of electoral dispute resolution is used when the usual models of dispute resolution do not produce decisions as expected. The main strengths of this model are its flexibility and the prospect of speedy dispute resolution compared with mechanisms through the courts. If it is designed well, the ADR model can be an effective and feasible settlement model, particularly in the context of transition, when the legitimacy of state institutions is being questioned or when institutions are weak and ineffective. In such situations, ADR models are formed by specialized institutions that consist of experts and are encouraged by relevant international agencies (ACE Project 2012). However, the ADR model may not be in accordance with international standards requiring the existence of an independent and impartial mechanism. This mechanism supports the existence of other mechanisms. Another limitation of this model is that resolution depends on the agreement of the parties.

The settlement model entrusted to an ad hoc agency may be formed after a conflict situation occurs in a country due to a transition agreement (International IDEA 2010: 17). This settlement model is temporary and is often sponsored by international organizations. In some cases, ad hoc bodies have been formed internally in a country. This is generally done after negotiations to avoid conflict in the future.

Reflections on the General Election
Supervisory Agency (*Bawaslu*)

Turning to Indonesia, the Election Supervisory Agency plays two main roles (Arts 93–96). The Election Supervisory Agency's duties include receiving alleged violations or requests for dispute resolution to resolving disputes and enforcing decisions. The Election Supervisory Board has a duty to review a complaint. The chairperson of the Election Supervisory Agency, Abhan, in the book *What and Who is the Election Supervisory Agency* suggested that commissioners of the Election Supervisory Agency play a role as both supervisor and judge: 'So in our clothes we are sometimes on one side as supervisors but on the other hand, we are also judges … On the other hand, I am also a supervisor' (*Bawaslu* 2018: 30). While the criminal justice system consists of three separate parts—police, prosecutors, and judges—electoral justice is delivered by one body, the Election Supervisory Agency.

A review of several cases shows that the Election Supervisory Agency is primarily a court or judge, rather than a supervisor.[22] One example regards a dispute over a petition filed by political parties that was rejected by the Election Commission to participate in the 2019 General Elections. By deciding that case, *Bawaslu* was considered to have a higher position than the Election Commission because it had to review a regulation under the general elections law.[23]

The Election Supervisory Agency's authority has been criticized by Supriyanto for three reasons:

> First, Election Supervisory Agency carries out judicial functions, but at the same time also carries out a supervisory function. This is a double function that can cause a conflict of interest. As an election supervision, the Election Supervisory Agency already has a certain assessment of a case or [election] administrative violation case. Whereas later this institution also adjudicates the case. Obviously, its judgment (when carrying out the supervisory function) will influence its decision (when it becomes a judicial institution). Secondly, the presence of an election court (institution) to deal with administrative violations clearly adds to the length of the election administration process, so that elections are not only more expensive, but also more bureaucratic, wordy, and alienate the substance of democracy. Third, specifically for the 2019 elections, members of Election Supervisory Agency, Provincial Election Supervisory Agency and Regency/City Election Supervisory Agency are recruited solely as election supervisors (Supriyanto 2017).

In addition to Supriyanto, a non-governmental organization engaged in the elections, known as KoDe Initiative, has also criticized the Election Supervisory Agency and how it conducts adjudication during administrative violation hearing. The Agency has been criticized for the lack of clear guidelines about the timeframe for the submission of documents; that the scheduling of its hearings is too close and makes it difficult for parties to prepare their response; and for being slow to provide its decision, both in print and online. There are also unclear guidelines about the code of conduct in the hearing (Ayuwuragil 2017).

Due to these criticisms, it is necessary to review whether and how the Election Supervisory Agency should play a role in the system of election supervision. The dual function held by the Election Supervisory Agency is also a feature of the other electoral management bodies, such as the Dominican Republic that has a dual function as an investigator and prosecutor. Therefore, the dual function of the Agency in Indonesia is not an anomaly in the holding of elections and the enforcement of election justice. Most importantly, the electoral management body must be supported by

---

[22] For the 2019 General Elections, *Bawaslu* handled 16,427 cases on election administration violation, 584 criminal cases on criminal election violation (in which 335 had a court verdict) and settled 773 election disputes.

[23] Election Commission Regulation 11/2017 on the Registration, Verification and Determination of Political Parties Participating in the General Elections of Members of the Representative Council and the Regional People's Representative Council to Law 7/2017 on General Elections.

members who are professional and who have integrity. However, if it is doubtful that electoral management body members can carry out both functions simultaneously, several options to reform the Election Supervisory Agency are available.

Alternative Options for Election Supervision Management in Indonesia

One alternative is the idea of a special election court. Several problems have arisen with the current model, including that separate legal remedies can be submitted to several judicial branches. Under these conditions, legal remedies for the election cycle face challenges with simultaneous election implementation because the cycles of the electoral process and legal remedies for each electoral cycle need to be carried out simultaneously. The current system of multiple legal avenues is not feasible in light of the electoral cycle.

According to the law, prior to simultaneous national elections, a special judicial body must be formed to dispute the results of the election.[24] However, this body has not yet been formed. Before the special election body has been formed, the Constitutional Court has the authority to examine and adjudicate disputes over the results of the election. However, to date, the Constitutional Court still adjudicates election result disputes.[25] In 2019, during a case concerning review of the Regional Election Law, Parliament Member Arteri Dahlan, as the DPR's representative, informed the Court that 'the parliament is still satisfied with the Constitutional Court's performance and has no intention to create special election court'.[26] This appears to suggest this option is not being considered by the government.

The Constitutional Court is the implementing agency of the judiciary branch that has authority to settle disputes over election results.[27] There is no arrangement in the General Elections Laws to establish a special judiciary outside the Constitutional Court. This is in line with the authority of the Constitutional Court (Art 24C(1)). Thus, the establishment of a special election court in Indonesia may be the answer to the current problems in electoral supervision.

A Special Electoral Court as Part of the Judicial Branch

The first possible model is a special election court as an ad hoc court under the Supreme Court. This option is viable because it is considered constitutional in Indonesia (Art 24(2), 24A(5)). At least three matters must be considered to establish a special election

---

[24] Article 157 of Law 10/2016 concerning the Second Amendment to Law 1/2015 concerning Establishment of Government Regulation in Lieu of Law 1/2014 concerning the Election of Governors, Regents and Mayors into Laws (Regional Head Election).

[25] Article 157(3): The Constitutional Court has the authority to examine and adjudicate disputes over the results of the election until a special judicial body has been formed.

[26] See   https://kabar24.bisnis.com/read/20191118/15/1171589/sengketa-pilkada-masih-percaya-mk-dpr-belum-bentuk-badan-khusus-, 26 February 2021.

[27] Article 474 of the General Elections Laws.

court under the Supreme Court. First, special courts can only be established under the Supreme Court. Referring to Law 48/2009 concerning Judicial Power, the institutional design of an election-specific court must be established in one of the judicial spheres under the Supreme Court, either the general judiciary, the religious justice branch, the military court branch, or the administrative court branch. The general judicial branch is the most relevant judicial environment as the host of the special election court.

Second, a special court must be established in a law. This understanding departs from the phrase 'a special court is a court ... regulated by law'. In the statutory approach, the phrase is 'delegative provision', which means that the formation of a special court is formed through a law that must specifically regulate the special election court. The formation and arrangement of special election courts cannot be inserted in the regulations in the Election Law[28] (Butt 2015: 129). Therefore, the establishment of a special election court must be carried out through a separate law, namely the Law on Election Court.

The third matter that must be considered in the design of a special election court relates to creating courts as ad hoc special courts. One example of an ad hoc court is the Human Rights Court (Setiawan 2019: 287; Crouch 2019). By using the definition of an ad hoc judge in the Law on Judicial Power, an ad hoc special court is interpreted as a special temporary court that has absolute and relative competence in certain fields to examine, hear, and decide on a case regulated in the law. If the ad hoc nature is to be adopted in the special election court design, later the court will only be formed before the election process, which starts no later than six months before the first stage of the election cycle and ends no later than one year after all cycles of the administration election are complete.

The final question that may arise regarding the special election court relates to the domicile of the court that is in line with its competence. I propose that the special election court is a domicile in accordance with its territory or competence. Election-specific courts for presidential, legislative (DPR), and regional (DPD) representative members should be attached to the Supreme Court. For the Provincial Regional Election (Governor election), a special election court should be attached to the Appeal Court at the provincial level. For the Regency and City Election (district head elections/mayor elections), a special election court should be attached to District Courts at the district/city level. This design will achieve efficiency in the settlement of cases given the relatively large number of regional head election cases and the demands to complete cases as quickly as possible. According to Utami (2018), establishing a special election court under the Supreme Court is realistic and necessary given the lack of coordination between the court and the Election Supervisory Agency, and will make sure that there is no conflict of authority and ensure there is consistency in the interpretation of the law (Utami 2018, 299).

However, two significant challenges arise if a special election court was formed. First, a judge who serves in the special election court under the Supreme Court would

---

[28] On 19 December 2006, the Constitutional Court, in reviewing Law 30/2002 on Corruption Eradication Commission (KPK), declared the establishment of an 'Anti-Corruption Court' in Law 30/2002 unconstitutional. The Court provides a three-year period for the DPR to regulate an anti-corruption court in a specific law.

ideally be a legal scholar with expertise in technical electoral matters. Unfortunately, in Indonesia, few law graduates have these qualifications, so it may be difficult to find someone to fill the bench.[29] Second, this option requires support from the Supreme Court. However, the option has been rejected by the Supreme Court itself, as conveyed by Chief Justice Ali (CR-23 2017). This poses a big challenge for the presence of a special election court in the Supreme Court.

A Special Election Court as an Autonomous Body

A special autonomous judicial body overcomes the criticism described earlier. In 2017, the Election Supervisory Agency became an investigative institution and a judge of election disputes and violations. This dual function phenomenon is welcomed as an effort to strengthen the Election Supervisory Agency's role in creating a fair election. However, it must also be recognized that the expansion of its authority has the potential for abuse, especially if the decision issued cannot be tested or appealed (International IDEA 2010: 17).

Regarding this situation, the proposal to transform the Election Supervisory Agency into an election-specific judicial body is becoming increasingly relevant. Ida Budhiati, in a dissertation entitled 'Reconstruction of the Political Law of Election Organizers in Indonesia' said that Election Supervisory Agency is no longer relevant (Handaka 2018). The Election Supervisory Agency should be transformed into an election court, and its oversight function should be transferred to civil society. Its dual role has moved the Election Supervisory Agency away from the principle of justice because every problem has been forced to act on behalf of the supervisory function. Refly Harun, in a dissertation entitled 'Settlement of Dispute over Election Results in Indonesia', stated that to create an honest and fair election, the perspective used should be law enforcement not a prevention mechanism (Sukamto 2016). Two principles can be used as the basis for structuring the existing election dispute settlement institution—namely, the integration of most electoral dispute resolution processes and the principle of electoral justice as a guide to the resolution of disputes. Harun emphasizes that the Election Supervisory Agency should be transformed into a special election court to handle the resolution of election disputes and disputes over election results (Harun 2016: 1).

The choice of forming an autonomous electoral judicial body is closely related to the model used in Latin American countries—especially in Brazil and Mexico, which form special autonomous election courts outside existing judicial bodies. Brazil formed the Superior Electoral Tribunal, which has broad authority and covers all aspects of elections and political parties.[30] Mexico formed the Judicial de la Federacion Tribunal

---

[29] Among the 2,107 permanent members of the Election Supervisory Agency from the national, provincial and regency levels, only 333 commissioners have legal backgrounds, equivalent to 15.8 per cent.

[30] As the highest institution in the electoral court in Brazil, the authority of the Superior Electoral Tribunal concerns the ratification of the registration of political parties as well as presidential and vice-presidential candidates, handling jurisdictional conflicts between regional electoral courts, handling disputes over the final election results, accepting appeals from regional electoral courts, authorizing state divisions to become constituencies, answering questions from political parties related to election issues, passing ballot counts, and taking other actions deemed necessary to implement electoral laws.

del Poder. In general, the formation of a special electoral justice institution by several Latin American countries has produced a strong combination of administrative duties and handling election disputes (Bisariyadi 2012: 550).

One of the main benefits of establishing a special autonomous court is that it prevents the courts that have been formed—both the Supreme Court and the lower judicial body, as well as the Constitutional Court—from interfering in matters of a political nature. In Indonesia, this was realized by the Constitutional Court and the Supreme Court because both institutions had expressly refused the additional task of resolving disputes over the results of regional head elections (Stefanie 2015). The choice to transform the Election Supervisory Agency into an autonomous special judicial body is the most ideal compared with establishing a special court under the Supreme Court.

To realize this, there are two options. First, a special judicial body can be designed that is in line with the Supreme Court and the Constitutional Court as applied in Mexico and Brazil. The establishment of an autonomous judicial institution in line with the Supreme Court and the Constitutional Court is the most ideal choice based on constitutional considerations. However, it is difficult to apply this option in Indonesia because it requires momentum for constitutional changes.[31] Also, as previously explained, the 1945 Constitution has given the role of resolving election result disputes over the presidential and vice-presidential elections and legislative elections to the Constitutional Court. Therefore, the constitutional amendment required to reduce the Constitutional Court's authority and transfer that authority to newly established institutions. This alternative would be challenging to achieve as the Constitutional Court has settled election result disputes since 2004 and is praised by the public for its role.

Second, the Election Supervisory Agency can be transformed into a semi-judicial institution with a focus on resolving election disputes. The choice to transform *Bawaslu* into a semi-judicial or quasi judicial institution is more realistic because it can be achieved by making changes at the regulation level. There is a precedent for this. Similar institutions for consumer disputes and information requests have been established in Indonesia—namely, the Consumer Dispute Settlement Agency (*Badan Penyelesaian Sengketa Konsumen*, BPSK) and the Central Information Commission (*Komisi Informasi Pusat*, KIP).[32] The special judicial body should become the central dispute settlement mechanism for election problems in Indonesia. However, establishing a semi-judicial institution that acts as a special electoral court outside the Supreme Court's judicial sphere may create further uncertainty. The parties may appeal all decisions by a semi-judicial institution to the general court or administrative court.[33] Judges of the administrative court may issue an injunction that may suspend

[31] Article 24C(1) of the 1945 Constitution states that the authority to decide on disputes over the results of general elections is the authority of the Constitutional Court. Regarding this provision, through Decision 96/PUU-XI/2013, the Constitutional Court narrowed the meaning of the general election in that Article, which was only related to disputes over the results of the presidential and vice-presidential elections and the results of legislative elections.

[32] The two institutions are autonomous institutions that have a duty to adjudicate cases in the field of consumer and information disputes. The legal basis for its formation can be seen in Art 47 of Law 8/1999 on Consumer Protection and Art 1 point (5) of Law 14/2008 on Public Disclosure.

[33] See Art 10(1) of the Law on Judicial Power.

the election process.[34] Those appeal processes may lead to more uncertainty in the process and will delay the election procedure itself.

Conclusion

The model of election supervision has been modified before every election in the post-constitutional reform period in Indonesia. The Election Supervisory Agency has changed from an ad hoc institution with special objectives to become a permanent institution created at the national level and down to the district/city level. The Election Supervisory Agency plays a dual function as supervisor and judge, which many critics suggest should be carried out by two separate institutions rather than one because it mixes the functions of prosecuting and judging. There is a need to reform the Election Supervisory Agency.

The first option is the formation of a special electoral justice body. This body must be under the Supreme Court, because the Constitution does not permit the possibility of judicial power emerging outside the Supreme Court and the Constitutional Court (Art 24(2)). Through a special judicial elections body, various forms of violations, disputes, and election crime can be solved by a single judicial institution and ensure legal certainty.

The second option is to transform the Election Supervisory Agency into a special court as an autonomous body. The difference to the first option is that the Election Supervisory Agency would become a special election court that is not under the Supreme Court. It is not clear whether this option is constitutional. A limited constitutional amendment may be needed to establish a special electoral justice body equal to the Supreme Court and the Constitutional Court, as in Mexico and Brazil. This choice is a long-term hope because the constitutional amendment process is difficult. Alternatively, steps can be taken to make the Election Supervisory Agency a special election court that is semi-judicial or quasi-judicial. This option is viable because it only requires revision to the law and other semi-judicial institutions that already exist in Indonesia.

Reform of the Election Supervisory Agency as a special election court is necessary because election supervision management is important. Given the complexities of the electoral process, it cannot be left to civil society alone. The Election Supervisory Agency's role in supervising the election process still needs to be maintained. The creation of a new institution as an election court brings the governance of election justice enforcement under one roof, including violations, disputes, disputes over regional head elections, and political criminal acts. However, to ensure its decision may be enforced, the election court should be established under the Supreme Court.

An Election Court is much needed in Indonesia. There are many lessons to be learnt from comparative institutions globally. It is a concept that must be encouraged[35] because the current system has at times failed to uphold electoral justice.

---

[34] Law on the Administrative Court, Art 113.

[35] It was also stated in one of the proposals in the 5th Constitutional Law Conference held on 9–12 November 2018 in Batusangkar, West Sumatra.

References

ACE Project (no date) 'Comparison of Countries by Model of Election Dispute Resolution Models, https://aceproject.org/epic-en/, accessed 27 February 2021.

ACE Project (no date) 'Distribution of Model of Electoral Dispute Resolution in Various Countries', https://aceproject.org/epic-en/.

ACE Project (2012) 'Legal Framework Encyclopaedia', Third Edition, https://aceproject.org/epic-en/.

Asshiddiqie, Jimly (2007) *Pokok-Pokok Hukum Tata Negara Indonesia Pasca Reformasi.* Jakarta: Bhuana Ilmu Populer.

Ayuwuragil, Kustin (2017) 'Lima Kritikan Terkait Kewenangan Mengadili Bawaslu', https://www.cnnindonesia.com/nasional/20171119163858-32-256677/lima-kritikan-terkait-kewenangan-mengadili-bawaslu.

Bawaslu (2018) *Apa dan Siapa Bawaslu: Di Balik Layar Penegak Demokrasi di Indonesia.* Jakarta: Bawaslu.

Bawaslu-International IDEA (2018) *Electoral Justice System Assesment Guide.* Jakarta.

Bisariyadi et al (2012) 'Komparasi Mekanisme Penyelesaian Sengketa Pemilu di Beberapa Negara Penganut Paham Demokrasi Konstitutional' 9(3) *Jurnal Konstitusi* 531–562.

Bomantama, Rizam (2017) *Miliki Kewenangan Baru, Bawaslu Harus Siap Dikonfrontasi dengan DPR,* http://www.tribunnews.com/nasional/2017/10/04/miliki-kewenangan-baru-bawaslu-harus-siap-dikonfrontasi-dengan-dpr.

Butt, Simon. (2015) *The Constitutional Court and Democracy in Indonesia.* Leiden: Brill.

Butt, Simon and Tim Lindsey (2012) *The Constitution of Indonesia: A Contextual Analysis.* Portland: Hart Publishing.

Chillcote, Ronald (2003) *Teori Perbandingan Politik, Penelusuran Paradigma.* Jakarta: Raja Grafindo Persada.

Commonwealth Electoral Act 1918, Section 353, http://www5.austlii.edu.au/au/legis/cth/consol_act//cea1918233/s353.html.

CR-23 (2012) *MK-MA Ingatkan Pembentukan Peradilan Khusus Sengketa Pilkada,* 10 March 2012, https://www.hukumonline.com/berita/baca/lt58c27a06d91c8/mk-ma-ingatkan-pembentukan-peradilan-khusus-sengketa-pilkada.

Crouch, Melissa (2019) 'The Judicial Reform Landscape in Indonesia: Innovation, Specialisation and the Legacy of Dan S Lev' in M Crouch (ed) *The Politics of Court Reform: Judicial Change and Legal Culture in Indonesia.* Cambridge: Cambridge University Press, pp 1–32.

Dahl, Robert and Michael Clegg (2011) 'Legal Frameworks for Effective Election Complaints Adjudication Systems' in Chad Vickery (ed) *Guidelines for Understanding, Adjudicating, and Resolving Disputes in Elections (GUARDE).* USA: International Foundation for Electoral System (IFES). pp 99–129.

Davis-Roberts, Avery (2009) 'International Obligations for Electoral Dispute Resolution', https://www.cartercenter.org/resources/pdfs/peace/democracy/des/edr-approach-paper.pdf.

Edy, Muhammad Lukman (2019) *Konsolidasi Demokrasi Indonesia (Original Intent Undang-Undang Pemilu).* Jakarta: Sinar Grafika.

Electoral Integrity Group (2011) 'Towards International Statement of the Principles of Electoral Justice (The Accra Guiding Principles)', Accra, Ghana, 15 September 2011.

Enriques, Jesus Orozco (2010) *Electoral Justice: The International Idea Handbook.* Oslo: International Institure for Democracy and Electoral Assistance.

Fahmi, Khairul (2016) 'Menelusuri Konsep Keadilan Pemilihan Umum Menurut UUD 1945' 4(2) *Jurnal Cita Hukum* 167–186.

Fleiner, Thomas (2005) *Continental Law: Two Legal System, Some Elements of Comparative Constitutional and Administrative Law with Regard to those two Legal Systems.* Fribourg: Director Institute of Federalism.

Gaffar, Janedjri M (2013) *Demokrasi dan Pemilu di Indonesia.* Jakarta: Konstitusi Press.

Hanan, Djayadi (2019) 'Meletakkan Pemilu dalam Kerangka Konsolidasi Demokrasi' in Hasyim Asy'ari (ed) *Konsolidasi Demokrasi Pergulatan Politik Pemilu di Indonesia.* Yogyakarta: Thafa Media. pp ix–x.

Handaka, Hermawan. (2018) *Ida Budhiati: Pemerintah Perlu Mentransformasi Bawaslu,* 21 July 2018, https://jateng.tribunnews.com/2018/07/21/ida-budhiati-pemerintah-perlu-mentransformasi-bawaslu?page=2.

Harun, Refly (2016). 'Rekonstruksi Kewenangan Penyelesaian Perselisihan Hasil Pemilihan Umum' 13(1) *Jurnal Konstitusi* 1–24.

Hidayat, Sardini Nur (2015) *Mekanisme Penyelesaian Pelanggaran Kode Etik Penyelenggara Pemilu.* Jakarta: LP2AB.

Ma'shum, Saifullah (2001) *KPU & Kontroversi Pemilu 1999.* Jakarta: Pustaka Indonesia Satu.

Inter-American Commission of Human Rights (2018) 'Strategic Plan 2011–2015' in Mirza Satria Buana (ed) *Menimbang Lembaga Peradilan Khusus Pemilu: Studi Perbandingan Hukum Tata Negara.* Padang: PUSaKO, pp 1334-1350.

International Foundation for Electoral System (2011) *Guidelines for Understanding, Adjudicating, and Resolving Disputes in Elections (GUARDE).* USA: International Foundation for Electoral System (IFES).

International IDEA (no date) 'Electoral Justice Database IDEA International', https://www.idea.int/data-tools/question-view/734, https://www.idea.int/data-tools/question-view/733.

International IDEA (2010) *Electoral Justice: An Overview of the International IDEA Handbook.* Stockholm: International Institute for Democracy and Electoral Assistance.

International IDEA (2010) *Electoral Justice: The International IDEA Handbook.* Sweden: Bulls Graphics.

International IDEA (2010) *Electoral Justice: The International IDEA Handbook Executive Summary.* Stockholm: International Institute for Democracy and Electoral Assistance.

International IDEA (2002) *International Electoral Standards, Guidlines for Reviewing the Legal Framwork of Elections.* Stockholm: International Institute for Democracy and Electoral Assistance.

Junaidi, Veri, M Ihsan Maulana and Mutiara Rahmah M (2020) *Electoral Justice System: Desain Peradilan dan Konsep Penegakkan Hukum Pemilu.* Jakarta: Yayasan Konstitusi Demokrasi Inisiatif.

Kelsen, Hans (1973) *General Theory of Law and State.* New York: Russel & Russel.

Lim, Jibong (2006) 'Korean Constitutional Court and Due Process Clause' 6(1) *Journal of Korean Law* 1–17.

Orozco-Henríquez, Jesus (2010) *Keadilan Pemilu: Ringkasan Buku Acuan International IDEA.* Stockholm: International Institute for Democracy and Electoral Assistance.

Pamungkas, Sigit (2009) *Perihal Pemilu.* Yogyakarta: Fisipol UGM.

Petit, Denis (2000) *Resolving Election Disputes in the OSCE Area: Towards a Standard Election Dispute Monitoring System (Organization for Security and Cooperation in Europe),* https://www.osce.org/odihr/elections/17567?download=true.

Pildes, Richard H (2004) 'The Constitutionalization of Democratic Politics' 118(1) *Harvard Law Review* 13–14.

Powell, G. Bingham (2000) *Elections as Instruments of Democracy (Majoritarian and Proportional Visions).* New Heaven: Yale University Press.

Ranawijaya, Usep (1983) *Hukum Tata Negara Indonesia Dasar-Dasarnya.* Jakarta: Ghalia.

Santoso, Topo (2011) 'Problem Desain dan Penanganan Pelanggaran Pidana Pemilu' 1 (29 December) *Jurnal Pemilu & Demokrasi* 25–47.

Santoso, Topo and Ida Budhiati (2019) *Pemilu di Indonesia: Kelembagaan, Pelaksanaan, dan Pengawasan.* Jakarta: Sinar Grafika.

Senate (2017). 'Certificates of Election' 163(1) *Congressional Record*, https://www.congress.gov/congressional-record/2017/1/3/senate-section/article/S1-4.

Setiadi, Wicipto (2008) 'Peran Partai Politik dalam Penyelenggaraan Pemilu yang Aspiratif dan Demokratis' 5(1) *Jurnal Legislasi* 29–39.

Setiawan, Ken (2019) 'The Human Rights Courts: Embedding Impunity' in Melissa Crouch (ed) *The Politics of Court Reform: Judicial Change in Legal Culture in Indonesia.* Cambridge: Cambridge University Press. pp 287–310.

Sorensen, G (2003) *Demokrasi dan Demokratisasi.* Yogyakarta: Pustaka Pelajar.

Stefanie, Christie (2015) *MA dan MK Ogah Tangani Sengketa Pilkada*, 3 February, https://www.cnnindonesia.com/nasional/20150213083549-32-31827/ma-dan-mk-ogah-tangani-sengketa-pilkada.

Strong, CF (1961) *Modern Political Constitution.* London: ELBS & Jackson.

Sukamto, Imam (2016) *Teliti Pemilu, Refly Harun Raih Gelar Doktor*, 21 May, https://nasional.tempo.co/read/772918/teliti-pemilu-refly-harun-raih-gelar-doktor/full&view=ok.

Supriyanto, Didik (2017) *Menyoal Bawaslu, Penampilan Baru, Wewenang Baru, Persoalan Baru*, https://nasional.kompas.com/read/2017/11/08/14273471/menyoal-bawaslu-penampilan-baru-wewenang-baru-persoalan-baru.

Suswantoro, Gunawan (2016) *Mengawal Penegak Demokrasi di Balik Tata Kelola Bawaslu & DKPP.* Jakarta: Erlangga.

Thoha, Miftah (2014) *Birokrasi Politik & Pemilihan Umum di Indonesia.* Jakarta: Kencana.

Tribunal Electoral del Poder Judicial de la Federacion (2012) *The Electoral Tribunal of the Federal Judicial Branch Guarantees The Constitutionality of The Elections.* Mexico: CIESAS.

Utami, Nofi Sri (2018) 'Pembentukan Badan Peradilan Khusus Perkara Pilkada Dalam Rangka Untuk Menjaga Integritas Penyelenggara Pilkada', Doktoral, Universitas Diponogoro.

PART 2
THE CONSTITUTIONAL COURT AND RIGHTS

9

Making Social Rights Real? The 1945 Constitution and Social Rights Litigation in Indonesia

Andrew Rosser

Introduction

Courts have become increasingly important forums for struggles over social rights in developing countries in recent years. This is particularly the case in countries with democratic political systems characterized by the separation of powers in which courts have a degree of autonomy (Gauri and Brinks 2008; Yamin and Gloppen 2011; Skelton 2017). Indonesia has been no exception in this respect. Social rights litigation was unheard of under Suharto's authoritarian New Order regime. But the country has witnessed a series of court cases related to social rights since the country transitioned to democracy in the late 1990s amidst the Asian economic crisis (1997–1998) and its aftermath (Nardi Jnr 2018). In many, if not all, cases, this litigation has involved claims to social rights provided for in the amended 1945 Constitution and/or in laws (*undang-undang*) that have sought to reinforce or expand constitutional provisions related to these rights (Susanti 2008; Rosser and Curnow 2014; Rosser 2017).

This chapter provides an overview of this litigation, an assessment of its impact vis-à-vis the fulfilment of social rights, and an analysis of the reasons for this impact.[1] It makes four main claims. The first is that that social rights litigation in Indonesia has typically been collective in orientation, focusing on policy-related matters rather than individual claims. The second is that it has had a positive effect vis-à-vis the fulfilment of social rights in Indonesia because it has precipitated policy changes that helped to enforce or realize these rights. The third claim is that this outcome has been supported by—and conditional upon—a number of factors including: (a) the presence of judicial and health institutions that have limited the scope for citizens to engage in individually focused litigation and—instead—enabled them to engage in collectively oriented litigation; (b) enhanced responsiveness by the political elite (including the judiciary) to social policy concerns as a result of the combined effects of the Asian economic crisis and democratization; and (c) the presence of non-governmental organizations

---

[1] This chapter draws heavily on my previous work on education rights litigation in Indonesia (Rosser and Curnow 2014; Rosser 2015; Rosser and Joshi forthcoming), health rights litigation in Indonesia (Rosser 2017), and the politics of social welfare in Indonesia (Rosser and van Diermen 2016; 2018). It seeks to draw this work together into a single overview piece on social rights litigation in Indonesia accompanied by an assessment of its likely effectiveness as a strategy looking forward.

Andrew Rosser, *Making Social Rights Real? The 1945 Constitution and Social Rights Litigation in Indonesia*
In: *Constitutional Democracy in Indonesia*. Edited by: Melissa Crouch, Oxford University Press. © Andrew Rosser, 2023.
DOI: 10.1093/oso/9780192870681.003.0009

(NGOs) that have had a strong commitment to social rights, the financial and technical resources to mobilize the law, and the ability to forge alliances with and mobilize popular forces. Fourth, and finally, it suggests that some of these conditions may no longer hold, raising doubts about the likely effectiveness of social rights litigation as a strategy for citizens to promote fulfilment of social rights in the foreseeable future.

In presenting this analysis, I begin by examining the political, policy, and legal context in which social rights litigation has occurred in Indonesia, providing an overview of this litigation, and giving an assessment of its impact. In the following section, I examine how factors (a) to (c) have helped to produce and shape this impact. I conclude the chapter by considering whether social rights litigation will remain an effective strategy for promoting the fulfilment of social rights in Indonesia in the future.

Before beginning with this analysis, it is necessary to briefly define three key terms as they are used in this chapter. *Social rights* refers to education and health rights.[2] These include general rights to education and health as well as more specific rights such as to free basic education, health services, a healthy environment, and social security (insofar as the latter relates to access to healthcare). *Social rights litigation* accordingly refers to litigation that (i) makes claims based on a constitutional, legislative, or internationally recognized education or health right, related right, or associated state obligation; (ii) seeks access to educational or health facilities, goods, and services; or (iii) concerns the underlying preconditions for realization of these rights (Gloppen and Roseman 2011: 15).[3] Finally, *social policy* refers to education and health policy.

Political, Policy, and Legal Context

Social rights litigation in Indonesia has been a product of long-standing struggles over social policy, which were reinvigorated by the collapse of the New Order and the country's transition to democratic rule. Broadly speaking, these struggles have pit three main sets of actors against one another. The first has consisted of liberal economic technocrats in government and their supporters within the donor community and other institutions controlling mobile capital (Winters 1996). This coalition has supported state investment in social policy as a way of building the country's human resources, creating a political and social environment conducive to market-oriented economic reform, and, in so doing, contributing to economic growth (Prawiro 1998; Boediono 2009). At the same time, it has sought to ensure that such investments are fiscally sustainable and promote efficiency in the use of public resources through measures of decentralization, competition/private provision, and corporatization

---

[2] My definition of social rights is narrower than the wider pool of rights defined by the United Nations as constituting 'economic, social and cultural rights'. The Office of the United Nations High Commissioner for Human Rights (2008: 1) has defined 'economic, social and cultural rights' as 'those human rights relating to the workplace, social security, family life, participation in cultural life, and access to housing, food, water, health care and education'.

[3] One important implication of this definition is that it excludes litigation involving civil or criminal claims against health, education, or other professionals involved in the delivery of public services or public service providers. Most notably it excludes malpractice suits, a common form of health-related litigation in Indonesia (Susanti 2008).

(Jalal and Musthafa 2001; Rokx et al 2009). The influence of this agenda has reflected powerful structural pressures on the government emanating from budget constraints, the power of mobile capital to relocate to alternative jurisdictions (Winters 1996), and the technocrats' direct access to the policymaking process as a result of their positions within the state apparatus.

The second set of actors has been predatory military and bureaucratic officials who have occupied the state apparatus (particularly the bureaucracy and the legislature) and the domestic and foreign business groups to which they have been connected (in many cases through family and other personal relationships) (Robison 1986). Members of this coalition have recognized that social policy is a useful way of promoting economic development through its contribution to human resource development and political and social stability (Hoemardhani 1975; Moertopo 1981). But they have had a stronger interest in limiting government spending on social policy to free up public resources for other areas (eg infrastructure, industrial projects, subsidized credit programmes) more central to their business activities (Riady 2013) and to create opportunities for private provision in the education and health sectors. To the extent that the government has invested in social policy, members of this coalition have had a further interest in the introduction of programmes that privilege military and bureaucratic officials—that is, by providing them with pensions and other benefits, opportunities for corruption, pay rises, or opportunities to fuel patronage networks and buy electoral votes. In this respect, managers of government-owned service providers such as public schools, universities, hospitals, community health centres, and food security agencies—the bodies most directly responsible for implementing the government's main social programmes—have been key actors, as have organizations representing relevant civil servant employees such as the Indonesian Teachers Union (PGRI) and the Indonesian Doctors Association (IDI) (Aspinall 2014; Irawan et al 2004). Members of this coalition have exercised influence over social policy and its implementation by virtue of their occupation of the state apparatus and consequent direct access to the policymaking process and central role in the implementation of social programmes.

The third main set of actors has been the poor and their allies in the NGO movement. Drawing on notions of human rights and a radical critique of neoliberalism (particularly the privatization of public services), this set of actors has sought to promote expanded and equitable access to quality public education and health services in line with social democratic notions of a welfare state and, in some cases, socialist principles (Irawan et al 2004; Tjandra 2014). Although its members have generally been excluded from policymaking and implementation processes, they have had some influence because of their ability to access the media, make strategic use of the court system, and leverage support from popular forces such as the labour movement and community groups, particularly since Indonesia's transition to a more democratic regime. Key actors in this coalition have included activists at NGOs such as Indonesia Corruption Watch (ICW), the Institute for Policy Research and Advocacy (ELSAM), Prakarsa, the Indonesian Human Rights Centre for Social Justice, the Ecosoc Institute, the Peoples Health Council (DKR), the Indonesian Poor People's Union (SRMI), the Jakarta Legal Aid Bureau (LBH Jakarta), the Trade Union Rights Centre (TURC), the Indonesian Consumers Foundation (YLKI), various parents groups, and the numerous poor and marginalized citizens represented by or aligned with these organizations. Members of this coalition have initiated most (although not all) instances of social rights litigation, doing so as a way of furthering their progressive cause.

Under the New Order, predatory officials and their business clients constituted the dominant political and social force within the country, while liberal technocrats and their allies exercised significant influence especially at times of economic crisis. The poor and their allies in the NGO movement, by contrast, were marginalized. The consequence in terms of social policy and its implementation was to ensure the underfunding of public health and education services, their capture by predatory elements, and increasing private provision. The New Order invested heavily in the country's public education and health systems during the oil boom of the mid to late 1970s and early 1980s when the country was awash with petrodollars. But following the collapse of international oil prices in the early to mid-1980s, the government reduced spending in these sectors in favour of increased private provision. At the same time, public education and health providers became mechanisms through which political elites sought to exercise political control, distribute patronage, mobilize political support, and generate rents. Combined with underfunding, this reduced their effectiveness in delivering quality education and healthcare, especially to the poor and marginalized (Irawan et al 2004; Rosser 2012). In short, Indonesia's social policy regime was one of 'predatory productivism' (Rosser and van Diermen 2018)—that is, one in which social policy was subordinated to economic policy and the interests of predatory elements.[4]

The onset of the Asian economic crisis in 1997 enhanced the structural power of international donors such as the World Bank and the International Monetary Fund (IMF) and other controllers of mobile capital, and in so doing the influence of liberal economic technocrats in government, at least for the period of the crisis and its immediate aftermath. It also strengthened the hand of the poor and their NGO allies by precipitating a social crisis which saw the poverty rate increase sharply and highlighted the need for more progressive social policies. At the same time, the demise of the New Order regime and transition to more democratic rule created an incentive for politicians and their political parties to promote policies favouring the poor and marginalized because of their electoral appeal; removed key obstacles to organization by NGOs and other groups that had previously been excluded from the policymaking process; and opened up new policy spaces that they could access in order to influence policy including within the court system (Rosser et al 2005).

In this context, Indonesia's social policies began to move in two distinct and, to some extent, contradictory directions. On the one hand, the government embarked on a programme of neoliberal education and health policy reform. This involved measures to devolve management of public education and health facilities to the facility level in accordance with a broader push towards decentralization; enhance the autonomy of these facilities and, in particular, their ability to generate income through fees; introduce minimum service standards; incentivize improved performance through new assessment and certification requirements; and promote greater competition in education and health through the participation of foreign providers (Rosser 2015; 2016;

---

[4] See Holliday (2000) for a discussion of the productivist model of welfare capitalism.

2017; Rosser and Fahmi 2018). These measures were aimed at improving the quality of public education and health services by bringing administration of these services closer to populations they serve and creating incentives for improved performance. But these measures did little to address the long-standing problem of unequal access to quality health and education services between the rich and poor and may have exacerbated this problem (Darmaningtyas et al 2009).

On the other hand, the government also moved to enhance social protection for the poor, initially through a series of social safety net schemes introduced during the Asian economic crisis and, from 2000, through a set second generation of programmes funded largely through cuts to government fuel subsidies (the benefits of which largely accrued to the middle class and business) (Sumarto and Bazzi 2011). In the education and health sectors, the most important of these programmes were School Operational Assistance (*Bantuan Operasional Sekolah*, BOS), a school grants scheme aimed at providing free basic education; the Family Hope Programme (*Program Keluarga Harapan*, PKH), a conditional cash transfer scheme providing cash to the poor on the grounds that education and health standards were met; Assistance for Poor Students (*Bantuan Siswa Miskin*, BSM), a scholarship scheme for poor students; Jamkesmas, a health insurance programme aimed at providing free healthcare to the poor and near poor; and Jampersal, a scheme providing women with free birth delivery and pre-natal and post-natal check-ups (van Diermen 2018: 89).

In 2011, the country's social protection regime moved into a third phase when four state insurance companies and Jamkesmas were merged into two state agencies: BPJS Health (which took over the health insurance-related programs) and BPJS Employment (which took over programmes related to employment including insurance for old age, death, pensions, and accidents). Both institutions are self-funded through members' premiums, with those for poor people being paid by the government. Taken together, some commentators have suggested that these changes amount to a transition away from the New Order's model of predatory productivism towards a more generous model of universal social welfare. In 2013, Aspinall and Warburton (2013), for instance, argued that: 'The tentative beginnings of universal social protection, even of an Indonesian welfare state, are now visible'.

In the midst of these changes, the government also revamped the legal framework related to the protection of social rights. The original 1945 Constitution provided citizens with few social rights. It provided them with a right to 'instruction' (*pengadjaran*) but neither it nor laws from the New Order period made provision for a wider right to education. Nor did it provide for a right to health. Between 1999 and 2002, the country's supreme legislative body, the People's Consultative Assembly (MPR), enacted wide-ranging amendments to the 1945 Constitution which included the introduction of new rights 'to obtain an education', 'to have a good and healthy environment', and 'to obtain health services'.[5] At the same time, the MPR also introduced new obligations for the government to provide health service facilities, to fund compulsory basic education (a requirement that effectively created a right to free basic education), and to spend at least 20 per cent of its budget on education. Before, during,

---

[5] See Arts 28C and 28H.

and after these amendments, the national parliament (DPR) passed several laws reaffirming and extending protection for these rights including Law 39/1999 on Human Rights, Law 23/2002 on Child Protection, Law 20/2003 on a National Education System, Law 11/2005 on the Ratification of the International Covenant on Economic, Social and Cultural Rights, and Law 36/2009 on Health.

Social Rights Litigation in Indonesia

There are considerable practical difficulties in identifying court cases related to specific subjects in Indonesia. Information and data on decisions made by Indonesian courts is limited (Susanti 2008: 230). Nevertheless, I was able to identify a set of cases that meet the aforementioned definition of social rights litigation by using a variety of techniques. These include: (i) reading previous academic studies on social rights litigation in Indonesia (eg Susanti 2008); (ii) conducting keyword searches in Indonesian and English in online case databases maintained by the Constitutional Court and the Supreme Court, media databases such as Factiva and that available through the *Kompas* Information Centre, and Google;[6] (iii) asking informants to nominate relevant cases during interviews; and (iv) reading through court documents to determine if education and/or health rights were invoked in legal argument or testimony. In carrying out this work, I focused on the period from 1998 to 2015, at which point my fieldwork in Indonesia came to an end.

The cases identified suggest that social rights litigation in Indonesia has been collectively oriented, focusing on policy issues rather than individual claims. In particular, social rights litigation has often been aimed at challenging the perceived commercialization or privatization of public services, contesting the capture of public service providers by political and bureaucratic elements, and/or promoting measures designed to improve access to education and health services for the poor and marginalized. I examine the reasons for this tendency towards policy-oriented rather than individually focused litigation in the next section of the chapter. In this section, I provide a brief overview of the issues on which social rights litigation has focused, its outcomes, and its impact on the fulfilment of social rights *via* its effect on policy.

Education

Education rights litigation in Indonesia has focused on the national exam, the size of the education budget, the legal status of education institutions, international standard schools, textbooks, and compulsory senior secondary education.

The national exam: After the fall of the New Order, the government introduced a new national exam administered at the end of primary, junior secondary, and senior secondary school in an effort to raise the quality of education. In contrast to the preceding system, where final results were partly determined by school grades and partly

---

[6] Search terms included 'right to education' (*hak atas pendidikan)*, 'right to health' (*hak atas kesehatan*), 'right to health services' (*hak atas pelayanan kesehatan*), and 'court' (*pengadilan, mahkamah*).

by national exam results, students' final results under the new system—and hence their ability to continue with their education—were made entirely dependent on their national exam scores. The logic was to give students greater incentive to do well in the exam by transforming it into a high-stakes test. Before long, human rights and education activists in Jakarta began receiving complaints from parents whose children had been unable to continue their education after failing the exam, in breach of their right to education. This was despite widespread cheating in the exam. In 2004, a group of Jakarta-based NGOs tried to have the regulations providing for the national exam overturned by lodging a judicial review case at the Supreme Court. But they were unsuccessful. In 2006, they returned to the courts as public attention towards the issue grew in the wake of increased media reporting. This time, they lodged a citizen lawsuit along with more than fifty individuals at the Central Jakarta District Court. Their submission called on the government to change various aspects of the exam and issue a public apology for failing to protect the right to education. They won the case the following year, with the Court ruling that the government had been 'negligent in providing fulfilment and protection of the human rights of its citizens who were victims of the national exam, especially the right to education and children's rights' (*HukumOnline* 2007: 30).[7] The government appealed the decision to the Jakarta High Court in 2008 and to the Supreme Court in 2009, but lost on both occasions.[8] In the wake of these decisions, the government introduced reforms that served to significantly reduce national exam failure rates (Rosser 2015: 201–203).

The size of the education budget: As noted above, among the amendments made to the 1945 Constitution between 1999 and 2002 was the introduction of a requirement for the government to allocate at least 20 per cent of its budget to education. In the wake of this amendment, the government moved slowly towards increasing education spending to the required level to the frustration of key education stakeholders. Between 2005 and 2008, a collection of parents, teachers, and students—including, in several cases, figures from the Indonesian Teachers Union (PGRI)—sought to force the central government to move more quickly by challenging various laws in the Constitutional Court. These included Law 20/2003 on a National Education System and a succession of budget laws. In challenging these laws, these actors invoked the constitutional right to education, as well as the provisions specifically establishing the minimum spending requirements. The Court ruled that the 20 per cent required should be fulfilled immediately and that budget laws were unconstitutional so long as they failed to fulfil this requirement. At the same time, though, it did not compel the government to revise its budget laws immediately to meet this requirement on the grounds that doing so would jeopardize economic stability.[9] In response to these decisions, in 2009, the government nevertheless increased spending on education up to the 20 per cent mark, albeit in part by incorporating some expenses of tangential relevance to the education system into this amount (Susanti 2008; Australia's Education Partnership with Indonesia 2016: 5).

---

[7] Central Jakarta District Court Decision 228/Pdt.G/2006/PN.JKT.PST.

[8] Jakarta High Court Decision 377/PDT/2007/PT.DKI and Supreme Court Decision 2596 K/PDT/2008.

[9] See Constitutional Court Decisions 011/PUU-III/2005, 012/PUU-III/2005, 026/PUU-III/2005, 026/PUU-III/2006, and 013/PUU-VI/2008.

The legal status of educational institutions: In 2009, the Indonesian parliament enacted legislation that changed the legal status of educational institutions to 'education legal entity' (*Badan Hukum Pendidikan*, BHP). Before that, public schools and universities had been units within the government bureaucracy. The change was intended to enhance the managerial autonomy of public educational institutions and was a requirement of a World Bank-funded higher education project. Parent, NGO, and university student activists strongly opposed this change in legal status, arguing that it amounted to the commercialization or privatization of public education. They said that it would lead to abrogation of the state's responsibility for funding education and consequently higher school and university fees. The law was also opposed by owners of private foundations for separate reasons: they feared losing control over the private educational institutions under their foundations. Following enactment of the law, all these groups challenged the law in the Constitutional Court. In their submission to the court, the activists argued that the change in the legal status breached citizens' constitutional rights to education and free basic education. In a late 2009 judgment, the Court found in their favour, declaring the law null and void.[10] After this decision, the government responded by enacting a new law on higher education in 2012 that, in effect, limited the proposed change in legal status to the country's top-ranked public universities. A subsequent Constitutional Court challenge to this law brought by university student activists—again invoking the right to education—was unsuccessful (Rosser 2015: 204–206).[11]

International standard schools: In 2009, the Indonesian government enacted new regulations providing for 'international standard' schools (SBI/RSBI), defined as schools with 'certain quality superiorities that originate from OECD member countries or other developed countries' (Government of Indonesia 2009, Art 1(8)). In contrast to 'regular' schools, SBI/RSBI were permitted to use international curriculums, install high-quality facilities for information and communication technology, employ foreign teachers, and use English in the classroom, among other means of enhancing quality. To support these schools in reaching international standards, the government allowed them to charge fees and furnished them with generous routine and additional funding. Such schools were meant to be academically selective and reserve 20 per cent of places for students from poor backgrounds but they generally failed to meet this target. The main beneficiaries (and supporters) of this policy were middle-class parents for whom SBI/RSBI promised a better-quality education for their children, and elements within the education bureaucracy, for whom SBI/RSBI opened up an array of new rent-seeking opportunities. The main opponents were parents of children excluded from SBI/RSBI for financial reasons, parents who could afford SBI/RSBI but were concerned about corrupt school management undermining educational quality, and teachers at SBI/RSBI who sympathized with either or both these groups of parents. In 2011, three parents—all from the first group above and supported by NGOs—lodged a judicial review request at the Constitutional Court challenging Article 50(3) of Law 20/2003 on a National Education System, the article that provided the legal foundation for the establishment of SBI/RSBI. In their submission

---

[10] Constitutional Court Decisions 11-14-21-126 and 136/PUU-VII/2009.
[11] Constitutional Court Decision 103/PUU-X/2012.

to the court, they argued, among other things, that SBI/RSBI policy amounted to an abrogation of state responsibility to provide free basic education because it allowed such schools to charge fees. They won, compelling the government to end the 'international standard' schools policy (Rosser and Curnow 2014).[12]

Textbooks: The cost of purchasing textbooks has long been a significant financial burden for poor parents in Indonesia. This problem has been worsened by the fact that teachers have supplemented their incomes by selling textbooks to students for inflated prices. In 2008, the central government issued a new regulation on textbooks that, in the eyes of its critics, did little to resolve these problems and, in fact, made them worse by proposing that 'society' (such as parents and students) share responsibility for ensuring that children had access to these books. In 2008, a group of NGO activists challenged this regulation by lodging a judicial review request at the Supreme Court. Among their reasons for challenging the regulation were that it breached the principle of free basic education (Kelompok Independen Untuk Advokasi Buku no date). In this case, the petitioners lost.[13]

Compulsory senior secondary education: In 1984, the central government made the first six years of school compulsory and in 1994 it extended this to nine years. In 2010–2011, it then announced a policy of *universal* senior secondary education covering the remaining three years of school. It stipulated that this was not an extension of compulsory education or free education, both of which only applied to the first nine years of school. It appears that the government backed away from such a change because of concerns among technocrats at the Ministry of Finance and Bappenas about the additional cost of free education at the senior secondary level.[14] In 2014, individuals and education organizations represented by lawyers from the Indonesian Human Rights Committee for Social Justice, an NGO, lodged a judicial review request at the Constitutional Court seeking an interpretation of Law 20/2003 on a National Education System that would effectively extend the government's compulsory and free education programmes to the senior secondary level. In so doing, they argued that limitation of these programmes to the basic education level infringed the right to education. The Court found against the petitioners, ruling that their petition lacked a legal basis (Rosser and Joshi, forthcoming).[15]

Health

Health rights litigation in Indonesia has focused on the following issues: the protection of migrant workers, hospital corporatization, the Social Security Implementing Agencies Law, and the size of the health budget.

Protection of migrant workers: Indonesian migrant workers are highly vulnerable while they are in transit or overseas. In 2002, eighty died after becoming stranded in Nunukan, East Kalimantan, without adequate access to food, water, shelter, sanitation,

---

[12] Constitutional Court Decision 5/PUU-X/2012.
[13] I wish to thank Ade Irawan at Indonesia Corruption Watch for this information.
[14] Interview with Satrio Soemantri Brojonegoro, Jakarta, November 2012.
[15] Constitutional Court Decision 92/PUU-XII/2014.

or health services upon return from Malaysia. This led a group of NGO activists, public figures, former migrant workers, and student activists to lodge a citizen lawsuit at the Central Jakarta District Court demanding that the government adopt new policies offering better protection for Indonesian migrant workers, including better access to adequate health services upon return from overseas. In their legal arguments, they contended that the government's negligence had breached migrant workers' constitutional right to obtain health services and the associated state obligation to provide health service facilities. In its decision, the court found that the government had provided insufficient protection to Indonesian migrant workers and sentenced the government to 'take concrete steps' to improve their management of migrant workers and their families.[16] Although the government won a subsequent appeal to the Jakarta High Court,[17] in 2004 the Indonesian parliament passed a new law on the Placement and Protection of Indonesian Migrant Workers. The new statute included articles on the protection of migrant workers' rights upon return to Indonesia, defining 'protection' of migrant workers in terms that encompassed fulfilment of their right to health services, and outlined the government's obligations in this respect. The Nunukan lawsuit also appears to have had the effect of pushing along—albeit slowly—moves within the Indonesian government to ratify the UN convention on the rights of migrant workers. The government finally ratified this convention in April 2012 (Susanti 2008: 252; Rosser 2017: 23–27).

Hospital corporatization: The cost of running public hospitals has been a continual challenge for successive governments, particularly within the context of consistently low overall government spending on health. This led to a series of policy initiatives to give public hospitals greater financial and managerial autonomy. In 2004, for instance, the Jakarta city government passed local bylaws converting three public hospitals under its control into limited liability companies, arguing that this change was necessary to improve their management and services and relieve pressure on the city government's budget. This move was met with condemnation from civil servant staff working at the hospitals who were concerned that it would reduce their job security and benefits, and members of local communities who were worried that it would make hospital services more expensive, placing them out of the reach of the poorest sections of the community. The Health Minister Siti Fadillah Supari weighed into the debate by arguing that transforming public hospitals into profit-seeking entities breached their social function. In the midst of these developments, activists from consumer and health-focused NGOs and clients of the hospitals lodged a request for judicial review with the Supreme Court. In their submission, they argued, among other things, that the change to the hospitals' legal status breached citizens' rights to obtain health services and the state's obligation to provide health service facilities. In 2006, the Supreme Court found in favour of the plaintiffs.[18] In the wake of this result, the Governor of Jakarta announced that his government would comply with the ruling and the city parliament voted to withdraw the bylaws (Rosser 2017: 27–32).

---

[16] Jakarta Central District Court Decision 28/PDT.G/2003/PN.JKT.PST.
[17] Jakarta High Court Decision 480/PDT/2005/PT DKI.
[18] Supreme Court Decision 05 P/Hum/Th.2005.

The Social Security Implementing Agencies (BPJS) Law: In Law 40/2004 on Social Security, the government committed to introducing a set of mandatory universal social security programmes including one providing healthcare benefits. But an ancillary law on Social Security Implementing Agencies (BPJS) required to implement these programmes ran up against stern opposition from a range of powerful actors including state-owned enterprises (SOEs) operating existing social security programmes, the Indonesian business community, and senior echelons of government. By the due date specified in Law 40/2004 (19 October 2009), the government had not yet submitted draft legislation to the DPR let alone secured its enactment. In this context, dozens of trade unions, NGOs, student organizations, professional bodies, and other organizations formed the Action Committee for Social Security (*Komite Aksi Jaminan Sosial*, KAJS) to lead a huge popular campaign to promote the passing of the bill. Their protests demanded the quick endorsement and subsequent enactment of the BPJS bill and, with that, healthcare for all Indonesians. As part of this campaign, in 2010, KAJS lodged a citizen lawsuit at the Central Jakarta District Court that was aimed at forcing the government and parliament to pass the bill. The lawsuit listed 120 individuals, mostly trade union activists, as plaintiffs, and it was supported by a legal team from a labour-oriented NGO. The lawsuit centered on a claim that, by failing to pass and enact the new law on BPJS, the government had committed illegal acts—in particular, breaching provisions of the 1945 Constitution, the 1999 Human Rights Law, and Law 40/2004 as well as other legislation providing citizens with a right to social security. At the same time, the KAJS also made reference to the state's constitutional obligation to provide health-service facilities as part of its argument that 'health insurance was a basic need that must be fulfilled by the State for all Indonesian people without exception and for the full term of people's lives (*universal coverage*)' (italics in original; Action Committee for Social Security 2010: 27). In July 2011, the Central Jakarta District Court found for the plaintiffs, declaring that the government had been negligent in implementing Law 40/2004 and instructing the executive to enact a new law on BPJS.[19] Faced with a court instruction and mass pressure, the parliament and government eventually passed a new law on BPJS on 28 October 2009 (Rosser 2017: 32–38).

The size of the health budget: Government spending on health has long been low by international standards. In 2009, the DPR sought to rectify this problem by including a requirement in the 2009 Health Law for the central government to spend at least 5 per cent of its budget on health-related expenses excluding salaries and wages (Art 171(1)). However, government spending on health in the aftermath of this law fell well short of this target. In this context, a group of individuals and NGOs lodged a request for judicial review with the Constitutional Court. They challenged the law on the 2010 budget on the grounds that it breached the 1945 Constitution by, among other things, allocating insufficient funds to health (specifically, less than 5 per cent of the total budget). One year later, they lodged a similar request for judicial review with the Constitutional Court, challenging the legislation on the 2011 budget as well. In both cases, they argued that the budget laws breached Articles 28H(1) and 34(3) of the 1945

---

[19] Jakarta District Court Decision 278/Pdt.G/2010/PN.JKT.PST.

Constitution—the provisions providing citizens with a right to obtain health services and imposing an obligation on the state to provide health-service facilities respectively. In legal terms, their case was similar to earlier successful Constitutional Court challenges brought between 2005 and 2008 against previous budget laws that allocated less than 20 per cent of the total central government budget to education. However, it was weaker to the extent that the 1945 Constitution specifies no minimum spending for either the central government or regional governments on health. In both cases, the plaintiffs were unsuccessful.[20] Under the 1945 Constitution, the court determined, the state is only obliged 'to make a real effort' (*mengupayakan secara sungguh-sungguh*) to fulfil citizens' health needs and provide adequate health services, not to ensure that all citizens are healthy (Mahkamah Konstitusi 2011: 13–14). Over time, however, the government has nevertheless moved towards compliance with the 5 per cent requirement, achieving this target for the first time in 2016 (Rosser 2017: 38–41).

Summary

In sum, then, social rights litigation in Indonesia has served to promote fulfilment of social rights by precipitating a variety of policy changes that have helped to enforce or realize them in practice. These policy changes have included: (i) policy changes that have halted the progress of neoliberal social policy reforms threatening to reduce access to public services for poor and marginalized citizens (eg those related to national exams, the legal status of educational institutions, international standard schools, and hospital corporatization); (ii) policy changes that increased the level of public funding to the education and health sectors (eg those related to the size of the government's education and health budgets); (iii) policy changes that have locked in promised changes to the country's social security system (eg that related to the BPJS law); and (iv) policy changes that have enhanced legal protection of the social rights of vulnerable groups (eg that related to migrant workers). In so doing, this litigation has served to promote the broader shift in the nature of the government's social policies— referred to earlier—away from predatory productivism and towards greater provision of social welfare to the poor and marginalized.

Explaining this Impact

This impact on policy has been contingent upon a number of factors. As noted earlier, this impact relates to the nature of judicial and health institutions; the responsiveness of the political elite to social policy concerns; and the characteristics of nongovernmental organizations in Indonesia. These factors have served to facilitate legal mobilization around social rights issues, steer this towards collective policy-oriented rather than individually focused litigation and improve the prospects of this litigation. In this section, I look in turn at each of these factors and their effects.

---

[20] Constitutional Court Decisions 60/PUU-IX/2011 and 58/PUU-X/2012.

Judicial and Health Institutions

Under the New Order, the government interfered extensively in court matters and encouraged the development of a culture of corruption within the judiciary (Thoolen 1987). At the same time, poor resourcing meant that decision-making processes moved slowly. The fall of the New Order produced some significant reforms to the country's judicial system that served to open up new opportunities for citizens to launch litigation invoking rights and/or associated state obligations in the 1945 Constitution and laws, especially in relation to policy issues. The most important of these was the establishment of the Constitutional Court in 2003. The Constitutional Court was given authority to, among other things, carry out judicial review of laws and their individual articles to determine whether they are consistent with the amended 1945 Constitution and strike them down if it determined that they were not. During the first few years of its existence, the court developed a reputation for fairness, efficiency, professionalism, and a willingness to support rights-oriented causes (Mietzner 2010; Butt et al 2016: 1113). A second important reform was an expansion in the powers of the Supreme Court with regards to the judicial review of regulations. Under the New Order, the Supreme Court had authority to review regulations and decrees for consistency with laws, but this authority was severely circumscribed. The fall of the New Order saw the Court's powers of judicial review strengthened, allowing for direct challenges to regulations/decrees (rather than merely via appeal), and enabling it to strike down regulations and decrees (Butt and Parsons 2014: 70–71). A third, and final, reform was a range of legal innovations such as citizen lawsuits, class actions, and legal standing (all of which were rare, if not unheard of, during the New Order period). These innovations opened up new ways for citizens and NGOs to engage with general courts and the Supreme Court over policy issues (Gatot 2007; Santosa 2007; Susanti 2008).

At the same time, the absence of effective mechanisms for facilitating individual rights claims in Indonesia's judicial system—such as the *amparo*-style mechanisms that exist in many Latin American countries—reduced the scope for individually oriented litigation. As Miguel-Stearns (2015: 100) has explained, the writ of *amparo* 'allows citizens to bring an action in court against the government for a violation of fundamental or constitutional rights. It is meant to be restorative as opposed to compensatory, and is a means of providing relatively immediate relief in otherwise overloaded and slow judicial systems'. In Latin America, health-rights litigation based on the writ of *amparo* (or equivalents such as *tutela* in Colombia) appears to have had regressive effects because middle-class citizens have been better placed than the poor to pursue their right to health through the court system given the costs involved (Ferraz 2011; Bergallo 2011; Young and Lemaitre 2013; Flood and Gross 2014). The absence of such mechanisms has helped Indonesia avoid this scenario.[21]

---

[21] See Crouch (2018) for a discussion of other 'prerogative writs' that can also facilitate individual rights claims. I have emphasized *amparo*-style mechanisms here because they have been widely discussed in the literature on health rights litigation in developing countries (Yamin and Gloppen 2011; Young and Lemaitre 2013; Flood and Gross 2014).

With regards to health institutions, the important point is that Indonesia lacked—at least until 2014—a universal, mandatory, and national public health insurance scheme akin to those in some Latin American countries. Such schemes contributed to the massive increase in individually focused health rights litigation in Latin America and its regressive effects by giving all citizens (including, most importantly, middle-class citizens) an entitlement to certain specified services and medicine. This fuelled a sense of entitlement to free healthcare and medication more generally. Most health rights litigation in these countries has related either to medicine or services that are covered under these schemes or for which there is no clear rationale for their exclusion (Wilson 2011; Young and Lemaitre 2013: 187–188; Flood and Gross 2014: 67–68).

Responsiveness of the Political Elite

The responsiveness of elites post-1998—including in the judiciary—to social policy pressures has also been a decisive factor in encouraging collective social rights litigation. As indicated earlier, democratization created an incentive for elites to promote social policies favouring the poor and marginalized, given the electoral appeal of such policies. For our purposes, two developments were especially important. The first was the appointment in 2004 of Siti Fadillah Supari as minister of health following Susilo Bambang Yudhoyono's election as president that year. A relative political unknown prior to her appointment, Supari, in keeping with the radical populist tradition in Indonesian economic thinking,[22] emerged as a strong critic of neoliberal health policies (Bari 2009; Supari 2010). She voiced stinging criticisms of the World Health Organization (WHO) and the World Bank and of Anglo-American donors who supported their policies and she dramatically reduced ministry of health cooperation with these organizations.

The second important development was growing judicial activism in the area of human rights, including social rights. Under the New Order, judges were widely regarded as 'gormless and corrupt functionaries who do the government's bidding in the government's courts' (Bourchier 1999: 233). To some extent, they have remained so in the post–New Order period (Tahyar 2012). But judicial reforms such as those mentioned above have nevertheless widened the scope for greater judicial activism in relation to human rights issues.[23] On the one hand, as noted above, these reforms created new legal pathways through which citizens and NGOs concerned about breaches of human rights could access the judicial system, especially for the purposes of collective litigation. On the other hand, these reforms also gave the judiciary greater independence from the executive, making it easier for judges to hand down decisions contrary to government positions considered to breach human rights. The reforms also created an opportunity for judges to build a political base among the poor and

---

[22] For an analysis of the radical populist tradition in Indonesia's economic thinking, see Chalmers and Hadiz (1997: Chs 5 and 8).

[23] Other important judicial reforms included the 'one roof' changes—whereby jurisdiction over court administration and the lower courts was granted solely to the Supreme Court rather than being shared with the government—and the establishment of a Judicial Commission (Crouch 2019: 4).

marginalized, both as a way of securing legitimacy for their respective courts and, in the case of some judges, positioning themselves for higher-level political office. The Constitutional Court, in particular, became a locus for such activism, especially under its first two chief justices, Jimly Asshiddiqie and Mahfud MD. Its judicial selection and funding arrangements gave it a greater degree of autonomy from government than other courts (Mietzner 2010), while the country's new rights-rich Constitution provided the Court with strong legal grounds for rights-friendly decisions. However, the shift in favour of greater judicial activism appeared to permeate the court system as a whole.

Characteristics of NGOs

The impact of social rights litigation in Indonesia has also been shaped by the nature of the country's NGO community. During the New Order, the government pursued a strategy of disorganizing civil society through harsh restrictions on freedom of organization and expression, the establishment of state-sponsored corporatist organizations to control representation of key professional and social groups, and the co-optation or repression of organizations that existed outside these corporatist structures (Robison and Hadiz 2004: 120–44). At the same time, to the extent that civil society organizations did engage in human rights advocacy, they tended to focus on issues of civil, political, land, environmental, and labour rights rather than the rights to education and health. However, the fall of the New Order triggered the establishment of a small number of NGOs explicitly focused on social rights. Post-1998 Indonesia also saw many NGOs with a core focus on other issues become more engaged with social rights as social policy became increasingly salient for the reasons mentioned above. Importantly for our purposes, these NGOs commanded sufficient financial and legal resources between them to utilize the courts to promote the rights to education and health, and were prepared to do so, as their involvement in the aforementioned cases illustrates. The development of these resources, in turn, was due to the NGOs' successes in tapping funding from external sources (and in some cases domestic sources) and the fact that many of them employed activist lawyers (Lindsey and Crouch 2013: 623). Moreover, they increased their mobilization capacity by forging close links to other groups within civil society, including public intellectuals with expertise on education and health issues, parents groups, and labour activists. This enhanced their capacity to engage in legal and political mobilization to promote the rights to education and health.

Conclusion

In this chapter, I have argued that social rights litigation in Indonesia has had a positive effect vis-à-vis the fulfilment of social rights because it has precipitated policy changes that helped to enforce or realize these rights—or, more precisely, that it did so during the period under review, 1998–2015. I have further argued that its effects in this respect were conditional upon factors such as the presence of particular judicial and health institutions; enhanced responsiveness by the political elite to social policy concerns in the post-New Order period; and the presence of NGOs with specific characteristics. In strategic terms, it would thus be easy to conclude that such litigation should remain an important element of the approaches employed by citizens to promote fulfilment of these rights in Indonesia. However, there are at least two reasons why social rights litigation may be less effective in this respect in the foreseeable future.

The first is that the judiciary and in particular the judges of the Constitutional Court appear to be becoming less receptive to rights-based claims. The Constitutional Court has been rocked by a series of corruption scandals. In 2013 it was revealed that then Chief Justice Akil Mochtar had taken bribes in relation to a series of regional election disputes. He was subsequently sentenced to life imprisonment. Four years later, Patrialis Akbar, who was appointed to the court in 2013, suffered a similar fate, being convicted of taking bribes in relation to a judicial review of a law on animal husbandry and animal health (Yuliawati 2017). At the same time, according to some commentators, the Constitutional Court has become more conservative in its outlook since the end of Mahfud MD's tenure as chief justice (Hendrianto 2016). If the Constitutional Court has now been captured by predatory elements with little commitment to the rule of law, let alone human rights specifically, and its overall outlook is more conservative in nature, it is unlikely that it will continue to take a progressive stance on issues of social rights. Moreover, after a radical overhaul of the country's political institutions following the fall of the New Order, Indonesia now appears to be going through a period of democratic decline as civil and political freedoms are wound back and elements in the military and hardline Islamist groups gain greater authority within government (Power 2018). In this context, the scope for judicial activism in favour of rights in general across the court system is likely to be more constrained.

The second reason is that progressive NGOs may shift their priorities with regards to education and health rights in the future, limiting the possibilities for legal mobilization around such rights. On the one hand, they may give renewed attention to struggles over civil and political rights as the country goes through a period of democratic decline. On the other hand, they may feel as if there is not much more that can be achieved with regards to the fulfilment of social rights. As we have seen, much social rights litigation in Indonesia has been motivated by a desire to defeat neoliberal social policy reforms introduced in the wake of the Asian economic crisis. This project has been largely successful and there seems to be little prospect of a renewed push for neoliberal social policy reform in the short to medium term—as several commentators have noted, Indonesia's development policies have become increasingly protectionist in nature over the past decade, not more neoliberal (Patunru and Rahardja 2015; Warburton 2017). Likewise, with the establishment of BPJS Kesehatan and BPJS Ketenagakerjaan and the government fulfilling constitutional and legal requirements for education and health spending, there seems little prospect of immediate further progress in terms of the development of Indonesia's social welfare regime. Finally, education and health policy debates are increasingly turning away from questions of access to questions of quality, the current focus on learning in education being a case in point (Rosser 2018). In general, the quality of education and health services is a domain in which progressive NGOs in Indonesia have relatively little expertise. It is also a domain less amenable to rights-based claims given that rights tend to focus on matters of access.

Of course, it is possible that the COVID-19 pandemic, which struck Indonesia during the first quarter of 2020, may offset both these factors, at least in relation to health rights. By most accounts, Indonesia handled the public health dimension of the pandemic poorly (Lindsey and Mann 2020a). By the time of writing (late August 2020), it had registered almost 150,000 confirmed cases of COVID-19, more than all other countries in Southeast Asia with the exception of the Philippines, and over 6,000 deaths, with many commentators suggesting that the actual figures were much higher in both cases (Barker and Souisa 2020; Lindsey and Mann 2020b). Most importantly for our purposes, the pandemic shone a light on the inadequacies of Indonesia's health system (eg its low number of doctors, hospital beds, ICU beds, and ventilators) and the poor quality of some of its health indicators (eg its high rates of tuberculosis and tobacco addiction) (Barker 2020). In contesting the government's handling of the pandemic, human rights activists have invoked the rights to health and health services in their public statements, calling on the government to fulfil these rights by improving its management of the crisis, and, in particular, by ensuring that Indonesian citizens can get needed healthcare (eg Sari 2020). It is possible that such sentiments may translate into both litigation against the government over its handling of the crisis and sympathy within the judiciary for the associated complaints. But this remains to be seen.

References

Action Committee for Social Security (2010) *Gugatan Perbuatan Melawan Hukum Atas Penyelengaraan Jaminan Sosial*, Jakarta.

Aspinall, Edward (2014) 'Health Care and Democratization in Indonesia' 21(5) *Democratization* 803–823.

Aspinall, Edward and Eve Warburton (2013) 'A Healthcare Revolution in the Regions' 111 *Inside Indonesia*.

Australia's Education Partnership with Indonesia (2016) *Education Partnership—Independent Completion Report*, https://www.dfat.gov.au/sites/default/files/indonesia-education-part nership-completion-report.pdf, accessed 24 August 2022.

Bari Syaiful (ed) (2009) *Kumpulan Wawancara Siti Fadillah Supari: Berkiblat Kata Hati Menggeser Tapal Batas Dunia*. Yogyakarta: SFS Fans Club and Lembaga Kajian Islam, dan Sosial.

Barker, Anne (2020) 'Indonesia's Health System is Vulnerable to COVID-19. Why Was it Late to Adopt Social Distancing?', https://www.abc.net.au/news/2020-04-20/an-exodus-of-milli ons-in-indonesia-could-fuel-covid-19-disaster/12154510, accessed 22 August 2020.

Barker Anne and Helena Souisa (2020) 'COVID-19 Death Rate in Indonesia is the Highest in the World. Experts Say it's Because Reported Case Numbers are too Low', https://www. abc.net.au/news/2020-03-23/why-is-indonesia-coronavirus-death-rate-highest-in-world/ 12079040, accessed 22 August 2020.

Bergallo, Paola (2011) 'Argentina: Courts and the Right to Health: Achieving Fairness Despite "Routinization" in Individual Coverage Cases' in A Yamin and S Gloppen (eds) *Litigating Health Rights: Can Courts Bring More Justice to Health?* Cambridge, MA: Harvard University Press. pp 43–75.

Boediono (2009) *Ekonomi Indonesia Mau ke Mana? Kumpulan Esai Ekonomi*. Jakarta: Gramedia and Freedom Institute.

Bourchier, David (1999) 'Magic Memos, Collusion and Judges with Attitude: Notes on the Politics of Law in Contemporary Indonesia' in K Jayasuriya (ed) *Law, Capitalism and Power: The Rule of Law and Legal Institutions*. London: Routledge. pp 233–252.

Butt, Simon and Nicholas Parsons (2014) 'Judicial Review and the Supreme Court in Indonesia: A New Space for Law?' 97 *Indonesia* 55–85.

Butt, Simon, Melissa Crouch, and Rosalind Dixon (2016) 'The First Decade of Indonesia's Constitutional Court' 16(2) *Australian Journal of Asian Law* 1113–1119.

Chalmers, Ian and Vedi Hadiz (eds) (1997) *The Politics of Economic Development in Indonesia: Contending Perspective*. London: Routledge.

Crouch, Melissa (2018) 'The Prerogative Writs as Constitutional Transfer' 38(4) *Oxford Journal of Legal Studies* 653–675.

Crouch, Melissa (2019) 'The Judicial Reform Landscape in Indonesia: Innovation, Specialisation and the Legacy of Dan S. Lev' in M Crouch (ed) *The Politics of Court Reform: Judicial Change and Legal Culture in Indonesia*. Cambridge: Cambridge University Press, pp. 1-28.

Darmaningtyas, Edi Subkhan and Fahmi-Panimbang (2009) *Tirani Kapital Dalam Pendidikan: Menolak UU BHP (Badan Hukum Pendidikan)*. Yogyakarta: Pustaka Yashiba and Damar Press).

Ferraz, Octavio (2011) 'Brazil: Health Inequalities, Rights, and Courts: The Social Impact of the Judicialization of Health' in A Yamin and S Gloppen (eds) *Litigating Health Rights: Can Courts Bring More Justice to Health?* Cambridge, MA: Harvard University Press. pp 76–102.

Flood, Colleen and Aeyal Gross (2014) 'Litigating the Right to Health: What Can We Learn from a Comparative Law and Health Care Systems Approach?' 16(2) *Health and Human Rights* 62–72.

Gatot (2007) 'Gugatan Citizen Law Suit Terhadap Kebijakan Ujian Nasional' in I Ridho (ed), *Menggugat Ujian Nasional*. Jakarta: Teraju. pp 101–116.

Gauri, Varun and Daniel Brinks (eds) (2008) *Courting Social Justice: Judicial Enforcement of Social and Economic Rights in the Developing World*. New York: Cambridge University Press.

Gloppen Siri and Mindy Roseman (2011) 'Introduction: Can Litigation Bring Justice to Health?' in A Yamin and Siri Gloppen (eds) *Litigating Health Rights: Can Courts Bring More Justice to Health?* Cambridge, MA: Harvard University Press. pp 1–16.

Government of Indonesia (2009) 'Minister of Education Regulation 78/2009 on the Implementation of International Standard Schools in Primary and Secondary Education'.

Hendrianto, Stefanus (2016) 'The Rise and Fall of Heroic Chief Justices: Constitutional Politics and Judicial Leadership in Indonesia' 25(3) *Washington International Law Journal* 489–563.

Hoemardani, Soedjono (1975) *Renungan Tentang Pembangunan*. Jakarta: Center for Strategic and International Studies.

Holliday, Ian (2000) 'Productivist Welfare Capitalism: Social Policy in East Asia' 48(4) *Political Studies* 706–723.

HukumOnline (2007) *Putusan Nomor 228/PDT.G/2006/PN.JKT.PST*, http://www.hukumonl ine.com/pusatdata/detail/lt4c1885f340a9f/node/lt49f802c936fc9/putusan-pengadilan-neg eri-jakarta-pusat-no-228_pdt.g_2006_pn.jkt.pst-kristiono-vs.-presiden-republik-indone sia, accessed 3 June 2013.

Irawan Ade et al (2004) *Mendagangkan Sekolah*. Jakarta: Indonesia Corruption Watch.

Jalal Fasli and Bachrudin Musthafa (eds) (2001) *Education Reform in the Context of Regional Autonomy: The Case of Indonesia*. Jakarta: MoNE, Bappenas, and World Bank.

Kelompok Independen Untuk Advokasi Buku (no date) 'Pers Release Pencabutan Permendiknas No 2 Tahun 2008 tentang Buku', mimeo.

Lindsey, Tim and Melissa Crouch (2013) 'Cause Lawyers in Indonesia: A House Divided' 31(3) *Wisconsin International Law Journal* 620–645.

Lindsey, Tim and Tim Mann (2020a) 'Indonesia was in Denial over Coronavirus. Now it May be Facing a Looming Disaster', *The Conversation*, https://theconversation.com/indonesia-was-in-denial-over-coronavirus-now-it-may-be-facing-a-looming-disaster-135436, accessed 22 August 2020.

Lindsey, Tim and Tim Mann (2020b) 'Indonesia's Coronavirus Fatalities are the Highest in Southeast Asia. So, Why is Jokowi Rushing to Get Back to Business?', *The Conversation*, https://theconversation.com/indonesias-coronavirus-fatalities-are-the-highest-in-southeast-asia-so-why-is-jokowi-rushing-to-get-back-to-business-144059, accessed 22 August 2020.

Mahkamah Konstitusi (2011) *Putusan Nomor 60/PUU-IX/2011*.

Mietzner, Marcus (2010) 'Political Conflict Resolution and Democratic Consolidation in Indonesia: The Role of the Constitutional Court' 10 *Journal of East Asian Studies* 397–424.

Mietzner, Marcus (2018) 'Fighting Illiberalism with Illiberalism: Islamist Populism and Democratic Deconsolidation in Indonesia' 91(2) *Pacific Affairs* 261–282.

Miguel-Stearns, Teresa M. (2015) 'Judicial Power in Latin America: a Short Survey' Librarian Scholarship Series. Paper 32.

Moertopo, Ali (1981) *Strategi Pembangunan Nasional*. Jakarta: Center for Strategic and International Studies.

Nardi Jnr, Dominic (2018) 'Can NGOs Change the Constitution? Civil Society and the Indonesian Constitutional Court' 40(2) *Contemporary Southeast Asia* 247–278.

Office of the United Nations High Commissioner for Human Rights (2008) *Frequently Asked Questions on Economic, Social and Cultural Rights*, Fact Sheet No 33, Geneva Office of the United Nations High Commissioner for Human Rights.

Patunru, Arianto and Sjamsu Rahardja (2015) *Trade Protectionism in Indonesia: Bad Times and Bad Policy*. Sydney: Lowy Institute.

Power, Tom (2018) 'Jokowi's Authoritarian Turn and Indonesia's Democratic Decline' 54(3) *Bulletin of Indonesian Economic Studies* 307–338.

Prawiro, Radius (1998) *Indonesia's Struggle for Economic Development: Pragmatism in Action*. Oxford: Oxford University Press.

Riady, John (2013) 'Jokonomics, Social Welfare and the Future of Indonesia', *Jakarta Globe*, 11 April, http://thejakartaglobe.beritasatu.com/opinion/jokonomics-social-welfare-and-the-future-of-indonesia/, accessed 8 October 2013.

Robison, Richard (1986) *Indonesia: The Rise of Capital*. Sydney: Allen and Unwin.

Robison, Richard and Vedi Hadiz (2004) *Reorganising Power in Indonesia: The Politics of Oligarchy in an Age of Markets*. London: Routledge.

Rokx, Claudia et al (2009) *Health Financing in Indonesia: A Reform Road Map*. Jakarta: World Bank.

Rosser, Andrew, Kornya Roesad, and Donni Edwin (2005) 'Indonesia: The Politics of Inclusion' 35(1) *Journal of Contemporary Asia* 53–77.

Rosser, Andrew (2012) 'Realising Free Health Care for the Poor in Indonesia: The Politics of Illegal Fees' 42(2) *Journal of Contemporary Asia* 255–275.

Rosser, Andrew (2015) 'Law and the Realisation of Human Rights: Insights from Indonesia's Education Sector' 39(2) *Asian Studies Review* 194–212.

Rosser, Andrew (2016) 'Neoliberalism and the Politics of Higher Education Policy in Indonesia' 52(2) *Comparative Education* 109–135.

Rosser, Andrew (2017) *Litigating the Right to Health: Courts, Politics and Justice in Indonesia*. Honolulu: East West Center.

Rosser Andrew (2018) *Beyond Access: Making Indonesia's Education System Work*. Sydney: Lowy Institute.

Rosser Andrew and Jayne Curnow (2014) 'Legal Mobilisation and Justice: Insights from the Constitutional Court Case on International Standard Schools in Indonesia' 15(4) *Asia-Pacific Journal of Anthropology* 302–318.

Rosser, Andrew and Mohamad Fahmi (2018) 'The Political Economy of Teacher Management in Decentralised Indonesia', World Bank Policy Research Working Paper no 7913.

Rosser, Andrew and Anuradha Joshi (forthcoming) 'Courts and the Rights to Education in Indonesia' in Z Sakhiyya, T Mulya, and A Aditomo (eds) *Education in Indonesia: Critical Perspectives on Equity and Social Justice*. Singapore: Springer.

Rosser, Andrew and Maryke van Diermen (2018) 'Law, Democracy and the Fulfilment of Social Rights in Developing Countries: Insights from Indonesia' 37(2) *Third World Quarterly* 336–353.

Rosser, Andrew and Maryke van Diermen (2018) 'Beyond Predatory Productivism? The Political Economy of Welfare Capitalism in Post-New Order Indonesia' in H Lim, S Hwang, and J Pieterse (eds) *Capitalism and Capitalisms in Asia*. Seoul: Seoul National University Press. pp 301–331.

Santosa, Mas (2007) 'Class Actions in Indonesia', http://globalclassactions.stanford.edu/cont ent/class-actions-indonesia, accessed 1 June 2013.

Sari, Haryanti (2020) 'Cegah Virus Corona, Komnas HAM Minta Pemerintah Yakinkan Publik soal Fasilitas Kesehatan', Kompas.com, 13 March, https://nasional.kompas.com/read/2020/ 03/13/16104281/cegah-virus-corona-komnas-ham-minta-pemerintah-yakinkan-publik-soal, accessed 11 April 2020.

Skelton, Ann (2017) *Strategic Litigation Impacts: Equal Access to Quality Education*. New York: The Open Society Foundation.

Sumarto, Sudarno and Samuel Bazzi (2011) 'Social Protection in Indonesia: Past Experiences and Lessons for the Future', paper presented at the 2011 Annual Bank Conference on Development Opportunities (ABCDE) jointly organized by the World Bank and OECD, 30 May–1 June 2011, Paris.

Supari, Siti (2010) 'IDI Harus Mencegah Terjadinya Neo Liberalisasi Bidang Kesehatan di Indonesia' in D Faqih and Z Abidin (eds) *60 Tahun Ikatan Dokter Indonesia: Rekam Jejak, Pandangan dan Harapan*. Jakarta: Ikatan Dokter Indonesia. pp 302–309.

Susanti, Bivitri (2008) 'The Implementation of the Rights to Health Care and Education in Indonesia' in Varun Gauri and Daniel Brinks (eds) *Courting Social Justice: Judicial Enforcement of Social and Economic Rights in the Developing World*. New York: Cambridge University Press. pp 224–267.

Tahyar, Ben (2012) 'Patrimonialism, Power and the Politics of Judicial Reform in Post-Soeharto Indonesia: An Institutional Analysis', unpublished PhD dissertation, School of Oriental and African Studies.

Thoolen, Hans (1987) *Indonesia and the Rule of Law: Twenty Years of the 'New Order' Government: A Study*. London: Pinter.

Tjandra, Surya (2014) 'The Indonesian Trade Union Movement under Reformasi', unpublished paper.

van Diermen, Maryke (2018) *Welfare in Transition: The Political Economy of Social Protection Reform in Indonesia*, unpublished PhD dissertation, University of Adelaide.

Warburton, Eve (2017) *Resource Nationalism in Post-Boom Indonesia: The New Normal?* Sydney: Lowy Institute.

Wilson B. (2011) 'Costa Rica: Health Rights Litigation: Causes and Consequences' in Alicia Yamin and Siri Gloppen (eds.) *Litigating Health Rights: Can Courts Bring More Justice to Health?* Cambridge, MA: Harvard University Press, pp 132–154.

Winters, Jeffrey (1996) *Power in Motion: Capital Mobility and the Indonesian State*. Ithaca, NY: Cornell University Press.

Yamin Alicia and Siri Gloppen (eds) (2011) *Litigating Health Rights: Can Courts Bring More Justice to Health?* Cambridge, MA: Harvard University Press.

Young, Katharine and Julieta Lemaitre (2013) 'The Comparative Fortunes of the Right to Health: Two Tales of Justiciability in Colombia and South Africa' 26 *Harvard Human Rights Journal* 179–216.

Yuliawati (2017) 'Setelah Akil Mochtar, Menyusul Patrialis Akbar', *CNN Indonesia*, 26 January, https://www.cnnindonesia.com/nasional/20170126130107-12-189189/setelah-akil-mochtar-menyusul-patrialis-akbar, accessed 21 August 2020.

Constitutional Court Decisions

Decision 011/PUU-III/2005
Decision 012/PUU-III/2005
Decision 026/PUU-III/2005
Decision 026/PUU-III/2006
Decision 013/PUU-VI/2008
Decisions 11-14-21-126 and 136/PUU-VII/2009
Decision 60/PUU-IX/2011
Decision 5/PUU-X/2012
Decision 58/PUU-X/2012
Decision 103/PUU-X/2012
Decision 92/PUU-XII/2014

Supreme Court Decisions

Decision 05 P/Hum/Th.2005
Decision 2596 K/PDT/2008

Jakarta High Court Decisions

Decision 480/PDT/2005/PT DKI
Decision 377/PDT/2007/PT.DKI

Jakarta Central District Court Decisions

Decision 28/PDT.G/2003/PN.JKT.PST
Decision 228/PDT.G/2006/PN.JKT.PST
Decision 278/PDT.G/2010/PN.JKT.PST

10

Indigeneity in the Indonesian Constitution

Yance Arizona[1]

Introduction

A salient issue in the constitution-making process of post-colonial countries is how to accommodate traditional political institutions and customary land rights that existed prior to the formation of a national constitution. Many post-colonial countries in the Global South face this problem, including Indonesia. The dominant characteristic of newly independent states is that a government establishes a legal system in favour of legal centralism rather than legal pluralism and this potentially undermines traditional political institutions (Allot 1968). Often, the establishment of a national legal system in post-colonial countries did not run smoothly because social and traditional property relations among native communities were diverse and did not fit with a new notion of the modern legal system. Constitution-makers faced great difficulties incorporating such diversity in the constitution-making process and creating a unified national law. Clifford Geertz highlights this tension between old societies and new nation-states that has resulted in the need for states to deal with multiculturalism (Geertz 1963). Contemporary studies in constitutional law have considered this topic through the lens of constitutional pluralism (Walker 2002) and pluralist constitutionalism (Neo and Son 2019).

Nevertheless, the dilemma of how or to what extent to respect and recognize traditional political institutions and customary land rights is not a new problem only faced by post-colonial states. In the past, during the colonial period, colonial rulers also encountered such a dilemma. Furnivall (2014) shows how British and Dutch colonial rulers in Asia faced a dilemma between applying European law or maintaining the customary law of the native peoples in the colonies. In the Dutch East Indies, the Dutch colonial rulers maintained legal pluralism by applying different laws and institutions to control the labour and land of native populations. This distinction was regulated in Articles 75 and 109 of *Regeeringsreglement*, which served as the constitution for the colony. Concerning land issues, the Dutch civil code applied for European settlers in the colony, while customary law operated for native populations (Luttikhuis 2013:541–542). In terms of administrative governance, the colonial rulers recognized that local traditional kingdoms and adat law communities exercised self-governance to support the colonisers' policy of indirect rule (Mamdani 2013).[2] In short, the

[1] I would like to thank Melissa Crouch and Adriaan Bedner for their valuable comments and advice in completing this chapter.
[2] Despite the colonial rulers distinguished legal category of population into European with Native and Foreign Oriental, among population groups from Native and Foreign Oriental can be subject to European

Yance Arizona, *Indigeneity in the Indonesian Constitution* In: *Constitutional Democracy in Indonesia*. Edited by: Melissa Crouch, Oxford University Press. © Yance Arizona, 2023. DOI: 10.1093/oso/9780192870681.003.0010

colonial government preserved a dual legal system for its own purposes, and to some extent also permitted autonomy for some indigenous communities under a policy of indirect rule (Fasseur 2007).

In the early post-colonial period, the Indonesian government created a constitution and legislation to reorganize political structures and land rights. Their main objective was to transform the colonial and feudalistic form of government to a new nationalistic and modern government system. For many decades, this transformative strategy undermined traditional political institutions and customary rights to pursue modernity. However, in the last three decades, the emergence of an international indigenous peoples movement has considerably changed the state's attitude towards indigenous claims. The Indonesian government reformulated the Constitution and legislation to accommodate indigeneity and customary land rights. As with Indonesia, there was a turning point in many countries that underwent political transition from authoritarian to democratic regimes. In Latin America, some countries such as Colombia, Venezuela, Chile, Brazil, Ecuador and Bolivia created new constitutions to recognize indigenous peoples rights. The new Latin American constitutionalism is characterized by respect for human rights, indigenous peoples' rights, environmental protection, and citizen participatory democracy (Uprimny 2011).

In line with the trend of recognition of indigenous rights in many countries, at the international level, the United Nations created a platform to discuss indigenous peoples rights. The United Nations designated two international decades of indigenous peoples (1995–2014) and created annual events and bodies to discuss indigenous peoples rights. In 2007, the crown of this development was the enactment of the United Nations Declaration on the Rights of Indigenous Peoples (UNDRIP). Indigenous peoples' advocacy has not only been successful in institutionalizing the recognition of indigenous peoples' rights at international law, but also reshaping the political relationship between native peoples and the state in many countries. To some extent, the indigenous peoples' movement also provides support for *adat* (custom) in reshaping the state–society relationship in Indonesia (Henley and Davidson 2007).

This chapter discusses how indigeneity has been accommodated, both in the constitution-making process and the implementation of constitutional provisions through legislation and judicial decision from 1945 until the present. I discuss two aspects of indigeneity in this chapter. The first aspect is concerned with the traditional political institutions, notably local kingdoms and adat law communities in Indonesia. These local political entities existed at different levels and they had different positions during the colonial period. The second issue is related to land rights, especially land rights claimed by local kingdoms as well as the customary land rights of adat law communities.

In order to analyse these two issues in Indonesian constitutional history, I describe the constitutional development in Indonesia chronologically. I draw upon the minutes of the Constituent Assembly to consider what constitution-makers understood by the term indigeneity in the constitution-making and constitutional amendment process.

---

jurisdiction after obtaining a declaration of 'applicable' (*toepasselijk*) by the Governor-General (Luttikhuis 2013:542).

Additionally, I analyse the political context surrounding the formulation and implementation of the Constitution regarding indigeneity in Indonesia.

In this chapter, I first discuss the definition of indigeneity used in the Dutch East Indies colonial setting. In the next section, I analyse the post-colonial context of constitutional development as it relates to indigeneity in six phases. It begins with the construction of indigeneity in the constitution-making process of the original 1945 Constitution. Furthermore, I analyse the formulation of indigeneity in the 1949 Federal Constitution and the 1950 Provisional Constitution. When President Soekarno released a president's decree on 5 July 1959, the 1945 Constitution was re-enacted in a different political context. Under the 1945 Constitution, President Soeharto, with his authoritarianism, suppressed indigenous rights as he perceived that such rights were an obstacle to the government's development agenda. After President Soeharto stepped down in 1998, a series of constitutional amendments were conducted in a democratic environment. Non-governmental organizations (NGOs) that were working on indigenous issues encouraged the government and legislature institutionalizing adat communities rights in law. This section discusses NGO's and adat community organization's efforts to expand the state legal framework on indigenous rights. Later in the chapter, I argue that the government created the conditional recognition clause to manage indigenous issues under state domination. This strategy is what Mahmood Mamdani (2013) calls define and rule politics. Moreover, I find that the conditionalities for the government to recognize indigeneity and customary land rights are changing over time, influenced by the social and political contexts. I conclude with a discussion on the conditional recognition clause concerning indigeneity and constitutional law, and its problems with the realization of indigenous rights in Indonesia.

Traditional Political Institutions and Customary Land Rights in the Dutch Colonial Policies

During the colonial period, two traditional political institutions functioned as self-governing units. The first political institution was traditional kingdoms that had autonomy and at the same time also functioned to support the colonial administration. Most of these local kingdoms entered into cooperation agreements with the Dutch colonial ruler, and the colonial ruler designated them as self-governing regions, or swapraja governments. For the implementation of the indirect rule policy, the Dutch colonial government made political contracts with swapraja governments in the form of extensive contracts (*lange contract*) and short declarations (*korte verklaring*) (Niessen 1999:44–45). Until the end of the Dutch colonial administration in 1942, there were 278 swapraja governments in the Dutch East Indies (Ranawidjaja 1955:49).

The second type of political institution was adat law communities. On a smaller scale, adat law communities are based on customary law that applies to all community members. During the Dutch colonial period, research on adat law communities was a key focus of Dutch researchers. Cornelis van Vollenhoven, the leading scholar on customary law, identified adat law communities (*rechtsgemeenschappen*) as a unit of self-governing communities with specific characteristics. In the colonial period, colonial rulers implemented a segregation policy by applying different laws between European settlers and native peoples in the colony (Wignjoeosbroto 2014). Customary law applied to native populations at the local level. The implication of this difference in status between colonizer and colonized peoples created a dual legal system. However, that does not mean that the colonial ruler did not intervene in adat law communities and customary law. In 1906, during the late colonial period, the Dutch colonial government released a regulation to reorganize village administration in Java and Madura.[3] Furthermore, in 1938 the colonial government expanded the village reorganization programmes to islands outside of Java.[4]

Both local kingdoms and adat law communities have land rights and control definite territories. Local kingdoms control particular territory and they can create contract agreements with business enterprises. At the local level, adat law communities also control definite territory as customary territories. Control of land and natural resources has been one of the main concentrations in Dutch colonial policies. In 1870, the Dutch colonial authorities issued the Agrarian Law (*Agrarische Wet 1870*), which was followed by a declaration domain decree (*domein verklaring*). The doctrine of domain declaration contained a principle that if ownership of land cannot be proven, then the land belongs to the state land. This doctrine facilitated colonial rulers to claim native lands and gave concessions to private companies. The implementation of this principle led to land dispossession of native populations. It was not only native populations who criticized the colonial agrarian policy but also scholars in the Netherlands.

The peak of this debate was in the 1910s when the Dutch colonial rulers intended to amend Article 62 of the 1854 general regulation for the colony (*Regeringreglemen*). The amendment of the proposed provision was intended to lead to legal unification and expand the domain declaration principle. The domain declaration is a decree by the colonial government which states that land for which no one could prove ownership would be classified as state land (Termorshuizen-Arts 2010). A decade later, debate regarding the amendment process arose between scholars from Utrecht University and Leiden University. The Utrecht group supported legal unification and the expansion of the principle of domain declaration. Meanwhile, the Leiden group wanted to protect and recognize the autonomy of adat law communities with their customary law in regulating land ownership (Burn 2004). Cornelis van Vollenhoven (1919) wrote a pamphlet to oppose the colonial government's plan to amend the basic rules of colonial land as he realized that the imposition of colonial law on native peoples would have a devastating impact.

The Dutch colonial government's plan to amend the regulation did not succeed. Still, the debate over the position of customary law and land rights of native peoples remained, and it has continued in the post-colonial period. The following section will analyse how traditional political institutions and customary land rights were part of the formation and implementation of the Constitution across different post-colonial political regimes in Indonesia.

---

[3] Inlandsche Gemeente Ordonnantie Java en Madoera (Stbld 1906 No 83).
[4] Inlandsche Gemeente Ordonnantie Buitengewesten (Stbld 1938 No 490 jo Stbld 1938 No 681)

The Six Phases of Constitutional Development
Concerning Indigeneity

For more than seventy-five years since independence, the Republic of Indonesia has had three constitutions—the 1945 Constitution, the 1949 Federal Constitution, and the 1950 Provisional Constitution. The contemporary 1945 Constitution has been implemented twice. The first period was 1945 to 1949, and the second period is 1959 up to the current period. From 1999 to 2002, the People's Consultative Assembly (*Majelis Permusyawaratan Rakyat*, MPR) conducted a series of constitutional amendments that significantly changed the original version of the 1945 Constitution. The contemporary amended version of the 1945 Constitution upholds principles of democracy, human rights, and the rule of law (Butt and Lindsey 2012). This chapter divides the constitutional development in Indonesia into six phases, as I discuss next.

Indigeneity in the Formulation and Implementation of the 1945
Constitution (1945–1949)

The first phase of constitutional development in Indonesia began with the 1945 Constitution (1945–1949). The formation of the first constitution was prepared by a constitution-making body created under the Japanese occupation: the Investigating Committee for the Preparation of Indonesian Independence (*Badan Penyelidik Usaha Persiapan Kemerdekaan Indonesia,* BPUPKI). Furthermore, on 18 August 1945, the draft of the Constitution was endorsed by the Preparatory Committee for Indonesian Independence (*Panitia Persiapan Kemerdekaan Indonesia*, PPKI), one day after the proclamation of independence. The majority of the members of the constitution-making body were nationalists who had a modern outlook. They had been trained by the Dutch or in Netherlands-Indies institutes of higher education and several of them were renowned jurists (Bedner 2017: 163). The constitution-makers came from a diverse set of political ideologies, including nationalist, Islamist, socialist, communist, liberalist, and traditionalist groups. Although they adhered to diverse political ideologies, they had a common purpose of creating a modern political constitution to establish a new nation-state replacing the colonial state.

The 1945 Constitution was designated to be a temporary constitution to meet the conditions for the formation of a new state after the proclamation of independence.[5] The main focus of this Constitution was to create a strong government and build territorial integrity in the form of a unitary state based on former Dutch East Indies colonial territory. The Constitution was concise (thirty-seven articles) and contained limited provisions concerning human rights.

Regarding the formation of a post-colonial government, the constitution-makers discussed a range of ideas to develop a new government structure by seeking inspiration from traditional political institutions. At the top level, to constitute the national

---

[5] Minutes of PPKI session on 18 August 1945, p 344. Soekarno stated that the 1945 Constitution was a temporary and revolutionary constitution (*revolutie grondwet*).

government, the constitution-makers debated the form of the state, that is, whether it should be a republic or a monarchy. At the mid-level, the position of swapraja governments and local traditional kingdoms were considered to be the base of provincial and municipality government units. At the lower level, the constitution-makers considered that adat law communities could be the base for village governments.

Constitution-makers encountered the question as to whether the newly independent state of Indonesia would be a republic or a monarchy. In a vote, fifty-five members voted for the republic, and six members voted for a monarchy.[6] This result indicates that since the beginning of the constitution-making process in Indonesia, the traditionalist group in favour of a monarchy had little support.

Muhammad Yamin, a jurist and an influential actor in the constitution-making process, rejected monarchy because in his view a monarchy government would create a political dynasty. Furthermore, Yamin was concerned it would be difficult to determine who would be the head of state in the monarchy because there were many local kingdoms. Although constitution-makers were in favour of a republic rather than a monarchy, they remained aware of the importance of the president as the head of state and as the symbol of the state.[7] This concern led to a discussion about the requirements to be a president of the Republic of Indonesia. The constitution drafters stipulated that 'The president must be an indigenous Indonesian'.[8] There has never been a clear definition of the meaning of this phrase. This provision was created amid discussions on citizenship and uncertainty about the status of Chinese and Arab descendants. The Chinese representatives were divided into two groups. One group supported the idea that all Chinese descendants should automatically become Indonesian citizens. Another group of Chinese descendants refused because they had privileged status during the colonial period. For the latter group, becoming Indonesian citizens would group them with the natives who were of lower status during the colonial period.[9] Implicitly, constitution-makers defined an indigenous person as a non-foreign descendant of the Chinese and Arabs. Consequently, this provision became a source for discriminatory action towards Chinese descendants by positioning them as non-indigenous Indonesian.

Another issue in the constitution-making process was the position of swapraja governments and adat law communities. Muhammad Yamin and Soepomo, both members of the Investigating Committee for the Preparation of Indonesian Independence and the Preparatory Committee for Indonesian Independence, and leading jurists in the early independence movement, had strong opinions regarding traditional political institutions. Muhammad Yamin argued that the ability and proficiency of society in running modern state administrations had emerged over thousands of years. Yamin

---

[6] Minutes of BPUPKI session, 10 July 1945, p 119.

[7] Ibid, p 105.

[8] Article 6(1) of the 1945 Constitution. Minutes of BPUPKI session, 11 July 1945, pp 195–196. Wahid Hasjim from the Islamist group proposed that the president must be a muslim as an addition of indigenous Indonesian. His proposal was accepted at the BPUPKI session on 16 July 1945, but during the enactment of the Constitution on 18 August 1945, his proposal was revoked. See minutes of PPKI session, 18 August 1945, p 336.

[9] See Liem Koen Hian and Wongsonegoro's accounts in the minutes of the BPUPKI session, 11 July 1945, pp 152–160. Including Oei Tjong Hauw's and Muhammad Yamin's accounts, pp 177–179.

used the traditional villages government as an example of native peoples' capability to manage social-political administrations such as the 21,000 villages (*desa*) in Java and 700 villages (*nagari*) in Minangkabau, as well as the other forms of village administration in Borneo, Bugis, Ambon, Minahasa, and so on. For Yamin, the role of traditional political institutions at the village level remained strong because it had not been affected by the arrival of Hinduism, feudalism, or European influences. Yamin proposed that these traditional political units should be used as the basis for supporting the new government of Indonesia.[10]

Similar to Muhammad Yamin, Soepomo also wanted to designate traditional political institutions of swapraja governments and adat law communities as the basis for building a new government of Indonesia. Soepomo stated that:

> The right of origin in special regions should be commemorated too. The special regions are, firstly, the monarchy territory (kooti), both in Java and outside Java, which in Dutch was called *zelfbesturendelanschapen* (self-government territories). Secondly is the smaller areas that have the original structures, which was *dorfgemeinschaften* (village communities), that have native folk structures such as *desa* in Java, *nagari* in Minangkabau, *dusun* and *marga* in Palembang, *huta* and *kuria* in Tapanuli, *gampong* in Aceh ... (they have to be) respected by improving its original structures.

Soepomo and Muhammad Yamin's accounts of respecting traditional political institutions influenced the inclusion of Article 18 in the 1945 Constitution. The explanation stated that:

> The division of Indonesia's region is divided into large and small regions, with the form of the structure of its government to be stipulated by law, by understanding and considering the basis of deliberation in the government system, and the rights of origin in the special regions.[11]

In reality, the government of Indonesia did not transform all the swapraja governments into special regions (*daerah istimewa*). The government enacted the first legislation concerning the Regional Government Committee to develop local government administration (Law 1/1945). In 1946, local kings from different regions created the Council of Kings (*Dewan Raja-Raja*) to secure their previous contract with the Dutch colonial rulers. The Council of Kings only lasted for a few years and their demands were not accommodated by the new republican government (Thufail 2013:17–18).

Nevertheless, the government used the designation of special autonomy as a way to respect the uniqueness of a particular region. Furthermore, the government enacted Law 22/1948 concerning the Basic Law of Self-Governing Regions. This law stipulated

---

[10] Minutes of BPUPKI session, p 18.

[11] The formal explanation of the 1945 Constitution, stated that: 'In the indonesian territoty, there were approximately 250 *zelfbesturende landchappen* (the swapradja governments) and *volksgetneenschappen* (adat law communities), such as *Desa* in Java and Bali, *Nagari* in Minangkabau, *Dusun* and *Marga* in Palembang and so on. These regions have original structures; therefore they have to be considered as special regions. The Republic of Indonesia respects the position of these special regions and all state regulations concerning those regions will respect the rights of the origin of the special regions.'

that special regions can be designated at the provincial, district, and village levels. Moreover, the head of a special region government would be elected by the president from a descendant of a traditional ruling family which had controlled a particular territory since the colonial period.[12] The government designated Pontianak District in West Kalimantan as a special region at the district level. At the provincial level, the government determined Aceh and Yogyakarta as special regions in the early period of the Republic of Indonesia.[13] These provinces contributed to the formation of the Republic of Indonesia, especially Yogyakarta, where Sultan and Pakualam declared their support to the new republican government (Thufail 2013:171). In exchange for the Yogyakarta Sultanate's support to the republic, the government designated Yogyakarta province as a special region. The Sultan of Yogyakarta was automatically the head of the province, and the government still recognizes the swapraja land of the Sultanates.

The constitution-drafters also considered adat law communities as the basis for village administration. According to Soepomo, building democracy at the state level through the establishment of national representative bodies should reflect political life in rural areas where citizens and their leaders are bound by voluntary cooperation and consensus. This idea is in accordance with the principle of integralism promoted by Soepomo during the sessions of the Investigating Committee for the Preparation of Indonesian Independence (Bourchier 2007; Bedner 2017). Although adat law communities and village administration were discussed in the constitution-making process, the constitutional provision on this topic was never clearly defined. The government's intervention into village administration occurred via an act of parliament. In 1946, the government introduced the Perdikan Village Act (13/1946). During the colonial period, traditional rulers released the *perdikan* village to their servants as a reward for their loyalty and service. This included special authority to control labour to work on their lands. Since independence, the government, with the strong support of nationalists and socialists, intended to eliminate feudalism and traditionalism in society and politics. The constitution-drafters did not provide for customary land rights in the 1945 Constitution. BPUPKI and PPKI members concentrated on presenting a counter-narrative to colonialism by strengthening state control over land and other natural resources. This position was stipulated in Article 33(3) of the 1945 Constitution: 'The land, the waters and the natural resources within shall be under the powers of the State and shall be used to the greatest benefit of the people.'[14] Moreover, sectors of production that are important for the country and affect the life of the people, such as providing water and electricity, were under the authority of the government.[15] During the first phase of the implementation of the 1945 Constitution until 1949, the government did not create legislation concerning land and natural resources, although in 1948, it did create the Yogyakarta Agrarian Committee to investigate what kind of law should replace the colonial agrarian law.

---

[12] Article 18(5) of the Law on Basic Law of Self-Governing Regions (22/1948).

[13] At that time, special areas were not only formed at the provincial level, but could also be formed at the municipality and village levels (Sujamto 1988).

[14] Article 33(3) of the 1945 Constitution.

[15] Article 33(2) of the 1945 Constitution.

It can be concluded that in the constitution-drafting process of the 1945 Constitution, the constitution-drafters emphasized the peoples' experience and ability to run local administration as the foundation of a new modern state. The goal of independence was in line with the spirit of modernism to end feudalism. Constitutional provisions recognizing traditional political institutions in the form of swapraja governments and adat law communities were brief and vague. During the uncertainty of the post-independence period, the government did not focus on implementing the Constitution. The main focus of the government at the time was to defend and consolidate independence from Dutch military aggression. After the end of the war in Indonesia in 1949, a peace treaty was finally constituted in the Hague. Amid heated debates in the roundtable meeting between the representatives of the Republic of Indonesia and the Netherlands, a new constitution was ratified by the Indonesian delegations prior to the roundtable meeting.

Indigeneity in the 1949 Federal Constitution (1949–1950)

The second phase of constitutional development was the 1949 Federal Constitution (1949–1950). This constitution was prepared in Yogyakarta and ratified on 29 October 1949 in the Netherlands during an intensive dialogue between Indonesia and the Netherlands in the decolonization period. At that time, political representatives were divided into two groups. The first group was the government as a result of the 1945 proclamation of independence. The second group was the Federal Consultative Assembly (*Bijeenkomst voor Federaal Overleg*, BFO) that consisted of local kings and local elites who supported a federalist system for the new state. Some representatives of the BFO came from influential local kingdoms across the archipelago. For instance, Sultan Hamid II who was the Sultan of Pontianak of West Kalimantan, Ida Anak Agung Gde Agung who was the King of Gianyar from Bali, and King Kaliamsyah Sinaga from East Sumatra. Representatives of local kingdoms in the BFO demanded recognition for local governments under a federalist system.

The federal system supported by the BFO was in line with Hubertus Johannes van Mook's proposal for a state that had strong political and economic ties to the Netherlands.[16] Aside from the federalist system, the 1949 Federal Constitution regulated more dimensions of governance and citizens' rights than the 1945 Constitution. The 1949 Federal Constitution consisted of 197 articles, and it included 27 articles concerning citizen's rights and freedoms, especially for individual rights in the social and political spheres. The 1949 Federal Constitution coined a blueprint for a liberal, democratic state, accountable government, and guaranteed an independent judiciary (Bedner 2017: 167–168). Similar to the 1945 Constitution, the 1949 Federal Constitution did not contain provisions on the recognition of adat law communities nor customary land rights. The only reference to indigeneity in the 1949 Federal Constitution was the position of swapraja governments.

---

[16] Hubertus Johannes van Mook served as the acting Governor-General of the Ducth East Indies from 1942 to 1948.

The 1949 Federal Constitution created regional governments in the form of states. In addition to sixteen states, the 1949 Federal Constitution also recognized the position of swapraja governments within states. The 1949 Federal Constitution stipulated that swapraja governments may make contracts with the states and the contract shall not eliminate or condense the swapraja governments' authority (Arts 64–67). However, such contracts shall not undermine the public interest and regulations made by the federal government. The Supreme Court could settle any disputes between the swapraja government and the regional state government.[17] Such provisions on swapraja governments in the federal constitution contained a paradox. On the one hand, swapraja governments could make contracts with regional states, allowing them to maintain deals and privileges struck with the Dutch colonial rulers. On the other hand, any contract was conditional because it should not disregard public interest and higher regulation. The conditional recognition clause in the 1949 Federal Constitution was the first constitutional provision that acknowledged the authority of traditional political institutions.

The 1949 Federal Constitution was only in force for a short period, less that one year. Accordingly, there is little information available to evaluate the implementation of the constitutional provisions. Some political groups rejected the outcome of the agreement between the Republic of Indonesia and the Netherlands, particularly concerning the formation of the federal state. They believed that a federalist system was another strategy by the Dutch to divide and rule the former colony. Therefore, they demanded that the national parliament repeal the 1949 Federal Constitution. Muhammad Natsir, the leading Islamic political party figure initiated the Integral Motion in parliament, which proposed constitutional reform to return to a unitary state. In response, the government and parliament revoked the 1949 Federal Constitution and created a provisional constitution.

Indigeneity in the 1950 Provisional Constitution (1950–1959)

The third phase was the 1950 Provisional Constitution (1950-1959). The 1950 Provisional Constitution was enacted on 17 August 1950 to replace the 1949 Federal Constitution. Soepomo, the Minister of Justice at that time, was the main drafter of the constitution. Soepomo combined the main elements of the 1945 Constitution and the 1949 Federal Constitution to be designated as the provisional constitution. The 1950 Provisional Constitution provided a balance between a strong centralist government and recognition of citizen rights. Many elements in the 1949 Federal Constitution, especially human rights provisions, were retained in the 1950 Provisional Constitution. The most crucial difference between the 1950 Provisional Constitution and the 1945 Federal Constitution concerned the form of the state, namely the reintroduction of the unitary state to replace the federal state.

Despite returning to the unitary state system, the 1950 Provisional Constitution kept provisions concerning the recognition of the swapraja governments from the

---

[17] Articles 64, 65, 66, and 67 of the 1949 Federal Constitution.

1949 Federal Constitution. Article 132 of the 1950 Provisional Constitution recognized the swapraja governments. The swapraja governments' authorities could not be eliminated or condensed by the national government, except for public interest reasons. The courts have the power to settle disputes between the swapraja governments and the state governments. Furthermore, the government enacted the Law on Basics of Regional Government (1/1957) to replace Law 22/1948. The new law on regional government provided a legal status for swapraja governments to be recognized as regional government units at the provincial, municipality, and village levels.[18]

Similar to the 1945 Constitution and the 1949 Federal Constitution, the 1950 Provisional Constitution did not specifically regulate the recognition of adat law communities or customary land rights. However, the government created several committees to prepare a new agrarian law to replace the colonial agrarian law. For instance, the government created the Jakarta Agrarian Committee (1951), the Soewahjo Committee (1956), and the Minister of Agriculture, Soenarjo (1958) issued the first draft of the new agrarian law. But the bill was not discussed in parliament.

The 1950 Provisional Constitution recommended the establishment of a constitution-making body to enact a new permanent constitution. In 1955, the first general election was held to elect members of parliament and the *Konstituante*. The *Konstituante* was the constitution-making body for the new constitution, which conducted meetings from 1956 to 1959. The *Konstituante* agreed to uphold human rights and democracy in the prospective constitution. But the debate on the foundations of the state remained unresolved with disputes between the nationalist and the Islamist camps. Ironically, before the *Konstituante* enacted a new constitution, on 5 July 1959, President Soekarno pissued a presidential decree dissolving the *Konstituante* and re-enacting the 1945 Constitution (Lev 2009).

Indigeneity under President Soekarno's Guided Democracy (1959–1966)

The fourth phase was the period of the 1945 Constitution during Soekarno's administration (1959–1966). The 1945 Constitution facilitated authoritarian government because it legitimized strong presidential power while at the same time also limiting human rights. With the re-enactment of the 1945 Constitution, the provision regarding 'the President must be an indigenous Indonesian' returned, while swapraja governments lost their constitutional basis.

Relying on strong executive authority in the 1945 Constitution, President Soekarno launched a political manifesto to shape Indonesia into a socialist state. During this period, political freedom was restricted. On the other hand, the government finally enacted a new agrarian law to replace the colonial agrarian law and provided a legal basis for the land reform programme. The formulation of the Basic Agrarian Law (5/1960) was key to understanding how indigeneity was seen by the government and parliament members.

---

[18] Article 2(2) of the Law on Basics of Regional Government (1/1957).

The discussion on the land rights of adat law communities and swapraja governments was discussed at length in the debates over the Basic Agrarian Law. The preparation of the Basic Agrarian Law begun in 1948 but was not discussed in the legislature until 1960. The Minister of Agriculture Sadjarwo created a new draft agrarian law based on previous works of agrarian committees. Intensive debate took place between the government and members of the legislature concerning the position of customary land rights of adat law communities and swapraja governments for the new agrarian law.

There were four approaches in relation to the accommodation of customary land rights in the Basic Agrarian Law. The first approach intended to use customary law and customary land rights as the main source for creating a new national land law. The government introduced the concept of the right of the nation to land and other natural resources reflecting the concept of customary land rights between adat communities and their territories.[19] Customary law was also used as the basis for the agrarian law, and customary law applied where the operating regulations of the Basic Agrarian Law had not yet been created.[20]

The second approach was a conditional recognition approach, in which customary law and customary land rights were recognized by the state as long as they met several conditionalities. This approach was reflected in Articles 3 and 5 of the Basic Agrarian Law, that formulated five conditions for the recognition and implementation of customary law and customary land rights. The government recognized customary law and customary land rights as long as they were not contrary to national and state interests, national integration, Indonesian socialism, higher laws and regulations, and respecting religious values. This conditional recognition approach became the dominant pattern towards legalizing customary land rights, which I discuss further later.

The third approach was the delegation approach. According to Article 2(4) of the Basic Agrarian Law, the state can delegate land to be managed by adat law communities. This model was not based on legal recognition, but the delegation of state land under the direct control of the government to be utilized by adat law communities. It was quite similar to the second approach because adat law communities could only use the land if the use was not contrary to the national interest and higher regulations.

The fourth approach concerned the land rights of swapraja governments. In contrast to the customary land rights of adat law communities, the Basic Agrarian Law eliminated the land rights of swapraja governments. The conversion provisions of the Basic Agrarian Law states that: 'The rights and authorities of swapraja governments or of former swapraja governments which still exist when this Act comes into effect shall be nullified and transferred to the State.'[21] The argument for the abolition of swapraja land was that the concept of feudalistic land ownership did not fit with modern land law and contradicted the objectives of land redistribution based on the framework of Indonesian socialism.

In this period, Soekarno's administration took a serious position to limit swapraja governments and adat law communities. In 1965, the government enacted another

---

[19] Article 1 of the Basic Agrarian Law (5/1960).
[20] Article 56 of the Basic Agrarian Law (5/1960).
[21] Article IV of the Conversion Terms in the Basic Agrarian Law (5/1960).

Law on Regional Government (18/1965) and the Law on Desapraja (19/1965). Similar to the provision in the Basic Agrarian Law, the Law on the Regional Government abolished swapraja governments, except for Yogyakarta (Art 88). This period was the peak of the anti-swapraja movement led by nationalists and socialists. Desapraja Law also had a similar spirit to transform adat law communities into a new form of modern village government to support the agenda of national revolution. This Law also undermined the village government in favour of national interests and agendas. The head of Desapraja must uphold the 1945 Constitution, Indonesian Socialism, and Guided Democracy, and 'Indonesian nationhood', which meant that he/she must actively implement the political manifesto of the Republic of Indonesia and its operational guidelines.[22] In short, the reorganization of village administration supported state development goals. However, the transformation of adat communities to a new form of a modern village was unsuccessful because government capacity to intervene in rural development was limited. In 1996, President Soekarno was removed from power and a new government under President Soeharto took over.

Indigeneity under President Soeharto's New Order regime (1966–1998)

The fifth phase of the relationship between indigeneity and constitutionalism was under the 1945 Constitution during Soeharto's New Order government (1966–1998). The political transition from Soekarno to Soeharto was not followed by constitutional reform. In 1966, Soeharto, who had just been appointed president, declared that he would not change the Constitution, stating that he would follow the 1945 Constitution. The 1945 Constitution gave Soeharto great powers without tenure restrictions, allowing him to run the country as president for thirty-two years.

Soeharto transformed the economy by focusing on natural-resource extraction with the support of foreign investment. The first legislation passed during President Soeharto's early presidency was the Law on Foreign Investment (1/1966) followed by the Forestry Law (5/1967) and the Mining Law (11/1967). The government expanded its control over forest areas by designating them as state property that should be free of individual land and customary land rights. The Forestry Law provided extra restrictions to customary land rights. Article 17 of the Forestry Law stated that:

> The implementation of peoples' rights, customary law and its members as well as individual rights to get benefit from forests either directly or indirectly based on customary rules as long as those rules remain to exist, should not interfere with the achievement of the objectives referred to in this Law.

Furthermore, in the explanation of the law, it was stated that customary land rights could not be used by local populations to reject government development projects— for instance, the government project to clear the forest for large national projects and

---

[22] Article 10, point c of the Law on Desapradja (19/1965).

transmigration programmes.[23] Local communities could not use customary law as a reason to clear the forest for their interests. The Forestry Law became the main source of land conflict between state agencies and corporations and adat law communities who have long lived in forest areas.

The New Order regime reduced the political role of local kingdoms, limiting them to traditional and cultural expression. In 1985, the government enacted Law 8/1985 on Mass Organizations (*Organisasi Kemasyarakatan*) and determined local kingdoms, or swapradja governments, as cultural institutions (*organisasi kebudayaan*). Another measure was the inclusion of local kingdoms into the discourse of cultural heritage. Law 5/1992 on the Protection of Cultural Heritage (*Perlindungan Cagar Budaya*) designated some sites and buildings in palace compounds as protected historical heritages. This law prevents anyone, including royal families, from changing anything or using the buildings for purposes other than activities endorsed by the state agencies, namely the Cultural Office (*Dinas Kebudayaan*) or the Office for Preservation and Protection of Historical and Ancient Heritages (*Balai Pelestarian and Perlindungan Sejarah dan Purbakala*) (Thufail 2013:173).

Similar to Soekarno's administration, Soeharto's New Order government used an analogous approach to reorganize village administration to support national development goals. In 1979, the government enacted the Village Government Law (5/1979). This law introduced a single model of village administration and required that adat law communities be transformed into the new uniformity of village administration model (Zakaria 2000). Regional government and adat law communities responded to this law in different ways. Most regional governments eliminated the existence of traditional villages to establish a new village model. In the province of West Sumatra, the original village government in the form of *Nagari* was dispersed into various villages based on a sub-group called *jorong* (von Benda-Beckmann and von Benda-Beckmann 2013). Meanwhile, in Bali, the regional government created a dual local government by adopting a new village administration, but at the same time also keeping the traditional villages. This dualistic model of village governance remains today in Bali (Warren 1993). Overall, Soeharto's government was successful in creating a new model of the corporate village across the country. The government also reorganized villages through its resettlement programme to displace local communities from forest areas into new administrative villages. The resettlement programme allowed the government to control the population, while at the same time also dispossessing local community members from their land and natural resources. Subsequently, the government allocated foresty concessions to large companies.

Local communities who experienced land dispossession looked for support in their struggle against the state agencies and corporations. The emerging environmental movement successfully shaped local communities' problems by constructing local problems as ecological, cultural, and indigenous problems (Tsing 2007. The environmental NGO commonly known as WALHI (*Wahana Lingkungan Hidup Indonesia* Indonesian Environmental Forum) and the Indigenous Peoples' Federation commonly known as AMAN (*Aliansi Masyarakat Adat Nusantara*) engaged with

---

[23] See the explanation of Art 17 of the Forestry Law (5/1967).

international indigenous peoples' movements and encouraged the government to expand its legal framework to incorporate legal recognition customary rights (Henley and Davidson 2007).

This demand is related to the legal aid movement and promotion of rule of law and environmental protection in Indonesia. In 1992, the active involvement of the government in the Earth Summit opened room for civil society to influence the government. Legal aid and environmental activists found momentum to revitalize customary law as an alternative for securing local land rights (Moniaga 2007). It was in line with the growing indigenous peoples' movement on a global scale. Across Indonesia, new adat community organizations were established as the base for the local struggle against land dispossession by state agencies and corporations.

Despite the absence of recognition of customary land rights through constitutional amendment or new legislation, this period is important as one in which the strength of adat community movements grew. The growing adat community movement provided a new necessary condition for the accommodation of indigeneity in the constitutional amendment process and the implementation of the Constitution in the next period (Inguanzo and Wright 2016).

Indigeneity after Amendments to the 1945 Constitution (1999–recent)

In 1998, President Soeharto stepped down and his resignation was the beginning of political reform. A new election was held in 1999, and a legislature with a truly democratic legitimacy was established. The MPR amended the 1945 Constitution as a response to people's aspirations regarding democracy, decentralization, and the rule of law. This is the beginning of the sixth phase of the constitutional development in Indonesia. The amendments have considerably changed the original text of the 1945 Constitution. The amended Constitution limits the tenure of a president for a maximum of two periods. The Constitution also upholds the rule of law and human rights. A new chapter on human rights was added to ensure individual and group rights regarding civil, political, economic, social, cultural, and environmental rights (ten articles).

Regarding the requirements to be president, the MPR revoked the provision that the president should be an indigenous Indonesian.[24] During the constitutional amendment process, a member of the MPR noted that the requirement for the president to be 'an indigenous Indonesian' was a form of racial discrimination.[25] One MPR member, JE Sahetapy, even suggested that the phrase 'an indigenous Indonesian' contained the seeds of Nazism that could cause social conflict.[26]

---

[24] Article 6(1) of the 1945 Constitution after constitutional amendments. The new provisions regarding the requirements of presidential and vice-presidential candidates stated that: 'Any candidate for President or Vice-President shall be a citizen of Indonesia since birth, shall never have acquired another citizenship by his/her own will, shall never have committed an act of treason against the State, and shall be mentally and physically capable of implementing the duties and obligations of President or Vice-President.'

[25] See the Comprehensive Document of the Amendment to the 1945 Constitution. Book IV, Vol I, pp 117.

[26] Ibid, p 127.

The amended Constitution acknowledged the status of special regions and adat law communities. Article 18B(1) and (2) of the 1945 Constitution states that:

(1) The State recognises and respects units of regional authorities that are special and distinct, which shall be regulated by law.
(2) The State recognises and respects adat law communities along with their traditional customary rights as long as they remain in existence and are in accordance with the societal development and the principles of the Unitary State of the Republic of Indonesia, and shall be regulated by law.

Compared to previous constitutions that had been in force in Indonesia, the amended Constitution accommodated traditional political institutions and the cultural rights of adat law communities. The existence of special regions as a platform to accommodate local demands of traditional kingdoms was stipulated in Article 18B(1). Yogyakarta Province, as a former Swapradja government, retained some privileges in local government administration, especially concerning the position of governor and traditional land rights. It is still the case that the Sultan of Yogyakarta automatically becomes the governor. Swapraja territory has been annulled by the Basic Agrarian Law, but still applies to the Yogyakarta Province territory.[27]

In addition to Yogyakarta, other provinces that have privileges based on indigeneity are the Province of Papua and West Papua. Law 21/2001 concerning the special autonomy for Papua Provinces contains recognition of the status of Papuans as indigenous peoples.[28] Only Indigenous Papuans can be the governors in Papua. Papuans have the right to engage and to obtain benefits from every development project in both provinces. Moreover, the Law on Special Autonomy in Papua also creates the Papuan People's Assembly as a representative institution to accommodate indigenous Papuans into the government institution at the provincial level. The experience of communities in Yogyakarta and Papua inspired other former swapraja governments to reclaim the privileged position that they had gained in colonial times.

Democracy and decentralization in this period provided opportunities for the descendants of local kingdoms to restore their political status in their respective regions. In some places, new kings were coronated such as in Buton, Gowa, and Sumbawa. However, occasionally there was a dispute about who the legitimate king was. These emerging kings across Indonesia gathered themselves in various federations and organized festivals of local kingdoms to show their cultural positions to the public (Thufail 2013:174). Local kingdoms took advantage of decentralization by encouraging regional governments to recognize their existence as *adat* custodians at the local level. They also lobbied national and regional governments during presidential and regional head elections with concessions to provide voters and cultural positions to candidates who supported the restoration of the kingdom's status in politics.

In terms of adat law communities and village governments, the government made a series of policies to decentralize authority to local governments. In 1999, President BJ Habibie enacted the Law on Regional Government (22/1999) replacing the Regional Government Law and Village Government Law of the Soeharto period. The new Law

---

[27] Law 13/2012 concerning the Speciality of Yogyakarta Province.
[28] This Law has been amended by Law 2/2021.

on Regional Government provided greater authority to local governments to endure decentralization. It provided an opportunity for regional governments to create regional regulations to restore former traditional village governments. In West Sumatra, the provincial government reinstated the *Nagari* system by merging several villages that had been dispersed during the Soeharto's period. Despite the regional government of West Sumatra employing the return to Nagari policy, the village administration model has not completely returned to the traditional government system. Instead, it has resulted in a hybrid model of government by amalgamating modern village administration and the traditional political structure of Nagari in Minangkabau society (von Benda-Beckmann and von Benda-Beckmann 2013).

Furthermore, in response to the emergence of aspirations for the recognition of adat law communities in various places, the government instituted a special form of customary villages in the Village Law (6/2014) (Vel, Zakaria, and Bedner 2017). The Village Law divided villages into two types: villages and customary villages. The customary village is an adat law community that has autonomy but also at the same time has responsibility for formal administrative affairs directed by higher government institutions. Some regional governments have been trying to recognize adat law communities as the basis for village administration such as in Jayapura (Papua) and Indra Giri Hulu (Riau). Nevertheless, until 2020, none of the customary villages had been officially registered with the Ministry of Home Affairs. In West Sumatra, which was expected to be a pilot for the implementation of the customary village model, it also did not occur as envisioned by lawmakers (Vel and Bedner 2015).

The Constitution and legislation have expanded the legal framework for recognition of indigenous law communities to exercise their traditional rights. Another example is Article 28I(3) of the Constitution, which guarantees 'respect for the cultural identity and rights of traditional communities in harmony with the changes in time and civilisation'. In the last two decades, almost all legislation concerning customary law, adat communities, and their traditional rights were stipulated with a conditional recognition clause. The conditional recognition clause reflects the continued preference for modernization, rather than for protecting 'old-fashioned' ways of living (Bedner 2017). Consequently, a local community has to be designated as an adat law community by a regional government before it is eligible to secure traditional rights.[29] In other words, adat law communities can only enjoy their traditional rights after the local government has determined them as a rights bearing subject (Rachman and Siscawati 2016).

The Constitutional Court strengthened the model of layered legal recognition of indigenous rights. Since its establishment in 2003, the Constitutional Court has reviewed a number of laws concerning indigenous rights. One of the landmark decisions was Decision 35/2012, in which the Court reinforced the status of customary forests. Adat law communities hope that the Constitutional Court's ruling will lead to an end to disputes over land between state agencies and corporations in the forestry sector. However, forest tenure conflict resolution through the legal recognition of customary forests must follow a complex procedure. Adat law communities must first

---

[29] While I do not discuss it in this chapter, other scholars have noted that regional regulations (*peraturan daerah*) concerning religion have also been justified on the basis of adat: see, eg, Crouch 2009.

gain recognition of their status as a legal subject from the local government through local regulations. Based on local regulations, adat law communities can submit an application for the recognition of customary forests to the Ministry of Environment and Forestry.

In short, in this period, constitutional amendment has resulted in more explicit provisions concerning the special regions and the recognition of indigeneity compared to the previous constitutions. However, legal recognition of indigenous rights is often granted by the government subject to conditionalities. The conditional recognition clause in the Constitution is similar to the conditional recognition clause from previous legislation. A clear and strong constitutional basis for the recognition of indigeneity does not necessarily ensure a proper realization of indigenous rights, while the government has the authority to define indigeneity.

The Conditional Recognition Clause: State Paternalism and Management of Indigeneity

These six phases of constitutional development in Indonesia show different approaches towards indigeneity. In the early period of independence, constitution-makers took into account traditional political institutions to build a post-colonial government. During the formulation of the 1945 Constitution, Muhammad Yamin and Soepomo stated the importance of the recognition of the right of origin, as well as the traditional model of governance in the form of swapradja governments and adat law communities. Yamin and Soepomo's accounts in the constitution-making process emphasized the ability of society to run a modern government system.

Although constitution-makers considered the important of swapraja governments and adat law communities during the constitution-making debate, the Constitution did not contain a clear provision on traditional political institutions. In practice, the government gradually reduced the role of swapraja governments to establish a new model of modern regional government corresponding with the idea of a unitary state. Furthermore, the 1949 Federal Constitution and the 1950 Provisional Constitution recognized swapraja governments with the conditionalities that the swapraja governments should not contradict national interests and higher legislation. The conditional recognition approach to indigeneity continues to influence contemporary Indonesian constitutionalism.

The conditional recognition clause was also the dominant approach in the preparation of legislation to implement constitutional provisions. In the formation of the Basic Agrarian Law (5/1960) during President Soekarno's administration, legislators had debated the position of customary law and customary land rights. On the one hand, the nationalist and communist groups demanded a fundamental transformation regarding tenurial relations based on customary law and traditional land rights. On the other hand, customary law is still needed as inspiration to build an anti-colonial land law, as well as to regulate information land relationships in the society. As a result, the Basic Agrarian Law recognized the application of customary law and customary land rights as long as it did not contradict national interests, national integrity,

Indonesian socialism, as well as religious norms. In contrast, the Basic Agrarian Law abolished swapraja's land rights.

In line with the abolition of swapraja lands, President Soekarno also obliterated the swapraja governments through the Regional Government Law (18/1965), as well as reorganizing the Village Government (19/1965). This radical transformation was taken under Soekarno's Guided Democracy. In this period, the government restructured political and economic institutions to support the government plan to develop Indonesian socialism. However, the dream of socialism soon disbanded after a political transition from Soekarno to Soeharto due to the assassination of a number of military officials in September 1965. Soeharto's New Order regime continued the same pattern inherited by Soekarno towards traditional political institutions and customary land rights. But this time the restrictions on customary law and customary land rights were no longer to realize the aim of Indonesian socialism, but to support national economic development. After President Soeharto's period (1998–recent), the government not only perceived customary land rights as an obstacle to the implementation of the national development agenda but was concerned by the potential of indigenous peoples' issues being associated with separatism. State legal recognition of customary land rights provides autonomy to indigenous communities to exercise the right to self-determination. The government was concerned about granting autonomy and self-determination to local communities because of its experience with East Timor's independence and the proposal of the Papuan independent movement to organize a referendum for self-determination in Papua.

Compared to the previous constitutions, the present Constitution clearly defines indigeneity, although this recognition is still relatively weak when compared to constitutions of other countries such as the Philippines, Bolivia, and Ecuador. In Indonesia, conditional recognition of adat law communities and customary land rights is reflected in Articles 18B(2) and 28I(3) of the 1945 Constitution. The conditional recognition clause is a legal standard for creating operational regulations as well as for evaluating legislation. Indigenous rights supporters have tried to challenge the conditional recognition clause in the Constitutional Court, but the Constitutional Court affirmed its validity. This clause became the main obstacle to realizing indigenous peoples rights. Currently, adat community rights supporters encourage the government and legislature to enact a special law concerning adat communities rights in Indonesia. However, this effort has not made progress despite being discussed for nine years by the legislature (Arizona and Cahyadi 2013).

The conditional recognition clause is a government tactic to control indigeneity. Such a clause is also found in various countries. In fact, the conditional recognition clause is a demonstration of state paternalism to indigeneity in the neoliberal age (Howard-Wagner, Bargh, and Altamirano-Jiménez 2018).

Conclusion

The contemporary debate over the incorporation of indigenous rights and traditional political institutions into the constitution-making process in Indonesia is a continuation of past debates that have taken place since colonial times. In the colonial period, the Dutch colonial rulers maintained the legal dualism to serve colonial interests while providing autonomy to traditional political entities such as swapraja governments and adat law communities. In contrast, after the independence in 1945, a common desire of the founding fathers was to create a modern nation-state that guarantees equality for citizens under a unified legal system. For this purpose, constitution-makers limited the role of traditional political institutions and customary land rights.

In pursuing a modern constitution and government, the constitution-makers recognized traditional political institutions and customary land rights with a conditional recognition clause. The conditional recognition clause is inherent in the Constitution as well as in legislation. In general, the conditional recognition clause requires that traditional political institutions and customary land rights should not be contrary to national interests and state laws and regulations. In different political regimes, there were several additional requirements attached to the conditional recognition clause. During Soekarno's Guided Democracy, one of the conditions for the recognition of customary law and customary land rights was that it could not be contrary to Indonesian socialism. During Soeharto's New Government, customary land rights must be consistent with national development projects promoted by the government. In the post-presidency of Soeharto's administration until today, the dominant requirement remains that indigeneity should not be contrary to national development. The government also sees the recognition of indigenous rights as a potential threat to the disintegration of the country due to the request by different indigenous peoples of political self-determination.

In the past three decades, the international and national indigenous peoples' movement in many countries has succeeded in reshaping the relationship between the state and indigenous peoples. Today, the international institution has designated indigenous rights as part of human rights on a global level. However, the constitutions in many countries have a different approach to incorporating indigenous rights, while at the same time also maintaining state authority. In Indonesia, the conditional recognition clause is used by the government as a means to control indigenous claims. The conditional recognition clause implies that the state is suspicious of customary land rights of indigenous communities. Consequently, customary land rights are not genuinely perceived as a human right where the government must conduct active measures to fulfil indigenous peoples rights. Due to the imbalance between the state and indigenous peoples' rights in the Constitution, the realization of indigenous rights faces considerable challenges in the future.

References

Allot, Antony (1968) 'The Unification of Laws in Africa' 15 *American Journal of Comparative Law* 51-87.

Arizona, Yance and Erasmus Cahyadi (2013) 'The Revival of Indigenous Peoples: Contestations Over a Special Legislation on *Masyarakat Adat*' in Brigitta Hauser-Schäublin (ed) *Adat and Indigeneity in Indonesia. Culture and Entitlements Between Heteronomy and Self-Ascription.*

Göttingen Studies in Cultural Property, Volume 7. Göttingen: Göttingen University Press. pp 43–62.

Bedner, Adriaan (2017) 'The Need for Realism: Ideals and practice in Indonesia's Constitutional History' in M Adams, A meuwese, and E Ballin (eds) *Constitutionalism and the Rule of Law: Bridging Idealism and Realism*. Cambridge: Cambridge University Press, pp. 159-194.

Benda-Beckmann, Franz von and Keebet von Benda-Beckmann (2013) *Political and Legal Transformations of an Indonesian Polity: The Nagari from Colonisation to Decentralisation*. Cambridge: Cambridge University Press.

Bourchier, David (2007). *Pancasila Versi Orde Baru dan Asal Muasam Negara Organis (Integralistik) di Indonesia*. Yogyakarta: Aditya Media Yogyakarta and Pusat Studi Pancasila Univeritas Gadjah Mada.

Burns, Peter (2004) *The Leiden Legacy: Concepts of Law in Indonesia*, Leiden: KITLV.

Butt, Simon and Tim Lindsey (2012) *The Constitution of Indonesia: A Contextual Analysis*. Oxford: Hart Publishing.

Crouch, Melissa (2019) 'The Judicial Reform Landscape in Indonesia: Innovation, Specialisation and the Legacy of Dan S Lev' in M Crouch (ed) *The Politics of Court Reform: Judicial Change and Legal Culture in Indonesia*. Cambridge: Cambridge University Press. pp 1–32.

Crouch, Melissa (2009) 'Religious Regulations in Indonesia: Failing Vulnerable Groups' 43(2) *Review of Indonesian and Malaysian Affairs* 53–103.

Fasseur, C (2007) 'Colonial dilemma Van Vollenhoven and the struggle between adat law and Western law in Indonesia,' in Jamie Davidson and David Henley (eds) *The Revival of Tradition in Indonesian Politics The deployment of adat from colonialism to indigenism*. London and New York: Routledge, pp. 50-67.

Furnivall, John SydenhamJS (2014) *Colonial Policy and Practice: A Comparative Study of Burma and Netherlands India*. Second Edition. Cambridge: Cambridge University Press.

Geertz, Clifford (eds) (1963) *Old Societies and New States: A Quest for Modernity in Asia and Africa*. New York: The Free Press of Glencoe.

Henley, David and Jamie Davidson (2007) 'Introduction Radical Conservatism—the Protean Politics of Adat' in Jamie Davidson and David Henley (eds) *The Revival of Tradition in Indonesian Politics The deployment of adat from colonialism to indigenism*. London and New York: Routledge, pp. 1-49.

Howard-Wagner, Deirdre, Maria Bargh, and Isabel Altamirano-Jiménez (2018) 'From New Paternalism to New Imaginings of Possibilities in Australia, Canada and Aotearoa/ New Zealand: Indigenous Rights and Recognition and the State in the Neoliberal Age' in Deirdre Howard-Wagner, Maria Bargh, and Isabel Altamirano-Jiménez (eds) *The Neoliberal State, Recognition and Indigenous Rights: New Paternalism to New Imaginings*. ANU University Press.

Inguanzo, Isabel and Claire Wright (2016) 'Indigenous Movements in Southeast Asia: An Analysis Based on the Concept of 'Resonance' 16(1) *Asia-Pacific Social Science Review* 1–17.

Lev, Daniel S (2009) *The Transition to Guided Democracy: Indonesian Politics, 1957–1959*. Singapore: Equinox Publishing.

Li, Tania Murray (2010) 'Indigeneity, Capitalism, and the Management of Dispossession' 51(3) *Current Anthropology* 385-414.

Luttikhuis, Bart (2013) 'Beyond Race: Constructions of "Europeanness" in Late-Colonial Legal Practice in the Dutch East Indies' 20(4) *European Review of History: Revue europeenne d'histoire* 539–558.

Mamdani, Mahmood (2013) *Define and Rule: Native as political identity*. Cambridge: Harvard University Press.

Martinez Cobo, J (1986/87) Study of the Problems of Discrimination against Indigenous Populations, UN Doc E/CN4/Sub2/1986/7 and Adds 1–4, paras 379–383.

Moniaga, Sandra (2007) 'From Bumiputera to Masyarakat Adat: A Long and Confusing Journey' in Jamie Davidson and David Henley (eds) *The Revival of Tradition in Indonesian Politics: The Deployment of Adat from Colonialism to Indigenism*. London and New York: Routledge. pp. 295-318.

Neo, Jaclyn L and Bui Ngoc Son (eds) (2019) *Pluralist Constitutions in Southeast Asia*. Oxford, UK: Bloomsbury Publishing.

Niessen, Nicole (1999) *Municipal Government in Indonesia: Policy, Law, and Practice of Decentralisation and Urban Spatial Planning*. Leiden: Research School CNWS, Universiteit Leiden.

Niezen, Ronald (2003) *The Origins of Indigenism: Human Rights and the Politics of Identity*. Berkeley: University of California Press.

Rachman, Noer Fauzi and Mia Siscawati (2016). 'Forestry Law, Masyarakat Adat and Struggles for Inclusive Citizenship in Indonesia' in *Christoph Antons* (ed) *Routledge Handbook of Asian Law*. London: Routledge, pp. 224-249.

Ranawidjaja, Usep (1955) *Swapradja: Sekarang dan dihari kemudian*. Jakarta: Djambatan.

Sujamto, (1988) *Daerah Istimewa dalam Negara Kesatuan Republik Indonesia*. Jakarta: Bina Aksara.

Syafrudin Bahar et al (eds) (1995) *Risalah Sidang Badan Persiapan Urusan Kemerdekaan Indonesia dan Panitia Persiapan Kemerdekaan Indonesia*. Jakarta: Sekretariat Negara Republik Indonesia.

Termorshuzen-Arts, M (2010) 'Rakyat Indonesia dan tanahnya: Perkembangan Doktrin Domein di masa kolonial dan pengaruhnya dalam hukum agraria Indonesia' in Myrna Safitri and Tristam Moeliono (eds) *Hukum agraria dan masyarkat di Indonesia*. Jakarta: HuMa, Van Vollenhoven Institute-Leiden University, KITLV-Jakarta. pp 33–74.

Thufail, Fadjar Ibnu (2013) 'Becoming Aristocrats: Keraton in the Politics of Adat' in Brigitta Hauser-Schäublin (ed) *Adat and Indigeneity in Indonesia: Culture and Entitlements between Heteronomy and Self-Ascription*. Göttingen Studies in Cultural Property, Volume 7, pp. 167-184.

Tsing, Anna (2007) 'Indigenous Voice' in Marisol de la Cadena and Orin Starn (ed) *Indigenous Experience Today*. London: Routledge.

Uprimny, Rodrigo (2011) 'The Recent Transformation of Constitutional Law in Latin America: Trends and Challenges' 89 *Texas Law Review* 1588-1609.

Vel, Jacqueline and Adriaan Bedner (2015) 'Decentralisation and Village Governance in Indonesia: The Return to the Nagari and the 2014 Village Law' 47(3) *Journal of Legal Pluralism and Unofficial Law* 493–507.

Vel, Jacqueline, Yando Zakaria, and Adriaan Bedner (2017) 'Law-Making as a Strategy for Change: Indonesia's New Village Law' 4 *Asian Journal of Law and Society* 447–471.

Walker, Neil (2002) 'The Idea of Constitutional Pluralism' 65(3) *Modern Law Review* 317-359.

Warren, Carol (1993) *Adat and Dinas: Balinese Communities in the Indonesian State*. Kuala Lumpur: Oxford University Press.

Wignjosoebroto, Soetandyo (2014) *Dari hukum kolonial ke hukum nasional: Dinamika sosial-politik dalam perkembangan hukum di Indonesia*. Jakarta: HuMa, Van Vollenhoven Institute, KITLV-Jakarta, and Epistema Institute.

Zakaria, Yando (2000) *Abih tandeh: Masyarakat desa di bawah rejim Orde Baru*. Jakarta: ELSAM.

11

The Indonesian Constitutional Court and Informal Constitutional Change

Stefanus Hendrianto

Introduction

Over the past decade, scholarship on comparative constitutional law has found that formal constitutional amendment is not the only or the most common way to change a constitution (Ginsburg and Melton 2015). Scholars distinguish between formal constitutional amendment and informal constitutional amendment. Formal constitutional amendment refers to the change in the wording of the constitutional text that has been engineered through the special amendment procedure typically included in the constitutional text itself. The concept of informal constitutional amendment refers to the change in the existing constitutional norms without a formal constitutional amendment (Albert 2017). In other words, an informal constitutional amendment is an alternative process of changing the Constitution.

With the rise of judicial review in the last century, judges often step in to interpret the constitutional text and adjust the meaning of the text over time. The Court's interpretations are often treated as a substitute for formal constitutional amendment. American constitutional theorists have argued that constitutional changes can and frequently do occur through constitutional decision-making by the US Supreme Court (Strauss 1996; Tushnet 2009).

Given the complexity of the informal constitutional amendment theory, in this chapter I will explore how the Indonesian Constitutional Court contributes to informal change. This chapter argues that in almost two decades since its inception, the Constitutional Court has generated informal constitutional change in two main ways. First, the informal constitutional changes initiated by a self-conscious effort of the Court. This informal constitutional change may occur when the Court intentionally gave a new meaning through its interpretation or when the Court repudiated a provision in the constitutional text.

The second means of informal constitutional change took place when the Constitutional Court unintentionally changed the meaning of the constitutional text (Passchier 2017). This mode of informal amendment takes place when the Court showed its support for, or condoned a repudiation of, specific constitutional text by the politicians. The public repudiation may take place when the politicians ignore, replace, or reorder constitutional rules. The effect of replacing, ignoring, or reordering one rule is to repudiate the original rule and to sanction the new one. The Court through its decision may affirm such repudiation and thus, through the Court's

Stefanus Hendrianto, *The Indonesian Constitutional Court and Informal Constitutional Change* In: *Constitutional Democracy in Indonesia*. Edited by: Melissa Crouch, Oxford University Press. © Stefanus Hendrianto, 2023.
DOI: 10.1093/oso/9780192870681.003.0011

decision, one constitutional rule is implicitly replaced by another. Alternatively, the unintentional informal amendment takes place through the sustained non-use of particular constitutional provisions. A provision may slowly lose its force when the Court has consistently declined to use a specific constitutional provision or refused to define the meaning of the text.

The Amendment Culture in Indonesia

Tom Ginsburg and James Melton postulate a theory of amendment culture to explain the typology of the formal and informal amendment (Ginsburg and Melton 2015: 687). Ginsburg and Melton define amendment culture as the set of shared attitudes about the desirability of amendment (Ginsburg and Melton 2015: 699). They explain that amendment culture is closely related to barriers to amendment—both institutional and political barriers. They explain that there are two types of amendment culture: flexible and rigid. The flexible culture is divided into an ultra-flexible and legislative centered amendment. On the other end, a rigid culture is divided into judicial centered and ultra-rigid culture. Moreover, there is an important factor in the equation: judicial review culture, which demonstrates that ultra-flexible and judicial centered types are related to activist judicial review culture. The legislative centered and ultra-rigid culture is closely related to the restrained judicial review culture. In sum, Ginsburg and Melton argue that the flexible amendment culture will allow more formal constitutional change. On the other hand, a rigid amendment culture will give more room for informal constitutional change.

Indonesia's amendment culture is unique because it falls between a rigid and flexible amendment culture. Under the rule of an authoritarian regime, it is common for powerful incumbent presidents to engineer constitutional change in order to cement his or her authority (Stilt 2014: 121). The original 1945 Constitution suited the interest of Soeharto's New Order regime (1966–1998) and, therefore, Soeharto abused the Constitution by making it practically unamendable.[1] After the fall of the New Order regime in 1998, the 1945 Constitution was no longer sacred, and while formal amendment still required a supermajority (two thirds) vote in the People's Consultative Assembly (*Majelis Permusvawarahan Rakyat*, MPR), the Constitution can be changed.

Several months after the first free election in June 1999, MPR convened to discuss the amendment of the Constitution. The constitutional reform process, however, took longer than people expected. In the end, the Assembly had to reconvene every year, finishing the fourth constitutional amendment in August 2002.

By amending the 1945 Constitution every year, the Assembly had turned the 1945 Constitution into a hyper-amendable constitution. By hyper-amendable, I am referring to the frequent revisions which have significant political consequences to the

---

[1] The 1985 Referendum Law prescribed that where a situation of constitutional change arises, a referendum must be held to gain the people's consent, and the constitutional change can be carried out if 90 per cent of the referendum participants voted in favour of it.

constitutional structure (Cain and Noll 2009).[2] Through these frequent revisions, the MPR revised various provisions and added many new ones to the Constitution, instead of focusing on altering specific items in existing constitutions as amendment processes are usually intended to do. Through the four years of amendments, the MPR created a new amendment culture in which the Constitution can be amended easily.

Interestingly, the formal constitutional amendment stopped in 2002. Nevertheless, Donald Horowitz argues that the accomplishment of the constitutional reform over several years is one of the distinctive features of the process in Indonesia (Horowitz 2013). Horowitz even argued that the enactment of the constitutional mandate stretched all the way to 2008 or even later. In other words, the constitutional reform process did not stop with the Fourth Amendment in August 2002, but it took almost the first entire decade of the twenty-first century. Horowitz never specifies his theory of constitutional amendment after 2002; presumably he was referring to the amendment in the context of 'small c' constitution, that is, all other sources of law that deal with constitutional matters (eg electoral acts, act on political parties, act on the Constitutional Court, etc). I concur with Horowitz's theory in so far as some changes to the small c constitution may have altered the meaning of the big C constitution (the formal text of the constitution). But I disagree with Horowtiz's theory in so far as the politicians who changed the small c constitution were merely seeking to preserve their political interests instead of changing the big C constitution. In sum, it is not easy to measure the amendment of the small c constitution. In this chapter, I would like to focus on the big C constitution (the formal constitutional text) and argue that although the formal amendment to the big C constitution stopped in 2002, the informal constitutional change continued all the way for more than a decade. Thus, in this chapter, I will investigate the involvement of the Indonesian Constitutional Court in the informal constitutional changes in the years after the formal constitutional amendment.

Informal Constitutional Change by the Indonesian Constitutional Court

In this chapter, I will focus on informal constitutional change in four major areas: elections; the economy; the bill of rights, and religion.

Informal Changes to Electoral Provisions

The original 1945 Constitution contains no provision on the general election. According to the Constitution, the president shall be elected by the MPR with a majority vote.[3] During the New Order, the general election is limited only to electing

---

[2] Cain and Noel used the term 'hyper-amendability' to describe the political culture in the State of California, in which the amendment rules allow voters to amend the Constitution by initiative without any legislative involvement.

[3] The Constitution of Republic of Indonesia 1945, Art 6(2) (original text).

members of the People's Representative Council (*Dewan Perwakilan Rakyat*, DPR). In contrast, the amended version of the 1945 Constitution contains at least five provisions on the elections: presidential election (Art 6A); the election of members of the DPR—(Art 19); the election of the member of Regional Representative Council (*Dewan Perwakilan Daerah*, DPD)—(Art 22C); the General Election (Art 22E); and the Regional Election (Art 18).

A major area that prompted the Court's engagement in informal constitutional change is the Regional Head Elections (*Pemilihan Kepala Daerah—Pilkada*). The Constitution states that 'Governors, Regents (*bupati*) and Mayors (*walikota*), respectively as head of regional government of the provinces, regencies, and municipalities, shall be elected democratically'.[4] During the amendment of the Constitution, regional heads were still elected by the Regional Assembly; therefore, the amendment drafters did not mention direct elections for the regional heads. The idea of direct elections for regional heads raised several constitutional issues, and therefore the Court must issue some decisions that led to informal constitutional changes (Erb and Sulistiyanto 2009).

The *Independent Candidate* Case

One of the issues is who is eligible to run in the local elections, known as *Pilkada*. In the *Independent Candidate* case,[5] the Court dealt with the issue of whether an independent candidate may run in the *Pilkada*. The Regional Governance (*Pemerintahan Daerah—Pemda*) Law required that gubernatorial candidates needed to secure a nomination of political parties or an alliance of political parties that had either 15 per cent of the seats in the regional Parliament or 15 per cent of the votes in the last local election.[6]

The claimant was an independent candidate with no party backers, and therefore legally barred from running for governor. The claimant argued that the Regional Governance Law was inconsistent with the equal protection clause of the Constitution (Art 28D(1)) because the law did not allow independent candidates to run in regional elections. In making the argument, the claimant referred to the provincial election in the special territory of Nanggroe Aceh Darussalam that allows independent candidates to run for local elections. This is provided for in the 2006 Aceh Governance Law,[7] which arose as the consequence of a 2005 peace deal between the Indonesian government and the Aceh rebel movement.

The Court ruled for the claimant and held that participation of independent candidates in regional elections should be allowed in other provinces outside the Naggroe Aceh Darussalam province.[8] The Court decision was meant to allow independent candidates to run in regional elections in the whole country; however, the Court realized that it had no authority to add new provisions in the statute that enabled independent

---

[4] Article 18(4) of the 1945 Constitution.
[5] Constitutional Court Decision 05/PUU-V/2007 (hereinafter the *Independent Candidate* case).
[6] See Art 59(2) of Law 32/2004 on Regional Governance.
[7] Article 67(1d) of Law 11/2006 on Aceh Governance.
[8] The *Independent Candidate* case, para 3.15.15.

candidates to run in regional elections. Therefore, the Court deferred to the legislature to make a new provision that allows independent candidates to run in regional elections nationwide.

In sum, while the Court deferred to the legislature to prepare a new law to allow an independent candidate to run in a regional election, it engaged in informal constitutional change by allowing an independent candidate to run in the *Pilkada*.

The Presidential Election Cases

Another major issue that prompted the Court's involvement in an informal constitutional change was the requirements for candidates who run in the presidential election. The Constitution provides that 'each ticket of candidates for President and Vice-President shall be proposed prior to the holding of general elections by political parties or coalitions of political parties which are participants in the general elections'.[9]

Since the Third Amendment of the Constitution in 2001, Indonesia has held four direct presidential elections (2004, 2009, 2014, and 2019). For the first direct presidential election in 2004, the lawmakers enacted the Presidential Election Law of 2003, which provided that presidential candidates could be nominated by a political party or a coalition of political parties who hold at least 15 per cent of seats in the House of Representatives or have obtained at least 20 per cent of the popular vote of the legislative election (DPR).[10]

In preparation for the second presidential election in 2009, the lawmakers increased the presidential threshold and provided that 'a presidential candidate shall be nominated by a political party or a coalition of political parties who hold at least 20 percent of seats in the House of Representative or obtain at least 25 percent of the popular vote in the legislative election'.[11] The DPR then kept the same requirement for the 2014 presidential election. In 2017, however, the DPR passed a new law, which states that a presidential candidate could be nominated by a political party or a coalition of political parties who hold at least 20 per cent of seats in the House of Representatives or have obtained at least 25 per cent of the popular vote in the last general election (in this case, the 2014 General Election).[12]

The Simultaneous Election Cases

The primary issue that arises from the presidential threshold rules is the schedule of the election. The Presidential Election Laws (2003 and 2008) state that the legislative and presidential elections must be held at least three months apart. The schedule arrangement makes sense because political parties cannot nominate a candidate until they know the official result of the legislative election.

In 2013, the Court had to deal with the constitutionality of the rules that prescribe two separate election schedules for legislative and presidential elections. In the

---

[9] The 1945 Indonesian Constitution, Art 6A(2).
[10] Article 5(4) of Law 23/2003 on the Election of President and Vice President.
[11] Article 9 of Law 42/2008.
[12] Article 222 of Law 7/2017 on General Elections.

Simultaneous Election I case,[13] the Court decided to strike down the provision that set the legislative and presidential elections to be scheduled three months apart. One of the primary reasons for the Court's decision was that the drafters of the Constitution never intended to hold two separate elections, but rather envisaged a simultaneous general election, which includes the presidential and legislative elections.[14] Nevertheless, the Court held that the decision could not be applied right away because it would disrupt preparations for the 2014 General Election.[15] In other words, the Court ruled that the decision would only be implemented in the 2019 General Election.

While the Court referred to the original intent of the drafters of the Constitution, it is hard to justify the Court's reasoning as following the original meaning of the constitutional text. The Court only referred to the committee reports written primarily by staff and read by few, if any, of the drafters. The 'intent,' which the Court found in these reports may have existed, but it was not clear whether there was a collective intent, which establishes an original meaning or involves the blending of many intentions from different groups. Moreover, the Court only relies on the testimony of a single member of the Working Committee, Slamet Effendi Yusuf. In 2013, he testified before the Court, twelve years after the amendment of the Constitution. So, it is hard to verify his memory on the drafters' collective intent. Even if Yusuf had a photographic memory, his statements did not automatically form a coherent drafters' intent. Thus, the Court's claim that his statement accurately captured the drafter's intent is dubious.

Regardless of the original meaning of the constitutional text, the Court has provided an informal constitutional change to the Constitution's operation. The constitutional text provides that 'General elections shall be conducted to elect the members of the DPR, DPD, the President and Vice-President, and the Regional People's Representative Council'. While the text of the Constitution does not explicitly mention the schedule of the elections, the legislators decided that it must be held in two separate elections. For two consecutive presidential elections (2004 and 2009), the General Election Commission held the presidential elections in a separate schedule after the legislative election. The Court then issued a decision that entirely changed the operation of presidential elections.

On 17 April 2019, Indonesia held a simultaneous general election for the first time, as mandated by the Court. Nevertheless, the Court was criticized as the general election turned out to be one of the most trying in Indonesia's history, with the death of more than 400 polling station workers. Most analysts and media blamed the Constitutional Court for the difficulties that arose when holding the presidential and legislative elections simultaneously.

Not long after the 2019 General Election, an NGO called the Association for Election and Democracy (*Perhimpunan Pemilu dan Demokrasi*, PERLUDEM) challenged the constitutionality of the simultaneous election. One of their arguments, among many, was that the simultaneous election was practically unmanageable and caused many casualties. In the *Simultaneous Election II* case,[16] the Court rejected the

---

[13] The Constitutional Court Decision 14/PUU-XI/2013 (hereinafter the *Simultaneous Election I* case).
[14] Ibid 82. The Court referred to the minutes of discussion of the Commission of 'A' on 5 November 2001.
[15] Ibid, para 3.20.
[16] Constitutional Court Decision 55/PUU-XVII/2019 (hereinafter the *Simultaneous Election II* case).

claimant's petition entirely and reaffirmed its previous decision on the simultaneous election. Nevertheless, the Court in the *Simultaneous Election II* case distinguished its decision from its earlier decision. First, the Court majority conducted a thorough investigation of the minutes of the meeting of the working committee on constitutional amendment. The Court concluded that there was no single collective intent of the drafters to have a simultaneous election.[17] The Court noted that there were many competing opinions and interests among the drafters on the General Election schedule. Thus, while the Court reaffirmed its previous ruling, it admitted that there was no collective intent of the drafters of having a simultaneous election.

The Court opined that the issue with the electoral system was that the multiparty system produces gridlock, in which different parties control the DPR rather than the president's party and often the president's party only controls a tiny minority of seats in parliament. The Court held that the simultaneous election was the solution to the gridlock between the executive and the legislature.[18] The Court posited that the simultaneous election would not only bring order to the chaos of the multiparty system, but it would also strengthen the presidential system, as the voters tended to vote for a presidential candidate and his party or parties coalition that nominated him.[19] Finally, the Court held that the simultaneous election was the logical consequence of the presidential system. The Court prescribed at least six options for the House to consider in designing the simultaneous election, but in the end, it deferred to the legislature on how to manage and design the simultaneous election as long as the new design did not negate the essence of the simultaneous general election schedule.

The Court's decision in the *Simultaneous Election II* case has elevated its involvement in informal constitutional change on to a new level. The Court admitted that there was no collective intent of the drafter to have a simultaneous election. Nevertheless, the Court moved to affirm the simultaneous election based on the necessity to preserve and strengthen the presidential system. Based on this decision, the Court boldly moved to support an informal constitutional change, which altered the constitutional text's operation regarding the General Election clause.

The Presidential Threshold Cases
Since 2008, the Court has reviewed the presidential threshold requirement multiple times (fourteen cases), and it has consistently argued that the policy is constitutional.[20] In this chapter, I will review three of the Court's decisions in the Presidential Threshold cases. The first decision was the *Presidential Threshold I* case.[21] In this case,

---

[17] Ibid, para 3.15.1.

[18] Ibid, para 3.15.2.

[19] Ibid.

[20] Constitutional Court Decision 51-51-59/PUU-VI/2008 (the *Presidential Threshold I* case); Decision 56/PUU-VI/2008 (the *Presidential Threshold II* case); Decision 26/PUU-VII/2009 (the *Presidential Threshold III* case); Decision 4/PUU-XI/2013 (the *Presidential Threshold IV* case); Decision 14/PUU-XI/2013 (the *Presidential Threshold V* case); Decision 46/PUU-XI/2013 (the *Presidential Threshold VI* case); Decision 108/PUU-XI/2013 (the *Presidential Threshold VII* case); Decision 49/PUU-XII/2014 (the *Presidential Threshold VIII* case); Decision 53/PUU-XV/2017 (the *Presidential Threshold IX* case); Decision 59/PUU-XV/2017 (the *Presidential Threshold X* case); Decision 70/PUU-XV/2017 (the *Presidential Threshold XI* case); Decision 71/PUU-XV/2017 (the *Presidential Threshold XII* case); Decision 72/PUU-XV/2017 (the *Presidential Threshold XIII* case); Decision 49/PUU-XVI/2018 (the *Presidential Threshold XIV* case).

[21] The *Presidential Threshold I* case.

a retired military general, Saurip Kadi, and several small political parties challenged the constitutionality of the 2008 Presidential Election Law, which imposes the 20 and 25 per cent threshold in nominating a presidential candidate.

Kadi was a military representative in the DPR during the last years of the New Order regime (1995–1997). In 2008, after he retired from the military, he continued to stay involved in politics and tried to run for the 2009 Presidential election. He argued that the presidential threshold was discriminatory and made it impossible for him to be nominated as a presidential candidate. The majority of the Court rejected his argument and held that the presidential election's procedure is the legitimate policy that is being delegated to the lawmakers; therefore, the presidential threshold is constitutional.[22] The Court held further that the presidential threshold is part of the democratic process, under which a party achieves a threshold that is determined by a democratic process left to voters.[23] Finally, the Court held that it could not strike down a statutory regulation, which contains a legitimate legal policy of the lawmakers.[24]

Three justices issued a joint dissent in which they expressed their disagreement with the majority opinion that the Constitution is loud and clear on this issue:

> [I]t does not provide any chance for the lawmakers to make legal policy based on 'fabrication', which is contaminated by ad hoc political motives in establishing a presidential threshold.[25]

Moreover, the dissenters argued that the Constitution never delegates any authority for the lawmakers to set the requirement for a presidential candidate, but the only authority for the lawmaker is to enact statutes on presidential election procedures. The dissenter argued that the Constitution had set the requirement for a presidential candidate, and therefore the lawmakers have mixed up these two issues.

The *Presidential Threshold I* case was decided in 2008 under the leadership of Mohammad Mahfud. Fast forward nine years, in 2017, under the leadership of Arief Hidayat, the Court had to deal with similar issues under different circumstances. Since the Court in the *Simultaneous Election I* case rendered null a decision that mandated a concurrent election, logically, political parties must now nominate their candidates before the parliamentary election. Nevertheless, the problem is that the Court never scrapped the 20 and 25 per cent presidential threshold and held that the legislature has the authority to decide the minimum percentage for votes or seats as a prerequisite for political parties to nominate a presidential candidate.

As the deadline for the implementation of the Court's decision for the 2019 Presidential Election was approaching, the DPR approved a bill that maintained the minimum support required by political parties to nominate presidential candidates. Nevertheless, and deeply problematically, lawmakers stipulated that the 20 and 25 per cent requirement must now be based on the official result of the last general election (in this case, the 2014 General Election).

---

[22] Ibid 185
[23] Ibid.
[24] Ibid 187.
[25] Ibid 193 (Abdul Mukthie Fadjar, Maruarar Siahaan, and Akil Mochtar dissenting).

Soon after President Jokowi signed the bill, several political parties and NGOs filed petitions with the Constitutional Court to challenge the 2017 General Election Law. One of the significant cases is the *Presidential Threshold IX* case, also known as the *Idaman Party* case.[26] The claimant, the Benign Islamic Party (*Partai Idaman*), argued that the provisions on the presidential threshold were discriminatory against new political parties. Moreover, the claimants across many of these cases posited that the presidential threshold would offer no real choice of presidential candidates.

The Court rejected the claimants' petitions and held that: first, the 20 and 25 per cent requirement is the legitimate policy of the lawmakers, and the requirement has no relationship whatsoever with the general election schedule. Second, the Court held that the basis for the 20 and 25 per cent requirement is to strengthen the presidential system. Third, the Court dismissed the claimant's argument and stated the claimant was merely speculating that the presidential threshold will offer the voters no true choice.

What was most jarring about the Court's decision in the *Idaman Party* case is that the idea that the 20 and 25 per cent requirement has no relationship with the general election schedule is implausible. These requirements made some sense under the old system: earlier legislative elections allowed political actors to await those results before carrying out presidential nominations. But the system makes much less sense now when it must be based on outdated legislative election results rather than on new ones.

Two justices, Suhartoyo and Saldi Isra issued a joint dissent, in which they argued that the so-called open legal policy of the legislators is only legitimate if it does not violate the principles of justice, rationality, and morality.[27] The dissenters argued that the presidential threshold requirement in the 2017 General Election Law is full of conflicts of interest because it was designed to provide benefits for political parties who hold the DPR seats. Thus, it concluded that the presidential threshold requirement violated the principles of justice, rationality, and morality.

Interestingly, the dissenting opinion in the *Presidential Threshold IX* case is quite different from the dissents in the *Presidential Threshold I* case. The former implicitly acknowledge that the lawmaker has the authority to regulate the presidential threshold as long as it respects the principles of morality, rationality, and justice. The latter decision, however, argued that the lawmakers have no authority to do so because the Constitution never delegates any authority for the lawmaker to set the presidential candidate's requirement.

In the *Presidential Threshold XIV* case,[28] different petitioners challenged the constitutionality of the 2017 General Election Law. They offered different arguments, pointing to the fact that the result of the previous election could not be used as a reference or requirement for the presidential threshold. The Court, however, rejected the claimants' argument entirely and reaffirmed its precedent that the presidential threshold was an open legal policy, and there is no compelling reason for the Court to undo its previous decisions.[29]

---

[26] Constitutional Court Decision 53/PUU-XV/2017 (the *Idaman Party* case).

[27] Ibid 142.

[28] Constitutional Court Decision 49/PUU-XVI/2008 (hereinafter the *Presidential Threshold XIV* case).

[29] Ibid 43, para 3.13.

Regardless of the correctness of the decision in the series of Presidential Threshold cases, the Court has been involved in informal constitutional change with regards to the requirement for a presidential candidate. Constitutional theorists have posited that written constitutions may be informally amended by desuetude. Adrian Vermeule postulates the notion of constitutional atrophy, in which constitutional power may atrophy from non-use (Vermeule 2012). Richard Albert suggests the theory of constitutional desuetude, in which a constitutional provision loses its binding force as a result of political actors' conscious sustained non-use and public repudiation (Albert 2014). These theories, in a sense, might inform the phenomenon of the presidential threshold in Indonesia. Although these theories are not fully applicable, their insights are relevant to understanding the informal constitutional amendment in Indonesia.

The Constitution never explicitly states that there is a presidential threshold of 20 and 25 per cent. But the political actors have repudiated the presidential election clause by adding additional requirements for a presidential candidate. In other words, the constitutional provisions on the presidential candidate have lost their power through political actors' public repudiation, which means that the legislators have informally amended the constitutional provisions on the presidential candidate. The Court has consistently refused to intervene when constitutional stakeholders ask the justices to review the constitutionality of the presidential threshold. The Court has condoned the public repudiation of the constitutional provision on the presidential requirement by its consistent refusal to review the constitutionality of the presidential threshold. In other words, the Court has affirmed informal constitutional amendment as initiated by the legislators.

Informal Changes to the Economic Clause

The Economic Clause in the Indonesian Constitution can be found in Article 33, which provides:

1. The economy shall be structured as a common endeavor based upon the family principle;
2. Branches of production that are important to the State, and that affect the common good, are to be controlled by the State; and
3. The earth and water and the natural resources within them are controlled by the State and used for the greatest prosperity of the people.[30]

Mohammad Hatta was credited with being the architect of Article 33. But Hatta was not alone in endorsing a strong role in state economic intervention and being suspicious of the workings of the market. After the revolution, the Indonesian elite were remarkably homogenous in their anti-capitalist economic outlook (McTurnan Kahin 1970). Many of the early Republican leaders believed that Article 33 was the middle way between communism and capitalism. Despite no clear definition of the economic

---

[30] Constitution of Republic of Indonesia 1945, Art 33(1), (2), and (3). The English translation of Art 33 is my own translation.

principle in Article 33, those leaders held in common the belief that Indonesia would not be developed along capitalist lines (Higgins 1968).

Article 33 has survived many changes in Indonesian politics from the left-leaning Soekarno regime to the right-wing Soeharto New Order military regime, and it also continued to survive in the post-authoritarian period. The constitutional reform process in the early 2000s left the original version of Article 33 untouched, but also added a new provision which states that 'the organization of the national economy shall be conducted on the basis of economic democracy upholding the principles of togetherness, the efficiency with justice, continuity, environmental perspective, self-sufficiency, and keeping a balance in the progress and unity of the national economy'.[31]

There has been no consensus on the precise meaning of Article 33, especially after the Fourth Amendment that added a new provision. The Fourth Amendment on Article 33 was part of the battle between the socialist camp and the neoliberal camp, yet the socialist camp came out as the victor (Susanti 2002). Nevertheless, the decisive moment occurred in 2004 when the Constitutional Court issued its interpretation on the meaning of Article 33.

The Court's decision in the *Electricity Law* case is the first case that involved Article 33.[32] The principal claimant was a human rights NGO called the Indonesian Human Rights Lawyers Association (*Assosiasi Penasehat Hukum dan Hak Asasi Manusia Indonesia*, APHI). The claimants challenged the constitutionality of the Electricity Law, which allowed for the establishment of a competitive electricity market with the involvement of private enterprises.[33]

The Court began its judgment by addressing the meaning of the term 'shall be controlled by the state' (*dikuasai oleh negara*). The Court held that the meaning of the phrase must be interpreted in the light of Article 33(4). The Court opined that the term 'shall be controlled by state' has a broader meaning than private ownership.[34] First, the Court defined the meaning of state-controlled as 'mandate to the state to perform a policymaking function (*kebijakan*), administrative function (*pengurusan*), regulative function (*pengaturan*), management function (*pengelolaan*) and supervisory function (*pengawsan*)'.[35]

Furthermore, the Court ruled that according to Article 33(4), the meaning of state control under the economic clause does not always mean 100 per cent ownership. The Court ruled that the state can have absolute majority control (over 50 per cent ownership of shares) or relative majority control (under 50 per cent ownership of shares), as long as the government, as the shareholders, can control the company's decision-making processes.[36]

Finally, the Court held that Article 33 does not prevent privatization, as long as privatization does not deprive the state control over natural resources. Nevertheless, the Court decided to strike down the Electricity Law because the privatization as mandated by the Law did not bring any benefits to the people as the private sectors would

[31] Constitution of Republic of Indonesia 1945, Art 33 (4)
[32] Constitutional Court Decision 001-021-022/PUU-I/2003 (hereinafter the *Electricity Law* case)
[33] *Undang Undang No 20 Tahun 2002 tentang Ketenagalistrikan* (Law 20/2002 on Electricity).
[34] The *Electricity Law I* case, 332.
[35] Ibid 334.
[36] Ibid 346

not be interested in providing electricity to underdeveloped areas; they would only focus on the profit that they can make from the well-developed and densely populated areas.[37] In other words, the privatization under the Electricity Law 'will not guarantee power supply to all sectors of the society', and, therefore, the Court held that the Law does not comply with Article 33.[38]

The Court's decision is a decisive moment as it informally changed the meaning of Article 33. First, the Court addressed the nature of state-owned enterprises and their different possible forms as private or public law entities. The Court referred to two models of business organization: the first one is public entities; the second one is private law companies owned by the state. The former does not necessarily exclude entrepreneurial freedom, as state influence is limited to policymaking, administrative, regulative, management, and supervisory functions. The second model allows mere partial state ownership (mixed enterprises) and may, in a holding structure, retain control despite small shareholdings (Grundmann and Möslein 2004; Papadopoulos 2015; Antonaki 2016).

The Court introduced the phenomenon of the golden share and the special rights it confers based on the second model. The Electricity Law or other privatization act does not introduce the notion of golden shares. Nevertheless, the Court has introduced an informal constitutional change by positing a notion of golden shares, in which the state's right is vested in a share (the golden share). The special rights vested in the golden shares relate to the company's decision-making processes and rights to influence the company's shareholder structure, which is not part of the company's business.

The proponents of the socialist view of Article 33 claimed that they were the torchbearers of Hatta's interpretation. Regardless of Hatta's real intention in proposing Article 33, he never envisioned the public/private ownership model as proposed by the Constitutional Court, let alone the notion of golden shares. Thus, the Court has given a new meaning to Article 33. In other words, the Court has informally changed the meaning of the constitutional text through its decision.

The *Electricity Law I* case was decided under the leadership of Jimly Asshiddiqie. The successive Court under the leadership of Mohammad Mahfud continued to engage in informal constitutional change in the area of Article 33 (Hendrianto 2018). In the *Coastal and Remote Islands Law* case,[39] the Mahfud Court began to solidify its decision regarding the interpretation of Article 33(4). In this case, some fishermen located in coastal areas and NGOs challenged various provisions of the 2007 Law on the Management of Coastal Areas and Remote Islands. The crux of the matter was whether some provisions in the Law, which authorized the government to grant a Coast Water Concessions Right (*Hak Pengusahaan Perairan Pesisir*—HP3) (Art 16) to a private business entity (Art 18), including foreigners (Art 23 § 7) were contrary to the Constitution.

The Court held that the Coastal Waters Concessions Right (HP3) is contrary to the principle of economic democracy based on the principle of togetherness and efficiency

---

[37] Ibid 347.
[38] Ibid.
[39] Constitutional Court Decision 3/PUU-VIII/2010 (hereinafter the *Coastal and Remote Islands Law* case).

with justice under Article 33(4). The Court ruled that the principle of togetherness in Article 33(4) must be interpreted in light of Article 33(3), especially the phrase 'the greatest benefit of the people' (*sebesar —besarnya kemakmuran rakyat*).[40] Thus, the Court held that the Coastal Waters Concessions Right (HP3) could not achieve the greatest benefit for the people because it would deprive the traditional or indigenous community of their rights to natural resources, upon which they relied for their subsistence needs and livelihoods.[41]

The Court's decision in the *Coastal and Remote Islands Law* case is a manifestation of an informal constitutional change because the Court held that Article 33(4) must be interpreted in light of Article 33(3). In other words, Article 33(4) is closely intertwined with Article 33(3). The unintended consequence of this interpretation is that the provision loses its force because it no longer has a significant meaning.

Another important decision from the Mahfud Court in the area of Article 33 is the *Oil and Gas III* case.[42] The claimants were twelve Islamic-based organizations and thirty individuals, chiefly led by *Muhammadiyah*, one of the largest Islamic organizations in the country. The claimants challenged some of the key statutory provisions in the Oil and Gas Law, which mandated the government to establish a Regulatory Agency (*Badan Pelaksana Minyak and Gas —BP Migas*) to supervise the oil and gas upstream sector and to take over *Pertamina*'s (state-owned oil company) regulatory and administrative functions.[43]

On the merits of the case, the Court began its judgment by referring to the *Coastal and Remote Islands Law* case, in which the Court held that the key point to determine state control is the phrase 'the greatest prosperity of the people' (*sebesar—besarnya kemakmuran rakyat*). The Court then moved to consider that the *BP Migas* only maintains a monitoring and supervisory function, and consequently, the services of *BP Migas* did not violate constitutional 'state control' within the meaning of Article 33.[44] The Court further considered that when *BP Migas* entered into a contract with private enterprises, the private companies would potentially control the benefits of oil and gas, and therefore it would minimize the benefits that the people were supposed to enjoy. Thus, the Court decided that the establishment of *BP Migas* contradicted the constitutional mandate of state control for the greatest benefit of the people.[45]

As mentioned earlier, constitutional theorists posit the notion of constitutional atrophy (Vermeulle 2012) and constitutional desuetude (Albert 2014), in which they argue that constitutional provisions lose their power or binding force as a result of their conscious non-use. In the *Oil and Gas III* case, the Court reaffirmed its holding in the *Coastal and Remote Islands Law* case, which interpreted Article 33(4) in light of Article 33(4). But in the *Oil and Gas III* case, the Court did not bother to consider Article 33(4) any longer, merely deciding the case based on Article 33(3). The Court's decision in the *Oil and Gas III* case was moving in the direction of constitutional atrophy and constitutional desuetude, in which the Court has engaged in an informal

---

[40] Ibid, para 3.15. 4.
[41] Ibid, para 3.15.4.
[42] Constitutional Court Decision 36/PUU-X/2012 (hereinafter the *Oil and Gas III* case).
[43] The Oil and Gas Law, Art 1(23) and Art 4(3).
[44] The *Oil and Gas Law III* case, para 3.13.3.
[45] For a critical analysis of the Court's decision in the *Oil and Gas III* case, see Butt and Siregar (2015).

constitutional amendment through a conscious decision not to use Article 33(4). In other words, the Court has engaged in an informal constitutional amendment through the non-use of Article 33(4).

Informal Changes to the Bill of Rights Provisions

In 2000, the adoption of the Bill of Rights Provisions in the 1945 Constitution in the Second Amendment enabled the Constitutional Court to engage in an informal amendment as those provisions require further interpretation. Before jumping into the discussion on the informal change on Bill of Rights provisions, a little caveat and clarification are necessary about constitutional interpretation. First, if a constitutional text is clear and decisive, a judge would interpret according to the written text. But often constitutional text cannot cover every individual issue and so the judge cannot make a decision based on the constitutional text. The Court may interpret constitutional text by reference to doctrine or to considerations of morality and public policy. But the constitutional text is still the starting point and still authoritative in significant ways. Some constitutional provisions, however, are interpreted in ways that are very difficult to reconcile with the text. Or constitutional interpretation may take place without any clear textual source are enforced. The authoritative entity is not the constitutional text any longer but what the judge appropriately defined. I think, at this point, the Court has engaged in an informal constitutional amendment.

Back to the interpretation of the Bill of Rights provision in the Indonesian Constitution, in this chapter, I will focus on the general rights-limitation clause, enshrined in Article 28J(2), which states:

> in the enjoyment of their rights and freedoms, each person is obliged to submit to the limits determined by law, with the sole purpose of guaranteeing recognition and respect for the rights of others and to fulfill the requirements of justice, and taking into consideration morality, religious values, security, and public order, in a democratic community.

The early case that dealt with the issue of Article 28J(2) is the *Bali bombing* case.[46] The claimant, an accomplice in the infamous Bali bombing incident, challenged the constitutionality of Law 16/2003 that allowed the retroactive application of the Anti-Terrorism Law that was passed *after* the Bali bombing. The claimant made an appeal based on Article 28I(1) of the Constitution, which states that 'the right not to be tried under the law with retrospective effect are all human rights that cannot be limited under any circumstances'. During the oral argument, the then minister of justice, Yusril Ihza Mahendra, argued that Article 28(1) was constrained by Article 28J(2).[47] Mahendra explained that based on Article 28J(2), the government has the authority to pass legislation to limit rights by requiring that any rights be balanced with other obligations.

---

[46] See Constitutional Court Decision 013/PUU-I/2003 (hereinafter the *Bali bombing* case).
[47] Ibid 15.

The Court—in a 5–4 decision—ruled that Law 16/2003 was unconstitutional. In its judgment, the majority concluded that human rights could be restricted unless the Constitution forbade the restriction. The Court held that Article 28I(1) prohibits a person from being put on trial under the Law with retrospective effect, and therefore, the Court declared the law unconstitutional.[48] The decision signified that Article 28J(2) could not trump Article 28I(1).

The Court, however, changed its approach in the *Soares* case.[49] The claimant was Abilio Soares, the former governor of East Timor, who challenged the constitutionality of Law 26/2000 that allowed the Human Rights Court to operate retrospectively. In response to the international condemnation of the alleged gross human rights violations in East Timor, the Indonesian government enacted Law 26/2000 on the Human Rights Court (Setiawan 2019). The DPR decided to allow Law 26/2000 to operate retrospectively but made it subject to a particular procedure, in which the President could only establish an ad hoc court on the explicit recommendation of the House of Representatives.[50] The Human Rights Court convicted Soares, and he challenged the constitutionality of Law 26/2000.

The Court—in a 6–3 decision—rejected the claimant's petition and repudiated its previous ruling in the *Bali bombing* case. The Court majority ruled that Article 28I(1) must be interpreted in light of Article 28J(2), which means that the prohibition against the application of retroactive Law is not absolute and can be abrogated based on the consideration of security and public order.[51] The Court ruled that the Human Rights Court generally adheres to the principle of non-retroactivity. Nevertheless, there is an exceptional specific procedure that sets aside the principle, whereby the president can establish an ad hoc court to try human right cases retroactively only on the explicit recommendation of the DPR.

The Court solidified its approach on Article 28J(2) in the *Death Penalty I* case.[52] The claimants were two Indonesian women and three Australian men who had been caught smuggling heroin, and all of them were sentenced to death under the Narcotics Law.[53] They asked the Court to review whether the Narcotics Law, which allowed the death penalty to be imposed, contradicted the constitutional guarantee of the right to life.[54] The claimants argued that while Article 28J(2) provides a general limitation for a bill of rights, not all rights can be limited. The claimants referred to Article 28I(1), which explicitly lists specific rights that cannot be limited under any circumstances, including the right to life.

In a split decision (6–3), the Court upheld the law and rejected the claimant's petition (Zerial 2007). The Court majority referred to the original intent of the Constitution by citing the testimony of two members of the Ad Hoc Committee of People Consultative Assembly. These two drafters had explained to the Court that the

---

[48] Ibid 46.
[49] Constitutional Court Decision 065/PUU-II/2004 (hereinafter the *Soares* case).
[50] Art 43(1) and (2) of Law 26/2000 on the Human Rights Court.
[51] The *Soares* case, 51.
[52] Constitutional Court Decision 2-3/PUU-V/2007 (hereinafter the *Death Penalty I* case).
[53] Law 22/1997 on Narcotics.
[54] The *Death Penalty I* case, 6.

regulatory scope of Article 28J(2) included Article 28I(1).[55] In other words, rights protection under Article 28I(1) is not absolute.

The Court's reliance on the drafter's original intent was problematic because it was unclear whether there was a communal intent of the drafters on the subject matter. The Court merely relied on the testimony of two members of the Ad Hoc Committee. Regardless of the drafters' intent, this declaration signified that the Court has engaged in informal constitutional amendment by deciding that Article 28J(2) can trump Article 28I(1), and consequently, Article 28I(1) lost its force.

In the *Death Penalty II* case,[56] the Court reaffirmed its decision that Article 28J(2) can trump Article 28I(1). Two claimants filed a judicial review against the death penalty provision contained in the Criminal Code. The claimants had been sentenced to death based on Article 364(4) of the Criminal Code, which imposes the death penalty on the crime of theft accompanied by force or threat of force resulting in serious physical injury or death. The claimants invoked Article 28I(1), which provides that the right to life is a right that cannot be limited under any circumstances.

The Court simply referred to the previous decision in the *Death Penalty I* case and declared that the limitation on the right to life could be justified based on Article 28J(2). One of the criticisms of the Court's decision was that it should not treat both cases the same, as the first case involved a drugs crime, and the second one only involved the crime of theft (Faiz 2016: 173). Nevertheless, the real issue is not which crime ought to be punished with the death penalty but rather the scope and meaning of the right to life. The Court did not define the scope and meaning of the right to life in the two death penalty cases. With the Court's ruling that Article 28J(2) can easily trump Article 28I(1), there seemed no need to define the meaning of the right to life because this provision has lost its force in the Indonesian constitutional milieu.

Informal Changes to the Religion Clauses

In 2000, the MPR adopted the Second Amendment, which guarantees the right of religious freedom:

> (1) Every person shall be free to choose and practice the religion of his/her choice ... ; (2) Every person shall have the right to the freedom to believe his/her faith (*kepercayaan*), and to express his/her views and thoughts, in accordance with his/her conscience.[57]

In addition to the constitutional amendment, in October 2005 Indonesia also ratified the International Covenant on Civil and Political Rights, which includes protection of religious freedom. The main issue is whether the amendments and ratification bind the Indonesian government to respect religious freedom.

---

[55] Ibid 411–412.
[56] Constitutional Court Decision 15/PUU-X/2012 (hereinafter the *Death Penalty II* case).
[57] The 1945 Constitution of the Republic of Indonesia, Art 28E.

In the *Blasphemy Law I* case,[58] the Court dealt with the constitutionality of the Blasphemy Law, which recognized that the majority of the Indonesian people adhere to six major religions—Islam, Protestantism, Catholicism, Hinduism, Buddhism, and Confucianism—and it mandated that the government protect these religions.[59] The Law also set criminal penalties for intentionally criticizing or attempting to undermine the six major religions, including a maximum penalty of five years' imprisonment.[60] The Law, however, recognized other religions such as Judaism, Shinto, Taoism as legitimate so long as they complied with the prohibition under the Blasphemy Law and other statutory regulations.[61]

Some NGOs and political activists requested that the Court declare the Blasphemy Law unconstitutional because it ran contrary to the religious freedom clause[62] and freedom of expression clause of the Constitution.[63] The Court rejected the petition and held that the Blasphemy Law is the manifestation of Article 28J(2);[64] therefore the state has the authority to limit liberty as long as it is based upon recognition of other people's rights and freedoms (Crouch 2012; Crouch 2014). This restriction pertains to morality, religion, and public order in a democratic society.[65] The Court held that the Blasphemy Law was never intended to curtail religious freedom, but rather it was aimed at protecting religion.[66]

In the *Blasphemy Law II* case,[67] the Court continued to deal with the interpretation of the religious freedom clause. The claimants were members of the Shiite Muslim minority (Formichi and Feener 2015; Crouch 2016). The first claimant, Tajul Muluk had been convicted by the Sampang District Court for Blasphemy because he propagated Shiite teachings.[68] Three other claimants—Hasan Alaydrus, Ahmad Hidayat, and Umar Shabab—had never been convicted of Blasphemy, but they asserted that as Shiite preachers, they were likely to be convicted in the future. The claimants argued that the Blasphemy Law had violated the religious freedom clause in the Constitution because it prevented the claimants from practising their religious belief.

The Court referred to the *Blasphemy Law I* case. Based on its previous ruling, the Court ruled that the claimants' petition had no legal basis and was irrelevant.[69] The Court ruled further that the applicants' concern involved the application of the Blasphemy Law, which falls under the ambit of the general court of jurisdiction. The Court held that the *Blasphemy Law II* case was about the application and implementation of the law instead of constitutional issues.[70] Therefore, the Court rejected the claimant's petition entirely (Crouch 2016).

---

[58] Constitutional Court Decision 140/PUU-VII/2009 (reviewing Law 1/1965 on Blasphemy) (hereinafter *Blasphemy Law* case).

[59] The Blasphemy Law 1/1965, Art 1 of Elucidation.

[60] Ibid, Art 4.

[61] Ibid, Art 1.

[62] The 1945 Constitution of the Republic of Indonesia, Art 28E(1) and Art 29.

[63] The Constitution of Republic of Indonesia, Art 28E(2) and (3).

[64] The *Blasphemy Law I* case, 293.

[65] Ibid 293

[66] Ibid 294

[67] Constitutional Court Decision 84/PUU-X/2012 (hereinafter the *Blasphemy II* case).

[68] See Decision of the Sampang District Court 69/Pid.B/2012/PN.Spg.

[69] Ibid, para 3.13.

[70] Ibid, paras 3.15–3.16.

In the *Blasphemy III* case,[71] some members of Ahmadiyah challenged the con-stitutionality of some provisions of the Blasphemy Law. Ahmadiyah is a religious movement that originated in India in the mid-1880s as part of the revival of Islam and Islamic missionary efforts. The teachings, however, differ from traditional Islamic doctrine in several important ways. The Ahmadiyah movement has been present in Indonesia since the 1920s. In the recent decade, the Ahmadi often gets inappropriate treatment from other Muslims. Moreover, many administrative regulations prohib-ited Ahmadiyah's activities based on the Blasphemy Law.[72] The claimants argued that their religious practice had been hampered by many administrative regulations based on the allegation that the Ahmadiyah is a deviant sect of Islam.

The Court, however, rejected the claimants' petition. The Court held that the main problem was with how these administrative regulations are implemented rather than the constitutionality of the challenged statute. The Court held that cabinet ministers and local governments have the authority to issue administrative regulations related to Ahmadiyah. The Court suggested that the claimants' main concern was vigilantism or persecution against Ahmadi rather than the constitutionality of the Blasphemy Law. The Court then recommended that the issue be addressed by revising the Blasphemy Law to provide better protection for citizens.

In the *Blasphemy IV* case,[73] the claimant challenged the anti-blasphemy provisions in the Criminal Code (Arts 156 and 157) and the Blasphemy Law on the ground of the constitutional guarantee of religious freedom and diversity. The claimant argued that there is a diversity of religious beliefs in Indonesia, and, therefore, the Blasphemy Law can be misused or abused for personal and political gain. The claimants argued that the blasphemy charges are routinely abused, and the Court must end such manifest injustice.

The Court addressed the petitioners' concerns based on the religious freedom clause in the Constitution (Art 29(2)). The Court argued that the provisions were ne-cessary to guarantee religious freedom because it does not allow any insults or defiles on religious teachings or books, which become a source of religious beliefs.[74] Finally, the Court believed that the abuse of the Blasphemy Law was a matter of the Law's im-plementation and had nothing to do with the constitutional issue.[75]

The series of decisions on the Blasphemy Law indicates that the Court never offered an interpretation of the meaning of the religious freedom clause. The Court either re-jected the claims based on Article 28J(2) or on a legal technicality. The Court chose not to use Article 29 in relation to the religious freedom clause. In this way, Article 29 has lost its force through consistent non-use by the Court. Indeed, religious freedom is a delicate issue, but the Court's consistent non-use of the provision, in which the judges are unwilling to interpret and apply the religious freedom clause, has created the un-intended consequences of losing the power of religious freedom. In other words, the

---

[71] Constitutional Court Decision 56/PUU-XV/2017.

[72] Ibid 18–19. The Ahmadis are prohibited from doing any religious activity according to policy regulated by the Minister of Religious Affairs, the Attorney General, and the Minister of Home Affairs. Several de-crees have also been published to prohibit Ahmadiyah's activity.

[73] Constitutional Court Decision 76/PUU-XVI/2018.

[74] Constitutional Court Decision 76/PUU-XVI-2018 (the *Blasphemy IV* case), para 3.15.

[75] Ibid, para 3.17.

Court has engaged in an informal amendment by the sustained non-use of the religious freedom clause.

Conclusion

The experience of the Indonesian Constitutional Court suggests that informal constitutional change may take different forms: first, informal constitutional change takes place when the Court intentionally changes the operation of the constitutional text. The informal change at this level can be manifested in two ways. The Court intentionally provided a new meaning of the constitutional text, such as the Court's decision to allow an independent candidate to run in the regional election or the decision that introduces the notion of golden shares in the context of Article 33. The Court may intentionally change the operation of the Constitution by repudiating the constitutional text. The informal amendment via constitutional repudiation occurred when the Court consistently repudiated the protection of the right to life under Article 28I(1). By consistently holding that Article 28J(2) can trump Article 28I(1), the Court has caused Article 28I(1)'s loss of force.

This silent constitutional change often took place in the Constitutional Court in two different forms: first, the Court's sustained support for the repudiation of political actors on the operation of the certain constitutional text. In the series of presidential threshold cases, the Court consistently supported the decision of political actors to change the requirement of the nomination of a presidential candidate. While the text of the Constitution never set any presidential threshold, the political actors have added requirements, which means that they have changed the text's operation. In other words, the Court has changed the operation of the constitutional text by extending its support to public reputation by political actors.

While there is a demonstrable intention of the change on the part of the Constitution through the Court's decision, the justices may not be aware of the impact of its decision to the operation of the constitutional text. In other words, the unintentional constitutional change takes place when the justices were not aware that they had bypassed formal constitutional hurdles, through their decision, to alter the operation of the existing constitutional text. Even if we have ample reason to suspect the justices deliberately try to change the constitutional text through its decision, they may be aware that they have engaged in a process of constitutional change. The unintentional constitutional change also takes place through the sustained non-use of certain constitutional provisions. Through the non-use of certain provisions, those provisions have lost their force and, therefore, the Court has engaged in informal constitutional change. For instance, Article 33(4) has lost its force because the Court decided not to use the article by declaring that Article 22(4) must be interpreted in light of Article 33(3). Similarly, concerning the religious freedom clause, the Court has consistently not used the provision by either avoiding deciding the merit of the case or trumping the religious freedom clause with Article 28J(2).

The phenomenon of informal constitutional change is still understudied, and there is much more to learn about the Indonesian case. Nevertheless, the subject matter is important because it invites us to think about amendment culture in Indonesia and the constitutional text itself. More importantly, informal constitutional change by the Constitutional Court has shifted attention away from the formal constitutional amendment by the MPR. The constitutional text still matters, but constitutional meaning has evolved through the Court's interpretations or by its omissions.

References

Albert, Richard (2014) 'Constitutional Amendment by Constitutional Desuetude' 63 *American Journal of Comparative Law* 641–686.

Albert, Richard (2017) 'Quasi-Constitutional Amendments' 65 *Buffalo Law Review* 739–770.

Antonaki, Ilektra (2016) 'Keck in Capital? Redefining 'Restrictions' in the 'Golden Shares' Case Law' 9(4) *Erasmus Law Review* 177–188.

Butt, Simon and Fritz Siregar (2015) 'State Control over Natural Resources in Indonesia: Implications of the Oil and Natural Gas Law Case of 2012' 31(2) *Journal of Energy & Natural Resources Law* 107–121.

Cain, Bruce E and Roger G Noll (2009) 'Constitutional Change: Malleable Constitutions: Reflections on State Constitutional Reform' 87 *Texas Law Review* 1517–1544.

Crouch, Melissa (2012) 'Law and Religion in Indonesia: The Constitutional Court and the Blasphemy Law' 7 *Asian Journal of Comparative Law* 1–46.

Crouch, Melissa (2014) *Law and Religion in Indonesia: Conflict and the Courts in West Java*. London, New York: Routledge.

Crouch, Melissa (2016) 'Constitutionalism, Islam and the Practice of Religious Deference: The Case of the Indonesian Constitutional Court' 1(2) *Australian Journal of Asian Law* 1–15.

Doyle, Oran (2017) 'Informal Constitutional Change' 65 *Buffalo Law Review* 1021–1038.

Erb, Maribeth and Priyambudi Sulistiyanto (ed) (2009) *Deepening Democracy in Indonesia? Direct Elections for Local Leaders (Pilkada)*. Singapore: ISEAS.

Faiz, PanMohamad (2016) 'The Protection of Civil and Political Rights by the Constitutional Court of Indonesia' 6(2) *Indonesia Law Review* 158–179.

Formichi, Chiara and RoyMichael Feener (2015) *Shi'ism in Southeast Asia: 'Alid Piety and Sectarian Constructions*. Oxford, New York: Oxford University Press.

Ginsburg, Tom and James Melton (2015) 'Does the Constitutional Amendment Rule Matter at All? Amendment Cultures and the Challenges of Measuring Amendment Difficulty' 13(3) *International Journal of Constitutional Law* 686–713.

Grundmann, Stefan and Florian Möslein (2004) 'Golden Shares—State Control in Privatized Companies: Comparative Law, European Law and Policy Aspects' 1 *European Banking & Financial Law Journal* (EUREDIA).

Hendrianto, Stefanus (2018) *The Law and Politics of Constitutional Court: Indonesia and the Search for Judicial Heroes*. London, New York: Routledge.

Higgins, Benjamin (1968) *Economic Development: Problems, Principles, and Policies*. London: Constable and Company.

Horowitz, Donal (2013) *Constitutional Change and Democracy in Indonesia*. Cambridge, New York: Cambridge University Press.

McTurnan Kahin, George (1970) *The Nationalism and Revolution in Indonesia*. Ithaca, NY: Cornell University Press.

O'Mahony, Conor (2014) 'If a Constitution Is Easy to Amend, Can Judges Be Less Restrained? Rights, Social Change, and Proposition 8' 27 *Harvard Human Rights Journal* 191–242.

Papadopoulos, Thomas (2015) 'Privatized Companies, Golden Shares and Property Ownership in the Euro crisis Era', 12 (1) *European Company and Financial Law Review* 1-18.

Passchier, Reijer (2017) 'Quasi-Constitutional Change Without Intent—a Response to Richard Albert' 65 *Buffalo Law Review* 1077–1099.

Setiawan, Ken (2019) 'The Human Rights Courts: Embedding Impunity' in M Crouch (ed) *The Politics of Court Reform: Judicial Change and Legal Culture in Indonesia*. Cambridge, New York: Cambridge University Press. pp 287–310.

Strauss, David (1996) 'Common Law Constitutional Interpretation' 63 *University of Chicago Law Review* 877–935.

Stilt, Kristen (2014) 'Constitutions in Authoritarian Regimes: The Egyptian Constitution of 1971' in T Ginsburg and A Simpser (eds) *Constitutions in Authoritarian Regimes*. Cambridge: Cambridge University Press. pp 111–140.

Susanti, Bivitri (2002) 'Neo-liberalism and its Resistance in Indonesia's Constitution Reform 1999-2002: A Constitutional and Historical Review of Indonesian Socialism and Neo-Liberalism', unpublished LLM thesis, University of Warwick.

Tushnet, Mark (2009) 'Constitutional Workarounds' 87 *Texas Law Review* 1499–1515.

Vermeule, Adrian (2012) 'The Atrophy of Constitutional Powers' 32(3) *Oxford Journal of Legal Studies* 421–444.

Zerial, Natalie (2007) 'Decision No. 2-3/PUU-V/2007 [2007] (Indonesian Constitutional Court)' 14 *Australian International Law Journal* 217–226.

12

The Constitutionalization of 'Religious Values' in Indonesia

Ahmad Rofii and Nadirsyah Hosen

Introduction

Much discussion on religion and the Indonesian Constitution has focused on Article 29, particularly the omitted famous seven words that stated '*dengan kewajiban menjalankan syariat Islam bagi pemeluk-pemeluknya*' (with the obligation to carry out Islamic Shariah for its adherents) (Hosen 2005; Elson 2009; 2013; Basalim 2002). However, the amendment to the 1945 Constitution introduced another interesting phrase: '*nilai-nilai agama*' (religious values). Among other reasons, this has led the Constitution to be characterized as 'very religious and godly at the same time' (Asshiddiqie no date: 14), or as establishing a 'religious nation state' (Mahfud MD 2006: 30). Although during the amendment process (1999–2002) the phrase 'religious values' were introduced and supported by Muslim-based factions, which were implicitly aiming to advance Islamic aspirations, the phrase used was not 'Islamic values'. Their final adoption by all factions from different political ideologies and religious affiliations demonstrated the inclusiveness and generality of the meaning of the words 'religious values' (Hosen 2007: 128). However, 'religious values' could be ambiguous since it entails a different understanding from various religious worldviews, and their different schools or denominations.

The phrase 'religious values' is mentioned twice in the Constitution, first, in Article 28J(2) on the limitations of constitutional rights, and second, in Article 31(5) on the duty of the government to uphold these values in education. In this chapter, we examine the meaning and the application of 'religious values' by specifically asking how far the Court has endorsed the limitation on religious freedom based on 'religious values' as a constitutional requirement.

In order to answer the question above, first, we will evaluate the constitutional debate surrounding the phrase during the 1999–2002 amendment. Notably, we want to understand the meaning of 'religious' and 'values' and the socio-legal-political context at that period. Second, we will discuss how the Indonesian Constitutional Court (*Mahkamah Konstitusi*) has interpreted the phrase in related cases. We argue that the words 'religious values' represents a compromise position of state and religion in the Indonesian Constitution. In order to maintain harmony and unity, the rights to religion are protected. Still, the application of these rights could be limited by the law. Therefore, the constitutionalization of religious values demonstrates that the Indonesian Constitution is not secular, nor is it hostile to religion (Kuru 2009;

Ahmad Rofii and Nadirsyah Hosen, *The Constitutionalization of 'Religious Values' in Indonesia* In: *Constitutional Democracy in Indonesia*. Edited by: Melissa Crouch, Oxford University Press. © Ahmad Rofii and Nadirsyah Hosen, 2023.
DOI: 10.1093/oso/9780192870681.003.0012

Ahdar 2013; Hosen 2013). Rather, it is a constitution that is designed to accommodate a highly religious society.

Religious Values in the Constitution

The place of religion in the Constitution is important. After the amendment, there is an increasing number of references to words related to religion in the amended Constitution. There are four models of mentioning religious terms in the amendment to the 1945 Constitution. First, the Constitution refers to 'religion' (*agama*) in many places in the Constitution such as on religion, on the presidential oath, on the Regional Representative Council, on the Religious Courts or judiciary (*Pengadilan Agama*) (Arts 29(2), 9, 22D, and 24(2) respectively).

Second, the Constitution also refers to religious rights, namely the right to have and to practice religion and freedom of religion as a non-derogable right (Arts 28E and 28I(1)). Third, the constitutional provisions on religious values are mentioned in the limitation clause on human rights and the clause on national education (Arts 28J(2) and 31(5)). Fourth, the Constitution also uses 'faith and piety' (*keimanan dan ketakwaan*') without mentioning religion in Article 31(3) on national education.

As stated at the outset, this chapter will only focus on the phrase 'religious values' (the third model). In this section, we will evaluate the ideas and proposals during the constitutional amendment debate that led to the use of such phrases so we can understand their meaning in the historical context. Such a phrase was not included in the original 1945 Constitution.

In 2000, during the Second Amendment, the members of the People's Consultative Assembly (*Majelis Permusyawaratan Rakyat*, MPR) discussed Chapter XA on Human Rights. Previously, in 1998, the MPR issued Decree XVII/1998 on human rights. In 2000, the constitution-makers used the 1998 MPR Decree as a basis for their constitutional debate. Therefore, it is essential to understand the socio-political context of 1998 that led to the issuance of this important decree.

In May 1998, when President BJ Habibie took over the presidency, he faced significant pressure, at both national and international levels, to improve human rights conditions in Indonesia. Many NGO activists and constitutional experts urged Indonesia to amend its Constitution to guarantee human rights protection, since the original 1945 Constitution had no adequate provisions on human rights. At the international level, the demands for reform came from the World Bank, when it raised its concerns over the human rights situation in Indonesia and East Timor. In a letter to President Habibie, the World Bank stressed the need for reform 'for the international financial community to be able to continue its full support'. The World Bank urged Habibie to take significant steps (Clark 2002).

Those pressures forced Habibie, in his State Address before the MPR session of 15 August 1998 to give strong support to the idea of the universality of human rights. He stated, 'We have firmly abandoned the uncertainty phase, which earlier always considered human rights as a Western cultural product (*Kompas* 1998). In addition, he also said, 'We are determined to make human rights principles the yardstick in our life as a nation and country. We will promote and safeguard human rights in accordance with our democratic and welfare-based approach' (Cassel 1998).

In order to deal with the protection of human rights, President Habibie issued Presidential Decree 129/1998 concerning the National Human Rights Plan. The Decree states that Indonesia, as a member of the international community, holds in high esteem the Universal Declaration of Human Rights, and the 1993 Vienna Human Rights Declaration and the Programme of Action. Article 1 of the Decree also states that the purpose of the National Action Plan is to increase the protection of human rights in Indonesia, by taking into account the values of indigenous and traditional communities, as well as national cultures and religions, based on the *Pancasila*, and the 1945 Constitution.

In 1998, the MPR, as the highest state institution, adopted Decree XVII/MPR/ 1998 on Human Rights. By this decree, for the first time in Indonesian history, an Indonesian Charter on Human Rights was introduced. Many of the clauses in this decree were drawn directly from the Universal Declaration of Human Rights (UDHR). For instance, Articles 19–21 of the decree protects citizens' rights to freedom of expression without interference and to seek, receive, and impart information and ideas through any media. In addition, the guarantee of the rights of assembly and association, if enforced, would end the president's ability to disband political parties. Presidents Soekarno and Soeharto banned certain parties and forced others to merge, as effective weapons against their political opponents.

On 23 September 1999, a month before the presidential election, President Habibie signed Law 39/1999 on Human Rights ('the Human Rights Law'). This law implemented MPR Decree XVII on Human Rights. The Human Rights Law sets out a long list of internationally recognized human rights, which Indonesia is obliged to protect. The law contains provisions on human rights and fundamental freedoms, the responsibilities and obligations of the government in the promotion and protection of human rights, and the plan to set up a Human Rights Court. The law also strengthens the powers of the National Commission on Human Rights (*Komnas HAM*), which had been established by presidential decision in 1993 to monitor and report on human-rights abuses. Most importantly for its future investigative role, the new law gave the National Commission on Human Rights the legal power to force the attendance of witnesses, including those against whom complaints have been made (Hosen 2002; Juwana 2003).

However, this law is not adequate to protect human rights since the legislature can easily replace or amend it. Laws and other regulations should be based on the Constitution, whereas too many of the key clauses of the original 1945 Constitution end with an injunction for further specification by laws, opening the door to subsequent manipulation by the legislature. The original Constitution also lacks guarantees of basic civil and political rights. We have shown that the human rights provisions in the Second Amendment were the result of a long process that started during the MPR Session of 1998.

For the drafters of the Chapter on Human Rights in the Amended Constitution, the acceptance of the universality of human rights should be balanced with limiting the application of human rights. Limitations on rights, including the right to freedom of religion, according to Article 28J(2), are legitimate provided that it is:

determined by legislation, with the sole purpose of guaranteeing recognition and respect for the rights and freedom of others, and of meeting just requirements, based upon considerations of morality, religious values, security and public order, in a democratic society.

The text above is similar to Article 36 of the MPR Decree XVII/1998 on human rights with one difference, namely the addition of the phrase 'religious values'. Originally based on Article 36, the draft constitutional article did not initially provide for 'religious values' as a limitation on rights. The other legitimate bases of limitations on rights echo common limitations found in international human rights instruments (*Majelis Permusyawaratan Rakyat Republik Indonesia* 2010b: 519–520; see Universal Declaration of Human Rights, Article 29(2); International Covenant on Economic, Social and Cultural Rights, Article 4; International Covenant on Civil and Political Rights, Article 19(3) concerning limitations on the right to freedom of conscience, religion, and belief). The wording of the 1998 MPR Decree seems to be similar to the general limitations clause in the UDHR. Similar grounds for limitations on rights are found in regional human rights instruments, such as the European Convention of Human Rights (Convention for the Protection of Human Rights and Fundamental Freedoms, Article 9(2) concerning limitations on the right to freedom of thought, conscience, and religion), and most national bills of rights (Gardbaum 2006; Ahmed and Bulmer 2017). Unlike all these instruments, the Indonesian Constitution peculiarly adopts the consideration of religious values as grounds for limiting constitutional rights.

Before we discuss the debate on religious values in detail, it is necessary to introduce the main factions that participated in the debate. We classify the MPR factions with regard to the issue of religious values into three groups. First, secular-nationalist factions, which includes the faction of the Indonesian Democratic Party of Struggle (*Partai Demokrasi Indonesia-Perjuangan*, PDI-P), the Party of Functional Groups (*Partai Golkar*, PG), and the Armed and National Police Forces (*Tentara Nasional Indonesia/Kepolisian Republik Indonesia*, TNI/POLRI). Second, Islamist factions, consisting of the faction of the Crescent Moon and Star Party (*Partai Bulan Bintang*, PBB), the United Development Party (*Partai Persatuan Pembangunan*, PPP), and the Union of Muslim Sovereignty (*Perserikatan Daulat Umat*, PDU). Third, religious-oriented factions, including the faction of the National Awakening (*Kebangkitan Bangsa*, KB) and the *Reformasi* faction (*Reformasi*), which consisted of two parties, National Mandate Party (PAN) and Justice Party (PK). When the idea of human rights was first debated, following the discussions on citizens and residents, the *Reformasi* faction suggested the inclusion of religious values, in line with the first principle of the state basis (Pancasila), *Ketuhanan Yang Maha Esa* (belief in One Supreme God), as a limiter of human rights (*Majelis Permusyawaratan Rakyat Republik Indonesia* 2010b: 335–336). The first draft chapter, however, did not make any such reference to religious values. It was then proposed again on the basis that it would constrain the unbridled exercise of individual freedom and the excessive enjoyment of rights (*Majelis Permusyawaratan Rakyat Republik Indonesia* 2010c: 253, 296). The *Reformasi* faction initially proposed the inclusion of the words 'religious values' directly after legislation (*undang-undang*) as a limitation on rights. This could be understood as suggesting that religious values would have authority equivalent to that of a law in limiting rights (*Majelis Permusyawaratan Rakyat Republik Indonesia* 2010c: 253, 305; Salim 2008: 110). Notwithstanding this, the matter of religious values was again left absent from the second draft chapter (*Majelis Permusyawaratan Rakyat Republik Indonesia* 2010c: 512).

Aware of this, AM Luthfi, of the *Reformasi* faction reminded other members of the MPR about 'religious values'. Instead of placing these words immediately after legislation, they suggested that 'religious values' be placed immediately after the word 'morality'. Some members from the secular-nationalist factions (TNI/POLRI and PDIP) opposed this inclusion, because the words 'religious values' had not been raised in the debates prior to the agreement on the draft. On the other hand, other members, particularly from the Muslim parties-based factions, supported the idea, arguing that the inclusion was a means to perfect the idea of morality, in accordance with the religious nature of the nation. Hamdan Zoelva (PBB Faction) specifically interprets this as 'no articles on human rights in the Second Amendment may contradict religious values' (Hosen 2007: 128). That is why his party accepted the human rights provisions in Chapter X of the 1945 Constitution. All factions, for their own reasons, finally agreed to the insertion of the term 'religious values' (*Majelis Permusyawaratan Rakyat Republik Indonesia* 2010b: 520–530).

The word 'values' was not crafted accidentally. It was deliberately chosen so that all MPR factions could agree with the insertion of the term 'religion'. By employing the word 'values', the consideration of the permissible limitations on rights can refer to general doctrines and principles of religion, rather than its rules and practical norms. This interpretation is consistent not only with the textual meaning of the word 'values' as 'important or beneficial qualities for humanity' (Pusat Bahasa Departemen Pendidikan Nasional 2001), but also its historical significance, as it was used during the amendment process. In the draft amendment proposed by the *Partai Golkar* Faction, for instance, religious doctrines are distinguished in terms of the values, norms, and laws of religion (*Majelis Permusyawaratan Rakyat Republik Indonesia* 2010b: 421–422: 566). Moreover, *Kebangkitan Bangsa* Faction, in its suggestions for amending Article 29, suggested that religious doctrines could be understood in four ways: creeds, rituals, social relations, and universal values and morality. Religious values, as used in this context, was understood as the most abstract and universal teachings of a religion, such as matters of honesty and kindness, and as providing the ethical foundations for the state (*Majelis Permusyawaratan Rakyat Republik Indonesia* 2010b: 423; 2010d: 427). Nonetheless, if religious values are understood in such an inclusive, general way, and therefore would include morality, public order, and all other considerations for limiting constitutional rights in accordance with Article 28J(2), the inclusion of the words 'religious values' would be repetitive and thus unnecessary. For this reason, these words could reasonably be taken to refer to the values of religion(s) other than those already mentioned. The phrase 'religious values' is placed alongside justice, morality, security, public order, and the concept of a democratic country.

Religious law, Islamic law in particular, could potentially have different roles, in the face of the religious values clause. It could act as an object of rights limitation. The exercise of the right to manifest religious freedom in the form of the implementation of Islamic law might be subject to state restrictions, whose legitimacy is determined by its consistency with, among others, religious values as the values of all religions. In the internal Islamic legal tradition, the application by Muslims of Islamic law is constitutionally confined by its compliance with the values and objectives of Islamic law itself (*maqāṣid al-sharī'ah*), namely to establish and maintain *maṣlaḥah* (the common good) which includes the preservation of religion, life, intellect, lineage, property, justice, liberty, equality, human dignity, social cooperation, and environment (Auda 2007; Duderija 2014).

In 2002, during the Fourth Amendment, members of the MPR discussed Article 31. After establishing the right to education for every citizen, Article 31(5), stipulates: 'The state advances science and technology by upholding religious values and national unity for the advancement of civilization as well as prosperity of mankind.' The original Article 31 consisted of only two paragraphs: the first guaranteed citizens' right to education and the second stipulated the establishment of a national educational system. Although no reference to religion was made in the article, the framers of the 1945 Constitution were certainly aware of the significance of religion in education. This can be read from the 'Broad Guidelines', a statement made by the subcommittee on education and teaching of the Committee to Investigate Preparations for Independence (*Badan Penyelidik Usaha Persiapan Kemerdekaan*, BPUPK) on 17 July 1945. The second paragraph of the Guidelines provided that: 'In line with the morality of humanity, as contained in all religious teachings, national education and teaching are founded on religion and national culture, and [directed] towards the safety and happiness of the people' (Kusuma 2009: 458). Furthermore, one might imply the connection of education with religion from the preamble. Its fourth paragraph provides that one of the objectives was 'to advance the intelligent life of the nation' (*mencerdaskan kehidupan bangsa*). It presumably has high relevance to education (*Tim Penyusun Naskah Komprehensif Proses dan Hasil Perubahan UUD 1945* 2010: 9–22). According to the preamble, the objective shall be based on, among others, the belief in One Supreme God.[1]

The idea of acknowledging the role of religion in education in a provision of the Constitution was raised in the course of debates regarding the goals of education during the process of the Second Amendment. The position of the MPR factions in many ways was an extension of their stance on the place of religious values in Article 28J(2). In 2002, two years after the Second Amendment of Article 28J(2), the debate appeared again in the Fourth Amendment.

The Islamist factions also proposed the inclusion of religious values as a limit to the advancement of education. A draft of paragraph 5 then would stipulate the government's responsibility for the development of science and technology 'that do not contravene (*yang tidak bertentangan dengan*) religious values'. This proposal resembled the Islamist factions' proposal regarding the limitation on human rights, as discussed earlier. Against the proposal, secular nationalist factions argued that the

---

[1] Attempts to ground education on religious values has in fact been made by way of pre-constitutional amendment legislation. For instance, the Law of the National Education System of 1989 stipulated in Art 4 that 'national education aims at advancing the intelligent life of the nation and developing Indonesian people as a whole, namely human beings who have faith in and piety towards One Supreme God and have noble characters...'

formulation was against the principle of neutrality and universality as the nature of science, and, as a result, would constrain the development of science. Furthermore, Article 29 has already provided religion as a guide for all matters relating to the state. They proposed a draft that only mentioned the 'advancement of civilisation and unity' without mentioning religion (*Majelis Permusyawaratan Rakyat Republik Indonesia* 2010a: 129–132; *Tim Penyusun Naskah Komprehensif Proses dan Hasil Perubahan UUD 1945 2010*: 118, 181–187).

Concerning the proposal to install religious values as a limit in draft paragraph 5, Ahmad Zacky Siradj of the *Utusan Golongan* Faction (F-UG) proposed a refinement to the words 'that do not contravene' which according to him assumed a mistaken conflict between science and religion. Instead of this negative wording, he suggested the positive words, namely 'with the highest respect for' (*dengan menjunjung tinggi*) (*Majelis Permusyawaratan Rakyat Republik Indonesia* 2010e: 53–54). This suggestion was accepted by the factions that had previously refused the addition of the words. Furthermore, together with religious values, the words 'national unity' were added. This addition aimed to make the advancement of science and technology have the highest respect for national interests. Yusuf Muhammad of the *Kebangkitan Bangsa* Faction proposed a formulation of draft paragraph 5 which eventually became an agreed draft of paragraph 5 (*Majelis Permusyawaratan Rakyat Republik Indonesia* 2010e: 269–275; 2010f, 8).

In our view, the meaning of the religious values clause in paragraph 5, like the religious values as a limiter of human rights, should be viewed inclusively and generally to include the values and principles of all religions, despite the fact that the clause was proposed and defended by the Muslim-based factions. Such values are acceptable in so far as they would be reasonably accepted by all religions. Upon this consideration, Islamic values as developed in the Islamic legal tradition, for instance, cannot be set as the sole consideration in the national education system. They rather have to be in harmony with values of other religions. Moreover, the reference to religion here should be read on the basis of the supremacy of the Constitution in which the preamble lies at the foundation of the Constitution. In other words, we suggest that religious values are not standalone values. Their legitimacy is derived from their consistency with the fundamental values and principles established in the preamble. In the current provision, the reference to religious values is inseparable from the consideration of national unity. This does not mean that 'the highest respect' is limited to these two values. They merely represent part of the values system, in which the Pancasila lies at its heart (Law 20/ 2003 on National Educational System, Art 2), that is considered by the drafters of the amendment to be important in the state's advancement of science and technology.

Analysis of Constitutional Cases

This constitutionalization of religious values implies the acknowledgment and support of religion by the state. How far has the Constitutional Court used the phrase 'religious values' in their interpretations of the Constitution and decisions in constitutional court cases to endorse the state's policy on religion? This section will analyse the related constitutional cases on this issue.

Religious Values and the Blasphemy Law Cases

It might not be an exaggeration to state that the current challenge to the constitutional right to freedom of religion is in the implementation of Law 1/1965 on the 'prevention of misuse and/or defamation of religion' (*penyalahgunaan dan/atau penodaan agama*), which is known as the Blasphemy Law. It is the law that laid the basis for state recognition of some religions and criminalization of minority religions or beliefs that are considered deviant from the religious orthodoxy, and of any person allegedly insulting religion. The Constitutional Court decisions on the constitutionality of this law in many respects legitimize this practice.

Prior to the issuance of the Blasphemy Law, the matter of religious deviation had been governed by some other regulations (for instance, Law 15/1961 on Provisions of the Public Persecution, Art 2(3); Presidential Decree 2/1962 on the Prohibition of Organizations which do not correspond to the Identity of Indonesia). These regulations targeted local beliefs (*aliran kepercayaan*) and organizations deemed contrary to the Revolution and national identity (for instance, the ban on Rotary Club and Baha'i organization as regulated in Presidential Decision 264/1962). In late January 1965, President Sukarno issued the Blasphemy Law as a Presidential Decree (*Penetapan Presiden*). In 1969, during the early years of Suharto, it was then promulgated as a law.

The purpose of the Blasphemy Law was made explicit in its Consideration part and the general section of its Elucidation. In the Elucidation, the Blasphemy Law was first explained in the context of the national ideology entrenched in the preamble of the Constitution, in which the first principle 'belief in One Supreme God' implied that religion constituted a basis for national unity and was part of the state's nation-building. In this sense, the law was arguably aimed at protecting religion for the purpose of maintaining state interests. It is under this consideration that the emergence of local beliefs, what the law calls mystical organizations (*kepercayaan/kebatinan*) were to be assessed. According to the decree, local beliefs were in conflict with the recognized teachings of religions. Their beliefs and activities allegedly abusive to those teachings were considered as contributing to national disunity and 'seriously endangering the existing religions' (Blasphemy Law, General Elucidation, para 2).[2] The objective of the regulation was to secure religious harmony, to guarantee freedom of 'religion', and to maintain national unity and security.

There are four constitutional cases related to this Blasphemy Law. It was in 2009 that the first historic attempt to test the constitutionality of the Blasphemy Law in the Constitutional Court was made. Since then, the law has been the subject of three

---

[2] Another issue that concerns the law is pertaining to hostility to and insulting religion. This related to the aggressive campaigns of the Indonesian Communist Party (PKI) between 1963 and 1965 prior to the law's promulgation that was considered as insulting the religious beliefs of Muslim communities. There were some incidents involving the PKI that presumably served as the background of the issuance of the law (see Zuhri 1987: 508–509, 517–518). This consideration was then accommodated in Art 4 of the Blasphemy Law.

consecutive challenges before the Court. All of them failed to strike down the law. The first decision delivered in 2010 constituted the main source of reasoning for the subsequent decisions.[3] This case drew huge attention both nationally and in the international fora. It has become a landmark case in matters of religious freedom (Isnur 2012; Crouch 2012; Butt and Lindsey 2012: 234–240; Menchik 2014). Two years later, a similar challenge to the law was brought before the Court, which decided the case mainly by quoting the arguments in the 2010 decision.[4] In 2018, the third and fourth cases were decided. This latter case made frequent references to the Court's arguments in the first and third cases.[5]

The Constitutional Court takes the position that Indonesia is a 'religious nation, not an atheist nation'.[6] The Court translated the principle 'belief in One Supreme God' as religious beliefs or religious values. It placed particular emphasis on the religiosity of the state on the basis of this principle and other constitutional provisions, including Article 28J(2) which stipulated 'religious values'. In the Blasphemy Law case No 1 (2009), the Court asserted that the Pancasila's first principle was a supreme principle that attested no separation of state and religion. It even suggested that religious values should be the basis of state policies, lawmaking, government, and the life of the people. The principle of belief in God and religious teachings and values should 'become a measuring instrument in determining [not only] good law from bad law but even constitutional law from unconstitutional law'.[7] It means the Court will not ignore God's law, as it is also reflected in the first pillar of Pancasila as a state ideology. In other words, the court decision is to justify the position of Indonesia as neither an Islamic state, nor a secular state. It should be understood that no law should contradict Pancasila, which is mentioned in the preamble to the Constitution.

Within this approach, religion is considered very special. The theocratic implications of this stand seem to have no limits. For the Court, the state had the duty to protect religions, their holy books, and teachings from decline, misuse, and defamation, as the impugned law aims to do. The state should make a campaign of freedom from religion impossible; international conventions and instruments should be read in light of religious values; and, above all, religion embodies the uniqueness of the Indonesian rule of law.[8] The Court in the Blasphemy Law case No 4, with reference to the 2010 decision, came to a similar view of the Indonesian model of religious freedom.[9]

This theocratic reading of the Pancasila and the 'radiating effect' of the principal belief in One Supreme God the Court demonstrated are problematic. Despite the inherent ambiguity of the meaning of the reference to religion, we argue that such reading would be an inaccurate implication of the historical and systematic interpretation of the Pancasila and principally contrary to the values contained in the preamble as a whole. The principle 'belief in One Supreme God' is qualified and limited by other Pancasila's principles. For instance, it is to be understood in line with the principle of

---

[3] Decision 140/PUU-VII/2009.
[4] Decision 84/PUU-X/2012.
[5] Decision 76/PUU-XVI/2018.
[6] Decision 140/PUU-VII/2009, 273, para 3.34.3, 274–275, para 3.34.8.
[7] Ibid 275, para 3.34.11.
[8] Ibid 273–275, para 3.34.4-11.
[9] Decision 76/PUU-XVI/2018, 30, para 3.15.

just civilized humanity. Upon this understanding, no theocratic reading could be concluded from reading the Pancasila's first principle. Moreover, the principle could not be understood in isolation from other values of the preamble, particularly the idea of a unitary state which protects and covers all people with no exceptions and guarantees the equality of all groups and individuals without regard to their religions and beliefs.

The Court in the Blasphemy Law case No 1 referred to the 'religious values' consideration of Article 28J(2) of the Constitution for limiting the right to freedom of religion. The limitation based on religious values was used by the Court as a principal justification for the constitutionality of the impugned law. The Court in the Blasphemy Law case No 4 again mentioned this consideration, although in a more modest way than previously.[10] How could religious values provide a basis for the law's constitutionality? In the Blasphemy Law case No 1, the majority of justices did not elaborate on what this reference meant. Which values? Whose religion(s)? The Court equated religious values with religious teachings and norms as in the state implementation of Islamic private law, or with the communal values of the society.[11] In another instance, the Court differentiated those values from the principle of separation of state and religion and pure individualism or collectivism.[12] One may argue that values are like principles and should be distinguished from rules. Values, therefore, are the most abstract and universal tenets of a religion. Moreover, they are not standalone values, because their acceptability requires their consistency with the Constitution.

In its defence of the impugned law's consistency with the right to religious freedom, the Court frequently made reference to the celebrated distinction within religious freedom, namely between internal (*forum internum*) and external aspects (*forum externum*) of religion.[13] The *forum internum* concerns the right to have, adopt, or change one's religion or belief that cannot be limited under any circumstances and cannot be criminalized because this aspect of freedom lies in the minds and hearts of people. The *forum externum*, on the other hand, is related to the right to manifestation and expression of religion that might be restricted for a specific reason. It is related to the rights of others and the interests of society and the state. This oft-quoted distinction became the main justification for the Court to restrict religious freedom.

In the Blasphemy Law case No 2, the Court agreed that religious interpretation was a part of the right to freedom of religion. It belonged to the *forum internum*. Nevertheless, the observance of religious freedom cannot be unrestrained. As the Court pointed out, 'freedom to interpret a religion is not absolute', because such an interpretation should abide by fundamental teachings of religion and its received methodology and have its basis in the holy books.[14] For the Court, this does not mean that the *forum internum* was limitable. In Blasphemy Law case No 1, the Court argued that a religious interpretation, even if it was deviant, would absolutely be protected if it was exercised internally and individually. The religious interpretation would potentially be restricted if it was manifested externally by making it known to others in the

---

[10] Ibid 29, para 3.13, 31, para 3.15.

[11] Decision 140/PUU-VII/2009, 275, para 3.34.8, 295, para 3.58.

[12] Ibid 275, para 3.34.10.

[13] Decision 56/PUU-XV/2017, 531, 532, para 3.16.5. See also Decision 140/PUU-VII/2009, 288, para 3.51; Decision 76/PUU-XVI/2018, 30–31, para 3.15.

[14] Decision 56/PUU-XV/2017, 531–532, para 3.16.5; Decision 140/PUU-VII/2009, 289, para 3.52.

public forum.[15] The Court's view in this case of the inevitable limitation of the *forum externum* and its absolute contrast to the *forum internum* would lead to unduly wide restriction on religious freedom. In our view, the *forum externum* is arguably inseparable from the *internum* freedom. A restriction on the former might result in severe impairment of the latter (Bielefeldt, Ghanea, and Wiener 2016: 85; Petkoff 2012).

The vulnerable guarantee of the external forum of religious manifestation in the case of religious interpretation would endanger minority interpretations. For the Court, a religious interpretation was called deviant and accordingly could be prohibited when it was not in line with the fundamental teachings of a religion. These fundamental teachings constituted the undisputed essence of a religion. They were the parameters and the basis of a 'controlling mechanism' in each religion. Because there is no further provision of how the fundamental teachings should be, the notion of fundamental teachings would be inevitably unclear and ambiguous in their form and content. Who should then define these parameters? According to the Court, it was the internal religious authorities, or *ulama* in the case of Islam, who would determine those teachings and the boundaries of religion by reliance on the holy books through a recognized methodology.[16] These authorities were the ones who would decide whether or not religious interpretation was acceptable. The state, as the Court pointed out, 'cannot by itself dictate the fundamental teachings of a religion, but rather will decide on the basis of the agreement from the relevant internal religious authorities'.[17]

The Court's decisions, according to Melissa Crouch, expose the state's practice of religious deference, which she defines as the court's deference to the leaders and institutions of the six religions recognized by the state. She argues that this practice of religious deference exists because the state 'seeks to capitalise on the legitimacy and moral authority that religious leaders generate in Indonesia' (Crouch 2016: 197). Religious deference is a concept that explains 'why religious leaders and religious texts have an influence over legal proceedings and practices in Indonesia'. In her study of two cases of the Blasphemy Law brought before the Court, Crouch argues that such deference is maintained through the Court's articulation of the constitutional limitation principles over public order and religious values, and by giving the authority to define religious identity to conservative religious leaders (Crouch 2012; Crouch 2016; Fenwick 2017). This means that 'religious values' seems to be taken in this context not only as morality but also as orthodoxy (ie correct theology) (Bagir, Suhadi, and Arianingtyas 2020: 39–56).

Whether the values of religion(s) may justify the criminalization of 'deviant' religious interpretations is contentious. How to deal with dissent or unorthodox interpretations is a controversial matter not only between different religions but also within each religious tradition (Chambers and Nosco 2015). Particularly in Islam, intramural diversity (*ikhtilāf*) is the rule rather than exception. This applies not only in the realm of law (*fiqh*) but also in the realm of creeds ('*aqīdah*). Muslim scholars have suggested what they consider to be the core tenets indisputable within Islam that determine whether someone would continue to be called Muslim. However, there

---

[15] Decision 140/PUU-VII/2009, 292, para 3.55.
[16] Decision 56/PUU-XV/2017, 532–534.
[17] Ibid 533. The Court here referred to the 2010 decision, Decision 140/PUU-VII/2009, 289.

is no agreement on most contents of these tenets (Modarressi 2016). Many scholars might argue that the first value of Islam according to the paradigm of the objectives of Islamic law (*maqāṣid al-sharī'ah*), namely the preservation of religion (*ḥifẓ al-dīn*), requires both the state's positive obligation to facilitate Muslims' observance of their religion and negative protection of religion by suppressing and punishing any Muslim whose beliefs are outside the core tenets of Islam (al-'Ālim 1994: 226–270; March 2011).[18] This is also the position generally held by the Indonesian Council of Ulama (*Majelis Ulama Indonesia*, MUI).[19] The view that deviants should be criminalized, including those accused of blasphemous acts, however, has been disputed by Muslim jurists of the classical period as well as the modern age. While those deviants might be considered theologically wrong, they would only be responsible before God in the hereafter (al-'Awwā 2006: 190–204; Kamali 1992; al-'Alwānī 2014; Saeed and Saeed 2017). We have argued in accordance with this latter stance that the state should not interfere in matters of religious interpretation considered deviant from the orthodoxy. Our stance is also consistent with the protection of the right to freedom of religion and belief. On this basis, instead of justifying the Blasphemy Law, the religious values consideration understood in combination with other constitutional principles would be appropriately employed to invalidate the law.

Religious Values and Zakat Management Law

We also discuss how the phrase 'religious values' has been used by the Court to decide on the constitutionality of Law 23/2011 on Zakat Management. Zakat is the obligation of almsgiving, which is an essential doctrine in the Islamic faith. It is due on Muslims' property for the benefit of the poor, the needy, and other beneficiaries.

The 2011 law contained provisions that significantly changed the previous administration of zakat particularly with regard to the role of the National Zakat Board (*Badan Amil Zakat Nasional*, BAZNAS). The law created a limited space for private zakat agencies. It even criminalized zakat committees traditionally found in parts of the country. It was because of these concerns that an application was made to the Constitutional Court to review those provisions of the law.

The Zakat Management Law was made by reliance on several articles of the Constitution including the Parliament's power to make laws and the President's assent (Art 20), the right of members of the Parliament to submit a bill (Art 21), the religious basis of the state and religious freedom (Art 29), and the state's duty to care for the poor and destitute children (Art 34(1)). The state's guarantee of a Muslim's right to religious freedom constitutes the main basis of the Zakat Management Law. With forty-seven articles and their elucidations, the new zakat law of 2011 disrupted the status

---

[18] According to the majority of Muslim jurists—even for many scholars, this is the consensus—a Muslim whose beliefs contrast with the core tenets of Islam would be considered to be an apostate (*murtadd*) and as a consequence would be punished by death. (Ibn Rushd 1982: 1:459; Abū Zahrah, no date: 154–155; Peters 2005: 64–65).

[19] In its recent fatwas concerning groups holding deviant religious interpretation, the MUI proposed recommendations for the government to ban and close down the deviant groups and punish their leaders.

quo of zakat management in Indonesia, even though it preserves the voluntary nature of the replaced law.

The former zakat law of 1999 introduced how the state articulates its power over the administration of zakat by, among other things, setting up governmental zakat agencies and requiring the involvement of the Ministry of Religious Affairs (MORA) in government and private zakat management. The Zakat Management Law of 2011 has further bureaucratized the management of zakat. It centralizes zakat management in the hands of BAZNAS. While the 1999 law equalized the power of both government supported *zakat* agencies (*Badan Amil Zakat*, BAZ(and private zakat agencies (*Lembaga Amil Zakat*, LAZ) so that they 'have the primary duty to collect, distribute and utilise zakat in line with the dictates of religion (Islam)' (Art 8), the law empowers the government to establish BAZNAS exclusively to deal with zakat management nationally (Arts 5(1) and 6). BAZNAS, located in the capital city, is an independent government institution that is responsible to the president through the Minister of Religious Affairs (Art 5(2) and (3). The functions of BAZNAS include planning the collection, distribution, and utilization of zakat, their implementation, supervision, and reporting, and being responsible for the application of zakat management (Art 7(1)). These comprehensive functions make BAZNAS both the regulator of zakat and operator of zakat management.

The law also provides that BAZNAS should provide a written report to the president through the Minister of Religious Affairs and the legislature at least once a year (Art 7(3)). In exercising its duty, BAZNAS can enter into cooperation with other related parties (Art 7(2)). The law also regulates membership of BAZNAS (Arts 8–13), its structure (Art 14), and the creation of BAZNAS in provinces and regencies/cities (Art 15). BAZNAS, either in the capital city, a province, or in a regency/city, can create a Zakat Collecting Unit (UPZ) to help them to collect zakat (Art 16). The law makes reference only to BAZNAS in cases where zakat payers (*muzaki*) cannot calculate their zakat (Art 21(2)). As part of the government, BAZNAS is funded by the state budget (Art 30).

Similar to the 1999 law, the Zakat Management Law of 2011 regulates non-governmental zakat agencies (LAZ), of which there are many in Indonesia. However, there are some differences in the institutional arrangement of LAZ between the two laws. First, in the former, provisions on LAZ are briefly formulated leaving its specification to the Minister (Art 7), but in the latter the law makes detailed provisions on LAZ. For instance, approval of the Minister or his/her appointed officials is required for the creation of LAZ (Art 18(1)). Article 18(2) stipulates that approval will be given if LAZ has fulfilled all minimum requirements: (a) registered as an Islamic mass organization that manages education, propagation of Islam, and social matters; (b) taken the form of a legal institution; (c) granted a recommendation from BAZNAS; (d) has Sharia supervisor(s); (d) has technical, administrative, and financial capabilities; (e) is a non-profit organization; (f) has a programme to manage zakat for the welfare of Muslim communities; and (g) is subject to regular Sharia and financial audits. In addition, LAZ should regularly submit a report of its activities to BAZNAS (Art 19) and 'regional government' (Art 29(3)). Secondly, unlike the previous law, the 2011 law makes LAZ subordinate to BAZNAS. The law stipulates that 'in order to *assist BAZNAS* in implementing the collection, distribution, and utilisation of zakat, society may found LAZ' (Art 7). This provision, together with other provisions on the centrality of BAZNAS as previously mentioned, seems to subordinate LAZ to the all-encompassing power of BAZNAS.

On 16 August 2012, several zakat organizations, including Yayasan Dompet Dhuafa and Yayasan Rumah Zakat Indonesia, two major national private zakat agencies, and several individuals applied to the Constitutional Court for review of some provisions of the Zakat Management Law of 2011. They challenged the provisions concerning the powers of BAZNAS, LAZ, and the provisions on criminal offences, arguing that these articles have injured or would injure the applicants' constitutional rights as they were not only discriminatory but also subjected the applicants as private zakat bodies to marginalization or even criminalization.

The Court unanimously held some of these provisions to be conditionally unconstitutional, while considering all the rest to be constitutional. For the Court, the provisions concerning the central role of BAZNAS in zakat management as both a regulator and an operator and the marginal role of LAZ did not represent a constitutional problem. On the other hand, the provision of the cumulative requirement of LAZ as both an Islamic mass organization and a legal entity (Art 18(2)(a) and (b)) is considered unconstitutional and not legally binding unless it is understood as an alternative ('or'), so that LAZ can be registered as an Islamic mass organization or alternatively be a legal entity only (a foundation). Moreover, the Court ruled that the provision should not bar traditional zakat agencies that are unreachable by BAZNAS or LAZ from managing zakat collected from their communities as long as they inform the authority of their activities.

With regard to the requirement that LAZ must be an Islamic mass organization (Art 18(2)(a), the Court referred to the Mass Organization Law (17/2013), in which the law stipulates that a mass organization could take the form of an association or foundation and it would be registered as such since its legality was authorized. This means that, in contrast to the impugned law, a LAZ established as a foundation was not required to change itself to be registered as a mass organization. The Court held that the cumulative requirement of Article 18(2)(a), as challenged by the applicants, and (b) (the requirement of being a legal entity) violated constitutional rights as stipulated in Article 28C(2), 28D(1), and 28E(2) and (3).[20] Instead of striking the provision down entirely, the Court stated that the requirement of being an Islamic mass organization was merely an alternative to the requirement of being a legal entity. Here, the Court employed the conditional unconstitutionality test to the impugned provision.

Furthermore, the Court found that the provision limited the right of individual Muslims or traditional zakat agencies to collect and distribute zakat as has long been the practice in Muslim societies. The limitation, however, was considered constitutionally unjustified according to Article 28J(2).[21] The Court suggested that the article would be unconstitutional unless it was amended so as to allow the traditional agencies to collect and distribute zakat provided that they resided in areas where no local BAZNAS or LAZ existed and provided they have informed the authorities of their activities. While the problem of the constitutionality of the limitation on traditional agencies might be raised, their inclusion in the (amended) article that particularly

---

[20] Decision 86/PUU-X/2012, 99–100, para 3.17.2–3.
[21] Ibid 100, para 3.17.4–5.

concerns the requirements of LAZ seems to be out of context. By making such an amendment, the traditional zakat agencies would be unduly required to fulfil all other requirements in the article.

The conclusion of unconstitutionality was also made for the provisions of offences in zakat management (Arts 38 and 41). According to the Court, the articles were in principle legitimate considering that they protected the right of zakat payers. In other words, they are generally justifiable not because they protect the enforcement of zakat as an Islamic institution as such. Nonetheless, for the Court, the words 'any person' were too general so as to criminalize the long-established practice of zakat by traditional zakat agencies.[22] By including them, the provisions have ignored the social reality embedded in the practice of zakat.[23] The Court then decided that the impugned provisions were unconstitutional unless they were interpreted as to exclude these agencies, as long as they informed the authority of their zakat-related activities. It argued that since BAZNAS or LAZ might not be present in some localities, it would be 'unreasonable' to force potential *muzakis* who live in these localities to come to a nearest BAZNAS or LAZ to pay zakat. The absence of a local BAZNAS and LAZ together with the criminalization of unregistered zakat collectors (traditional zakat agencies) would prevent potential *muzakis* from exercising their obligation to pay zakat. This, according to the Court, violated the constitutional right to religious freedom enshrined in Articles 28E(2) and 29(2).[24]

From the aforementioned examination, we notice that the Court's argument on the illegitimacy of the limitation on traditional zakat agencies is because of its inconsistency with the limitation clause (Art 28J(2)) and violation of religious freedom. The Court's reference to morality, religious values, safety, and public order unfortunately provides no further explanation on how the impugned provision has not satisfied each or one of those considerations. For instance, in what sense is the restriction on the right of traditional zakat agencies inconsistent with religious values? Do the values of Islam authorize individual Muslims to collect and distribute zakat? While it was agreed by traditional Muslim jurists that zakat administrators (*al-ʿāmilīn ʿalayhā*) are to be appointed by the government (al-Qarāḍāwī 1973: 579–580; Singer 2008: 45–50), contemporary jurists allow non-governmental zakat committees to collect and distribute zakat (al-Hayʾah al-Sharʿiyyah li Bayt al-Zakāt 2019: 173–174; al-Zuḥaylī 2012: 463–468). Within this discourse, there is no religious right granted to individual Muslims to collect and distribute zakat in the name of a zakat agency.

Conclusion

This chapter has demonstrated how the religious values limitation in the Constitution, based on historical debate and socio-political context during the constitutional

---

[22] Ibid 104–105, para 3.19.1–2.
[23] The Court earlier in its decision stated: 'In any arrangement in any form of law, the state must pay attention to matters that are sociologically effective. With due regard to such conditions, each arrangement according to the Court cannot be justified if it negates the existing social institutions. [T]he state through legislation instruments is obliged to guide and foster it so that it can coincide with the dynamics of progress of a nation that has become a state.' Decision 86/PUU-X/2012, 91, para 3.13.3.
[24] Ibid 105–106, para 3.19.3–5.

amendment, should reasonably be understood in general and universal terms. Consequently, we argue that these values should reasonably be accepted by various religious traditions. Some specific contexts, however, should be put into consideration, for example when legislation is made by reference to laws of a certain religion, such as Islamic law. Moreover, because religious values are not standalone values, in understanding the significance of religious values it is necessary to refer to the basic values and principles established in the Constitution, particularly those found in the preamble. The fact that religious values are not the highest values in the rights limitation and that they submit to the principle of constitutional supremacy suggests that the Constitution should not be treated as a religious constitution.

The constitutional cases on 'religious values' discussed above are all about Article 28J(2) on limitations of constitutional rights. At the time of writing, we have not found any cases related to Article 31(5) on the duty of government to uphold 'religious values' in education. Therefore, most interpretations of the Court are on how to use 'religious values' in endorsing government law and policy that may infringe on religious freedom. While the arguments can vary, we found at least four meanings of 'religious values' from the cases above.

The first meaning is that the Court treats religious values as the basis of state policies, lawmaking, government, and the life of the people. The Court did not interpret the phrase only as a limitation on human rights as originally stipulated in Article 28J(2). The Court went further by connecting the phrase to the concept of God and religion in Pancasila, the state's ideology, and other references to religion in the constitutional provision, while ignoring other values contained in the preamble.

Second, the Court has used the phrase 'religious values' to limit the interpretation of the right to religious freedom and religious interpretation. This position would significantly impact minority groups who have different religious interpretations to mainstream groups. The Court effectively failed to protect religious freedom in giving the meaning and application of 'religious values'. This leads to the third meaning of 'religious values' discussed in the above cases: the correct theology. The universality of 'religious values' has been reduced to orthodoxy. The Court seems to have the power to determine which religion or institution is correct, and which one is incorrect, in terms of the correct theology. In other words, the Court has protected religious orthodoxy against unorthodox interpretation and teachings and justified the criminalization of the latter.

Finally, the Court seems to take the phrase 'religious values' for granted without the need to explain how the impugned laws are inconsistent with 'religious values'. The phrase 'religious values' is ambiguous, and the Court has used it as a panacea to validate or invalidate law, whichever suits the Court. This unclear explanation did not assist our understanding of which values and whose religion(s) the Court refers to. The Court did not distinguish religious values from religious teachings and norms as in the state implementation of Islamic law, or with the communal values of the Indonesian society.

While it is sometimes exploited in the decisions of the Court, there is no clear pattern of how the phrase 'religious values' has been used in the Court's reasoning. The Court also justified state interference in determining religious deviation and in prosecuting religious minorities. We hope in future cases, when dealing with the phrase 'religious values' in national education, stipulated in Article 31(5), that the Court will have the chance to revisit its position and provide further clarification on the meaning of this important term.

References

Abū Zahrah, Muḥammad (no date) *Al-Jarīmah Wa al-'Uqūbah Fī al-Fiqh al-Islāmī: Al-'Uqūbah*. Cairo: Dār al-Fikr al-'Arabī.

Ahdar, Rex (2013) 'Is Secularism Neutral?' 26(3) *Ratio Juris* 404–429, doi: 10.1111/raju.12020.

Ahmed, Dawood and Elliot Bulmer (2017) *Limitation Clauses*. Second Edition. Stockholm: International IDEA.

al-Hay'ah al-Shar'iyyah li Bayt al-Zakāt (2019) *'Aḥkām Wa Fatāwā al-Zakāt Wa al-Ṣadaqāt Wa al-Nużur Wa al-Kafārāt*. Kuwait: Maktab al-Shu'ūn al-Shar'iyyah.

'Ālim, Yūsuf Ḥāmid al- (1994) *Al-Maqāṣid al-'Āmmah Li al-Sharī'ah al-Islāmiyyah*. Herndon, Virginia: The International Institute of Islamic Thought.

'Alwānī, Ṭāhā Jābir al- (2014) *Lā Ikrāha Fī Al-Dīn: Ishkāliyyah al-Riddah Wa al-Murtaddīn Min Ṣadr al-Islām Ilā al-Yaum*. Casablanca: al-Markaz al-Thaqāfī al-Ārabī.

Asshiddiqie, Jimly (no date) "'Tuhan' Dan Agama Dalam Konstitusi: Pergesekan Antara Ide-Ide "Godly Constitution Versus Godless Constitution"', http://www.jimly.com/makalah/namafile/130/Tuhan_Dalam_Konstitusi.pdf, accessed 24 June 2021.

Auda, Jaser (2007) *Maqāṣid Al-Sharī'ah as Philosophy of Islamic Law: A Systems Approach*. London: The International Institute of Islamic Thought.

'Awwā, Muḥammad Salīm al- (2006) *Fī Uṣūl Al-Niẓām al-Jinā'ī al-Islāmī: Dirāsah Muqāranah*. Cairo: Nahḍah Miṣr.

Basalim, Umar (2002) *Pro-Kontra Piagam Jakarta Di Era Reformasi*. Jakarta: Pustaka Indonesia Satu.

Bielefeldt, Heiner, Nazila Ghanea, and Michael Wiener (2016) *Freedom of Religion or Belief: An International Law Commentary*. Oxford: Oxford University Press.

Butt, Simon and Tim Lindsey (2012) *The Constitution of Indonesia: A Contextual Analysis*. Oxford and Portland, Oregon: Hart Publishing.

Cassel, Doug (1998) 'Universal Rights and Asian Culture: Indonesia Converts' 19(2) *Worldview Commentary*.

Chambers, Simone and Peter Nosco (eds) (2015) *Dissent on Core Beliefs: Religious and Secular Perspectives*. Cambridge: Cambridge University Press.

Clark, Dana L (2002) 'The World Bank and Human Rights: The Need for Greater Accountability' 15 *Harvard Human Rights Journal* 205.

Convention for the Protection of Human Rights and Fundamental Freedoms. Opened for signature 4 November 1950, 213 UNTS 221 (entered into force 3 September 1953).

Crouch, Melissa (2016) 'Constitutionalism, Islam and the Practice of Religious Deference: The Case of the Indonesian Constitutional Court' 16(2) *Australian Journal of Asian Law* 6: 1–15.

Crouch, Melissa A (2012). 'Law and Religion in Indonesia: The Constitutional Court and the Blasphemy Law' 7(1) *Asian Journal of Comparative Law* 3: 1–46, doi: 10.1017/S2194607800000582.

Duderija, Adis (ed) (2014) *Maqāṣid Al-Sharī'a and Contemporary Reformist Muslim Thought: An Examination*. New York: Palgrave Macmillan.

Elson, RE (2009) 'Another Look at the Jakarta Charter Controversy of 1945' 88 *Indonesia* 105–130.

Elson, RE (2013) 'Two Failed Attempts to Islamize the Indonesian Constitution' 28(3) *SOJOURN: Journal of Social Issues in Southeast Asia* 379–437.

Fenwick, Stewart (2017) *Blasphemy, Islam and the State: Pluralism and Liberalism in Indonesia*. London and New York: Routledge.

Gardbaum, Stephen (2006) 'Limiting Constitutional Rights' 4 *UCLA Law Review* 789–854.

Hosen, Nadirsyah (2002) 'Human Rights and Freedom of the Press in the Post-Soeharto Era: A Critical Analysis' 3(2) *Asia-Pacific Journal on Human Rights and the Law* 1–104.

Hosen, Nadirsyah (2005) 'Religion and the Indonesian Constitution: A Recent Debate' 36 *Journal of Southeast Asian Studies* 419.

Hosen, Nadirsyah (2007) *Shari'a and Constitutional Reform in Indonesia*. Singapore: ISEAS.

Hosen, Nadirsyah (2013) 'Religious Pluralism, Inclusive Secularism, and Democratic Constitutionalism: The Indonesian Experience' in Lili Zubaidah Rahim (ed) *Muslim Secular Democracy: Voices from Within*. New York: Palgrave Macmillan. pp 211–232.

Ibn Rushd, Abū al-Walīd (1982) *Bidāyah Al-Mujtahid Wa Nihāyah al-Muqtaṣid*. Sixth Edition. Volume 1. Beirut: Dār al-Maʿrifah.

International Covenant on Civil and Political Rights. Opened for signature 19 December 1966, 999 UNTS 171 (entered into force 23 March 1976).

International Covenant on Economic, Social and Cultural Rights. Opened for signature 16 December 1966, 993 UNTS 3 (entered into force 3 January 1976).

Isnur, Muhamad (ed) (2012) *Agama, Negara, Dan Hak Asasi Manusia: Proses Pengujian UU 1/PNPS/1965 Tentang Pencegahan, Penyalahgunaan, Dan/Atau Penodaan Agama Di Mahkamah Konstitusi*. Jakarta: LBH Jakarta.

Juwana, Hikmahanto (2003) 'Special Report: Assessing Indonesian's Human Right Practice in the Post-Soeharto Era' 7 *Singapore Journal of International & Comparative Law* 644–677.

Kamali, Mohammad Hashim (1992) 'Freedom of Religion in Islamic Law' 21(1) *Capital University Law Review* 63–82.

Kompas (1998) 'Presiden Habibie Minta Maaf', 16 August.

Kuru, Ahmet T (2009) *Secularism and State Policies toward Religion: The United States, France and Turkey*. New York: Cambridge University Press.

Kusuma, AB (ed) (2009) *Lahirnya Undang-Undang Dasar 1945: Memuat Salinan Dokumen Otentik Badan Oentoek Menyelidiki Oesaha2 Persiapan Kemerdekaan*. Revised. Jakarta: Badan Penerbit Fakultas Hukum Universitas Indonesia.

Mahfud MD, Moh (2006) *Membangun Politik Hukum, Menegakkan Konstitusi*. Jakarta: Pustaka LP3ES Indonesia.

Majelis Permusyawaratan Rakyat Republik Indonesia (2010a) *Risalah Perubahan Undang-Undang Dasar Negara Republik Indonesia Tahun 1945: Tahun Sidang 2000, Buku Enam*. Revised. Jakarta: Sekretariat Jenderal.

Majelis Permusyawaratan Rakyat Republik Indonesia (2010b) *Risalah Perubahan Undang-Undang Dasar Negara Republik Indonesia Tahun 1945: Tahun Sidang 2000, Buku Lima*. Revised. Jakarta: Sekretariat Jenderal.

Majelis Permusyawaratan Rakyat Republik Indonesia (2010c) *Risalah Perubahan Undang-Undang Dasar Negara Republik Indonesia Tahun 1945: Tahun Sidang 2000, Buku Tujuh*. Revised. Jakarta: Sekretariat Jenderal.

Majelis Permusyawaratan Rakyat Republik Indonesia (2010d) *Risalah Perubahan Undang-Undang Dasar Negara Republik Indonesia Tahun 1945: Tahun Sidang 2001, Buku Satu*. Revised. Jakarta: Sekretariat Jenderal.

Majelis Permusyawaratan Rakyat Republik Indonesia (2010e) *Risalah Perubahan Undang-Undang Dasar Negara Republik Indonesia Tahun 1945: Tahun Sidang 2002, Buku Dua*. Revised. Jakarta: Sekretariat Jenderal.

Majelis Permusyawaratan Rakyat Republik Indonesia (2010f) *Risalah Perubahan Undang-Undang Dasar Negara Republik Indonesia Tahun 1945: Tahun Sidang 2002, Buku Tiga.* Revised. Jakarta: Sekretariat Jenderal.

March, Andrew F (2011) 'The *Maqṣad* of *Ḥifẓ al-Dīn*: Is Liberal Religious Freedom Sufficient for the *Sharīʿah?*' 2(2) *Islam and Civilisational Renewal* 358–378.

Menchik, Jeremy (2014) 'Productive Intolerance: Godly Nationalism in Indonesia' 56(3) *Comparative Studies in Society and History* 591–621, doi: 10.1017/S0010417514000267.

Modarressi, Hossein (2016) 'Essential Islam: The Minimum That a Muslim Is Required to Acknowledge' in Camilla Adang et al, *Accusations of Unbelief in Islam: A Diachronic Perspective on* Takfīr. Leiden and Boston: Brill. pp 395–412.

Peter Petkoff (2012) '*Forum Internum* and *Forum Externum* in Canon Law and Public International Law with a Particular Reference to the Jurisprudence of the European Court of Human Rights' 7(3) *Religion & Human Rights* 183–214, doi: 10.1163/18710328-12341236.

Peters, Rudolph (2005) *Crime and Punishment in Islamic Law: Theory and Practice from the Sixteenth to the Twenty-First Century.* Cambridge: Cambridge University Press.

Pusat Bahasa Departemen Pendidikan Nasional (2001) *Kamus Besar Bahasa Indonesia.* Third Edition. Jakarta: Balai Pustaka.

Qarāḍāwī, Yūsuf al- (1973) *Fiqh Al-Zakāt: Dirāsah Muqāranah Li Aḥkāmihā Wa Falsafatihā Fī ḌawʾI al-Qurʾān Wa al-Sunnah.* Beirut: Muʾassasah al-Risālah.

Saeed, Abdullah and Hassan Saeed (2017). *Freedom of Religion, Apostasy and Islam.* London: Routledge.

Salim, Arskal (2008) *Challenging the Secular State: The Islamization of Law in Modern Indonesia.* Honolulu: University of Hawaii Press.

Singer, Amy (2008) *Charity in Islamic Societies.* Cambridge: Cambridge University Press.

Tim Penyusun Naskah Komprehensif Proses dan Hasil Perubahan UUD 1945 (2010) *Naskah Komprehensif Perubahan Undang-Undang Dasar Negara Republik Indonesia Tahun 1945: Latar Belakang, Proses, Dan Hasil Pembahasan 1999-2002, Buku IX Pendidikan Dan Kebudayaan.* Revised. Jakarta: Sekretariat Jenderal dan Kepaniteraan Mahkamah Konstitusi.

Universal Declaration of Human Rights. GA Res 217A (III), UN GAOR, UN Doc A/810 (10 December 1948).

Zainal Abidin Bagir, Asfinawati, Suhadi, and Renata Arianingtyas (2020) 'Limitations to Freedom of Religion or Belief in Indonesia: Norms and Practices' 15(1–2) *Religion & Human Rights,* 39–56. doi: 10.1163/18710328-BJA10003.

Zuḥaylī, Wahbah al- (2012) *Mawsūʿah al-Fiqh al-Islāmī Wa l-Qaḍāyā al-Muʿāṣirah.* Damascus: Dār al-Fikr, vol 13, pp 446–470.

Zuhri, Saifuddin (1987) *Berangkat Dari Pesantren.* Jakarta: Gunung Agung.

Constitutional Court Decisions

Decision 140/PUU-VII/2009.
Decision 84/PUU-X/2012.
Decision 86/PUU-X/2012.
Decision 56/PUU-XV/2017.
Decision 76/PUU-XVI/2018.

13

LGBT Rights and the Constitutional Court

Protecting Rights without Recognizing them?

Abdurrachman Satrio

Introduction

At the end of 2017, the Constitutional Court handed down one of its most contro-versial cases ('the *LGBT case*'). This case originated from a petition by conservative Muslim organizations under the banner of the Love Family Alliance (*Aliansi Cinta Keluarga*, AILA), which asked the Constitutional Court to interpret several provisions of the Criminal Code, including Article 292 that criminalizes adults who commit ob-scene acts against children. The petitioners asked the Constitutional Court to expand the interpretation of Article 292 in order to criminalize adults who have same-sex re-lations (Hendrianto 2018a).

The petitioners claimed that they wanted to protect the importance of marriage. In Indonesia, there is no law that prohibits same-sex relations, except in the special regions of Aceh where Islamic law (*qanun*) applies (Cammack 2016: 624–625). The petitioners argued that the 1945 Constitution recognizes religious values in Article 29, which states that: 'The state shall be based on the One and Only God.' According to the claimants, although the article does not refer to any one religion, it does place a duty on the state to protect religious values in society.[1] This petition appealed to conserva-tive Islamic views. It included a survey that alleged that the majority of Indonesians feel threatened by the existence of the LGBT (lesbian, gay, bisexual, and transgender) community and therefore claimed that most people would support the criminaliza-tion of same-sex relations (Reuters 2018).

As a result of this case, the Constitutional Court was under public pressure to crim-inalize same-sex relations. However the Court did not do this. Instead, in a split de-cision (5–4), the Court declared that it could not accept the claimants' petition to criminalize same-sex relations. The Court rejected the petition on the basis that it did not have the power to review it because only the legislature has the authority to create a new legal norm, especially one that related to criminal matters. In this decision, the Court advised the applicants to take their demands to the government and to legisla-tors in the People's Representative Council (*Dewan Perwakilan Rakyat*, DPR).[2]

In this decision, the Court did not make a bold interpretation in support of LGBT rights[3] and indeed failed to declare that the attempt to criminalize same-sex relations

---

[1] Constitutional Court Decision 46/PUU-XVI/2016, 58 (hereafter 'the *LGBT case*').
[2] The People's Representative Council is the lower house of the Indonesian Parliament.
[3] This chapter uses the term 'LGBT' rather than LGBTQI, as it is the phrase commonly used in Indonesia.

Abdurrachman Satrio, *LGBT Rights and the Constitutional Court* In: *Constitutional Democracy in Indonesia*. Edited by: Melissa Crouch, Oxford University Press. © Abdurrachman Satrio, 2023. DOI: 10.1093/oso/9780192870681.003.0013

was unconstitutional. The Court simply stated that it did not have any authority to decide this issue, so the petitioners' should instead submit their views as part of the process of revising the Criminal Code (*hereinafter the 'Draft Criminal Code'*), which was being discussed by the government and the People's Representative Council at that time.[4] Some human rights activists and constitutional law scholars were concerned by this decision (Hendrianto 2018a; Iskandar 2018) and expressed concerns that it failed to prevent future threats to LGBT rights. The Court exercised caution by avoiding taking a position on the issue and deferring to the legislative process. In its reasoning (*pertimbangan hukum*), the Court also emphasized that it is bound by the doctrine of judicial restraint.[5] Therefore, most constitutional scholars in Indonesia view the *LGBT case* as an example of the application of the doctrine of judicial restraint, rather than a case for the protection of human rights (Latipulhayat 2017; Faiz 2017).

In contrast to the views of most scholars, this chapter suggests that the *LGBT case* was implicitly able to protect the rights of LGBT people. The Constitutional Court decision is an example of what Mark Tushnet calls weak-form review, a type of judicial review that emphasizes dialogue between the court and the legislature (Tushnet 2013). Weak-form judicial review positions the political branches of government as the final interpreter of the constitution, allowing the legislature to reject or accept the Court's interpretation (Tushnet and Dixon 2014: 102). That is why Tushnet considers this model of judicial review suitable in cases relating to the fulfillment of socio-economic rights rather than civil and political rights, because in these cases the enforcement of rights has major implications for government budgets (Tushnet 2008: xi).

However, this chapter shows that the Constitutional Court in the *LGBT case* is able to use the weak-form technique in regard to civil and political rights. Apart from that, the *LGBT case* also shows that in a country that has transitioned in recent decades from authoritarianism to democracy, sometimes the weak-form review can be an alternative for the Constitutional Court to decide politically sensitive cases because this technique allows the court to still perform its function to protect human rights in a less confrontational manner.

The Political Background of the *LGBT Case*

The Constitutional Court petition to criminalize LGBT relations is closely related to the growing trends towards Islamic conservatism in Indonesian society. In 2016, there was false news claiming that LGBT people are a disease in society and this discourse was shamelessly exploited by the government, politicians, and religious leaders to increase their popularity (Larasati et al 2017). This created a hostile environment for the LGBT community (Siregar 2018), which led to a petition to criminalize same-sex relations in the Constitutional Court. Historically, there is a variety of traditional expressions of gender in Indonesia. This includes those known as '*Bancis*' and '*Warias*' (the terms to describe male-to-female transgender people) and the recognition

---

[4] The *LGBT case*, 453.
[5] The *LGBT case*, 444–445.

of the third gender alongside heterosexual men and women by some communities (Polymenopoulo 2018: 30–32).

The growth of Islamic conservatism cannot be separated from Indonesia's transition to democracy in 1998. Before the transition, for thirty-two years (1966–1998) Indonesia was under the grip of Suharto's New Order authoritarian regime. During his reign, Suharto was threatened by public support for a greater role for Islam. That is why his government repressed Islamic political groups and limited the use of Islamic identity in public spaces (Lindsey and Pausacker 2016: 1).

This situation changed near the end of the New Order when in 1990 Soeharto's government sought to generate popular support by openly sponsoring the establishment of the Indonesian Muslim Intellectual's Association (ICMI) —the only major Islamic organization that was established during the New Order (Ramage 1995). In 1998, these changes increased when the New Order collapsed, and Indonesia entered the era of reformation (popularly known as 'reformasi'). At this time, almost all restrictions on the use of Islamic identity were lifted. In this era, comprehensive amendments were made to the 1945 Constitution to democratize the political system. The amendments established new organs of state tasked with the duty of limiting governmental powers including a new Constitutional Court with the power of judicial review, expanding the human rights provision, limiting the president's term of office, and introducing a direct mechanism for the election of the president (Harijanti and Lindsey 2006: 138).

The new political atmosphere created space for Islamic groups with a political goal to ensure that shari'a (Islamic law) be enforced by the state (Crouch 2013; Lindsey and Pausacker 2016: 1). The concept of the state in Indonesia has been described by Jeremy Menchik (2014: 599–600) as 'godly nationalism'. In this form, the state is positioned in the middle between religion and secularism. However, this does not mean the state has a neutral position on religious matters. In fact, the state views a good citizen as the one who believes in God and uses that belief to motivate his or her behaviour. That is why godly nationalism requires the state to promote religious values. This strange position was caused by a sharp disagreement between Indonesia's founding fathers and mothers during the drafting process of the 1945 Constitution, where some wanted Indonesia to make Islam the basis of the state, while others wanted Indonesia to be a country that did not prioritize one particular religion. As a result of these competing views, Indonesia took a middle ground in Article 29 of the 1945 Constitution:'The State shall be based on the One and Only God'. The provision allows for the accommodation of the values of all religions (pan-religious value) but does not give a special position to one religion (Iskandar 2019).

The ambiguous position at first did not create a problem, because, during the New Order era, the Soeharto government tended to limit the Islamic political movement. However, the situation changed drastically after the reformasi, with no more obstacles to the Islamic political movement. Conservative Islamic groups now often use Article 29 of the 1945 Constitution to expand their influence. They argue that the statement 'Belief in one and only God' is an embodiment of the monotheist God that is derived from Islamic values (Iskandar 2019). By drawing on this constitutional provision and offering this interpretation, they aim to force the state to enforce Islamic values (shari'a-isation or syariahisasi). One of their strategies is to propose many regulations at the regional and national levels to implement aspects of Islamic law (Crouch 2009).

This idea is problematic since there are many interpretations regarding the Islamic penal tradition among Muslim scholars. However, as stated by Lukito, the proponents of Islamic law seem more concerned with the orthodox and traditional understanding that views Islamic penal tradition 'as not receptive towards the modern view of punishment' (Lukito 2016: 410). The petition to the Constitutional Court in the *LGBT case* is also an example of efforts to introduce this orthodox understanding of Islamic penal law.

Despite the benefits that *reformasi* brought to conservative Islamic groups to strengthen their influence in Indonesian constitutional politics, it also gave the same benefits of freedom of speech and association to groups who are fighting for pluralism and human rights. In fact, there is evidence that after the *reformasi* the groups that engaged in the field of pluralism and human rights—usually cause lawyers and non-government organizations (NGOs)—often use the Constitutional Court as a means to influence policy (Crouch 2011; Lindsey and Crouch 2013: 624-625). However, human rights NGOs often do not have the same level of social support as conservative Islamic groups. This is why NGOs rely more on their ability to create legal arguments to influence policymakers, and this strategy is suited to advocacy through the Constitutional Court (Nardi 2018: 250).

The involvement of human rights NGOs in many of the Constitutional Court's cases is also illustrated by Dominic J Nardi (2018). From 2003 to 2013, in cases of judicial review handled by the Constitutional Court, NGOs were the stakeholders who submitted the second highest number of petitions. Specifically, human rights NGOs are the most frequent NGOs to file a petition. Not only that, but Nardi's (2018: 255) study also found that the Constitutional Court often cited arguments presented by NGOs in their petition. This is a sign that the Constitutional Court relies on the data presented by NGOs when deciding a case and the Constitutional Court has also openly admitted this. This point has been acknowledged by one of the former justices of the Constitutional Court, Maruarar Siahaan. According to Siahaan, public opinion and NGOs are important sources of support for the Court. That is why the Constitutional Court has sometimes allowed public pressure to influence its decisions. As a result, the NGOs and public opinions are effective weapons to protect the Constitutional Court from intervention by the political elite (Mietzner 2010: 414).

In the *LGBT case*, human rights NGOs were actively opposing the case, such as the Institute for Criminal Justice Reform (ICJR), a prominent NGO that works on the issues of criminal reform.[6] The ICJR is one of the related parties that opposed the position of the petitioners (AILA). The ICJR influenced the Constitutional Court decision to reject the petition during the hearing process. The ICJR argued that the concerns of the petitioner should be dealt with by the legislature rather than the Constitutional Court. ICJR also explained in its argument that the government and the legislature had discussed the matter claimed by the petitioner in the Draft Criminal Code, so they suggested the petitioner channel their aspirations in the drafting process of the Draft Criminal Code.[7] Surprisingly, the Constitutional Court's reasons were very similar to

---

[6] The ICJR's mission is to change the orientation of Indonesian criminal law to make it an instrument to support the democratic political system and for the protection of fundamental rights. See https://icjr.or.id/about-us/ (accessed 21 March 2020).

[7] The *LGBT case*, 219–220.

the ICJR argument, stating that the claimants aspirations should be channelled to the legislative drafting process of the Draft Criminal Code since it was the authority of the legislature to introduce limitations on human rights.

The Constitutional Court can still claim it was not influenced by the ICJR arguments (Sahbani 2017) because in the Court's reasons it only referred to its previous decisions, namely Decision 132/PUU-XIII/2015 which confirms that the Court cannot make new norms in cases relating to criminal matters.[8] However, the fact that the Constitutional Court frequently cites arguments from NGOs in its decisions thus strengthens the notion that the Constitutional Court's reasons in the *LGBT case* were influenced by the ICJR argument. Moreover, it is also unreasonable for the Constitutional Court to reject the petition by using a reason if what the petitioner was asked is outside their authority. If the petitioner's request was outside the authority of the Court, then the Court should have denied (*tidak menerima*) the petitioner's claim in the standing examination process and not rejected it (*menolak*).[9] To have standing, the petitioner must show in their petition that the Constitutional Court has the authority to handle their claim.[10] Standing was established in this case, and so the Constitutional Court could also receive the ICJR's proposal after the question of standing was resolved.

The Attempt to Criminalize Same-Sex Relations: A Surprising Result

At the end of 2017, when the *LGBT case* was decided by the Constitutional Court, the decision was not immediately praised by human rights activists. Even though the decision rejected AILA's petition, this ruling also allowed for the possibility that same-sex relations may be criminalized by the legislature.

Four Constitutional Court justices had dissenting opinions in the *LGBT case*. These four dissenters, including the then chief justice, Arief Hidayat,[11] considered that homosexual activities contradicted the 1945 Constitution, because in their view the 1945 Constitution was based on religious values as reflected in Article 29 of the 1945 Constitution that stated: 'The State shall be based on the One and Only God.'[12]

The dissenting opinion gave some support to members of the public who felt that the majority had wrongly decided the case (Rahadian 2017). In fact, this dissenting opinion almost became the majority view. At that time Hidayat together with Patrialis Akbar were the two justices who seemed to be the most vocal in supporting the criminalization of same-sex relations. In mid-2017, Justice Akbar lost his position suddenly

---

[8] Ibid 444–445.

[9] There are three types of Constitutional Court decisions for judicial review cases. First, the Court can deny (*tidak dapat menerima*) the petition, in cases where the claimant does not fulfill the standing requirement. Second, the Court may declare that a specified article, sub-article, and/or parts of a law are unconstitutional, and in this case, the petition for judicial review shall be granted (*dikabulkan*). Third, the Court can reject (*menolak*) the petition, when the challenged law remains constitutional: (Hendrianto 2018b: 63).

[10] See Art 51A(2) Law 24/2003, which requires every petitioner in the judicial review case to show whether the Court has the authority to handle their petition.

[11] The *LGBT case*, 453–467.

[12] Ibid 465–466.

due to a bribery case. If he had not been subject to criminal charges of corruption, it is very possible that the Constitutional Court would have decided otherwise and criminalized same-sex relations. Fortunately, Akbar's replacement, Saldi Isra, an academic-cum-activist, has more liberal views, and joined the majority of justices who decided to reject this case.

The dissenting opinion in this case also reveals the differences in views on the bench. In Indonesia, a dissenting justice can request his dissent to not be included in the decision to give the impression of legitimacy for the Court decision (Butt 2018: 12). However, in the *LGBT case*, the dissenting decision of the four justices (Arief Hidayat, Aswanto, Wahiduddin Adams, and Anwar Usman) was included in the final decision. This shows the sharply different views among the Constitutional Court justices about this issue (Kelemen 2013: 1365). There is also evidence that Arief Hidayat was appointed to the Constitutional Court by the legislature because of his personal views opposing the LGBT community and atheism. One of the members of the legislature, Dewa Pasek Suardika, explained that the legislature voted in favour of Hidayat because of his opposition to same-sex marriage as Hidayat has publicly declared that there is no constitutional right to same-sex marriage under the Indonesian Constitution (Hendrianto 2018b: 217–218).

This case was disappointing for LGBT communities. So why did this decision not offer more explicit protection for LGBT rights? The answer to this can be seen in the development of the attempts to criminalize LGBT in the legislature.

In the *LGBT case*, the Constitutional Court avoided public pressure by stating that the legislature is the proper institution to make policies that can criminalize same-sex relations. In this decision, the Constitutional Court acknowledges that the case was related to the issue of human rights restrictions, so they must comply with Article 28J of the Constitution that only permits the state to limit rights based on limited justifications such as national security. Any such limitation requires a law whose formation involves the legislature as the people's representative.[13] That is why the Constitutional Court suggested that the petitioners channel their aspirations to the drafting process of the Draft Criminal Code.[14]

The Constitutional Court's choice to direct the claimants' aspirations into the legislature turned out to have unexpected results. In early 2018, not long after the *LGBT case* had been decided, the legislature rejected the proposal to criminalize same-sex relations in the Draft Criminal Code (Wardhani 2019). This refusal cannot be separated from the Constitutional Court's choice to borrow the ICJR argument in the *LGBT case* as before the *LGBT case*, the government and parliament had already tried to criminalize same-sex relations in the Draft Criminal Code.[15] The ICJR, as an NGO that engages in advocacy on criminal reform issues, rejected the proposal to criminalize same-sex relations. Together with other NGOs, a movement called the National Alliance for Reform of the Criminal Code (*Aliansi Nasional Reformasi, KUHP*) was

---

[13] Ibid 442.
[14] Ibid 453.
[15] See Art 454 in the March 2018 version of the Draft Criminal Code, which regulates sexual abuse by same-sex persons. This article has been criticized because the new penal code already contains a provision on sexual abuse. So the existence of a specific article about sexual abuse by same-sex persons is suspected of discriminating against the LGBT community (Anggara, 2018: 93-94).

formed. The National Alliance for Reform of the Criminal Code channelled their rejection through their involvement in the government and the legislative hearing process when formulating the Draft Criminal Code (Reformasi KUHP 2015).

Since the issue of the recognition and protection of the LGBT community is a very sensitive topic for many Indonesians, the majority of politicians have agreed to the idea of criminalizing same-sex relations. The National Alliance for Reform of the Criminal Code has advocated for the rights of the LGBT community (Rahmawati 2022). To convince the legislators not to criminalize same-sex relations, they also relied on economic arguments based on data that shows that the Indonesian prisons are over-populated,[16] so if the legislators criminalize same-sex relations, the prisons will become more crowded and impact the government budget (Anggara 2019: 81). As a result of the advocacy of the National Alliance, the government realized that it does not have the capacity to enforce the criminalization of same-sex relations.[17]

The decision of legislators not to criminalize same-sex relations was surprising because it happened at a time when many Indonesian people still see the LGBT community as a threat to religious morals. In my opinion, this successful advocacy campaign cannot be separated from the Constitutional Court's choice to move the claimants' aspirations in the *LGBT case* to the legislative path.

The *LGBT Case*: The Pragmatic Use of Weak-Form Review

According to Mark Tushnet, the weak-form technique is a form of judicial review which emphasizes the dialogue between the constitutional court and the legislative body. It places political institutions as the last interpreter of the constitution, where they can re-examine the court interpretation and then decide to accept or reject it through the laws they make to follow up the court decision (Tushnet 2013: 2251). Tushnet considered these techniques more suitable for application in cases related to socio-economic rights because the enforcement of socio-economic rights is dependent on the financial capabilities of the executive and legislative. He argues it is more appropriate if the final decision regarding the enforcement of socio-economic rights is held by the political branches of government through their choice of policy since they will be more aware of the limits of their abilities to enforce those rights (Tushnet 2013: 2258–2259).

On the contrary, Tushnet suggests civil and political rights can be enforced through a strong-form technique or a form of judicial review that positions the constitutional court as the last interpreter of the constitution, where the court's interpretation can only be defeated through constitutional amendments that require a super-majority or through the court's interpretation to repudiate an old decision, because these types of rights can be upheld directly, and it also does not have the same financial implications

---

[16] Erasmus Napitupulu, Executive Director of ICJR, acknowledged the use of this strategy through personal communication with the author on 16 October 2019.

[17] See the 2019 version of the Draft Criminal Code, especially in Art 418, which does not distinguish the conditions for a person to be subjected with the crime of sexual abuse, whether it was performed heterosexually or homosexually (Amindoni 2022).

for government, so it would be better for the court to issue a constitutional interpretation that forces the legislators to follow their decision in the context of civil and political rights (Tushnet 2013: 2260).

By interpreting whether the authority to limit a person's rights can only be performed through laws, and emphasizing that they cannot make a new norm, the Constitutional Court in the *LGBT case*, is conducting a weak-form review, because it made the political branches of government the last interpreters of constitutional norms. The Constitutional Court's choice to give the legislators authority to make a final decision about this case was clearly unusual because they could have accepted the petitioner's claim and formed a new norm as exemplified in some of their previous cases,[18] or they could have rejected the petition on the grounds that the petitioner's claim was unconstitutional since the 1945 Constitution has several clauses that can protect LGBT people from discrimination such as Article 27, which mentions equality before the law or Article 28D(1), which states that 'every person shall be entitled to recognition, guaranty, protection, and equitable legal certainty as well as equal treatment before the law' (Wieringa 2019: 3).

Interestingly, the *LGBT case* is related to the enforcement of civil and political rights, given that the essence of this case is an attempt to discriminate against sexual minorities. Thus, the *LGBT case* proves that in certain situations weak-form review can be performed to uphold civil and political rights, because the efforts to enforce the criminalization of same-sex relations would require significant financial investment by the government. This shows that if the traditional categorization of rights which, based on positive–negative dichotomy cannot be maintained, since the civil and political rights which are seen as having a negative dimension or require the state to not intervene in the implementation of this right by citizens may have a positive dimension (Klatt 2015: 354–355).

This case also reveals that sometimes the application of the weak-form technique might be appropriate in some politically sensitive cases that are handled by the Constitutional Court. As argued by Stephen Garbaum (2015: 308), a country that has just transitioned to democracy is not yet completely stable, so there is a greater risk that political institutions have a tendency to weaken the independence of the constitutional court. This is because these countries do not have a tradition to respect the independence of the court as a result of their experience under the authoritarian regime. Gardbaum suggests that in these countries it would be better to prioritize the independence of the constitutional court rather than strengthening the court's power to invalidate legislation. One of the most appropriate ways to maintain the independence of the constitutional court, according to Gardbaum (2015: 309), is to apply weak-form techniques that emphasize dialogue between the constitutional court and political institutions and place political institutions as the last interpreter of the Constitution. This choice will place the constitutional court as partner to the political branches of government when forming laws. On the contrary, if the constitutional court positions itself as the final interpreter of the constitution, it has the potential to make political

---

[18] See the Decision 102/PUU-VII/2009 (*Electoral roll* case); Decision 11/PUU-VIII/2010 (the *Panwaslu* case); Decision 34/PUU-X/2012; and Decision 110-111-112-113/PUU-VII/2009 (the *left over votes* case).

institutions see it as an opponent or potential rival, which in turn can trigger political attacks that threaten its independence (Gardbaum 2015: 306).

In the Indonesian context, Gardbaum's approach is quite relevant, given that political institutions do not have a tradition that respects the independence of the court as a result of the past successive authoritarian regimes (Nardi 2013). There was also evidence of political institutions in Indonesia attempting to launch political attacks when it felt that the Constitutional Court acted too strongly. Some of these efforts include the attempt in 2008 by the Susilo Bambang Yudhoyono's administration to overthrow Jimly Asshiddiqie—the first chief justice of the Court—from his position as chief justice. They did this by convincing several justices of the Constitutional Court not to vote for him in the process to re-elect the chief justice's position. This attempt was carried out by Yudhoyono's administration due to the Constitutional Court's decision that invalidated the state budget (Hendrianto 2018b: 157–159). Prior to this, in 2011, parliament passed several laws that amended the Constitutional Court Law, and tried to limit the power of the Constitutional Court. For example, the laws prohibit the Court from making a decision that goes beyond what the claimant requested (commonly known as 'ultra petita'). It also forbids the Constitutional Court from issuing declarations of 'conditionally constitutional' or 'conditionally unconstitutional' (Hendrianto 2018b: 171). The reason behind this amendment was that at that time the government and the legislature felt that the Constitutional Court, under the leadership of its second chief justice, Mahfud MD, often acted beyond its jurisdiction. This amendment was issued to return the Constitutional Court to the original terms of its mandate (Roux and Siregar 2016: 14).

Responding to an amendment that was carried out in 2011, the Constitutional Court found several articles that limit its authority to be unconstitutional.[19] At that time, Indonesia's political constellation was heavily fragmented, so even though the legislature and the government succeeded in making laws that weakened the Constitutional Court, it was difficult for them to find a way around the Constitutional Court's decision which annulled many core articles of the law (Roux and Siregar 2016: 13). Moreover, in 2011, the Constitutional Court also enjoyed strong public support and the Court built upon this to assert its authority against political institutions (Siregar 2013). Although the Constitutional Court enjoyed strong public support under the leadership of chief justices Jimly Asshiddiqie and Mahfud MD, this did not last.

By 2017, the Constitutional Court no longer enjoyed the same level of public support. In 2013, public support for the Court had dropped dramatically after the arrest of its third chief justice, Akil Mochtar, on bribery charges (Nardi 2018: 254). In 2016, Justice Patrialis Akbar was arrested on similar grounds. In addition, in 2017 the Joko Widodo government also managed to consolidate its power by obtaining the support of more than 60 per cent of the votes in the legislature (Hendrianto and Siregar 2017: 93). The government also publicly indicated that it wanted to criminalize same-sex relations (Kine 2017), and it had widespread public support. The Constitutional Court was therefore in a much more difficult position in the *LGBT* case.

---

[19] Constitutional Court Decision 48/PUU-IX/2011.

For that reason, the Constitutional Court's choice to reject the petition by borrowing the ICJR arguments and applying a weak-form technique is a clever strategy. The Constitutional Court did not explicitly protect LGBT rights in order to avoid public backlash. Of course, the Constitutional Court was not completely free from public criticism, with some people perceiving the decision to legalize LGBT rights. However, this criticism did not affect the legitimacy of the Court.[20] The majority justices sought to protect LGBT rights in a way that balanced internal and external pressures on the court (Garoupa and Ginsburg 2009).

But the most important point is that the Constitutional Court's decision reduced the momentum gained by the conservative Islamic movement to criminalize same-sex relations. The Constitutional Court's hearing process is open to the public. This situation coupled with media coverage of the Constitutional Court's trial process (Hendrianto 2016), meant that the AILA petition made the headlines in several Indonesian media outlets (Ginanjar 2016). This publicity generated support for the proposal to criminalize same-sex relations.

The conservative Islamic groups then shifted their efforts to the drafting process of the Draft Criminal Code. In contrast to the judicial review process, the legislative process usually occurs behind closed doors and the media are not able to cover it as intensely as in the Constitutional Court trial process, due to the ability of the political elites to control the mainstream media (Tapsell and Dewi 2019: 351). The public were also distracted for several reasons. The legislative process is often prolonged. The drafting process of the Draft Criminal Code was also crowded with many other unrelated topics that were discussed.[21] The efforts to criminalize same-sex relations through the Draft Criminal Code failed to obtain public support as it did during the *LGBT case*.

Overall, in this situation the National Alliance for Reform of the Criminal Code succeeded to thwart the efforts to criminalize same-sex relations by silently persuading the government and the legislature not to do so, based on economic arguments.

Conclusion

The *LGBT case* is an interesting example of how the Constitutional Court used its power pragmatically to implicitly protect the rights of sexual minorities. Although scholars like Tushnet doubted that weak-form review would be able to uphold civil and political rights, the Constitutional Court was able to protect the LGBT community from attempts to criminalize them by some conservative Islamic groups (AILA) that had wide public support. By holding that the authority to criminalize same-sex relations is in the hands of the legislators (the government and the DPR), and not in its power to review the law, the Constitutional Court succeeded in reducing public

---

[20] This happened because some supporters of the proposal to criminalize LGBT still perceived that this decision was not intended to legalize LGBT rights in Indonesia (Muhammadin 2017).

[21] There are some crucial issues which were discussed in the Draft Criminal Code other than the criminalization of LGBT, including the death penalty, legal pluralism, adultery, terrorism, corruption, narcotics, and the *lese majeste* provision (CNN 2009).

support for this proposal and prevented efforts to amend the Criminal Code. The Draft Criminal Code has not yet become law, so there remains future concern that same-sex relations may still be criminalized.

This case also provides important lessons for the constitutional courts in a fragile democracy when deciding politically sensitive cases, especially in a country where political institutions do not adhere to a tradition of respect for the independence of the court. In this situation, maintaining the independence of the constitutional court is far more important than strengthening its power, so using the weak-form technique rather than the strong-form as exemplified by the Constitutional Court in the *LGBT case* can be an alternative. In addition to being able to maintain the ability of the constitutional court to protect the values of human rights and democracy, this technique is also able to maintain the court's legitimacy in the eyes of the public.

References

Amindoni, Ayomi (2022) 'RKUHP: Wacana kriminalisasi LGBT, 'Indonesia akan jadi negara paria''. *BBC Indonesia*, https://www.bbc.com/indonesia/indonesia-61567481, accessed 3 August 2022.

Anggara et al (2019) *Kebangkitan Penal Populisme di Indonesia*. Jakarta: Institute of Criminal Justice Reform.

Anggara et al (2018) *Catatan dan Rekomendasi ICJR terhadap beberapa ketentuan dalam RKUHP*. Jakarta: Institute for Criminal Justice Reform.

Butt, Simon (2018) 'The Function of Judicial Dissent in Indonesia's Constitutional Court' 4 *Constitutional Review* 1–26.

Cammack, Mark (2016) 'The Punishment of Islamic Sex Crimes in a Modern Legal System: The Islamic Qanun of Aceh Indonesia' 45 *Southwestern Law Review* 595–630.

CNN Indonesia (2019) 'RKUHP Fokus Tujuh Isu Krusial, Ditargetkan Tuntas Juli', *CNN Indonesia*, https://www.cnnindonesia.com/nasional/20190628204118-12-407481/rkuhp-fokus-tujuh-isu-krusial-ditargetkan-tuntas-juli, accessed 18 March 2020.

Crouch, Melissa (2013) *Law and Religion in Indonesia: Conflict and the Courts in West Java*. New York: Routledge.

Crouch, Melissa (2011) 'Cause Lawyering, the Legal Profession and the Courts in Indonesia: The Bar Association Controversy' *LawASIA Journal* 63–86.

Crouch, Melissa (2009) 'Religious Regulations in Indonesia: Failing Vulnerable Groups?' 43(2) *Review of Indonesian and Malaysian Affairs* 53–103.

Faiz, Pan Mohamad (2017) 'Judicial Restraint vs Judicial Activism' 130 *Majalah Konstitusi* 8–9.

Gardbaum, Stephen (2015) 'Are Strong Constitutional Courts Always a Good Thing for New Democracies?' 53 *Columbia Journal of Transnational Law* 285–320.

Garoupa, Nuno and Tom Ginsburg (2009) 'Judicial Audiences and Reputation: Perspectives from Comparative Law' 47 *Columbia Journal of Transnational Law* 451–490.

Ginanjar, Ging (2016) 'Mengapa ada upaya mempidanakan LGBT di MK?', *BBC Indonesia*, https://www.bbc.com/indonesia/berita_indonesia/2016/08/160804_indonesia_lgbt_mk, accessed 18 March 2020.

Harijanti, Susi Dwi and Tim Lindsey (2006) 'Indonesian General Election Tests the Amended Constitution and the New Constitutional Court' 4 *International Journal of Constitutional Law* 138–150.

Hendrianto, Stefanus and Fritz Siregar (2017) 'Indonesia: Development in Indonesian Constitutional Law' in R Albert et al (eds) *2016 Global Review of Constitutional Law*. Boston: ICONnect-Clough Center. pp 93–97.

Hendrianto, Stefanus (2018a) 'Not #LoveWins: On the Indonesian LGBT Case' *International Journal of Constitutional Law Blog*, http://www.iconnectblog.com/not-love-wins-on-theind onesian-, accessed 21 March 2020.

Hendrianto, Stefanus (2018b) *Law and Politics of Constitutional Courts Indonesia and the Search for Judicial Heroes*. London, New York: Routledge.

Hendrianto, Stefanus (2016) 'The Puzzle of Judicial Communication in Indonesia: The Media, The Court and the Chief Justice' in Richard Davis and David Taras (eds) *Justices and Journalists: The Global Perspective*. Cambridge: Cambridge University Press. pp 141–163.

Iskandar, Pranoto (2019) 'Religious Constitutionalism: An Indonesian-esque interpretive venture' 2 *Oxford University of Comparative Law Forum*, https://ouclf.iuscomp.org/religi ous-constitutionalism-an-indonesian-esque-interpretive-venture/#more-683, accessed 29 January 2020.

Iskandar, Pranoto (2018) 'Another take on LGBT: No reason to cheer', *Jakarta Post*, https://www. thejakartapost.com/news/2018/01/13/another-take-lgbt-no-reason-cheer.html, accessed 21 March 2020.

Kelemen, Katalin (2013) 'Dissenting Opinion in Constitutional Courts' 14 *German Law Journal* 1345–1371.

Kine, Phelim (2017) 'Indonesian Religion Minister Contradictory LGBT "Embrace"', *Human Rights Watch*, https://www.hrw.org/news/2017/12/19/indonesian-religion-ministers-contra dictory-lgbt-embrace, accessed 18 March 2020.

Klatt, Matthias (2015) 'Positive Rights: Who Decides? Judicial Review in Balance' 13 *International Journal of Constitutional Law* 354–382.

Larasati, Ajeng et al (2017) *LGBT=Nuklir? Indonesia Darurat Fobia*. Jakarta : Lembaga Bantuan Hukum Masyarakat.

Latipulhayat, Atip (2017) 'Editorial: Mendudukan Kembali Judicial Activism dan Judicial Restraint dalam Kerangka Demokrasi' 4 *Padjadjaran Jurnal Ilmu Hukum* i–vi.

Lindsey, Tim and Helen Pausacker (2016) 'Introduction' in Tim Lindsey and Helen Pausacker (eds) Religion, Law, and *Intolerance in Indonesia*. New York: Routledge. pp 1–15.

Lindsey, Tim and Melissa Crouch (2013) 'Cause Lawyers in Indonesia: A House Divided' 31(3) *Wisconsin International Law Journal* 620–645.

Lukito, Ratno (2016) 'Islamisation as Legal Intolerance: The Case of GARIS in Cianjur, West Java' 54(2) *Al-Jami'ah* 393–425.

Menchik, Jeremy (2014) 'Productive Intolerance: Godly Nationalism in Indonesia' 56(3) *Comparative Study in Society and History* 591–621.

Mietzner, Marcus (2010) 'Political Conflict Resolution and Democratic Consolidation in Indonesia: The Role of the Constitutional Court' 10 *Journal of East Asian Studies* 397–424.

Muhammadin, Fajri Matahati (2017) 'Putusan MK tentang LGBT: Menelusuri Akar Kesalahpahaman', *Republika.co.id*, https://www.republika.co.id/berita/jurnalisme-warga/ wacana/17/12/17/p13ola291-putusan-mk-tentang-lgbt-menelusuri-akar-kesalahpahaman, accessed 5 April 2020.

Nardi, Dominic J (2018) 'Can NGOs Change the Constitution? Civil Society and Indonesian Constitutional Court' 40(2) *Contemporary Southeast Asia* 247–278.

Nardi, Dominic J (2013) 'A Comparative Analysis of Judicial Accountability in the People's Republic of China and New Order Indonesia' 4(1) *Yonsei Law Journal* 1–41.

Polymenopoulo, Eleni (2018) 'LGBT Rights in Indonesia: A Human Rights Perspectives' 19 *Asia-Pacific Journal on Human Rights and the Law* 27–44.

Rahadian, Lalu (2017) "MUI Pertanyakan Putusan MK yang Tolak Kriminalisasi LGBT", *Tirto,* https://tirto.id/mui-pertanyakan-putusan-mk-yang-tolak-kriminalisasi-lgbt-cBMh,   accessed 5 June 2020.

Rahmawati, Maidina (2022) 'RKUHP: Wacana Kriminalisasi LGBT, 'Indonesia akan jadi Negara Paria', *Aliansi Nasional Reformasi KUHP,* https://reformasikuhp.org/rkuhp-wacana-kriminalisasi-lgbt-indonesia-akan-jadi-negara-paria/, accessed 3 August 2022.

Ramage, Douglas E (1995) *Politics in Indonesia: Democracy, Islam and the Ideology of Tolerant.* London, New York: Routledge.

Reuters (2018) 'Most Indonesians feel "threatened" by LGBT Community survey', Reuters, https://www.reuters.com/article/us-indonesia-lgbt/most-indonesians-feel-threatened-by-lgbt-community-survey-idUSKBN1FE1KG, accessed 29 January 2020.

Reformasi KUHP, Aliansi Nasional (2015) 'Aliansi Nasional Reformasi KUHP dan Dirjen PP Kemenkumham sepakat dorong pembahasan Rancangan KUHP', *Institute for Criminal Justice Reform,* https://icjr.or.id/aliansi-nasional-reformasi-kuhp-dan-ditjen-pp-kemenkum ham-sepakat-dorong-pembahasan-rancangan-kuhp/, accessed 4 May 2020.

Roux, Theunis and Fritz Siregar (2016) 'Trajectories of Curial Power: The Rise, Fall and Partial Rehabilitation of the Indonesian Constitutional Court' 16(2) *Australian Journal of Asian Law* 1–21.

Sahbani, Agus (2017) 'MK Tegaskan Tak Bisa Kriminalisasi Delik Kesusilaan', *Hukumonline* https://www.hukumonline.com/berita/baca/lt5a38f093ef7d0/mk-tegaskan-tak-bisa-krimin alisasi-delik-kesusilaan/, accessed 29 January 2020.

Siregar, Kiki. (2018) 'Moral panic target Indonesia's LGBT community', *Jakarta Post,* https://www.thejakartapost.com/news/2018/11/18/moral-panic-targets-indonesias-lgbt-commun ity.html, accessed 29 January 2020.

Siregar, Fritz. (2013) 'Indonesian Constitutional Politics', *International Journal of Constitutional Law Blog,* http://www.iconnectblog.com/2013/10/indonesianconstitutional-politics, accessed 5 April 2020.

Tapsell, Ross and Sita Dewi (2019) 'The Media Megaspectacles and Transparency in the Courts', in M Crouch (ed) *The Politics of Court Reform: Judicial Change and Legal Culture in Indonesia.* Cambridge: Cambridge University Press. pp 334–352.

Tushnet, Mark (2013) 'Relation Between Political Constitutionalism and the Weak-Form Review' 14(12) *German Law Journal* 2249–2263.

Tushnet, Mark (2008) *Weak Courts, Strong Rights Judicial Review and Social Welfare Rights in Comparative Constitutional Law.* Princeton: Princeton University Press.

Tushnet, Mark and Rosalind Dixon (2014) 'Weak-Form Review and its Constitutional Relatives: An Asian Perspective' in R Dixon and T Ginsburg (eds) *Comparative Constitutional Law in Asia.* Cheltenham: Edward Elgar. pp 102–119.

Wardhani, Wulan Kusuma (2019) 'Aliansi Nasional: RKUHP Masih Berpotensi Kriminalisasi Kelompok Rentan', *Magdalene,* https://magdalene.co/story/aliansi-nasional-rkuhp-masih-berpotensi-kriminalisasi-kelompok-rentan, accessed 4 May 2020.

Wieringa, Saskia Eleonora (2019) 'Criminalisation of Homosexuality in Indonesia: The Role of the Constitution and Civil Society' 20 *Australian Journal of Asian Law* 1–19.

14

Legal Certainty in the Indonesian Constitutional Court

A Critique and Friendly Suggestion

Mark Cammack[1]

Introduction

In 2001 Indonesia's People's Consultative Council (*Majelis Permusyarawatan Rakyat*, MPR) approved an amendment to the Constitution mandating the creation of a Constitutional Court with the power to review the conformity of laws with the Constitution. Two years later, the People's Representative Assembly (*Dewan Perwakilan Rakyat*, DPR) implemented the constitutional mandate with the passage of the Constitutional Court Law prescribing rules for the appointment of judges and regulating court organization and procedure. Nine Constitutional Court justices were sworn in on 16 August 2003, and in December of 2004 the Court announced its first decisions.

By some accounts, it was not the intention of the creators of the Constitutional Court to charter a tribunal with broad powers to review the constitutionality of legislation. According to this version of events, the principal reason motivating the creation of a constitutional court was to impose constraints on the legislative branch's power to impeach the president, and the Court's constitutional review authority was added so the Court would not be left with nothing to do. But as one observer has noted, if the Court was initially regarded as a joke, it is a joke that in short order turned serious (Hendrianto 2018: 41). In its very first decision, the Court invalidated in its entirety a statute regulating the country's electric power industry.[2] During its first term, the Court also issued decisions invalidating a comprehensive oil and gas law[3] striking down a statute that prohibited supposed communist sympathizers from holding political office,[4] and annulling a provision of the Constitutional Court law that regulates the Court's organization and procedure that sought to drastically limit the Court's constitutional review jurisdiction.[5] During its first nineteen years in

---

[1] I am grateful to Adriaan Bedner, Melissa Crouch, and Jonathan Miller for comments on earlier drafts of this chapter, and to Southwestern Law School students Alexandra Christensen and Kimberly Morosi for superb research assistance.
[2] Decision 01/PUU-I/2003.
[3] Decision 02/PUU-I/2003.
[4] Decision 11-17/PUU-I/2003.
[5] Decision 04/PUU-I/2003. Technically, this first decision 'set aside' the provision limiting the Court's jurisdiction without formally overruling it. The article was formally overruled during the Court's next term: Decision 66/PUU-II/2004.

Mark Cammack, *Legal Certainty in the Indonesian Constitutional Court* In: *Constitutional Democracy in Indonesia*. Edited by: Melissa Crouch, Oxford University Press. © Mark Cammack, 2023. DOI: 10.1093/oso/9780192870681.003.0014

operation, the Constitutional Court received nearly 1,500 petitions for judicial review. Approximately 670 of the filings were either withdrawn or declared inadmissible. Of the 814 cases decided on the merits, the Court denied 532 and granted 282 in whole or in part.

The response to the Court's exercise of its judicial review powers has been generally very positive. This favourable assessment is based in part on the Court's independence and willingness to stand up to entrenched interests. The decision invalidating the disqualification from political office of a broad and loosely defined category of former 'communists' defied a sacrosanct dogma about the dangers of communism supported by three decades of intense indoctrination. In a case challenging parts of the Marriage Law, the Court granted new rights to children born out of wedlock contrary to standard interpretations of Islamic law. While the Constitutional Court has been praised for decisions demonstrating independence and a commitment to principle, the Court is valued primarily not for what it has accomplished but for what it represents as an instrument of citizen empowerment. The Court offers a broad category of individuals and groups who feel that their constitutional rights have been impaired by the existence of any statute an avenue for obtaining unmediated access to the means for effecting change. Those who invoke the jurisdiction of the Court are assured that their grievances will receive serious consideration in a public and participatory process in which they present their arguments and evidence directly to judges with the power to give them redress. Litigants are also assured accountability in the form of a decision backed up with reasons and available for public scrutiny and criticism.

The Constitutional Court has earned the public's approbation for its accessibility, transparency, and integrity. Reviews of the quality of the Court's decision-making have been more guarded (eg Butt and Lindsey 2012: 104). Observers have commented that there is a lack of clarity and precision in the identification, articulation, and application of constitutional norms, and it is often not possible to determine the precise basis for the Court's decision (Butt 2015: 63). The Court often identifies one or more provisions of the Constitution as the basis for the decision without identifying the specific language that is relied on or explaining how the text of the law applies to the facts of the case.[6] In many decisions the Court does not cite any authority other than the text of the Constitution and the law that is under review. The Court cites its own decisions when the precise statutory language or issue under review has been addressed in an earlier decision (Augustine 2018). The Court rarely, however, cites its prior interpretations of the constitutional texts that form the law the Court is charged with applying and makes no attempt to reconcile the application of a constitutional text in one

---

[6] See, eg, Decision 14-17/PUU-V/2007 (finding provision disqualifying persons convicted of crimes from government office conditionally constitutional unless it excludes from its coverage crimes of minor negligence because conviction for such crimes indicates lack of care rather than criminal character); Decision 115/PUU-VII/2009 (finding provisions of the Labour Law conditionally unconstitutional without specific constitutional basis); Decision 46/PUU-VIII/2010 (finding provision of Marriage Law relating to rights of out-of-wedlock children conditionally unconstitutional without specific constitutional basis); Decision 05/PUU-X/2012 (invalidating law requiring establishment of schools based on international standards because it will 'erode and reduce pride in Indonesia's national language and culture, and result in differential access to quality education in violation of the mandate of the constitution'); Decision 18/PUU-XII/2014 (finding provisions of Law on Protection and Management of the Environment relating to hazardous waste conditionally unconstitutional because 'not fair').

case with the way that text has been applied in other cases (Butt 2015: 66).[7] As a result, capacious concepts and principles stated in the Constitution never achieve any degree of definition or precision.

The Court's strengths and weaknesses are a reflection of its priorities. The Court has been more interested in doing justice to the people it serves than in becoming a model of rational-legal decision-making (Faiz 2016).[8] Not accidentally, the fact that the Court performs badly as a court of law has facilitated its success as a court of justice. This is nowhere clearer than in the Court's application of the principle of 'legal certainty'. Article 28D(1) of the Constitution guarantees the right of every person 'to recognition, security, protection and legal certainty that is just as well as equal treatment before the law'. In applying this language, the Court has focused primarily on the guarantee of legal certainty. Early applications of the rule reflected an understanding of the requirement of legal certainty as establishing a narrow and essentially formal test for the validity of the law; statutory language found to be ambiguous or inconsistent with other language created legal uncertainty that rendered the law invalid. Inevitably, however, the use of a claim of legal uncertainty to bring a constitutional challenge began to grow, and once unloosed its potential reach was unlimited. This is because the rule requiring that the law be certain is unlike other constitutional requirements. Constitutional constraints on the content of the law, like legal rules generally, specify a defined factual context in which the rule is applicable. The constitutional prohibition against laws that infringe freedom of speech only applies to laws that address conduct that qualifies as speech. The applicability of the rule that law must be certain has no such limits. There is no law that this requirement does not apply to.

The versatility of the constitutional requirement of legal certainty makes it irresistible as a tool for anyone wishing to challenge the constitutionality of legislation. A claim that the law is uncertain is not guaranteed to succeed, but it is guaranteed to make it through the courthouse door. The Court could have found a way to control the flow of legal certainty claims, but for a court anxious to establish itself as an engine for reform, the fact that any law is subject to constitutional challenge is not at all a bad thing. Leaving the legal certainty door open allows the court to weigh in on any matter it deems important. Which is exactly what the Constitutional Court has done.

The Principle of Legal Certainty

The post-Suharto constitutional amendments added an extensive list of human rights guarantees to the Indonesian Constitution. The set of rights included in the amendment was based on the Universal Declaration of Human Rights, but the drafters also made a number of additions and modifications to the UDHR. One of the more

---

[7] One situation in which the Court has cited and followed its previous interpretations of the Constitution is in cases applying Art 33 requiring that the country's natural resources be 'controlled by the state'.

[8] This tendency was less pronounced during the Court's first five years in operation under Chief Justice Jimly Asshidiqie. As Simon Butt (2015: 63) has put it, with the ascendance of Mahfud MD as the Court's second chief justice in 2008, 'the Court moved towards emphasizing "substantive justice" over "procedural justice"'. The shift in the Court's priorities under the leadership of Mahfud MD has also been noted by others (Hendrianto 2018; Siregar 2016; Roux 2018; Roux 2019) and has continued since.

significant modifications was Article 28D. Article 6 of the Universal Declaration of Human Rights on which Article 28D of the Indonesian Constitution is based guarantees the right to 'recognition everywhere before the law'. This implements the principle that all people possess fundamental human rights. Article 28D(1) restates the essence of this right but expands on it. In addition to guaranteeing the right to legal recognition, the Indonesian Constitution guarantees a right to 'legal certainty that is just'.

Construed broadly, the concept of legal certainty expresses a value that is found in all legal systems. Indeed, the requirement that the meaning of a legal norm be to some degree certain is inherent in the very idea of law. The feature that distinguishes law from other forms of social control is that the decisions of judges are thought to be obedient to commands of an external will. This is possible only if the law is expressed in terms that control the decision. Law cannot serve as a means of social regulation unless the rules are accessible, meaning both public and understandable. In order to resolve disputes based on rules, the rules must have a meaning that is sufficiently definite to serve as a guide to decision.

While some conception of legal certainty is recognized in all legal systems, the concept plays a particularly significant role in national legal systems that trace their origins to France and Germany (Merryman 1969: 48). In civil law systems, '[l]legal certainty is central to the creation of the legal methods by which law is made, interpreted, and applied' (Maxeiner 2008: 38). It has a meaning and importance similar to the idea of the rule of law in the common law world (Paunio 2020 54) and is intimately related to the protection of personal autonomy (Maxeiner 2007: 553).

Legal certainty is a protean concept whose concrete requirements are not easily pinned down. In a narrow juridical sense, legal certainty requires 'that there are clear, consistent, and accessible legal rules, issued or acknowledged by or on behalf of the state' (Bedner and Wiratman 2019: 134n1 quoting Otto 2002: 25).[9] But beyond the requirement that the law be formulated in publicly stated intelligible rules, legal certainty requires that the techniques of the law operate to ensure predictability and protect legitimate expectations more broadly. The principle of *res judicata* and the prohibition against laws with retroactive effect, for example, are understood as aspects of legal certainty. Scholars have also identified what is referred to as 'substantive legal certainty' which relates to the rational acceptability of legal decision-making (Paunio 2020: 51; see also Suominen 2014). Substantive legal certainty requires that legal decision-making follows patterns of consistent, 'predictable reasoning' in accordance with standards regarded as legitimate in the relevant legal community (Paunio 2020: 80–81), and that legal reasoning exhibit 'coherence' in the sense that the reasoning supporting a ruling must cohere (Paunio 2020: 84).

Indonesian law absorbed the concepts and methods of the civil law tradition from the Dutch, including an emphasis on the importance of legal certainty. The Constitutional Court is unusual in the way the principle of legal certainty is used, however. For the most part, the concept of legal certainty functions not as a test for

---

[9] Jan Michiel Otto (2002: 25) has defined 'Real Legal Certainty' as requiring, in addition to this first requirement, that 'the government institutions apply these rules consistently and themselves comply with them; most citizens in principle conform to such rules; in the course of dispute settlement, independent and impartial judges apply such rules consistently; and their judicial decisions are actually put into practice'.

the validity of law but as the basis for an argument about how the law should be interpreted (Popelier 2008: 65–66). In Dworkin's terms, legal certainty is not a rule but a principle (Dworkin 1967: 25). Both rules and principles provide standards that guide legal decision-making, but they differ in the degree to which they compel a particular outcome. 'Rules are applicable in an all-or-nothing fashion' (Dworkin 1967: 25). If the facts that trigger the rule are present, then the rule prescribes the answer that must be accepted. Like other principles, legal certainty does not prescribe answers to specific questions. It operates as a higher order consideration that is weighed with other principles, policies, and values as a guide to interpretation (Maxeiner 2007: 553).

While the concept of legal certainty is not ordinarily applied as an enforceable test of the law's validity, there are some contexts in which a lack of semantic clarity in the formulation of the law renders the law invalid. One widely recognized situation where precision and certainty is required is in the definition of crimes. In US law, for example, a requirement that crimes be defined with clarity is enforced as an aspect of the constitutional guarantee of due process. This rule was initially rationalized as a requirement of the doctrine of separation of powers. Criminal statutes that failed to meet a required standard of clarity were declared invalid because they allowed police and prosecutors to exercise the power assigned to the legislature to determine what conduct is punishable as crime. The so-called 'void-for-vagueness' doctrine is currently understood in pragmatic terms as necessary to prevent arbitrary enforcement of the criminal law (Goldsmith 2003). The rule is defined functionally as requiring that penal statutes 'define the criminal offense with sufficient definiteness that ordinary people can understand what conduct is prohibited and in a manner that does not encourage arbitrary and discriminatory enforcement'.[10]

Indonesia's is not the only constitution that incorporates the principle of legal certainty. A search using the term 'legal certainty' of the *Oxford Constitutions of the World* database showed that ten of the world's 664 current national and subnational constitutions use the term. Apart from Indonesia, however, legal certainty is guaranteed as an enforceable right in only one Constitution, and that provision is narrowly focused on specifically defined circumstances: the Constitution of the Dominican Republic contains a sentence in an article prohibiting laws with retroactive effect stating: 'In no case may the public powers or the law affect or alter the legal certainty resulting from the situations established in accordance with previous legislation.' In all other cases, the term is used as a label for specifically described rights or denotes a general principle that is to be used in the application of the law. The Serbian Constitution uses the term 'legal certainty' in the heading of an article that recognizes a range of doctrines applicable to the prosecution of crimes, including the presumption of innocence and the right not to be prosecuted twice for the same offence. Three constitutions—those of Portugal, Angola, and the Democratic Republic of Sao Tome and Principe—permit limitations on the effect of a finding of unconstitutionality 'when required for the purposes of legal certainty, reasons of fairness or matters of exceptionally important public interest'.

---

[10] *Kolender v Lawson*, 461 US 352, 357 (1983).

The concept of legal certainty has also emerged as a central principle of contemporary international law (Paunio 2020; Usher 1998). Although the European Convention on Human Rights does not mention legal certainty, the European Court of Human Rights referred to the principle in nearly 1,000 cases between 1975 and 2021.[11] The ECHR has stated that the principle of legal certainty is 'inherent in all Convention provisions'[12] and is a fundamental aspect of the rule of law which is implied in the Convention.[13] The Court has also interpreted a number of specific provisions of the Convention to include a requirement of legal certainty. Article 7(1), which prohibits the retroactive application of criminal law, has been construed to include a requirement similar to the void-for-vagueness doctrine in US law that criminal offences be clearly defined. This requirement is satisfied where 'the individual can know from the wording of the relevant provision and, if need be, with the assistance of the courts' interpretation of it, what acts and omissions will make him liable'.[14] The ECHR has also derived a requirement of legal certainty from language contained in several provisions stipulating that restrictions on rights guaranteed in the Convention must be 'prescribed by law'. A limitation which on the face of it is prescribed by law may be invalid if it is not formulated with the necessary degree of certainty. In a case challenging restrictions on freedom of expression guaranteed by Article 10, the ECHR explained this requirement as follows:

> In the Court's opinion, the following are two requirements that flow from the expression 'prescribed by law'. Firstly, the law must be accessible: the citizen must be able to have an indication that is adequate in the circumstances of the legal rules applicable to a given case. Secondly, a norm cannot be regarded as 'law' unless it is formulated with sufficient precision to enable the citizen to regulate his conduct: he must be able—if need be with appropriate advice—to foresee, to a degree that is reasonable in the circumstances, the consequences which a given action may entail.[15]

Finally, the ECHR has found an enforceable guarantee of legal certainty in the language of Article 6(1) guaranteeing that civil and criminal rights be determined through 'a fair and public hearing ... by an independent and impartial tribunal'. The Court has applied the right derived from this article in two principal contexts. First, the ECHR has held that the principle of legal certainty contained in Article 6(1) requires that 'where courts have finally determined an issue, their ruling shall not be called into question'. Exceptions to this rule are 'justified only when made necessary by circumstances of a substantial and compelling character, such as a correction of fundamental defects or a miscarriage of justice'.[16] A violation of the legal certainty guaranteed by Article 6(1) also results if the decisions of the courts are in conflict. The Court has said:

---

[11] This is based on a search of the Lexis-Nexis database of decisions of the ECHR using the search term 'legal certainty'. The search returned 976 cases in which the term is used.

[12] *M and others v Bulgaria* [2011] ECHR 41416/08, para 69.

[13] *Vusic v Croatia* [2010] ECHR 4810/07, para 44.

[14] *Kokkinakis v Greece* [1993] ECHR 14307/88, para 52.

[15] *Sunday Times v United Kingdom* [1979] ECHR 6538/74, para 49.

[16] *Bezrukovy v Russia* [2012] ECHR 34616/02, para 32 (citations omitted).

The principle of legal certainty guarantees, inter alia, a certain stability in legal situations and contributes to public confidence in the courts. The persistence of conflicting decisions, on the other hand, can create a state of legal uncertainty likely to reduce public confidence in the judicial system, whereas such confidence is clearly one of the essential components of a State based on the rule of law.[17]

This is the broadest and most nebulous application of the principle of legal certainty, and the ECHR has taken pains to ensure that it does not become an open-ended invitation to challenge any decision on the grounds of inconsistency with other decisions. The Court has stated that '[t]he requirements of legal certainty and the protection of the legitimate confidence of the public do not confer an acquired right to consistency of case law', and '[i]t is not in principle the Court's function to compare different decisions of national courts, even if given in apparently similar proceedings'.[18] In applying the rule, the ECHR looks to 'whether "profound and long-standing differences" exist in the case-law of the domestic courts'.[19] In one case, for example, the Court declined to find a violation of legal certainty notwithstanding the fact that the national court issued flatly contradictory decisions in two cases decided three months apart with identical facts but different parties. In explaining the decision, the Court said that it had not been shown that 'the divergence on [the] specific issue [decided in the two cases] went against a well-established case law' or that 'the divergence extended over any longer period than between the judgments [in the two cases]'.[20]

Legal Certainty in the Indonesian Constitutional Court

One of the changes defining the boundary between Suharto's New Order and the *reformasi* era was the emergence of a consensus that the Constitution should be taken seriously. Under Suharto, the terms of the Constitution shaped the forms of governance, but it had little bearing on the exercise of governmental power; parliamentary elections were held every five years, but the elections did not operate as the mechanism for determining membership in the group that actually ruled the country. The *reformasi* amendments to the Constitution set up rules that were expected to be followed. By the time the MPR entered the third round of constitutional amendments there was a broad consensus on the need to include some mechanism for providing authoritative answers to what those rules require (Butt 2015: 28).

The MPR considered a number of different mechanisms for assuring that the law conforms to the requirements of the Constitution. The first approach would have vested the power to assess the constitutionality of legislation in the MPR itself (Butt 2015: 28–29). The obvious problem with this option was that the membership of the MPR was comprised primarily of members of the DPR. There is little point in having the same people who created the law evaluating its constitutionality afterwards.

---

[17] *Albu and others v Romania* [2012] ECHR 34796/09, para 34.
[18] *Lupeni Greek Catholic Parish and others v Romania* [2016] ECHR 76943/11, para 116.
[19] *Albu and others v Romania* [2012] ECHR 34796/09, para 34.
[20] *Melgarejo Martinez de Abellanosa v Spain* [2021] ECHR 11200/19, paras 35–36.

Consideration was also given to expanding the jurisdiction of the Supreme Court to include the power of constitutional review (Butt 2015: 28). The principal objection to this option was that the Supreme Court was not up to the task. Forty years of autocratic rule had degraded the integrity and professionalism of the Court to the point that it could not be relied on to resolve ordinary legal disputes competently and impartially, never mind policing the legislature (Pompe 2005). Aside from the problems of corruption and incompetence, Indonesian political culture incorporates traditional civil law assumptions about the low status and narrow role of the judiciary that would have made it difficult for the Supreme Court to be accepted as a credible arbiter of the meaning of the Constitution. If the MPR was serious about establishing a system of constitutional review, the only real option was the creation of a new body designed to perform that function, and that is what it did.

The third round of amendments completed in November 2001 added Article 24C providing for the creation of a Constitutional Court. The Court's constitutional review power is limited to examining the constitutionality of *statutes*; executive and administrative regulations are not subject to review. The limitation of the Court's review power to statutes also places the enactments of regional level governments outside the Court's constitutional review authority.[21] The DPR sought to further limit the Court's constitutional review powers in the Constitutional Court Law which contained a provision prohibiting the Court from reviewing statutes enacted prior to 1999. This provision would have prevented the Court from reviewing precisely those laws most likely to present constitutional problems, and the Court declared it unconstitutional on the grounds that the legislature cannot reduce the powers granted to the Court by the Constitution.[22]

Article 28D(1) is one of if not the most commonly relied upon rights in the Court's constitutional review cases (Butt and Lindsey 2012: 130). The Court has applied the guarantee of legal certainty in a broad range of contexts and given it a variety of meanings. In some cases, the Court has identified Art 28D(1) with specific rights that apply in narrowly defined circumstances. In many cases, however, the meaning of the rule and the interests it protects are not stated, and the character of the right it guarantees is difficult to discern. It is not my intention to seek to disentangle all the ways the right of legal certainty has been interpreted. The analysis here is limited to applications of Article 28D(1) in which legal certainty is identified with consistency and clarity of expression. I argue that the Court has used its authority to review the language of the law for legal certainty to entertain a constitutional challenge to almost any law on any grounds.

---

[21] The Supreme Court possesses the authority to review the conformity of central government regulations to statutes. The Department of Home Affairs is charged with determining whether regional regulations are properly within the lawmaking authority of the local legislatures. There is, however, no process for reviewing the constitutionality of either central government regulations or regional laws.

[22] Decision 066/PUU-II/2004.

Supreme Court Law Case

In 2004, the Constitutional Court first applied the constitutional guarantee of legal certainty to strike down a law in a case that was decided during the Court's second term. The case, referred to as the *Supreme Court Law* case, involved a challenge to the law that governs the Supreme Court.[23] The challenge was based on a conflict between an amendment to the Supreme Court Law, which was passed in 2004, and the law governing the Indonesian legal profession, which was passed in 2003.

The 2004 enactment was a revision of an earlier law passed in 1985.[24] Article 36 of the 1985 law assigned the Supreme Court and the government responsibility for regulating the legal profession. When the law was revised in 2004, Article 36 regarding Supreme Court regulation of the legal profession was retained unchanged.

The Advocates Law was passed in 2003.[25] A principal purpose of the law was to transfer control over the regulation of lawyers from the government to the profession itself. In accordance with this objective, Article 12(1) of the Advocates Law assigned responsibility for the supervision of lawyers to a (yet to be created) Advocates Organization. As a result, the two laws were irreconcilably at odds—the Advocates Law vested the power to oversee advocates in the legal profession, and the Supreme Court Law gave that authority to the Supreme Court and the government.

The petitioners in the case based their argument on Article 24 of the Constitution. That provision states that 'the judicial power shall be independent and shall possess the power to organize the judicature to enforce law and justice'. The petitioners argued that the Advocates Law that assigned supervisory authority over the legal profession to the profession itself implemented the spirit of the constitutional guarantee of judicial independence. The Supreme Court Law, it was argued, was not only inconsistent with the Advocates Law, it was also inconsistent with the Constitution.

The Court expressly rejected the petitioners' argument that assigning the Supreme Court supervisory power over the legal profession was contrary to Article 24 of the Constitution, but nevertheless found a violation of the Constitution in the existence of two conflicting statutes. 'It is apparent', the Court wrote, 'that the legislature was less than careful in the exercise of its authority resulting in inconsistencies between one statute and another'. Inconsistencies in the law 'raise doubts over the implementation of the law, which causes legal uncertainty, and the potential violation of Article 28D(1)'.[26]

The Court found that the existence of laws that are inconsistent or contradictory violates the Constitution. Eliminating this defect and rendering the law constitutional requires that one of the two laws be declared invalid. The problem, of course, is that to the extent the defect in the law consists solely in the existence of inconsistent statutes that create legal uncertainty, there is nothing in the Constitution to guide the determination of which provision is to be invalidated and which is to be retained. In the

---

[23] Decision 67/PUU-II/2004.
[24] Law 14/1985 on the Supreme Court.
[25] Law 18/2003 on Advocates.
[26] Decision 67/PUU-II/2004, 31.

Supreme Court Law case, the Court found the general principle of statutory interpretation that *lex specialis derogat lex generalis*—a more specific law takes precedence over a law that is more general—as inapplicable to the facts. The rule commonly applied in other contexts in Indonesia that *lex posteriori derogat lex priori*—a more recent law takes precedence over a law that is older—does appear to be applicable but was not discussed. If it had applied that rule, the Court would have decided the case differently than it did. The Court did not explain its reason for choosing to invalidate the Supreme Court Law provision rather than the provision in the Advocates Law. It may have been that the decision was based on no better reason than that this is what the petitioners in the case had asked for.

Surplus Votes Case

In the *Supreme Court Law* case, the Court found a violation of legal certainty based on the existence of inconsistencies between two statutes. The Court has also found a violation of the requirement of legal certainty based on a finding that the terms of a statute were ambiguous.

The first case in which the Court found a violation of the Constitution on the basis of ambiguous statutory language involved a challenge to a law governing the election of members of national and regional legislatures.[27] Indonesia follows a system of proportional representation for electing members of the legislature. For purposes of filling seats in the DPR, the country is divided into electoral districts each of which has between three and ten seats. The parties contesting the election are allocated seats in proportion to the number of votes cast for that party in the district. The issue in the case concerned the method to be used in allocating unassigned seats based on what the case referred to as 'surplus votes'.

The process of converting votes into seats in the legislature begins with the calculation of a quota for each electoral district. The quota represents the number of votes needed to secure one seat in the district. It is calculated by dividing the total number of votes cast in that district for all parties by the number of seats assigned to that district. During the first stage of the process, each party that receives enough votes to meet the quota or some multiple of the quota receives a seat or seats in the DPR. This process, however, will inevitably leave some number of 'surplus votes'—votes cast for a party whose sum is less than the number required to fill a quota and therefore not converted into a seat—and some number of unassigned seats. The issue in the case concerned the method to be used in allocating seats among parties with surplus votes in a second stage.

The procedure to be followed in converting surplus votes into seats in the DPR is set forth in Article 205(4) of Law 10/2008. That provision states:

> In the event there are surplus seats [ie seats not filled by converting a quota into a seat], the allocation of seats in the second stage is calculated by assigning the surplus

---

[27] Decision 110-111-112-113/PUU-VI/2009 challenging Law 10/2008 on General Election of DPR, DPD, and DPRD.

seats to the parties that receive votes equal to at least 50 percent of the quota [ie the votes necessary to secure a seat].

The petitioners in the case challenged the constitutionality of this provision on the grounds that the word 'votes' in this article was subject to multiple interpretations and therefore violated the constitutional guarantee of legal certainty. This ambiguity, the petitioners argued, was demonstrated by the fact that the General Election Commission (*Komisi Pemilian Umum*, KPU) and the Supreme Court had interpreted the word differently. The KPU had issued a regulation in which it interpreted the word 'votes' to mean surplus votes, that is, votes received by a party that had not been converted into a seat. In a case reviewing the conformity of a regulation issued by the KPU with the statute, the Supreme Court interpreted the word 'votes' to mean all of the votes cast for a particular party in that district.

The Court agreed with the petitioners that the provision did not satisfy the requirements of legal certainty. The Court explained that Article 28D(1) constitutionalizes a principle of legislative drafting requiring that the contents and language of statutes must be clear and not subject to multiple interpretations. The Court wrote that this principle is both stated in a 2004 Indonesian statute on legislative lawmaking and recognized as a general principle of legal drafting. General principles of lawmaking include the principles that law must be certain (*lex certa*) and written (*lex scripta*) 'so as not to produce differing interpretations and guarantee legal certainty'.[28]

The Court's explanation of the concept of legal certainty in the *Surplus Votes* case describes a formal rather than substantive constraint on legislative lawmaking.[29] This is clear from the fact that the Court's finding of unconstitutionality was based on the challenged provision's failure to meet standards of clarity required by the statute governing the process of legislative drafting. The constitutional guarantee of legal certainty demands that the law be expressed in terms that are clear and precise. But a requirement that the meaning of a statute be definite and unambiguous does not limit the permissible content of the law. In its application of the principle, however, the Court has treated the requirement of legal certainty as prescribing not only criteria for how the law must be written but also criteria for what the content of the law should be. In order to explain the Court's substantive use of the principle of legal certainty, it is first necessary to explain the approach the Court has adopted to providing a remedy for a finding of unconstitutionality.

---

[28] Decision 110-111-112-113/PUU-VI/2009, 100, citing Law 10/2004 on Legislative Lawmaking. The Court quoted Art 6(i) of the Legislative Lawmaking Act which states that one of the principles of lawmaking is that law must be orderly and certain. The Elucidation of this provision explains the principle of orderliness and certainty as requiring that 'the terms of a statute must be capable of creating order in society through legal certainty'. The 2004 statute was subsequently repealed and replaced by Law 12/2011 on Legislative Lawmaking.

[29] The distinction between formal and substantive validity is expressly recognized in the Constitutional Court Law which differentiates between claims alleging that the creation or formulation of a statute fails to satisfy constitutional requirements and claims alleging that the substantive content of the law is unconstitutional. Despite the fact that the Court cited the Legislative Lawmaking Act as the basis for the statute's unconstitutionality, the Court treated the petition as a challenge to the substance of the law rather than the process of its enactment.

The Constitutional Court Law clearly contemplates that the Court shall function exclusively as what Hans Kelsen called a 'negative legislature'. Article 56(3) of the Law requires that decisions finding a statute to be unconstitutional must expressly identify the paragraph, article, or section that is contrary to the Constitution, and Article 57(1) states that any paragraph, article, or section of the statute found to violate the Constitution does not have binding legal effect. The legislature intended that the Court have the power to invalidate laws; it was not intended that the Court have the power to fix a law found to be defective so as to render it constitutional.[30]

Relatively early in its history, the Court adopted the position that in deciding questions of constitutionality its options were not limited to those of either finding a law to be constitutional and upholding it or finding the law to be unconstitutional and invalidating it. The Court took the position that, in addition to either granting or denying a petition to declare a statute unconstitutional, the Court could also make a finding that the law was constitutional only if interpreted in a particular way (Rahman and Wicaksono 2016). Initially, the Court entered these qualified holdings by finding a law to be 'conditionally constitutional'. The Court would admonish the government that the law must be interpreted in accordance with its decision in order for the law to conform to the requirements of the Constitution. In its formal order, then, the Court would deny the petition to declare the law unconstitutional. The Court came to realize that these findings of conditional constitutionality were simply advisory opinions that did not have the force of law; because the formal order of the Court denied the request to find the law unconstitutional, it was left to the government to decide whether to follow the Court's interpretation of the meaning of the law. The Court then began declaring laws found to be contrary to the Constitution to be 'conditionally unconstitutional' and entering an order granting the petition. In cases where a law is found to be conditionally unconstitutional, the decision specifies the circumstances necessary for the law to comply with the Constitution. This often entails prescribing language that must be deemed to be included in the statute.[31]

When a law is found to be inconsistent with a substantive principle of constitutional law, the principle that provides the basis for the finding of unconstitutionality also guides the determination of the conditions necessary for the law to conform to

---

[30] As Theunis Roux (2018: 258) has pointed out, there is nothing in the language of Art 24C of the Constitution that obviously limits the Court's remedial powers to invalidating laws found to be unconstitutional. Roux attributes the common assumption that the Court is limited to exercising the powers of a negative legislature to a statement made at a press conference by the Court's first chief justice, Jimly Asshiddiqie.

[31] The change in approach is clearly illustrated by two cases decided two years apart in 2007 and 2009 that both involved challenges to statutes that disqualified persons who had been convicted of a crime carrying a prison sentence of five years or more from holding certain positions in government. In the 2007 case the Court found the statutes conditionally constitutional, denied the petition, and stated that the challenged provisions were 'not contrary to the Constitution insofar as they are not interpreted in such a way as to include criminal acts resulting from minor negligence or criminal acts committed for certain political reasons'. Decision 14-17/PUU-V/2007, 134. In the second case, the Court noted that it had found the challenged statutory language 'conditionally constitutional' in its 2007 decision, but the legislature failed to take action to revise the statute in accordance with its instructions. It was therefore necessary, the Court said, 'to push [lawmakers] harder' by declaring the statutes at issue in the present case to be 'conditionally unconstitutional'. Decision 4/PUU-VII/2009, 80–81. In its order the Court granted the petition and stated that the challenged provisions 'have no binding legal force' insofar as they fail to meet four conditions stated in its decision. Decision 4/PUU-VII/2009, 84.

constitutional requirements. For example, if a law is found to violate the guarantee of due process of law, the demands of due process supply the criteria for the law to be constitutional, and if some interpretations of a law result in an unconstitutional infringement of free speech, the scope of the right to freedom of expression determines the proper interpretation of the statute. As explained above, the principle of legal certainty imposes requirements that are purely formal. As such, the concept of legal certainty can be used to identify constitutional violations, but legal certainty in itself does not point the way to making the law constitutional. Legal certainty tells us that a statutory provision that is subject to more than one interpretation violates the Constitution, it does not provide criteria for determining which if any of the possible interpretations is required by the Constitution.

The Court has treated violations of legal certainty in the same way it treats violations of other constitutional norms: when a provision of a law has been found to be uncertain, the Court often finds the law conditionally unconstitutional and prescribes the interpretation that must be given to the law for it to have the force of law. The Court has never explained the approach to be followed in deciding how uncertain language should be interpreted. In some cases, the Court resolves the uncertainty by undertaking an inquiry into the probable intent of the legislature. In other cases, the Court appears to be prescribing an interpretation that accords with the Court's understanding of sound legal policy.

In the *Surplus Votes* case the Court found the language of Article 205(4) to be conditionally unconstitutional and specified the interpretation that must be given to the provision in order for it to have the force of law. In deciding how the provision should be interpreted, the Court looked to both the apparent intent of the legislature and general principles of democratic governance and Indonesia's system of proportional representation. The Court wrote that the concept of democracy requires that the votes of minorities be given effect, and that the system of proportional voting mandated by the General Election Law seeks to achieve the closest possible fit between the percentage of votes that a party receives and the percentage of seats the party obtains.[32] The Court found that the Supreme Court's interpretation of the statute was not consistent with the objective of avoiding to the extent possible deviations from exact proportionality, and declared Article 205(4) unconstitutional unless the word 'votes' is interpreted to mean votes received by a political party that remain after the party's votes have been used to satisfy the quota for securing a seat.[33]

Pretrial Dismissal Case

A second example of a case in which the Court found a violation of legal certainty on the basis of linguistic ambiguity concerned a challenge to an article in the Code of Criminal Procedure regarding a procedure called the 'pretrial'.[34] The pretrial procedure is a mechanism by which both defendants and prosecutors can obtain a judicial

---

[32] Decision 110-111-112-113/PUU-VI/2009, 101–102.
[33] Ibid 102–103.
[34] Decision 102/PUU-XIII/2015.

determination of the legality of the initiation and termination of a criminal prosecution before the case goes to trial.[35] The case before the Constitutional Court arose out of a corruption prosecution in which the defendant filed a pretrial petition challenging the legality of his designation as a suspect. Before the petition was decided, the prosecution registered the case dossier in the trial court. The judge hearing the pretrial petition then dismissed the petition without decision on the authority of Article 82(1)d of the Criminal Procedure Code which requires that a pretrial petition be dismissed if the trial of the case begins before the examination of the petition is completed. The defendant petitioned the Constitutional Court seeking to have this article declared unconstitutional.

The Constitutional Court's decision focused on language in the challenged provision marking the point at which a pretrial petition is dismissed without decision. The article stated that dismissal is required if the pretrial petition had not yet been decided when 'the case has begun to be heard' in the trial court. The issue as framed by the Court was whether this language was fatally uncertain. The Court found it was on the basis that judges had interpreted the phrase differently. Some judges interpreted the provision to require dismissal if the pretrial petition had not been decided at the time of the first hearing of the case in the trial court. Other judges found that a case had begun to be heard at the point at which the dossier is registered in the trial court. These differences, the Court wrote, 'are not merely a matter of application or implementation of the rule,' but rather 'the differing interpretations arise as a result of a lack of clarity in the formulation of the rule itself'.[36] The provision therefore violated the legal certainty guaranteed by Article 28D(1) of the Constitution unless interpreted to mean that the pretrial lapses at the point when the first hearing on the case is convened.

The *Pretrial Dismissal* case raised a question relating to the rights of the accused to challenge the legality of the actions of police and prosecutors in charging him with a crime; the petitioner alleged that prosecutors exploited the ambiguity in Article 82(1)d and rushed to file the case dossier with the trial court in order to prevent the pretrial petition from being decided. This implicates issues that are commonly the subject of constitutional regulation. The Court's discussion of the matter, however, focused not on the question of what rights should be guaranteed to citizens confronting an attempt by the state to deprive them of life or liberty, but focused instead on the seemingly tangential question whether the language of the rule was susceptible to more than one interpretation. As part of its discussion, the Court observed that 'the essence of the pretrial procedure is to evaluate whether there has been an abuse of authority by the police or prosecutor' in bringing the charges,[37] but at no point did the Court directly address what would seem to be the real issue of whether the rights of the accused are violated if prosecutors short-circuit the pretrial procedure by filing the dossier before the defendant's petition challenging the charges has been decided.

---

[35] Law 8/1981 on Criminal Procedure.
[36] Decision 102/PUU-XIII/2015, 50.
[37] Ibid 50–51.

Office of Deputy Minister Case

In the earliest cases applying Article 28D(1)'s requirement of legal certainty, the provision was described in a way that defined an essentially formal constraint on lawmaking. But if the guarantee of legal certainty were useful only as a mechanism for vindicating the values of consistency and clarity in the formulation of statutes, it would attract little interest among potential litigants. Parties who file claims in the Constitutional Court are invariably pursuing objectives that are unrelated to formal aspects of the way the law is written. The requirement of legal certainty is invoked because it offers would-be litigants a means for pursuing those objectives. To challenge a law with which one disagrees, a party need only convince the Court that the law contains inconsistencies or ambiguities. And while the determination that a statutory provision is subject to more than one interpretation and the determination of which interpretation should be adopted are in principle separate questions, in practice the two issues are often conflated.

One case in which a claim of legal certainty was used to raise a broader set of policy issues involved a challenge to a statute creating the office of deputy minister.[38] The decision arose out of a suit by an NGO called the National Movement to Eradicate Corruption challenging a provision of the Law on State Ministries that created the office of deputy minister. Then President Susilo Bambang Yudhoyono had used the authority granted by the statute to appoint some twenty deputy ministers. These appointments were widely regarded as political favours and a waste of money. The petitioner sought to have Article 10 of the statute that created the position of deputy minister declared invalid on the ground that it is not mentioned in the Constitution. They also argued that, if the creation of the office of deputy minister was found to be constitutional, the position should be open to any qualified candidate. The Elucidation to Article 10 which contains the legislature's official interpretation of the provision, described the position of deputy minister as a member of the civil service. The applicant argued that limiting the position to career civil servants violated Article 28D(3) of the Constitution that guarantees the right of every citizen to an equal opportunity to be part of the government.

The Constitutional Court rejected the argument that the absence of any mention of the office of deputy minister in the Constitution precluded the legislature from creating the position. With respect to the second issue, the constitutionality of the requirement that a deputy minister be a member of the civil service, the Court granted the petition to invalidate the requirement, but not on the grounds argued by the applicant. Without even addressing the applicability of Article 28D(3), the Court held that the Elucidation to Article 10 stating the requirement that deputy ministers be civil servants failed to satisfy the constitutional requirement of legal certainty.

The Court found that the Elucidation to Article 10 violated legal certainty for two reasons. The first reason, which was discussed only briefly in the decision, was that the Elucidation contained a legal norm not stated in the article itself.[39] This was found to

---

[38] Decision 79/PUU-IX/2011 challenging Law 39/2008 on State Ministries.
[39] Decision 79/PUU-IX/2011, 77.

violate the Law on Legislative Lawmaking. The second reason, which consumed the majority of the Court's decision, was that designating the office of deputy minister as a non-cabinet civil service position was not in accordance with both the Law on State Ministries and various requirements applicable to members of the civil service. On the one hand, the Yudhoyono administration's record in appointing deputy ministers created the strong impression that the positions were being created and filled to bestow political favours rather than in response to actual needs. This, the Court said, was 'contrary to the philosophy and intent of the Law on State Ministries' that contemplates that the president will use his/her appointment powers to achieve effective and efficient governance.[40] On the other hand, the rule that a deputy minister must be a civil servant conflicts with various formalistic requirements applicable to civil servants. All civil servants must be one of two types—administrative or functional—yet the actual practice used to select and swear in deputy ministers does not comply with the requirements of either. The requirement that deputy ministers be civil servants also creates uncertainty regarding their term of service, since civil service jobs are not tied to the term of a president or her political appointees.[41] Finally, the organizational structure of state ministries specified in the statute does not accommodate the existence of the office deputy minister who holds civil service status.[42]

Commonhold Property Case

Many of the cases argued and decided on legal certainty grounds also implicate other constitutional doctrines. The petitioner's claim in the *Office of Deputy Minister* case challenging the rule limiting the position to members of the civil service raises issues that are commonly subject to constitutional regulation. The legal certainty doctrine, however, can be used to turn any legal issue into a constitutional question. The scope of the Court's judicial review powers under Article 28D(1) and the willingness of the Court to open its doors to an array of essentially private civil disputes is illustrated by a case decided in 2015 challenging a provision of the statute on Commonhold Property.[43] The petitioners in the case were seven individuals who owned units in commonhold properties. They challenged two articles in the law relating to the role of property developers in the creation of an owners organization with the responsibility to manage the property. The petitioners argued that the challenged provisions failed to provide them with the protection of law that is certain in violation of the Constitution.

The Constitutional Court challenge focused on Article 75(1) of the statute. That provision states that the property developer is required to facilitate the formation of the owners association to take over management of the property within one year after the first transfer of property to an owner. The petitioners argued that the term 'the developer' in this article failed to provide them with legal certainty unless the term 'the developer' is interpreted to mean 'the government'. The petitioners argued that legal

---

[40] Ibid 78.
[41] Ibid 78–79.
[42] Ibid 80.
[43] Decision 21/PUU-XIII/2015 challenging Law 20/2011 on Commonhold Property.

certainty demands that the Act be interpreted to vest responsibility for establishment of the owners association in the government rather than the developer because developers were using their power to control the formation of the owners association to benefit themselves.

The Court rejected the petitioners' argument that legal certainty demands that Article 75(1) be interpreted to vest responsibility for ensuring the establishment of the owners association in the government rather than the developer. This interpretation, the Court wrote, is precluded by the fact that another part of the statute assigns specific responsibilities to the government in regard to non-commercial commonholds, whereas the petitioners' claim related to commercial property.[44] Although the Court rejected the petitioners' specific grounds for challenging Article 75(1), the Court found the provision unconstitutional because of uncertainty created by Article 59(2) which is referenced in Article 75(1) as defining the deadline for creation of the owners association.[45] The uncertainty with respect to this provision arose because, while the text of the article set a deadline of one year for creation of the owners association, the language of the Elucidation, which used completion of all sales to mark the end of the transition period, was used by developers as justification for retaining management authority beyond one year.

The Court acknowledged the validity of the petitioners' complaints but refused to rewrite the statute in the way the petitioners had requested. The Court did, however, give the government a role. Relying on language in the statute that gives the state ultimate responsibility to provide guidance in the construction of commonhold housing, the Court stated that the government cannot simply stand idle if there is evidence that developers are exploiting the uncertainty with respect to the period of transition to delay formation of the owners association to retain the management of the property for their own economic benefit.[46] When this is the case, according to the Court, the statute justifies the government in taking steps to ensure enforcement of the Commonhold statute in accordance with its objectives.

2013 and 2014 *Labour Law* Cases

The theory underlying the doctrine of legal certainty is that inconsistencies or ambiguity in the law creates the need to invalidate or interpret it. In some cases, though, it works the other way around—it's the need for interpretation or invalidation that results in a determination of ambiguity. The issue for the Court is how should the law be written or interpreted. If the Court and the petitioner agree on the answer to that question, the law is declared uncertain and invalidated or revised.

An illustration of the way policy judgments about the law drive assessments of legal certainty can be found in a pair of cases decided in 2013 and 2014 involving challenges to provisions of the Labour Law.[47] The petitioners in the two cases challenged

---

[44] Decision 21/PUU-XIII/2015, 125–126.
[45] Ibid 125.
[46] Ibid 126.
[47] Decisions 96/PUU-XI/2013 and 07/PUU-XII/2014 challenging Law 13/2003 on Labour.

the same language in the same articles of the law. In both cases it was argued that the term failed to guarantee legal certainty. The Court denied the petition in the first case but granted it in the second.

The petitioners in the first case were officers of the Association of Indonesian Entrepreneurs, an organization that represents the interests of business. They challenged the constitutionality of three provisions of the Labour Law stipulating that the employment status of workers would in specified conditions be altered 'by law' (*demi hukum*). One of the provisions, for example, stated that a fixed-term employment contract would become an indefinite-term contract by operation of law if the statutory requirements for fixed-term contracts were not satisfied.[48] The petitioners argued that this provision violated the guarantee of law that is certain and just unless the phrase by law was interpreted to mean 'after there has been a final decision of the Industrial Relations court'. In rejecting the petition, the Court stated that the petitioners' contention that the phrase 'by law' is subject to multiple interpretations raises an issue regarding the implementation of a legal norm and not an issue of the consistency of a legal norm with the Constitution.[49]

The petitioners in the second case were a number of individual workers and officers of the Indonesian Federation of Labour Unions. They also argued that for the phrase 'by law' to satisfy the requirement of legal certainty it must be interpreted to include means for enforcing their rights. This was said to be necessary because employers often fail to implement findings by state labour inspectors that the conditions of employment did not satisfy the requirements for a fixed term contract. The petitioners argued that the Constitution guaranteed workers a right to seek court enforcement of inspection reports if employers failed to comply with the inspector's findings. The Court agreed and held that 'the phrase "by law" [in the challenged articles] is conditionally unconstitutional insofar as it is not interpreted':

> Workers may seek confirmation of an inspection report by a state labour inspector in the district court provided (1) bipartite negotiations have failed to reach an agreement or one of the parties refuses to negotiate, and (2) an inspection has been conducted by a labour inspector in accordance with the law.[50]

Protection of Teachers Case

The use of Article 28D(1) to challenge the law based on policy grounds is so well accepted that legal uncertainty is sometimes explicitly equated with the petitioner's policy arguments. In the *Protection of Teachers* case[51] decided in 2017 both the petitioners and the Court framed the issue in terms of whether the challenged statute was '*multitafsir*', a word meaning susceptible to multiple interpretations, but none of the arguments or analysis addressed possible ambiguities in the language of the law.

---

[48] Article 59(7).
[49] Decision 96/PUU-XI/2013, 135.
[50] Decision 07/PUU-XII/2014, 51–52.
[51] Decision 06/PUU-XV/2017.

The claim focused on two articles in the Child Protection Act[52] guaranteeing school children the right to be protected from acts of physical violence by teachers and a provision of the Teachers and Lecturers Law that guaranteed legal protection for teachers from violence by students.[53] The petitioners claimed that the articles protecting children 'are *multitafsir* in character because they ignore the principles of criminal law as the remedy of last resort, substantive justice in criminal law, and collide with general principles of education'.[54] They argued, among other things, that because teachers exercise authority *in loco parentis* they can use appropriate physical punishment to discipline students and that the use of physical punishment to create an environment conducive to learning cannot be against the law. The article designed to protect teachers allegedly failed to protect them from being criminalized for doing their job which prevented teachers from providing students with the best possible education. The Court accepted the admissibility of the petitioners' argument and stated the issues to be:

- Are the provisions [regarding the rights of children to be protected from violence] *multitafsir* in character causing criminalization and violence against teachers in violation of the Constitution?
- Does the provision [regarding the protection of teachers] fail to provide legal protection for teachers from acts of criminalization for doing their job such that it violates the Constitution?[55]

The Court's discussion addressing these issues focused on the state's obligation to protect and educate children. It stated that the challenged statutes implement the commands of Article 28B(2) of the Constitution guaranteeing the rights of children to grow and develop and to be free from violence and discrimination and Article 31B(2) giving all citizens a right to education. The disciplining of students should promote moral maturity, and punishments should be administered with love and sincerity based on a sound pedagogical foundation and not out of hatred or anger. This requires preparation and capacity building on the part of schools and educators to keep up with developments in educational theory related to the positive disciplining of students that does not rely on corporal punishment. Teachers need safety and a sense of security both physically and emotionally, but the fact that students and parents have reported large numbers of teachers to the police for disciplining students does not mean that the challenged law fails to provide teachers with protection and is therefore unconstitutional.[56]

---

[52] Articles 9(1a) and 54(1) of Law 35/2014 on Protection of Children.
[53] Article 39(3) of Law 14/2005 on Teachers and Lecturers.
[54] Decision 06/PUU-XV/2017, 111–112
[55] Ibid 113–114.
[56] Ibid 117.

Constitutional Court Law Amendment Case

In 2011 the DPR passed and the president approved a law amending portions of the 2003 Constitutional Court Act.[57] The amendment made a number of changes that were clearly intended to assert greater control over the Court and rein in practices that the legislature disapproved of. One of the practices targeted in the law was the Court's use of the legal certainty guarantee as the basis for finding laws to be unconstitutional.[58] Article 50A of the statute stated:

> When reviewing the constitutionality of statutes, the Constitutional Court shall not use another statute as the basis for its legal considerations.

The DPR did not explain the intent behind this rule, but the Court typically refers to a statute other than the law under review in two situations, both of which involve review of statutes on legal certainty grounds. First, legal certainty challenges based on a claim of inconsistency necessarily require a comparison between the language that is the subject of the challenge and the language of another statute or another part of the same statute. Second, cases finding statutory language uncertain because it is ambiguous have referred to the DPR's statute on legislative lawmaking.

Within weeks of the amendments being approved, they were challenged as unconstitutional. In a pair of decisions announced on the same day, the Court struck down a total of sixteen provisions of the law, including its ban on the use of statutes as a part of the Court's analysis. The Court declared the DPR's attempt to limit legal certainty review unconstitutional by finding that it violated (you guessed it) the guarantee of legal certainty. The Court denied that it had in fact used a statute in its legal considerations. The Court also stated, however, that the use of a statute other than the one under review serves the goal of ensuring legal certainty that is just.[59] It is sometimes necessary, according to the Court, 'to examine the entire body of legislation as a unitary system in which individual statutes may not be in conflict with each other, and if the Court does find that one statute conflicts with another statute there has been a violation of the principle of legal certainty that is just'.[60]

In another portion of the decision addressing the constitutionality of a different provision of the law the Court did the very thing the law prohibits—referred to another law to find that the Amendment to the Constitutional Court Law was unconstitutional. One change included in the amendment was a revision of the Elucidation to Article 10. Article 10 includes language stating that the decisions of the Constitutional

---

[57] The 2011 Law and the Court's response are summarized in Butt and Lindsey 2012: 144–156.

[58] The amendments addressed two other aspects of the Court's exercise of its constitutional review powers. Article 45A sought to prohibit the Court from issuing orders which are referred to in Indonesia as '*ultra petita*'—orders that grant more than what the petitioner requested. Another change was intended to put an end to the Court's practice of curing constitutional violations by prescribing language necessary to remedy the constitutional defect through an order of conditional unconstitutionality: Art 57(2a). The Court found both of these changes unconstitutional.

[59] Decision 49/PUU-IX/2011, 74.

[60] Ibid 74–75.

Court are final. The amendment added a sentence to the Elucidation stating that because the decisions are final, they are also binding.[61] The Court declared the attempted change invalid based on a failure to adhere to the requirements of the 2011 Legislative Lawmaking Act.[62] That Act stipulates, according to the Court, that the material content of a norm must be contained in the statute itself, and the Elucidation functions as 'the lawmaker's official interpretation of the norm'. The problem here was that although the legislature clearly intended to change the Elucidation, the heading immediately preceding the newly added language labelled it as 'Article 10' rather than 'Elucidation to Article 10'.[63] The effect of this error was to create a second Article 10 resulting in confusion that violated the guarantee of legal certainty.

Conclusion

There is irony in the way the Constitutional Court has used the guarantee of legal certainty to enable it to interpret laws without interpreting the Constitution. Article 28D(1) is useful as a mechanism for expanding the Court's jurisdiction precisely because, in the Court's application of the principle, legal certainty lacks a definite meaning that would limit the scope of its applicability.

Discussions of legal certainty in Indonesia tend to focus exclusively on clarity of expression in statutory language. This is perhaps a legacy of civil law understandings of separation of powers and attitudes towards judicial lawmaking. Historically, clear and precise statutory language was viewed as a means for making the law judge-proof.[64] It is now widely accepted, even in the civil law world, that the language of the law, however precise, is not itself sufficient to ensure consistent application, and that even the most broadly worded rules can, through a process of judicial application, acquire sufficient definition to serve as a guide to action (Lasser 1995). This is all the more the case when it comes to constitutional texts which express broad precepts and principles applicable across a wide range of circumstances. Instructing police officers to conform their actions to the US Constitution's prohibition against 'unreasonable searches and seizures' would achieve nothing. Decades of judicial application has refined that language to produce a set of narrowly focused rules that can be learned and applied by police officers in a wide variety of factual contexts.

The essence of legal certainty is predictability. Since the language of the constitution cannot alone produce predictability, some mechanism is needed to ensure that constitutional norms are interpreted and applied in a consistent manner. This can be achieved through a broader application of the principle of precedent—the rule that the

---

[61] This change was presumably intended to prevent the Court from declaring a statute unconstitutional but allowing the law to remain in effect.

[62] Law 12/2011 on Legislative Lawmaking.

[63] Decision 49/PUU-IX/2011, 67–68.

[64] Sebastiaan Pompe (2005: 428–435) has shown that the Dutch understanding of the civil law tradition did not have the same hostility to judicial lawmaking found in the French system, and that during the period of Dutch colonization courts in Indonesia exercised robust lawmaking power. However, 'jurisprudence all but lost its lawmaking authority after independence and was actually reduced to having legal effect only on both litigating parties, as required by strict civil law doctrine' (Pompe 2005: 433).

court is bound to follow its decisions in earlier cases. The Court currently recognizes a narrow doctrine of precedent that is little more than a modified rule of constitutional *res judicata*. The Court considers itself bound by an earlier decision that addressed the same statutory language that is the subject of a later challenge (Kurnia 2016). A broader doctrine of precedent extends the requirement of consistency beyond the decision itself to the law on which the decision is based. It requires that the court interpret and apply specific constitutional texts in a consistent manner. To take an example from the Court's jurisprudence, if in one case the presumption of innocence is found inapplicable to the dismissal from office of a government official suspected of criminality because the presumption applies exclusively to criminal punishment and dismissal from office is an administrative sanction,[65] the Court cannot thereafter interpret the presumption to prohibit dismissal from a different government position without a judicial finding of guilt.[66] The Court may, of course, decide the second case differently from the first, but it must do so using an interpretation of the presumption of innocence that is consistent with its earlier decision.

I concur that, generally, the Constitutional Court is a very welcome addition to the Indonesian state. Indeed, the Court's expansion of its jurisdiction beyond what is prescribed in the Constitution may be justified as necessary to compensate for the failings of the Supreme Court and the DPR.[67] It has been observed, for example, that lawyers sometimes file petitions with the Constitutional Court 'merely to get "statutory interpretation" to push the consistent application of the law of the general court' (Assegaf 2019: 52). But the Court cannot effectively promote the goal of legal certainty in Indonesian law as a whole unless it gives more attention to the problem in its own decisions.

The Constitutional Court has in many ways served as both an example and a rebuke to the Indonesian legal system generally. Adoption by the Court of the principle that its decisions must demonstrate that the interpretation and application of a particular constitutional text in one case is consistent with the way that same text has been interpreted and applied in other cases would do much to promote legal certainty in both the Constitutional Court and the Indonesian judiciary more broadly.

References

Agustine, Oly Viana (2018) 'Keberlakuan Yurisprudensi pada Kewenangan Pengujian Undang-Undang dalam Putusan Mahkamah Konstitusi' 15(3) *Jurnal Konstitusi* 642–665.

Assegaf, Rifqi (2019) 'The Supreme Court: *Reformasi*, Independence and the Failure to Ensure Legal Certainty' in Melissa Crouch (ed) *The Politics of Court Reform: Judicial Change and Legal Culture in Indonesia*. Cambridge: Cambridge University Press. pp 31–58.

Bedner, Adriaan and Herlambang Perdana Wiratman (2019) 'Administrative Courts: The Quest for Consistency' in Melissa Crouch (ed) *The Politics of Court Reform: Judicial Change and Legal Culture in Indonesia*. Cambridge: Cambridge University Press. pp 133–148.

---

[65] Decision 024/PUU-III/2005.
[66] Decision 133/PUU-VII/2009.
[67] Notably, the Indonesian Constitutional Court is not the only tribunal that has used its constitutional review powers to engage in ordinary statutory interpretation (Brewer-Carias 2011: 115–124).

Brewer-Carias, Allan R (2011) 'Constitutional Courts' Interference with the Legislator on Existing Legislation' in Allan R Brewer-Carias (ed) *Constitutional Courts as Positive Legislators: A Comparative Law Study*. Cambridge: Cambridge University Press. pp 73–124.

Butt, Simon and Timothy Lindsey (2012) *The Constitution of Indonesia: A Contextual Analysis*. Oxford: Hart Publishing.

Butt, Simon (2015). *The Constitutional Court and Democracy in Indonesia*. Leiden: Brill.

Dworkin, Ronald (1967) 'The Model of Rules' 35(1) *University of Chicago Law Review* 14–46.

Faiz, Pan Mohamad (2016) 'Dimensi Judicial Activism dalam Putusan Mahkamah Konstitusi' 13(2) *Jurnal Konstitusi* 406–430.

Goldsmith, Andrew E (2003) 'The Void-for-Vagueness Doctrine in the Supreme Court, Revisited' 30(2) *American Journal of Criminal Law* 279–314.

Hendrianto, Stefanus (2018) *Law and Politics of Constitutional Courts: Indonesia and the Search for Judicial Heroes*. London: Routledge Taylor & Francis Group.

Kurnia, Titon Slamet (2016) 'Prediktabilitas Ajudikasi Konstitusional: Mahkamah Konstitusi dan Pengujian Undang-Undang' 13(2) *Jurnal Konstitusi* 259–277.

Lasser, Mitchel (1995) 'Judicial (Self-)Portraits: Judicial Discourse in the French Legal System' 104(6) *Yale Law Journal* 1325–1410.

Maxeiner, James R (2007) 'Legal Certainty: A European Alternative to American Legal Indeterminacy' 15(2) *Tulane Journal of International and Comparative Law* 541–608.

Maxeiner, James R (2008) 'Some Realism about Legal Certainty in the Globalization of the Rule of Law' 31(1) *Houston Journal of International Law* 27–46.

Merryman, John Henry (1969) *The Civil Law Tradition: An Introduction to the Legal Systems of Western Europe and Latin America*. Stanford California: Stanford University Press.

Otto, Jan Michiel (2002) 'Toward an Analytical Framework: Real Legal Certainty and Its Explanatory Factors' in Jianfu Chen, Yuwen Li, and Jan Michiel Otto (eds) *The Implementation of Law in the People's Republic of China*. The Hague: Kluwer Law International. pp 23–34.

Paunio, Elina (2020) *Legal Certainty in Multilingual EU Law: Language, Discourse and Reasoning at the European Court of Justice*. London: Routledge Taylor & Francis Group.

Pompe, S (2005) *The Indonesian Supreme Court: A Study of Institutional Collapse*. Ithaca, NY: Southeast Asia Program, Cornell University.

Popelier, Patricia (2008) 'Five Paradoxes on Legal Certainty and the Lawmaker' 2(1) *Legisprudence* 47–66.

Rahman, Faiz and Dian Agung Wicaksono (2016) 'Eksistensi dan Karakteristik Putusan Bersyarat Mahkamah Konstitusi 13(2) *Jurnal Konstitusi* 348–378.

Roux, Theunis (2018) 'Indonesia's Judicial Review Regime in Comparative Perspective' 4(2) *Constitutional Review* 188–221.

Roux, Theunis (2019) 'The Constitutional Court: A Levian Take on Its Place in *Reformasi*' in Melissa Crouch (ed) *The Politics of Court Reform: Judicial Change and Legal Culture in Indonesia*. Cambridge: Cambridge University Press. pp 245–264.

Siregar, Fritz Edward (2016) 'Indonesian Constitutional Politics', PhD dissertation, University of New South Wales.

Suominen, Annika (2014) 'What Role for Legal Certainty in Criminal Law Within the Area of Freedom, Security and Justice in the EU?' 2(1) *Bergen Journal of Criminal Law and Criminal Justice* 1–31.

Usher, John Anthony (1998) *General Principles of EC Law*. London: Longman.

Index

For the benefit of digital users, indexed terms that span two pages (e.g., 52–53) may, on occasion, appear on only one of those pages.